The Human Experience
Readings in Sociocultural
Anthropology

The Human Experience

Readings in Sociocultural Anthropology

edited by

David H. Spain
The University of Washington

 **1975**

The Dorsey Press Homewood, Illinois 60430
Irwin-Dorsey Limited Georgetown, Ontario L7G 4B3
Irwin-Dorsey International London, England WC2H 9NJ

First Printing, March 1975

ISBN 0-256-01708-5
Library of Congress Catalog Card No. 74–25810
Printed in the United States of America

for *Andrew* and *Ryan*

Preface

It has been my intention to create a book of readings which can be used to amplify the issues raised in basic textbooks in anthropology. I believe this book can also be used successfully as a core text, especially when coordinated with ethnographic case studies and similar introductory materials. In general, selections that emphasize ethnographic data were chosen over those which were literature reviews, theoretical platforms, or devoted to interesting but relatively minor theoretical fine points. As a whole, the selections present many theoretical points, although sometimes only indirectly. I have also sought to balance the more formal and technical selections typically found in anthropological monographs and journals with selections that are less formal and technical. Observations about people from all parts of the world, including Africa, Asia, Australia, India, Native North and South America, the Near East, Oceania, and contemporary United States are included in order to present the beginning student with a reasonably wide sample of anthropological literature.

I have done a bit of personal "theoretical axe grinding" in the introductory and concluding sections, but otherwise have made selections in an effort to represent diverse theoretical and doctrinal viewpoints in modern anthropology. Included are such "ism's" as cultural materialism, structuralism, and functionalism, as well as such orientations as are implied by the labels "ecological," "cognitive," and "hologeistic" anthropology (among others). Another major concern has been to provide examples of anthropological thinking on a wide range of the human experience, from incest and warfare to stratification and baseball. Moreover, although it was not possible to include separate readings on all the issues within the basic topic areas of a typical introductory course in sociocultural anthropology, each area is represented by a sampling of the key issues.

Insofar as practical, this book has been organized to support either of two widespread but somewhat conflicting approaches to introductory courses in anthropology. First, there is what may be termed the "topical-theoretical" approach. In such an approach, the goal is to give an overview of the basic topical and theoretical areas of sociocultural anthropology (such as religion, kinship, economics, politics, and change, for example). With this approach, the sequence and number of topics tend to be variable. For example, some instructors may wish to combine several of the parts of this book into even larger units such as "process," "organization," "ideology," and "change." Other instructors may wish to begin with the parts on religion and symbolism, or family and kinship. The assignment of articles to the various parts is also flexible since most presentations in anthropology seem to be relevant to more than one topic area.

Second, there is what may be termed the "problems" approach. With this approach, the goal is to present the anthropological view of the human experience through a more-or-less Malinowskian discussion of human solutions to various individual and group problems, such as the "need" for food, shelter, reproduction, socialization, social order, answers to "ultimate questions," and so on. The arrangement of selections in this book is intended to be adaptable to this approach, too.

Achieving all of these diverse goals within the constraints of a book of this length and with only 34 selections was more challenging than I thought it would be, but it was far more stimulating, too. I can only hope the reader also will find this to be true.

Acknowledgments

Many people have assisted me in my efforts to produce this book. I appreciate the extensive advice and assistance given me by my colleagues in anthropology, most notably Pamela Amoss, John Atkins, Victor Barnouw, Carol Eastman, Charles Keyes, James Nason, William O'Barr, James Watson and Edgar Winans. In addition, William Madsen, Richard T. Curley, Robert F. Spier, and Allen S. Erlich offered numerous valuable comments and suggestions. I wish to thank those authors and publishers represented in this volume for permitting their material to be reprinted. Special acknowledgment is due, in this regard, to professors Beidelman, Edgerton, and Spiro, each of whom permitted their articles to be edited rather extensively in order to meet space limitations, and to Professor Suttles, who added a valuable "postscript" to his already important essay.

Particular thanks are due my immediate family and close friends, for they have had to live with and around me while I have essentially been living with a manuscript. I envy their patience, value their friendship, and am grateful for their support and encouragement.

February 1975   D.H.S.

Contents

INTRODUCTION

Questions about Variety: An Introduction to Anthropology and *The Human Experience*

The purpose of this introduction is to indicate the outlines of what I think sociocultural anthropology is and what sociocultural anthropologists have tried to find out about the human experience. This is done to assist the reader in developing a perspective for undertaking a critical examination of the diverse selections which comprise the bulk of this book. An overview of what I think are some of our main understandings and misunderstandings regarding the human experience is presented as *a* conclusion to this volume. This introduction and the conclusion are closely related conceptually, if not spatially; the adventurous may wish to read them together, both before and after studying the other selections.

IMAGES AND REALITIES

A young high school student once asked my wife why we had lived for nearly two years in Nigeria. When she answered that we were there as part of my work as an anthropologist, the student, with widening eyes, and in a soft, lingering voice, replied, "Faaarr out." That may well be the most succinct summary yet of one of the oldest and most common images of anthropology and anthropologists. Anthropology, in this view, is the study of exotic people, old stones and bones, and faraway places. Anthropologists, similarly, are odd people who do all these strange but exciting things—and get paid for it!

The problem with stereotypes is often not one of "facts" but of proportions. How typical are the facts implicit and explicit in our "far out" image? I would argue they are not typical at all, but rather (and more importantly), the reality is far more exciting than the image. But what, then, is the reality? What is anthropology?

As most introductory textbooks in anthropology state at the outset, anthropology is the study of humanity. But many people who study humans do not call themselves anthropologists and many others who call themselves anthropologists rarely (if ever) study humans. So there must be "something more"; there must be something which welds together the diverse membership of the discipline and, indeed, I think there is.

FINDING OUR ROOTS

In order to discover and understand what this "something more" is, it will be necessary to consider a few of the major developments which produced the academic discipline of anthropology we know today. It has been conventional, within anthropology, to state that ours is a young discipline with a history of just about a hundred years. This is accurate enough if, by anthropology, we mean a formal, academic, scholarly discipline with a recognized place in universities and other scholarly centers around the world. But anthropological thinking, it must be remembered, has been going on for much more than a century. People have reflected upon the nature of the human experience since the dawn of human existence itself. Many profound insights have emerged from these reflective moments; a surprising number of these, although distant in time and place, are strikingly contemporary in their content. Although these will not be sampled in great number here, I will be arguing, following Harris (1968), that while anthropology emerged as a formal academic discipline during only the last years of the 19th century, it has its most immediate and significant roots in the revolutionary ideas about mankind that were developed during the 18th century in Europe. It was during this period—the heart of the Enlightenment—that the unique and multifaceted anthropological view of the human experience began to take shape. Only by understanding the principles, assumptions, and orientations of this period can we see the "something more" that gives anthropology its distinctive role in the social sciences today.

LOCKE AND TURGOT

But, the reader may ask, why do we begin with the Enlightenment when, in fact, there have been productive ruminations about the human experience for thousands of years? Why not start with the ideas of classic Greece, ancient Mesopotamia, or imperial China? In part, the answer lies in the particular impetus given the inquiry into the human experience by two of the most impressive figures of the 18th century, at least as far as the study of humanity is concerned. These two are the English philosopher, John Locke, and the French politician and historian, Anne Robert Jacques Turgot.

To appreciate their contributions, we will do well to pause for a moment and consider the character of ideas about humanity, in all of its presumed variety, then reigning. The most ancient and universal observation made by people, of course, is that there are *other* distinctive groups of people. Indeed, the very word "other" implies or assumes differences that are important enough to be detected and remembered. People did not stop, however, with the obvious discovery that there were other people who behaved differently; they evaluated the behavior of these other people in moral terms, generally, with the standard being the moral tenets and behavioral tendencies of the group doing the evaluating. This process has occurred throughout history and across the face of the earth; westerners by no means have a monopoloy on making invidious distinctions. Many groups, for example, refer to themselves by using names which translate as "true humans" or "people," while the names for "others" are the equivalent of such words as "savage," "barbarian," or other more descriptive indications of their distinctive and inhuman qualities such as "the-ones-who-walk-on-their-heads."

In Christian Europe and America, for centuries it was held that people who were deemed inferior were in their deplorable state because they had fallen further from Grace than had the members of more moral groups. By the early 19th century, this view had reached its most elaborate form as the "theory of degeneration"—a theory which may be described as assuming that "all contemporary primitives are descended from peoples who enjoyed civilization prior to the construction of the Tower of Babel" (Harris 1968:54). Many other people were convinced that "inferior" people were not fully human, or were at best differently human (recalling once again the implication of the names groups of people have tended to give themselves and others over the ages). And still others, on hearing the numerous tales then being told, were convinced there were fantastic humanoids, with duck-like necks or no necks or heads at all, etc., inhabiting many of the far corners of the earth.

It was in this context that John Locke made his vitally important contribution to the study of humanity. This well known contribution, quite simply, is the assertion that humans do what they do and are what they are by virtue of *experience*. People do not, in the idiom of Locke's day, have innate ideas which cause them to behave differently. In the idiom of our day, we might say that if people have any innate ideas (as it is suggested they do in the realm of language, for example) then such "ideas" cause people to behave alike, not differently. It is this emphasis on variation in experience as the cause of variation in behavior which is the basis for a most fundamental anthropological assumption. It can be assumed that any *individual* differences in biogenetic endowment can generally be ignored because at the level of group differences in human behavior, these differences cancel each other out. This assumption is found in several disciplines that study humanity; in anthropology, it is the essence of the principle of the "psychic unity of mankind." In more familiar terms, perhaps, this principle holds that when comparing groups, the emphasis can be on nurture (experience) rather than nature (individual biogenetic endowment).

Carried to extremes (as sound principles almost inevitably are) this assumption leads to the scientific disaster of ignoring nature altogether, and this is exactly what some of Locke's more ardent supporters have done (and continue to do). As Harris tells us for example (1968:16), the Scotsman, Lord Monboddo argued, in 1774, that with sufficient training, apes could learn to talk. (What would he think of the reports on language learning among chimpanzees summarized by Peter Farb below in Chapter 4?) He was convinced, moreover, that orangutans were "wild men." "It is," he said,

> difficult to determine how far the natural capacities of the brutes may go with proper culture; but man, we know, may, by education and culture continued for many years, be transformed into an animal of another species. Thus with respect to his body, though he is undoubtedly by nature a terrestrial animal, yet he may be so accustomed to the water, as to become perfectly amphibious as a seal or an otter. —And, with respect to the mind, it is impossible to say how far science and philosophy may carry it. The Stoics pretended, in that way to make a *god* of a *man* [Monboddo 1774:22–23; cited in Harris 1968:16].

Nevertheless, there can be little doubt about the value of Locke's ideas for the scientific study of the human experience. Indeed, the very phrase juxtaposes Locke's key variable—experience—with the focal subject matter—humanity. And so it is to Locke that anthropology must trace its interest in showing how variation in experience, acting upon humans who as a whole are essentially equal (psychic unity), produces group variations in behavior.

One of the more useful and contemporary sounding expressions of the implications of Locke's principle for the study of humanity was given by the historian, Turgot, who was writing an outline for what was to be a "universal history." Although his masterwork was never completed, the outline provides this impressive challenge (then to his colleagues in history; today to his descendents in anthropology):

> Universal history embraces the consideration of the successive progress of humanity; and the detailed causes which have contributed to it: the earliest beginnings of man, the formation and mixture of nations; the

origins and revolutions of government; the development of language; of morality, custom, arts and sciences; the revolutions which have brought about the succession of empires, nations, and religions [Turgot 1844:627; orig. 1750; cited in Harris 1968:14].

This, then, is one of the most basic goals of anthropology—a goal which comes from the leaders of the Enlightenment, but which continues to animate anthropology today.

But, if Locke's principle and Turgot's charge are so important, why has it been conventional to take so shallow a view of anthropology's history? The answer to this is in some dispute, but one place to begin lies again with Locke and his influence on the course of politics in the United States. As is well known, Locke's principle formed a key part of the mood which produced the Declaration of Independence and the revolutionary assertion that all men are created equal. But it is also well known that Thomas Jefferson, to whom much of the credit goes for insisting that this phrase remain in his astounding document, had serious doubts about the endowments of the slaves he himself owned. And, as Harris emphasizes (1968:14), even Locke, along with many other 18th and 19th century students of the human experience, continued to cling to some version of the notion that "there were universally valid moral beliefs and right and wrong rules and modes of conduct." So firm were they in these beliefs that in spite of Locke's other arguments, it had become the case by the middle of the 19th century that "no 'truth' had become more 'self-evident' than that all men were created *unequal*. And no 'truth' was to exert a more noxious influence upon the course of social science" (Harris 1968:80).

In short, racial determinism became, for many, the dominant basis for explaining why groups of people behaved differently. And it is this episode in the history of anthropology, coupled with the intense reaction against it by early twentieth century anthropologists, which appears to have led to the neglect of the role of Locke, Turgot, and others in laying the foundations of modern anthropology.

19TH CENTURY EVOLUTIONISM

Interest in explaining why groups of people behaved differently continued throughout the 19th century. But by the last quarter of the century, when academic anthropology was in its infancy, one of the most significant concerns—and by all accounts the concern which has given this period its distinctive character—was with the development of a new intellectual framework which could give some sort of order to the ever increasing data anthropologists had about the lifestyles of people, both in the present and the past. The arrangements of data varied, but all of these schemes were influenced extensively by Darwinian evolutionary theory. In typical versions, anthropologists sought to order data on all aspects of human behavior by arranging the available facts (and some fancies) into what they thought were precise evolutionary sequences. They held that each form or institution developed out of earlier and simpler forms and that all of these developments could be ordered in time along a single broad line. The general practice was to subdivide this line of development into periods or "stages." Thus, in one of the more famous and widely adopted of such schemes, Lewis Henry Morgan (1877) wrote of the "Period of Savagery" (complete with "older," "middle," and "later" subdivisions followed by the "Period of Barbarism" (also with these subdivisions) and, ultimately, the "Period of Civilization" (with the zenith represented by the lifeways of people in England and America).

Such schemes were used not only for ordering particular human institutions (such as marriage forms, which were ranked in sequences from lowest or most savage or most immoral to highest or most civilized or most moral) but also whole groups of people (so that, for example, groups were placed at one or another level of development). All too often, selected and biased data were forced into preordained sequences with little regard for context, logic, or completeness. As we shall see shortly, this was a key factor leading to the downfall of such schemes for ordering the variety of human behavior.

To be sure, the evolutionary schemes of the late 19th century have their near counterparts in certain theories used in anthropology today. But of the many differences between the older and more contemporary evolutionary frameworks, two contrasts are of particular importance. First, in the late 19th century versions, evolutionism was characterized by a key assumption which no anthropologist makes today. This assumption was that groups of people can make "progress" along the evolutionary scale only by passing through all the "stages" or "periods" of cultural development, from a group's current position (whatever it was thought to be) through each succeeding level to, ultimately, the highest level of civilization. For example, people classified as savages, could not become "civilized" without first passing through the stage of "barbarism" (and all the relevant substages).

A second major difference stems from the moral implications implicit in these hierarchical systems. Not only were certain peoples lagging in terms of technical and social institutions, but these deficiencies, to the extent that they acted to separate people from civilization, also separated them from "true morality." In extreme cases, people were thought to have no morals at all. This assumption, along with the revolutionary developments occurring then in the technologic and economic sectors of European and American society, combined to give the period of the late 19th century a very dynamic and optimistic tone (at least from the vantage point of Europeans and Americans). "Progress" was indeed their "most important product." The older theories such as those which suggested people varied because they were in varying degrees fallen from Grace or were less than human were replaced, in most evolutionary frameworks, with an insistance that the course of history and the fate of all peoples was ultimately one of *progress* (not degeneration). It is easy to see, then, how all of these ideas and developments gave support to the colonization process which was beginning to move so rapidly (one hesitates to say "forward"). The technological capability was there, the moral justification was there, and the economic and political needs of Europe, particularly, were there. In short, the economic and political demands of late 19th century Europe were fulfilled with the justification that it was the obligation of more advanced people to lift the burden of ignorance and sin from the peoples of the "savage" world, and, in this way, to speed them along the long road to their ultimate destiny—civilization.

Mixed rather thoroughly among the proponents of such evolutionary schemes in anthropology were the racial determinists noted previously in our discussion of the traditionally shallow view of anthropological history. They argued, with effect, and in direct if unrecognized defiance of Locke's bold arguments of a century before, that the different levels of development exhibited by the various groups of people in the world, now and in the past, were simply further bits of evidence that these groups differed in their biogenetic or biophysical capacity for "civilization." And thus, the evolutionary schemes put forward as a way of ordering available data became linked with racial determinist answers to questions about why groups of people behaved the way they did.

EARLY 20TH CENTURY PARTICULARISM

As we noted, the tendency in the late 19th century was to use selected and biased data of a rather limited sort (albeit more abundant than in previous years) to bolster essentially heuristic evolutionary conceptions which, in fact, were not very faithful renderings of the biological principles upon which they ostensibly were based. Thus, in the early 20th century, under the leadership of anthropologists of a new generation on both sides of the Atlantic, students began to fan out into all parts of the world seeking solid data about the particulars of what people actually did. The goal was to collect extensive data first hand, rather than rely upon fragments of data which came to anthropologists by second, third and *n*th hand. The goal was also to record the behavior of groups of people who, it seemed clear by then, were not likely to survive the onrush of the western world. And, finally, rather than pushing the data into the preordained sequences developed in the 19th century or looking for racial explanations of group differences, the goal was "simply" to find out more about the range of human behavior.

This search had many appealing dimensions to it, not the least of which was the fact that as the data came in, more and more weaknesses were found in the already shaky 19th century conceptions of the human experience. Evolutionary schemes fell apart faster than they could be repaired, and racial determinism was crushed by the sheer weight of evidence. There simply was no way the behavior of groups of peoples could be ranked and ordered into such simple, unilinear schemes as had been proposed by Morgan and others, and there simply was no correlation between the complexity of human lifeways and human physical or biogenetc characteristics.

There continued to be interest in giving order to the data, to be sure. Particular attention was given to finding new ways to organize the ethnographic facts that were pouring in. Much effort was devoted to the discovery of internal order and logic (or "configurations" or "patterns") in the lifeways of specific groups of people. Rather than trying to make sense out of the variety of human groups by ranking them on a scale of human development, interest shifted to comparing selected groups in terms of general patterns and configurations they were thought to exhibit. More importantly, groups were not ranked in moral terms as had been the practice in the previous century. Indeed, many anthropologists went in the opposite direction and declared all distinctive lifeways to be morally equal. Although varying in form and degree from one anthropologist to another, most adopted some version of the still debated doctrine of "cultural relativism." It asserts, fundamentally, that no single standard of morality can be used in the assessment of the various human lifeways and that, as a consequence, a particular bit of human behavior can properly be evaluated only on the basis of the moral standards of the context in which the behavior occurs.

THREE QUESTIONS ABOUT HUMAN BEHAVIORAL VARIETY

By approximately the outbreak of World War II, anthropology had passed through at least three major and distinct historical periods, each characterized by a different principal concern. We will examine the main themes of the more recent decades of our history in the conclusion. But I believe we can now identify, through the historical record thus far presented (brief though it necessarily has been), the "something more" for which we have been searching. I think we can find the clues to the distinctive character of anthropology in the issues and orientations of the past two hundred years. For as people are known by the company they keep seeing, sciences, it seems to me, are known by the questions their practioners keep asking. And today, as in the past, anthropologists are asking three very general, fundamental, and closely interrelated questions about the human experience. All three, moreover, are about the same thing: *human behavioral variety*. They are:

1.   *Why* is there variety in human societies?
2.   *What order* can be discovered in and/or given to this variety?
3.   *How much* variety is there?

Although these are not the only questions about human behavioral variety that can be asked, they are the ones which have held center-stage in anthropology over the past two centuries. Each has been in the spotlight in its own turn, but always with the other two close at hand.

Anthropology, then, is not "simply" the science of humanity. Distinctively, it is the science oriented to answering, at a pan-human level, these three very general questions. They are, as we have seen, rooted in the views of humanity developed principally by John Locke in the 18th century. Thus, it is assumed that biogenetic differences between societies[1] are sufficiently minor that they can be given secondary consideration when attempting to answer these three questions. It must be emphasized, however, that another of the hallmarks of anthropology has been and continues to be the contention that humans must be recognized for what they are—very distinctive animals, but animals none the less.

The great importance of these questions cannot be over stressed. No other human science has asked all three so consistently for so long. Their importance is intrinsic and individual as well as extrinsic and collective. They are ancient and modern; they seem simple but are terribly complex. They can stand alone and yet they are highly interconnected. If we can appreciate the answers anthropologists have tended to give to them, we will have come a long way toward understanding both anthropology and the human experience, for they are the essence of each.

---

[1] In this discussion, the term "society" is used in a very particular way. This must be emphasized since this term has been given many meanings over the years. Here, a society will be understood to refer to a population of humans that is sufficiently diverse in age and sex (and other relevant characteristics of this sort) that it can, barring disasters, survive and grow through time. In this sense, a society is analogous to a "population" as the term is generally used in genetics. In particular, it is analogous to such sub-specific taxonomic terms as "variety" and "race" (the latter term being very different from its ostensible social "counterpart)." In this sense, then, a society, like a genetic population, is a statistical reality. That is, gene flow in the "population" and the flow of symbolic information (and genes, too) in a society is most frequent within these statistical units but *not* limited to them. The utility of such a definition is elaborated upon in the conclusion.

Part I

CULTURE AND FIELDWORK

CULTURE

We have said that anthropologists ask three basic questions about human behavioral variety. In seeking answers to these questions, anthropologists utilize numerous concepts. Among them is one which is undoubtedly the discipline's most venerated, vexatious and vital concept. This is the concept "culture." The word culture has been used to denote many things. Not surprisingly, this has been a cause of considerable confusion and misunderstanding. Indeed, for many, such variability in the use of what seems to be so central a concept is extremely disconcerting. (It is curious that anthropological scientists should be disconcerted rather than intrigued by such variation but apparently such is the nature of scientists.)

That "culture" has been defined in many ways can be documented easily. It may be sufficient to note that in 1952, a review of the conceptions of culture was published by two of the most influential anthropologists of the day—Alfred Kroeber and Clyde Kluckhohn. Their review listed hundreds of specific definitions of culture. Many of them were essentially duplicates or were seriously incomplete or deficient in some other way. But even if these are eliminated from consideration, 164 reasonably distinct definitions remain. Kroeber and Kluckhohn felt these definitions could be grouped into six major types, and from all of them they distilled a definitional blend which asserts that culture is

> patterns, explicit and implicit, of and for behavior, acquired and transmitted by symbols, constituting the distinctive achievement of human groups, including their embodiments in artifacts . . . [Kroeber and Kluckhohn 1952:357].

This definition is not given here because it is right or because it is accepted by most anthropologists. (Indeed, this definitional distillate is probably no more popular among anthropologists than blend whiskeys are

13

among people in Kentucky and Tennessee.) Rather, it is given because it illustrates most of the usual referents of the term as well as some of its principal excesses—e.g., that culture is the distinctive achievement of *Homo sapiens*. It also serves as a benchmark for considering some of the developments in the decades since their review was published.

Since 1952, there have been many attempts to define culture in more limited terms, with anthropologist *a* asserting (and sometimes arguing) that culture should denote only phenomenon *X,* anthropologist *b* asserting (and also sometimes arguing) that culture should only denote phenomenon *Y,* and so on through anthropologists *c, d, . . . n.* Some of these definitions have had significant impact on recent anthropological inquiry; it is these definitional statements that will be noted briefly here.

First, Marvin Harris (1964:183) states that [human] culture is "the sum of the entities [concepts] constructed from the observation of the behavior of [people]." "Culture is any and all . . . nomothetic nonverbal and verbal data language units" pertaining to behavior and defined in operational terms. Examples of "data language units" include such comparatively familiar things as words, phonemes, and behavior plans, and such unfamiliar things as "actones," "scenes," "permaclones," and "permaclonic supersystems." The latter unfamiliar words, just as the more familiar ones, are labels which refer to observed regularities in behavior. They are all cultural things in that they are concepts (or data language units) which are constructed from the observation of humans behaving.

Ward Goodenough (1963:258–59) states that culture consists of

> standards for deciding what is, standards for deciding what can be, standards for deciding how one feels about it, standards for deciding what to do about it, and standards for deciding how to go about doing it.

Goodenough insists, therefore, that culture as he defines it not be confused with "the patterns of recurring events and arrangements that characterize the community as a relatively stable system" (1963:Ibid.). Even though such patterns of behavior have been called "culture" in some other definitions, Goodenough argues that culture consists of whatever standards for behavior one has to know in order to behave in a manner acceptable to "natives."

The last definitional statement to be considered here is that of Clifford Geertz. He states (1973:92) that "culture patterns, that is systems or complexes of symbols . . . are extrinsic sources of information." By "symbols," Geertz means (1973:91)

> any object, act, event, quality, or relation which serves as a vehicle for a conception—the conception is the symbol's "meaning" . . . they are tangible formulations of notions, abstractions from experience fixed in perceptible forms, concrete embodiments of ideas, attitudes, judgments, longings, or beliefs.

By "extrinsic," Geertz means that the information or symbols

> lie outside the boundaries of the individual organism as such in that intersubjective world of common understandings into which all human individuals are born, in which they pursue their separate careers, and which they leave persisting behind them after they die.

By "sources of information," Geertz means that these symbols, like genes, "provide a blueprint or template in terms of which processes external to themselves can be given a definite form." But, he adds (1973:93–4), unlike genes which are *only* models or guides for reality, "culture patterns have an intrinsic double aspect: they give meaning, that is objective conceptual form, to social and psychological reality both by shaping themselves to it [i.e., by being a model of reality] and by shaping it to themselves [i.e., by being a model or guide for reality]." Culture patterns serve not only as "sources of information in terms of which other processes can be patterned," but also as representations of "those patterned processes as such, [expressing] their structure in an alternative medium . . ." (Geertz 1973:94).

These definitions appear to exhibit far more differences than similarities. Certainly the authors of these definitional statements act as though this were true. Harris has denounced Goodenough; Goodenough has denounced Harris, Geertz has denounced Goodenough, and so on and on. Although there certainly are differences in the import of these statements as worded and as they are used by the authors and their followers, there are several important similarities. A brief consideration of these, as well as some of the key differences, will provide a starting point for gaining a good working understanding of "culture."

One of the more important points of convergence is that all three of these definitional statements suggest that cultural things are more or less symbolic things. For Harris, these symbols are scientific abstractions from behavior. For Goodenough, they are symbol-like standards for conduct that exist in the human mind. For Geertz, cultural things are symbols par excellence—i.e., Janus-like, shared, public, meaningful things. As can be seen, however, these are similarities and not congruencies.

Also, none of these definitions would reduce culture to human behavior itself. Some have thought Harris' definition amounts to this; a few have even believed he was only interested in nonverbal behavior. This is not correct. He specifically states (1964:172) that individual human behavior per se is not a cultural thing. It is clear that Goodenough is not claiming human behavior is itself culture. Although this is less clear in the statements by Geertz, he does stress that culture refers to the meaning of behavior and not merely the behavior itself.

Of the many differences, the following may be noted. Harris appears to be more interested in scientific abstractions than in the abstractions that exist in the heads of "natives." This does not mean, however, that he is completely uninterested in the things natives think and believe. Harris' concepts apparently do not have the dual "of" and "for" qualities posited by Geertz. Rather, the nomothetic concepts used by Harris appear to be *models of* reality only. Goodenough is most interested in the standards for behavior which are in the native's head, but Geertz strongly dissents (1973:11–12), arguing that meaning is public not private; symbolic patterns and cultural acts are, he say, "as public as marriage and as observable as agriculture" (1973:91). Harris is interested in observable reality, as is Geertz, but both Goodenough and Geertz see cultural things as "standards" or as "templates" that guide behavior. Harris does not see cultural things as guides for behavior, or at least this is not emphasized. For Harris, behavior is shaped by the material, techno-environmental circumstances faced by a group of people; culture is simply the set of concepts used to describe that behavior.

For the moment, this is all that will be said about what culture is; the issue is complex and will be taken up again briefly in the conclusion (see especially pages 420–21). I think it is fair to say, however, that none of these formulations tells the whole story. In the first essay in this book, however, Clifford Geertz does give us a forceful statement about one of the most important lessons which comes from the culture concept. Seeing culture primarily as "a set of control mechanisms" (or guides for behavior), he argues that "man is precisely the animal most desperately dependent upon such extragenetic, outside-the-skin control mechanisms." Humans emerged at the end of an evolutionary process (which really hasn't ended) that involved *both* culture and physiology. The physical organism that is "man" would be just as inhuman without a particular culture as a particular culture would be impossible without "man." On this fundamental point, there is very strong agreement within anthropology.

FIELDWORK

In the late 1950s, when the Russian government amazed the world by launching its Sputnik, it also launched an amazing response in America—the crash programs in science. Perhaps the only other crash program in those days which was more dramatic was our space effort itself, with rocket after rocket falling in fiery ignominy. As part of the science crash program, it was common for university science departments to invite interested high school seniors to campus for "science day." I remember my visit very well. Complex scientific apparatuses had been erected on demonstration tables in various laboratories. As we moved from room to room, imposing looking instructors in the required long white lab coats gave us a glimpse of "science." They dropped chemicals which made blue liquids turn pink and pink liquids clear. They dipped roses into liquid nitrogen, transforming them into frozen monuments to the fragility of nature and the power of science. And, as if to demonstrate this realistically as well as symbolically, they dashed these icy blooms against the laboratory tables, shattering the petals into countless crystalline fragments. This sort of drama was continued for several hours. At the end, of course, the scientists expressed the hope that we prospective college students would major in biology, physics or chemistry, thus enabling us to participate in the sort of excitement we had witnessed that day (and, of course, to do our part in helping the United States catch up with the Soviets in the race for space).

I actually don't care very much for roses, but neither do I care for this way of presenting the activity of scientists. Indeed, to my mind, one of the more pathetic developments in a science is the extent to which scientists themselves come to accept the caricature of the enterprise in place of its character. In doing so, a very real risk is that the caricature will become the character. To be sure, doing anthropology is exciting and it is often very dramatic indeed. Few other aspects of anthropology hold out as much mystery and public awe as "fieldwork." Next to the word "culture" it is most certainly true that "fieldwork" is the hallmark of both the image and reality of anthropology.

For sociocultural anthropologists, fieldwork may be defined minimally as the collection of data about human behavior through extended first hand observation of humans in their normal habitats (normal except for the presence of the anthropologist, a fact that is of some significance to the overall field situation, as George Devereux would remind us; Devereux 1967). To borrow an apt phrase from Geertz, fieldwork is the way anthropologists "descend into detail."

But anthropologists have not always relied upon such extended experiences with people as the means of gathering data; indeed, the tradition is only about 60 years old, but once developed, anthropology has never looked back. The older more or less secondhand and cursory approaches to learning about human behavior were found to be inadequate by comparison to the newer ways. Details emerged that not only had been missed before but which changed radically our assumptions about what it was we were viewing. At times, early fieldworkers became bogged down in almost mindless data collecting, but on balance, the improvements which came from "simply" living on a firsthand, day-to-day basis with the people whose lifeways were of interest proved to be a great aid to understanding.

Good accounts of anthropological fieldwork are rare. The better ones, moreover, tend to be long, complex, tightly integrated, and autobiographical in nature. Consequently, they are not easily fragmented for use in anthologies. These facts in themselves shed some light on what the field experience can be like. Anthropologists often reveal selected aspects of their fieldwork, especially in lectures and in the context of scholarly discourse on other topics. The selections in this book by Lee, A. Wolf, Sinha, and Fox (among others), contain several comments which give us at least a glimpse of what their fieldwork was like. The two brief essays on fieldwork included in Part I probably will not tell most readers all they would like to know about this almost mystical anthropological rite of passage, but together they do provide many very valuable insights.

The first of the two is by Margaret Mead, perhaps the most famous anthropologist of all time. She is famous for many reasons, not the least of which is her almost legendary ability as a fieldworker. She has done fieldwork in eight cultures—far more than is typical. She has been a pioneer in the use of data gathering techniques now considered standard, and the published record of her research is almost without parallel. In her essay in Chapter 2, she reveals only a small portion of her broad interests. One of her concerns is the phenomenon of cultural continuity in the midst of sweeping change—a theme of great importance in anthropology that will be considered in more detail in Part X. In her reflective and almost melancholy comments about fieldwork, she reveals a wisdom that has become the trademark of all her observations about the human experience.

She speaks of the "ordinary business" of fieldwork and, at the same time, documents the many ways in which it is truly a most extraordinary experience. Fieldwork is very demanding, it has a remoteness which permits concentration, it requires the response of a whole person, it involves continual "active waiting," it thrives upon the helter-skelter of everyday life, and it involves paradoxes of involvement and detachment. And, as she suggests, it has become one of the most significant challenges for anthropologists today.

A view of fieldwork from this more recent perspective is provided in Chapter 3 by Victor Uchendu. His comments about fieldwork are representative in that he describes problems and concerns many anthropologists of this generation face, but it is also somewhat unique because we have very few discussions of fieldwork by those among us who are not westerners. It is noteworthy, then, that Uchendu should emphasize the significance of the ethnographer's "cultural load." Because most anthropologists are westerners, the discipline has probably given less attention than it should to the potential biasing effect of these cultural factors. There are many other valuable points of emphasis on Uchendu's essay. For example, he correctly notes the importance of gaining appropriate entry into the lives of the people whose culture is to be studied. The word "appropriate" is crucial here because it raises many questions about the ethical responsibilities of an ethnographer that are difficult to answer. One might think, perhaps, that it should be easy to live up to these ethical responsibilities but often they are in conflict (e.g., the rights of the people being studied vis-à-vis the constraints of the host government). These issues are not solved simply by raising them, and to a certain extent, since they are ethical issues, they are unlikely to be resolved to the satisfaction of all concerned. Nevertheless, it remains true that each anthropologist must consider the implications of what he or she does during fieldwork and afterwards, and should attempt, insofar as this is possible, to do the work in a way which contributes the greatest good to the greatest number.

But in the final analysis, two brief essays can convey only a minor portion of the complexity that is anthropological fieldwork. Those who would know more of what it is like but who cannot do it themselves must, paradoxically, do a little fieldwork about fieldwork among those anthropologists they encounter. As in all fieldwork, if the questions are specific and probing (and not the equivalent of "What is fieldwork really like?"), the sought after details will emerge.

Clifford Geertz

1. The Impact of the Concept of Culture on the Concept of Man*

I

Toward the end of his recent study of the ideas used by tribal peoples, *La Pensée Sauvage,* the French anthropologist, Lévi-Strauss, remarks that scientific explanaation does not consist, as we have been led to imagine, in the reduction of the complex to the simple. Rather, it consists, he says, in a substitution of a complexity more intelligible for one which is less. So far as the study of man is concerned, one may go even farther, I think, and argue that explanation often consists of substituting complex pictures for simple ones while striving somehow to retain the persuasive clarity that went with the simple ones.

Elegance remains, I suppose, a general scientific ideal; but in the social sciences, it is very often in departures from that ideal that truly creative developments occur. Scientific advancement commonly consists in a progressive complication of what once seemed a beautifully simple set of notions but now seems an unbearably simplistic one. It is after this sort of disenchantment occurs that intelligibility, and thus explanatory power, comes to rest on the possibility of substituting the involved but comprehensible for the involved but incomprehensible to which Lévi-Strauss refers. Whitehead once offered to the natural sciences the maxim: "Seek simplicity and distrust it"; to the social sciences he might well have offered "Seek complexity and order it."

* Reprinted by permission of author and publisher from *New Views of the Nature of Man,* John R. Platt, ed., University of Chicago Press, 1965:93–118.

21

Certainly, the study of culture has developed as though this maxim were being followed. The rise of a scientific concept of culture amounted to, or at least was connected with, the overthrow of the view of human nature dominant in the Enlightenment—a view that, whatever else may be said for or against it, was both clear and simple—and its replacement by a view not only more complicated but enormously less clear. The attempt to clarify it, to reconstruct an intelligible account of what man is, has underlain scientific thinking about culture ever since. Having sought complexity and, on a scale grander than they ever imagined, found it, anthropologists became entangled in a tortuous effort to order it. And the end is not yet in sight.

The Enlightenment view of man was, of course, that he was wholly of a piece with nature and shared in the general uniformity of composition which natural science, under Bacon's urging and Newton's guidance, had discovered there. There is, in brief, a human nature as regularly organized, as thoroughly invariant, and as marvelously simple as Newton's universe. Perhaps some of its laws are different, but there *are* laws; perhaps some of its immutability is obscured by the trappings of local fashion, but it *is* immutable.

A quotation that Lovejoy (whose magisterial analysis I am following here) gives from an Enlightenment historian, Mascou, presents the position with the useful bluntness one often finds in a minor writer:

> The stage setting [in different times and places] is, indeed, altered, the actors change their garb and their appearance; but their inward motions arise from the same desires and passions of men, and produce their effects in the vicissitudes of kingdoms and peoples [Lovejoy 1960:173; orig. 1948].

Now, this view is hardly one to be despised; nor, despite my easy references a moment ago to "overthrow," can it be said to have disappeared from contemporary anthropological thought. The notion that men are men under whatever guise and against whatever backdrop has not been replaced by "other mores, other beasts."

Yet, cast as it was, the Enlightenment concept of the nature of human nature had some much less acceptable implications, the main one being that, to quote Lovejoy himself this time, "anything of which the intelligibility, verifiability, or actual affirmation is limited to men of a special age, race, temperament, tradition or condition is [in and of itself] without truth or value, or at all events without importance to a reasonable man" [Lovejoy 1960:80]. The great, vast variety of differences among men, in beliefs and values, in customs and institutions, both over time and from place to place, is essentially without significance in defining his nature. It consists of mere accretions, distortions even, overlaying and obscuring what is truly human—the constant, the general, the universal—in man.

Thus, in a passage now notorious, Dr. Johnson saw Shakespeare's genius to lie in the fact that "his characters are not modified by the customs of particular places, unpractised by the rest of the world; by the peculiarities of studies or professions, which can operate upon but small numbers; or by the accidents of transient fashions or temporary opinions" [Johnson 1931:11–12]. And Racine regarded the success of his plays on classical themes as proof that "the taste of Paris . . . conforms to that of Athens; my spectators have been moved by the same things which, in other times, brought tears to the eyes of the most cultivated classes of Greece" [from the Preface to Iphigénie].

The trouble with this kind of view, aside from the fact that it sounds comic coming from someone as profoundly English as Johnson or as French as Racine, is that the image of a constant human nature independent of time, place, and circumstance, of studies and professions, transient fashions and temporary opinions, may be an illusion, that what man is may be so entangled with where he is, who he is, and what he believes that it is inseparable from them. It is precisely the consideration of such a possibility that led to the rise of the concept of culture and the decline of the uniformitarian view of man. Whatever else modern anthropology asserts—and it seems to have asserted almost everything at one time or another—it is firm in the conviction that men unmodified by the customs of particular places do not in fact exist, have never existed, and most important, could not in the very nature of the case exist. There is, there can be, no backstage where we can go to catch a glimpse of Mascou's actors as "real persons" lounging about in street clothes, disengaged from their profession, displaying with artless candor their spontaneous desires and unprompted passions. They may change their roles, their styles of acting, even the dramas in which they play; but—as Shakespeare himself of course remarked—they are always performing.

This circumstance makes the drawing of a line between what is natural, universal, and constant in man and what is conventional, local, and variable extraordinarily difficult. In fact, it suggests that to draw such a line is to falsify the human situation, or at least to misrender it seriously.

Consider Balinese trance. The Balinese fall into extreme dissociated states in which they perform all sorts of spectacular activities—biting off the heads of living chickens, stabbing themselves with daggers, throwing themselves wildly about, speaking with tongues, performing miraculous feats of equilibration, mimicking sexual intercourse, eating feces, and so on—rather more easily and much more suddenly than most of us fall asleep. Trance states are a crucial part of every ceremony. In some, fifty or sixty people may fall, one after the other ("like a string of firecrackers going off," as one observer puts it), emerging anywhere from five minutes to several hours later, totally unaware of what they have been doing and convinced, despite the amnesia, that they have had the most extraordinary and deeply satisfying experience a man can have. What does one learn about human nature from this sort of thing and from the thousand similarly peculiar things anthropologists discover, investigate, and describe? That the Balinese are peculiar sorts of beings, South Sea Martians? That they are just the same as we at base, but with some peculiar, but really incidental, customs we do not happen to have gone in for? That they are innately gifted or even instinctively driven in certain directions rather than others? Or that human nature does not exist and men are pure and simply what their culture makes them?

It is among such interpretations as these, all unsatisfactory, that anthropology has attempted to find its way to a more viable concept of man, one in which culture, and the variability of culture, would be taken into account rather than written off as caprice and prejudice and yet, at the same time, one in which the governing principle of the field, "the basic unity of mankind," would not be turned into an empty phrase. To take the giant step away from the uniformitarian view of human nature is, so far as the study of man is concerned, to leave the Garden. To entertain the idea that the diversity of custom across time and over space is not a mere matter of garb and appearance, of stage settings and comedic masques, is to entertain also the idea that humanity is as various in its essence as it is in its expression. And with that reflection some well-fastened philosophical moorings are loosed and an uneasy drifting into perilous waters begins.

Perilous, because if one discards the notion that Man, with a capital "M," is to be looked for "behind," "under," or "beyond" his customs and replaces it with the notion that he, uncapitalized, is to be looked for "in" them, one is in some danger of losing sight of him altogether. Either he dissolves, without residue, into his time and place, a child and perfect captive of his age, or he becomes a conscripted soldier in a vast Tolstoian army, engulfed in one or another of the terrible historical determinisms with which we have been plagued from Hegel forward. We have had, and to some extent still have, both of these aberrations in the social sciences —one marching under the banner of cultural relativism, the other under that of cultural evolution. But we also have had, and more commonly, attempts to avoid them by seeking in culture patterns themselves the defining elements of a human existence which, although not constant in expression, are yet distinctive in character.

II

Attempts to locate man amid the body of his customs have taken several directions, adopted diverse tactics; but they have all, or virtually all, proceeded in terms of a single over-all intellectual strategy: what I will call, so as to have a stick to beat it with, the "stratigraphic" conception of the relations between biological, psychological, social, and cultural factors in human life. In this conception, man is a composite of "levels," each superimposed upon those beneath it and underpinning those above it. As one analyzes man, one peels off layer after layer, each such layer being complete and irreducible in itself, revealing another, quite different sort of layer underneath. Strip off the motley forms of culture and one finds the structural and functional regularities of social organization. Peel off these in turn and one finds the underlying psychological factors—"basic needs" or what-have-you—that support and make them possible. Peel off psychological factors and one is left with the biological foundations—anatomical, physiological, neurological—of the whole edifice of human life.

The attraction of this sort of conceptualization, aside from the fact that it guaranteed the established academic disciplines their independence and sovereignty, was that it seemed to make it possible to have one's cake and eat it. One did not have to assert that man's culture was all there was to him in order to claim that it was, nonetheless, an essential and irreducible, even a paramount ingredient in his nature. Cultural facts could be interpreted against the background of non-cultural facts without either dissolving them into that background or dissolving that background into them. Man was a hierarchically stratified animal, a sort of evolutionary deposit, in whose definition each level—organic, psychological, social, and cultural—had an assigned and incontestable place. To see what he really was, we had to superimpose findings from the various relevant sciences—anthropology, sociology, psychology, biology—upon one another like so many patterns in a *moiré*; and when that was done, the cardinal importance of the cultural level, the only one distinctive to man, would naturally appear, as would what it had to tell us, in its own right, about what he really was. For the eighteenth-century image of man as the naked reasoner that appeared when he took his cultural costumes off, the anthropology of the late nineteenth and early twentieth centuries substituted the image of man as the transfigured animal that appeared when he put them on.

At the level of concrete research and specific analysis, this grand strategy came down, first, to a hunt for universals in culture, for empirical uniformities that, in the face of the diversity of customs around the world and over time, could be found everywhere in about the same form, and, second, to an effort to relate such universals, once found, to the established constants of human biology, psychology, and social organization. If some customs could be ferreted out of the cluttered catalogue of world culture as common to all local variants of it, and if these could then be connected in a determinate manner with certain invariant points of reference on the subcultural levels, then at least some progress might be made toward specifying which cultural traits are essential to human existence and which merely adventitious, peripheral, or ornamental. In such a way, anthropology could determine cultural dimensions of a concept of man commensurate with the dimensions provided, in a similar way, by biology, psychology, or sociology.

In essence, this is not altogether a new idea. The notion of a *consensus gentium* (a consensus of all mankind)—the notion that there are some things that all men will be found to agree upon as right, real, just, or attractive and that these things are, therefore, in fact right, real, just, or attractive—was present in the Enlightenment and probably, has been present in some form or another in all ages and climes. It is one of those ideas that occur to almost anyone sooner or later. Its development in modern anthropology, however—beginning with Clark Wissler's elaboration in the nineteen-twenties of what he called "the universal cultural pattern," through Bronislaw Malinowski's presentation of a list of "universal institutional types" in the early forties, up to G. P. Murdock's elaboration of a set of "common-denominators of culture" during and since World War II —added something new. It added the notion that, to quote Clyde Kluckhohn [1953:516], perhaps the most persuasive of the *consensus gentium* theorists, "some aspects of culture take their specific forms solely as a result of historical accidents; others are tailored by forces which can properly be designated as universal." With this, man's cultural life is split in two: part of it is, like Mascou's actors' garb, independent of men's Newtonian "inward motions"; part is an emanation of those motions themselves. The question that then arises is, Can this halfway house between the eighteenth and twentieth centuries really stand?

Whether it can or not depends on whether the dualism between empirically universal aspects of culture rooted in subcultural realities and empirically variable aspects not so rooted can be established and sustained. And this, in turn, demands (1) that the universals proposed be substantial ones and not empty categories; (2) that they be specifically grounded in particular biological, psychological, or sociological processes, not just vaguely associated with "underlying realities"; and (3) that they can convincingly be defended as core elements in a definition of humanity in comparison with which the much more numerous cultural particularities are of clearly secondary importance. On all three of these counts it seems to me that the *consensus gentium* approach fails; rather than moving toward the essentials of the human situation, it moves away from it.

The reason the first of these requirements—that the proposed universals be substantial ones and not empty or near empty categories—has not been met is that it cannot. There is a logical conflict between asserting that, say, "religion," "marriage," or "property" are empirical universals and giving them very much in the way of specific content, for to say that they are empirical universals is to say that they have the same content, and to say they have the same content is to fly in the face of the undeniable fact that they do not. If one defines religion generally and indeterminately—as man's most fundamental orientation to reality, for example

—then one cannot at the same time assign to that orientation a highly circumstantial content, for clearly what composes the most fundamental orientation to reality among the transported Aztecs, lifting pulsing hearts torn live from the chests of human sacrifices toward the heavens, is not what comprises it among the stolid Zuñi, dancing their great mass supplications to the benevolent gods of rain. The obsessive ritualism and unbuttoned polytheism of the Hindus expresses a rather different view of what the really real is really like from the uncompromising monotheism and austere legalism of Sunni Islam. Even if one does try to get down to less abstract levels and assert, as Kluckhohn did, that a concept of the afterlife is universal or, as Malinowski did, that a sense of Providence is universal, the same contradiction haunts one. To make the generalization about an afterlife stand up alike for the Confucians and the Calvinists, the Zen Buddhists and the Tibetan Buddhists, one has to define it in most general terms, indeed—so general, in fact, that whatever force it seems to have virtually evaporates. So, too, with any notion of a "sense of Providence," which can include under its wing both Navaho notions about the relations of gods to men and Trobriand ones. And as with religion, so with "marriage," "trade," and all the rest of what A. L. Kroeber aptly called "fake universals," down to so seemingly tangible a matter as "shelter." That everywhere people mate and produce children, have some sense of mine and thine, and protect themselves in one fashion or another from rain and sun are neither false nor, from some points of view, unimportant; but they are hardly very much help in drawing a portrait of man that will be a true and honest likeness and not an untenanted "John Q. Public" sort of cartoon.

My point, which should be clear and I hope will become even clearer in a moment, is not that there are no generalizations that can be made about man as man, save that he is a most various animal, or that the study of culture has nothing to contribute toward the uncovering of such generalizations. My point is that such generalizations are not to be discovered through a Baconian search for cultural universals, a kind of public-opinion polling of the world's peoples in search of a *consensus gentium* that does not in fact exist, and, further, that the attempt to do so leads to precisely the sort of relativism the whole approach was expressly designed to avoid. "Zuñi culture prizes restraint," Kluckhohn writes; "Kwakiutl culture encourages exhibitionism on the part of the individual. These are contrasting values, but in adhering to them the Zuñi and Kwakiutl show their allegiance to a universal value; the prizing of the distinctive norms of one's culture" [Kluckhohn 1962:280]. This is sheer evasion, but it is only more apparent, not more evasive, than discussions of cultural universals in general. What, after all, does it avail us to say, with Herskovits [1955:364], that "morality is a universal, and so is enjoyment of beauty, and some standard for truth," if we are forced in the very next sentence, as he is, to add that "the many forms these concepts take are but products of the particular historical experience of the societies that manifest them"? Once one abandons uniformitarianism, even if, like the *consensus gentium* theorists, only partially and uncertainly, relativism is a genuine danger; but it can be warded off only by facing directly and fully the diversities of human culture, the Zuñi's restraint and the Kwakiutl's exhibitionism, and embracing them within the body of one's concept of man, not by gliding past them with vague tautologies and forceless banalities.

Of course, the difficulty of stating cultural universals which are at the same time substantial also hinder fulfillment of the second requirement facing the *consensus gentium* approach, that of grounding such universals in particular biological, psychological, or sociological processes. But there is more to it than that: the "stratigraphic" conceptualization of the relationships between cultural and non-cultural factors hinders such a grounding even more effectively. Once culture, psyche, society, and organism have been converted into separate scientific "levels," complete and autonomous in themselves, it is very hard to bring them back together again.

The most common way of trying to do so is through the utilization of what are called "invariant points of reference." These points are to be found, to quote one of the most famous statements of this strategy—the "Toward a Common Language for the Areas of the Social Sciences" memorandum produced by Talcott Parsons, Kluckhohn, O. H. Taylor, and others in the early forties—

> in the nature of social systems, in the biological and psychological nature of the component individuals, in the external situations in which they live and act, in the necessity of coordination in social systems. In [culture] . . . these "foci" of structure are never ignored. They must in some way be "adapted to" or taken account of."

Cultural universals are conceived to be crystallized responses to these unevadable realities, institutionalized ways of coming to terms with them.

Analysis consists, then, of matching assumed universals to postulated underlying necessities, attempting to show there is some goodness of fit between the two. On the social level, reference is made to such irrefragable facts as that all societies, in order to persist, must reproduce their membership or allocate goods and services, hence the universality of some form of family or some form of trade. On the psychological level, recourse is had to basic needs like personal growth—hence the ubiquity of educational institutions—or to panhuman problems, like the Oedipal predicament—hence the ubiquity of punishing gods and nurturant goddesses. Biologically, there is metabolism and health; culturally, dining customs and curing procedures. And so on. The tack is to look at underlying human requirements of some sort or other and then to try to show that those aspects of culture that are universal are, to use Kluckhohn's figure again, "tailored" by these requirements.

The problem here is, again, not so much whether in a general way this sort of congruence exists but whether it is more than a loose and indeterminate one. It is not difficult to relate some human institutions to what science (or common sense) tells us are requirements for human existence, but it is very much more difficult to state this relationship in an unequivocal form. Not only does almost any institution serve a multiplicity of social, psychological, and organic needs (so that to say that marriage is a mere reflex of the social need to reproduce, or that dining customs are a reflex of metabolic necessities, is to court parody), but there is no way to state in any precise and testable way the interlevel relationships that are conceived to hold. Despite first appearances, there is no serious attempt here to apply the concepts and theories of biology, psychology, or even sociology to the analysis of culture (and, of course, not even a suggestion of the reverse exchange) but merely a placing of supposed facts from the cultural and subcultural levels side by side so as to induce a vague sense that some kind of relationship between them—an obscure sort of "tailoring"—obtains. There is no theoretical integration here at all but a mere correlation, and that intuitive, of separate findings. With the levels approach, we can never, even by invoking "invariant points of reference," construct genuine functional interconnections between cultural and non-cultural factors, only more or less persuasive analogies, parallelisms, suggestions, and affinities.

However, even if I am wrong (as, admittedly, many anthropologists would hold) in claiming that the *consensus gentium* approach can produce neither substantial universals nor specific connections between cultural and non-cultural phenomena to explain them, the question still remains whether such universals should be taken as the central elements in the definition of man, whether a lowest common denominator view of humanity is what we want anyway. This is, of course, now a philosophical question, not as such a scientific one; but the notion that the essence of what it means to be human is most clearly revealed in those features of human culture that are universal rather than in those that are distinctive to this people or that is a prejudice we are not necessarily obliged to share. Is it in grasping such general facts—that man has everywhere some sort of "religion"—or in grasping the richness of this religious phenomenon or that—Balinese trance or Indian ritualism, Aztec human sacrifice or Zuñi rain dancing—that we grasp him? Is the fact that "marriage" is universal (if it is) as penetrating a comment on what we are as the facts concerning Himalayan polyandry, or those fantastic Australian marriage rules, or the elaborate bride-price systems of Bantu Africa? The comment that Cromwell was the most typical Englishman of his time precisely in that he was the oddest may be relevant in this connection, too: it may be in the cultural particularities of people—in their oddities—that some of the most instructive revelations of what it is to be generically human are to be found; and the main contribution of the science of anthropology to the construction—or reconstruction—of a concept of man may then lie in showing us how to find them.

III

The major reason why anthropologists have shied away from cultural particularities when it came to a question of defining man and have taken refuge instead in bloodless universals is that, faced as they are with the enormous variation in human behavior, they are haunted by a fear of historicism, of becoming lost in a whirl of cultural relativism so convulsive as to deprive them of any fixed bearings at all. Nor has there not been some occasion for such a fear: Ruth Benedict's *Patterns of Culture,* probably the most popular book in anthropology ever published in this country, with its strange conclusion that anything one group of people is inclined toward doing is worthy of respect by another, is perhaps only the most outstanding example of the awkward positions one can get into by giving oneself over rather too completely to what Marc Bloch called "the thrill of learning singular things." Yet the fear is a bogy. The notion that unless a cultural phenomenon is empirically universal it cannot reflect anything about the nature of man is about as logical as the notion that because sickle-cell anemia is, fortunately, not universal it cannot tell us anything about human genetic processes. It is not whether phenomena are empirically common that is critical in science—else why should Becquerel have been so interested in the peculiar behavior of uranium?—but whether they can be made to reveal the enduring natural processes that underlie them. Seeing heaven in a grain of sand is not a trick only poets can accomplish.

In short, we need to look for systematic relationships among diverse phenomena, not for substantive identities among similar ones. And to do that with any effectiveness, we need to replace the "stratigraphic" conception of the relations between the various aspects of human existence with a synthetic one; that is, one in which biological, psychological, sociological, and cultural factors can be treated as variables within unitary systems of analysis. The establishment of a common language in the social sciences is not a matter of mere coordination of terminologies or, worse yet, of coining artificial new ones; nor is it a matter of imposing a single set of categories upon the area as a whole. It is a matter of integrating different types of theories and concepts in such a way that one can formulate meaningful propositions embodying findings now sequestered in separate fields of study.

In attempting to launch such an integration from the anthropological side and to reach, thereby, an exacter image of man, I want to propose two ideas. The first of these is that culture is best seen not as complexes of concrete behavior patterns—customs, usages, traditions, habit clusters —as has, by and large, been the case up to now, but as a set of control mechanisms—plans, recipes, rules, instructions (what computer engineers call "programs")—for the governing of behavior. The second is that man is precisely the animal most desperately dependent upon such extrage-netic, outside-the-skin control mechanisms, such cultural programs, for ordering his behavior.

Neither of these ideas is entirely new, but a number of recent devel-opments, both within anthropology and in other sciences (cybernetics, information theory, neurology, molecular genetics) have made them sus-ceptible of more precise statement as well as lending them a degree of empirical support they did not previously have. And out of such reformu-lations of the concept of culture and of the role of culture in human life comes, in turn, a definition of man stressing not so much the empirical commonalities in his behavior, from place to place and time to time, but rather the mechanisms by whose agency the breadth and indeterminate-ness of his inherent capacities are reduced to the narrowness and speci-ficity of his actual accomplishments. One of the most significant facts about us may finally be that we all begin with the natural equipment to live a thousand kinds of life but end in the end having lived only one.

The "control mechanism" view of culture begins with the assumption that human thought is basically both social and public—that its natural habitat is the house yard, the market place, and the town square. Think-ing consists not of "happenings in the head" (though happenings there and elsewhere are necessary for it to occur) but of a traffic in what have been called, by G. H. Mead and others, significant symbols—words for the most part but also gestures, drawings, musical sounds, mechanical devices like clocks, or natural objects like jewels—anything, in fact, that is disengaged from its mere actuality and used to impose meaning upon experience. From the point of view of any particular individual, such sym-bols are largely given. He finds them already current in the community when he is born, and they remain, with some additions, subtractions, and partial alterations he may or may not have had a hand in, in circulation there after he dies. While he lives he uses them, or some of them, some-times deliberately and with care, most often spontaneously and with ease, but always with the same end in view: to put a construction upon the events through which he lives, to orient himself within "the ongoing course of experienced things," to adopt a vivid phrase of John Dewey's.

Man is so in need of such symbolic sources of illumination to find his bearings in the world because the non-symbolic sort that are constitution-ally ingrained in his body cast so diffused a light. The behavior patterns of lower animals are, at least to a much greater extent, given to them with their physical structure; genetic sources of information order their actions within much narrower ranges of variation, the narrower and more thoroughgoing the lower the animal. For man, what are innately given are extremely general response capacities, which, although they make possible far greater plasticity, complexity, and on the scattered occasions when everything works as it should, effectiveness of behavior, leave it much less precisely regulated. This, then, is the second face of our argument: Undirected by culture patterns—organized systems of significant symbols—man's behavior would be virtually ungovernable, a mere chaos of pointless acts and exploding emotions, his experience virtually shapeless. Culture, the accumulated totality of such patterns, is not just an ornament of human existence but—the principal basis of its specificity—an essential condition for it.

Within anthropology some of the most telling evidence in support of such a position comes from rec nt advances in our understanding of what used to be called the descent of man: the emergence of *Homo sapiens* out of his general primate background. Of these advances three are of critical importance: (1) the discarding of a sequential view of the relations between the physical evolution and the cultural development of man in favor of an overlap or interactive view; (2) the discovery that the bulk of the biological changes that produced modern man out of his most immediate progenitors took place in the central nervous system and most especially in the brain; (3) the realization that man is, in physical terms, an incomplete, an unfinished, animal; that what sets him off most graphically from non-men is less his sheer ability to learn (great as that is) than how much and what particular sorts of things he *has* to learn before he is able to function at all. Let me take each of these points in turn.

The traditional view of the relations between the biological and the cultural advance of man was that the former, the biological, was for all intents and purposes completed before the latter, the cultural, began. That is to say, it was again stratigraphic: Man's physical being evolved, through the usual mechanisms of genetic variation and natural selection, up to the point where his anatomical structure had arrived at more or less the status at which we find it today; then cultural development got underway. At some particular stage in his phylogenetic history, a marginal genetic change of some sort rendered him capable of producing and carrying culture, and thenceforth his form of adaptive response to environmental pressures was almost exclusively cultural rather than genetic. As he spread over the globe he wore furs in cold climates and loin cloths (or nothing at all) in warm ones; he didn't alter his innate mode of response to environmental temperature. He made weapons to extend his inherited predatory powers and cooked foods to render a wider range of them digestible. Man became man, the story continues, when, having crossed some mental

Rubicon, he became able to transmit "knowledge, belief, law, morals, custom" (to quote the items of Sir Edward Tylor's classical definition of culture) to his descendents and his neighbors through teaching and to acquire them from his ancestors and his neighbors through learning. After that magical moment, the advance of the hominids depended almost entirely on cultural accumulation, on the slow growth of conventional practices, rather than, as it had for ages past, on physical organic change.

The only trouble is that such a moment does not seem to have existed. By the most recent estimates the transition to the cultural mode of life took the genus *Homo* over a million years to accomplish; and stretched out in such a manner, it involved not one or a handful of marginal genetic changes but a long, complex, and closely ordered sequence of them.

In the current view, the evolution of *Homo sapiens*—modern man— out of his immediate pre-*sapiens* background got definitively underway nearly [four] million years ago with the appearance of the now famous Australopithecines—the so-called ape men of southern and eastern Africa —and culminated with the emergence of *sapiens* himself only some one to [three] hundred thousand years ago. Thus, as at least elemental forms of cultural, or if you wish protocultural, activity (simple toolmaking, hunting, and so on) seem to have been present among some of the Australopithecines, there was an overlap of, as I say, well over a million years between the beginning of culture and the appearance of man as we know him today. The precise dates—which are tentative and which further research may alter in one direction or another—are not critical; what is critical is that there was an overlap and that it was a very extended one. The final phases (final to date, at any rate) of the phylogenetic history of man took place in the same grand geological era—the so-called Ice Age—as the initial phases of his cultural history. Men have birthdays, but man does not.

What this means is that culture, rather than being added on, so to speak, to a finished or virtually finished animal, was ingredient, and centrally ingredient, in the production of that animal itself. The slow, steady, almost glacial growth of culture through the Ice Age altered the balance of selection pressures for the evolving *Homo* in such a way as to play a major directive role in his evolution. The perfection of tools, the adoption of organized hunting and gathering practices, the beginnings of true family organization, the discovery of fire, and most critically, though it is as yet extremely difficult to trace it out in any detail, the increasing reliance upon systems of significant symbols (language, art, myth, ritual) for orientation, communication, and self-control all created for man a new environment to which he was then obliged to adapt. As culture, step by infinitesimal step, accumulated and developed, a selective advantage was given to those individuals in the population most able to take advantage of it—the effective hunter, the persistent gatherer, the adept toolmaker, the resourceful leader—until what had been a small-brained, protohuman *Homo australopithecus* became the large-brained fully human *Homo sapiens*. Between the cultural pattern, the body, and the brain, a positive feedback system was created in which each shaped the progress of the other, a system in which the interaction among increasing tool use, the changing anatomy of the hand, and the expanding representation of the thumb on the cortex is only one of the more graphic examples. By submitting himself to governance by symbolically mediated programs for producing artifacts, organizing social life, or expressing emotions, man determined, if unwittingly, the culminating stages of his own biological destiny. Quite literally, though quite inadvertently, he created himself.

Though, as I mentioned, there were a number of important changes in the gross anatomy of genus *Homo* during this period of his crystallization—in skull shape, dentition, thumb size, and so on—by far the most important and dramatic were those that evidently took place in the central nervous system; for this was the period when the human brain, and most particularly the forebrain, ballooned into its present top-heavy proportions. The technical problems are complicated and controversial here; but the main point is that though the Australopithecines had a torso and arm configuration not drastically different from our own, and a pelvis and leg formation at least well launched toward our own, they had cranial capacities hardly larger than those of the living apes—that is to say, about a third to a half of our own. What sets true men off most distinctly from protomen is apparently not over-all bodily form but complexity of nervous organization. The overlap period of cultural and biological change seems to have consisted in an intense concentration on neural development and perhaps associated refinements of various behaviors—of the hands, bipedal locomotion, and so on—for which the basic anatomical foundations—mobile shoulders and wrists, a broadened ilium, and so on—had already been securely laid. In itself, this is perhaps not altogether startling; but, combined with what I have already said, it suggests some conclusions about what sort of animal man is that are, I think, rather far not only from those of the eighteenth century but from those of the anthropology of only ten or fifteen years ago.

Most bluntly, it suggests that there is no such thing as a human nature independent of culture. Men without culture would not be the clever savages of Golding's *Lord of the Flies* thrown back upon the cruel wisdom of their animal instincts; nor would they be the nature's noblemen of Enlightenment primitivism or even, as classical anthropological theory would imply, intrinsically talented apes who had somehow failed to find themselves. They would be unworkable monstrosities with very few useful instincts, fewer recognizable sentiments, and no intellect: mental basket cases. As our central nervous system—and most particularly its crowning curse and glory, the neocortex—grew up in great part in interaction with culture, it is incapable of directing our behavior or organizing our experience without the guidance provided by systems of significant symbols. What happened to us in the Ice Age is that we were obliged to abandon the regularity and precision of detailed genetic control over our conduct for the flexibility and adaptability of a more generalized, though of course no less real, genetic control over it. To supply the additional information necessary to be able to act, we were forced, in turn, to rely more and more heavily on cultural sources—the accumulated fund of significant symbols. Such symbols are thus not mere expressions, instrumentalities, or correlates of our biological, psychological, and social existence; they are prerequisites of it. Without men, no culture, certainly; but equally, and more significantly, without culture, no men.

We are, in sum, incomplete or unfinished animals who complete or finish ourselves through culture—and not through culture in general but through highly particular forms of it: Dobuan and Javanese, Hopi and Italian, upper-class and lower-class, academic and commercial. Man's great capacity for learning, his plasticity, has often been remarked, but what is even more critical is his extreme dependence upon a certain sort of learning: the attainment of concepts, the apprehension and application of specific systems of symbolic meaning. Beavers build dams, birds build nests, bees locate food, baboons organize social groups, and mice mate on the basis of forms of learning that rest predominantly on the instructions encoded in their genes and evoked by appropriate patterns of external stimuli: physical keys inserted into organic locks. But men build dams or shelters, locate food, organize their social groups, or find sexual partners under the guidance of instructions encoded in flow charts and blueprints, hunting lore, moral systems, and aesthetic judgments: conceptual structures molding formless talents.

We live, as one writer has neatly put it, in an "information gap." Between what our body tells us and what we have to know in order to function, there is a vacuum we must fill ourselves, and we fill it with information (or misinformation) provided by our culture. The boundary between what is innately controlled and what is culturally controlled in human behavior is an ill-defined and wavering one. Some things are, for all intents and purposes, entirely controlled intrinsically: we need no more cultural guidance to learn how to breathe than a fish needs to learn how to swim. Others are almost certainly largely cultural: we do not attempt to explain on a genetic basis why some men put their trust in centralized planning and others in the free market, though it might be an amusing exercise. Almost all complex human behavior is, of course, the vector outcome of the two. Our capacity to speak is surely innate; our capacity to speak English is surely cultural. Smiling at pleasing stimuli and frowning at unpleasing ones are surely in some degree genetically determined (even apes screw up their faces at noxious odors); but sardonic smiling and burlesque frowning are equally surely predominantly cultural, as is perhaps demonstrated by the Balinese definition of a madman as someone who, like an American, smiles when there is nothing to laugh at. Between the basic ground plans for our life that our genes lay down—the capacity to speak or to smile—and the precise behavior we in fact execute—speaking English in a certain tone of voice, smiling enigmatically in a delicate social situation—lies a complex set of significant symbols under whose direction we transform the first into the second, the ground plans into the activity.

Our ideas, our values, our acts, even our emotions, are, like our nervous system itself, cultural products—products manufactured, indeed, out of tendencies, capacities, and dispositions with which we were born, but manufactured none the less. Chartres is made of stone and glass. But it is not just stone and glass; it is a cathedral, and not only a cathedral, but a particular cathedral built at a particular time by certain members of a particular society. To understand what it means, to perceive it for what it is, you need to know rather more than the generic properties of stone and glass and rather more than what is common to all cathedrals. You need to understand also—and, in my opinion, most critically—the specific concepts of the relations between God, man, and architecture that, having governed its creation, it consequently embodies. It is no different with men: they, too, every last one of them, are cultural artifacts.

IV

Whatever differences they may show, the approaches to the definition of human nature adopted by the Enlightenment and by classical anthropology have one thing in common: they are both basically typological. They endeavor to construct an image of man as a model, an archetype, a Platonic idea or an Aristotelian form, with respect to which actual men —you, me, Churchill, Hitler, and the Bornean headhunter—are but reflections, distortions, approximations. In the Enlightenment case, the elements of this essential type were to be uncovered by stripping the trappings of culture away from actual men and seeing what then was left —natural man. In classical anthropology, it was to be uncovered by factoring out the commonalities in culture and seeing what then appeared— consensual man. In either case, the result is the same as tends to emerge in all typological approaches to scientific problems generally: the differences among individuals and among groups of individuals are rendered secondary. Individuality comes to be seen as eccentricity, distinctiveness as accidental deviation from the only legitimate object of study for the true scientist: the underlying, unchanging, normative type. In such an approach, however elaborately formulated and resourcefully defended, living detail is drowned in dead stereotype: we are in quest of a metaphysical entity, Man with a capital "M," in the interests of which we sacrifice the empirical entity we in fact encounter, man with a small "m."

The sacrifice is, however, as unnecessary as it is unavailing. There is no opposition between general theoretical understanding and circumstantial understanding, between synoptic vision and a fine eye for detail. It is, in fact, by its power to draw general propositions out of particular phenomena that a scientific theory—indeed, science itself—is to be judged. If we want to discover what man amounts to, we can only find it in what men are: and what men are, above all other things, is various. It is in understanding that variousness—its range, its nature, it basis, and its implications—that we shall come to construct a concept of human nature that, more than a statistical shadow and less than a primitivist dream, has both substance and truth.

It is here, to come round finally to my title, that the concept of culture has its impact on the concept of man. When seen as a set of symbolic devices for controlling behavior, extrasomatic sources of information, culture provides the link between what men are intrinsically capable of becoming and what they actually, one by one, in fact become. Becoming human is becoming individual, and we become individual under the guidance of cultural patterns, historically created systems of meaning in terms of which we give form, order, point, and direction to our lives. And the cultural patterns involved are not general but specific—not just "marriage" but a particular set of notions about what men and women are like, how spouses should treat one another, or who should properly marry whom; not just "religion" but belief in the wheel of karma, the observance of a month of fasting, or the practice of cattle sacrifice. Man is to be defined neither by his innate capacities alone, as the Enlightenment sought to do, nor by his actual behaviors alone, as much of contemporary social science seeks to do, but rather by the link between them, by the way in which the first is transformed into the second, his generic potentialities focused into his specific performances. It is in man's *career,* in its characteristic course, that we can discern, however dimly, his nature, and though culture is but one element in determining that course, it is hardly the least important. As culture shaped us as a single species—and is no doubt still shaping us—so too it shapes us as separate individuals. This, neither an unchanging subcultural self nor an established cross-cultural consensus, is what we really have in common.

Oddly enough—though on second thought, perhaps not so oddly—many of our subjects seem to realize this more clearly than we anthropologists ourselves. In Java, for example, where I have done much of my work, the people quite flatly say, "To be human is to be Javanese." Small children, boors, simpletons, the insane, the flagrantly immoral, are said to be *ndurung djawa,* "not yet Javanese." A "normal" adult capable of acting in terms of the highly elaborate system of etiquette, possessed of the delicate aesthetic perceptions associated with music, dance, drama, and textile design, responsive to the subtle promptings of the divine residing in the stillnesses of each individual's inward-turning consciousness, is *sampun djawa,* "already Javanese," that is, already human. To be human is not just to breathe; it is to control one's breathing, by yoga-like techniques, so as to hear in inhalation and exhalation the literal voice of God pronouncing His own name—*hu Allah.* It is not just to talk; it is to utter the appropriate words and phrases in the appropriate social situations in the appropriate tone of voice and with the appropriate evasive indirection. It is not just to eat; it is to prefer certain foods cooked in certain ways and to follow a rigid table etiquette in consuming them. It is not even just to feel but to feel certain quite distinctively Javanese (and essentially untranslatable) emotions—"patience," "detachment," "resignation," "respect."

To be human here is thus not to be Everyman; it is to be a particular kind of man, and of course men differ: "Other fields," the Javanese say, "other grasshoppers." Within the society, differences are recognized, too —the way a rice peasant becomes human and Javanese differs from the way a civil servant does. This is not a matter of tolerance and ethical relativism, for not all ways of being human are regarded as equally admirable by far; the way the local Chinese go about it is, for example, intensely dispraised. The point is that there are different ways; and to shift to the anthropologist's perspective now, it is in a systematic review and analysis of these—of the Plains Indian's bravura, the Hindu's obsessiveness, the Frenchman's rationalism, the Berber's anarchism, the American's optimism (to list a series of tags I should not like to have to defend as such)—that we will find out what it is, or can be, to be a man.

We must, in short, descend into detail, past the misleading tags, past the metaphysical types, past the empty similarities to grasp firmly the essential character of not only the various cultures but the various sorts of individuals within each culture if we wish to encounter humanity face to face. In this area, the road to the general, to the revelatory, simplicities of science lies through a concern with the particular, the circumstantial, the concrete, but a concern organized and directed in terms of the sort of theoretical analyses that I have touched upon—analyses of physical evolution, of the functioning of the nervous system, of social organization, of psychological process, of cultural patterning, and so on—and, most especially, in terms of the interplay among them. That is to say, the road lies, like any genuine quest, through a terrifying complexity. . . .

Margaret Mead

2. Letter from Peri—Manus, II*

MAY, 1966

I am writing in the little house made of rough wood and sago-palm thatch that was built for me by the people of Peri village. The wind brings the sound of waves breaking on the reef, but my house, its back to the sea, looks out on the great square where the public life of the village takes place. At the opposite end of the square is the meetinghouse, and ranged along the sides are the houses of eminent men. Everything is new and paint sparkles on the houses. The handsomest ones are built of corrugated iron; the others are built of traditional materials, with decorative patterns woven into the bamboo.

This is the fourth version of Peri that I have lived in over the last thirty-seven years. The first was the primitive village. When I first came to study the Manus, they were an almost landless sea people and all the houses of Peri were built on stilts in the shallow sea. When I returned twenty-five years later, in 1953, the Manus had moved ashore and the new Peri, located on a small strip of marshy land, was their first attempt to build a "modern" village, designed in accordance with their notions of an American town. By 1964, when I came back on a third field trip, this village had degenerated into a kind of slum, noisy, dilapidated, cramped and overcrowded, because the people of a neighboring village

*Reprinted by permission of William Morrow & Co., Inc. from *A Way of Seeing* by Margaret Mead and Rhoda Metraux. Copyright © 1968 by Margaret Mead and Rhoda Metraux.

had moved in so that their children too could go to school. Now, a year later, an entirely new village has been built on a spacious tract of land bought with the people's own savings, and here Peri villagers, for so long accustomed only to sea and sand, are planting flowers and vegetables.

For two months everything went along quietly, but now the whole village is humming with activity. Last-minute preparations are in progress for a tremendous celebration at which Peri will entertain some two thousand members of the Paliau movement—all the people who, under the leadership of Paliau Moluat, have taken part in the strenuous and extraordinary effort to create a new way of life. It is the holiday season, and every day more of the adolescents who have been away at school and the young people who have become teachers in faraway parts of New Guinea are returning home to visit their families, see the new village and join in the festivities. Some families have built special rooms for the visitors. In one house there is a real room in which bed, chair and bench, all made by hand, are arranged to make a perfect setting for a schoolboy—the bed neatly made, pictures of the Beatles on the wall, schoolbooks on the table and a schoolbag hung in the window. In another house a few books piled on a suitcase in one corner of a barnlike room are all that signal the return of a school child. But whatever arrangements families have managed to make, the village is alive with delight in the visitors.

The children have come home from modern schools. But some of the young teachers have been working all alone in small bush schools among alien peoples only a few years removed from cannibalism and head-hunting. So the tales circulating in the village are extremely varied. There are descriptions of boarding-school life, stories of examinations and of prizes won in scholarship or sports. But there are also stories about the extraordinary customs of the people in the interior of New Guinea. Listening, I ask myself which is harder for the people of Peri to assimilate and understand—a savage way of life, which in many ways resembles that of their own great-grandfathers but which now has been so enthusiastically abandoned; or the new way of life the Manus have adopted, which belongs to the modern world of the planes that fly overhead and the daily news on the radio. Nowadays this may include news of the Manus themselves. Yesterday morning a newscaster announced: "At the first meeting of the new council in Manus, Mr. Paliau Moluat, member of the House of Assembly, was elected president."

I have come back to Peri on this, my fourth trip to Manus, to witness and record the end of an epoch. The new forms of local self-government, supported by an insistent and originally rebellious leadership, all are legalized. Paliau, the head of what the government once regarded as a subversive movement, now holds elective office and is immersed in work that will shape the future of the Territory of Papua—New Guinea. On a small scale this handful of people living on the coast of an isolated archipelago have enacted the whole drama of moving from the narrow independence of a little warring tribe to participation in the development of an emerging nation.

During the last two months I have been aware of all the different stages of change, as they can be seen simultaneously. On weekdays I see men and women passing by, stripped bare to the waist and holding pandanus hoods over their heads to keep off the rain. On holidays some of the younger women dress in fashionable shifts, bright with splashed flower designs. The oldest men and women, people I have known since 1928, were born into a completely primitive world, ruled over by ghosts, dominated by the fear of disease and death and endlessly preoccupied by the grinding work entailed in meeting their obligations and making the exchanges of shell money and dogs' teeth for oil and turtles, grass skirts and pots. The middle-aged grew up in the period when warfare was ending; as young men they still practiced throwing and dodging the spears they would never use as weapons of war. The next-younger group, in whose childhood the first Christian mission came, lived through the Japanese occupation and reached manhood when the people of the whole south coast were uniting in a small, decisive social revolution. And the youngest group, adolescents and children, are growing up in a world of school and clinic talk. Before them lies the prospect of career choice and the establishment of a new university, the University of Papua—New Guinea, in Port Moresby. These are the first-comers to a new epoch.

Yet, in spite of everything, the Manus have preserved their identity as a people and their integrity as individuals. The shy little boys I knew in the past have grown up into shy, quiet men. The boastfully brash still are brash. The alert-minded are keen and aware. It is as if the changes from savagery to civilization were new colors that had been laid on over the hard, clear outlines of their distinct personalities. At the same time, where once the Manus feared and plotted war, they now hear only echoes of distant battlefields in places of which formerly they were totally unaware. Where once they suffered hunger when storms kept the fishermen at home, they now can buy food for money in the village shops. Where once flight to live precariously among strangers was the outcome of a quarrel, now it is proud ambition that takes the Manus abroad.

One outcome of the chance that brought me to their village to do field work in 1928 is that their history has been chronicled. Unlike most simpler peoples of the world, the Manus can bridge past and present. Here in my house I hang up photographs of all the "big-fellow men belong before," who would otherwise be no more than half-remembered names. Seen from the vantage point of the present, pictures taken ten years ago and thirty-seven years ago have a continuity that overcomes strangeness. Instead of being ashamed of the life that has been abandoned, young people can be proud of an ancestral mode of life that is being preserved for others to know about and is mentioned in speeches made by visitors from the United Nations. Then old pride and new pride merge and the old men, nodding agreement, say: "After all, the Manus people started in Peri."

Each day I go about the ordinary business of fieldwork. I accept the presents of fresh fish and accede to small requests for tobacco, matches, a postage stamp or perhaps four thumbtacks. Whatever I am working at, I listen to the sounds of the village, ready to go quickly to the scene of wailing or shouting or some child's uncharacteristic cry. As I type notes I also watch the passers-by to catch the one person who can answer a question, such as: "Is it really true that the same two women first married Talikat and then later married Ponowan?" Or word comes that two turtles, necessary for the coming feast, have been brought in, and I hurriedly take my camera out of its vacuum case and rush to record the event.

At the same time I think about fieldwork itself. For an anthropologist's life is keyed to fieldwork. Even at home, occupied with other activities, writing up field notes and preparing for the next field trip keeps your mind focused on this aspect of your life. In the past, actual fieldwork has meant living with and studying a primitive people in some remote part of the world. The remoteness has been inevitable, for the peoples anthropologists have studied were primitive because they lived far from the centers of civilization—in the tropics or in the Arctic, in a mountain fastness or an isolated atoll. Remoteness also has set the style of fieldwork. Cut off from everything else, your attention is wholly concentrated on the lives of the people you are working with, and the effort draws on all your capacities, strength and experience. Now, as the most remote places become known, the conditions of fieldwork are changing. But the need to see and respond as a whole does not change.

I am especially aware of the conditions of fieldwork on this trip because for the first time since my original field trip to Samoa forty years ago I am working alone, without any collaborators in the same or a nearby village. This and the fact that I am using only one camera, a notebook and a pencil—instead of all the complex paraphernalia of the modern field team—throws me back to the very core of fieldwork: one person, all alone, face-to-face with a whole community. Equipped principally with a way of looking at things, the fieldworker is expected somehow to seize on all the essentials of a strange way of life and to bring back a record that will make this comprehensible as a whole to others who very likely never will see this people in their living reality. The role of the fieldworker and the recognition that every people has a culture, the smallest part of which is significant and indicative of the whole, go together. Once the two were matched, our fieldwork helped us to learn more about culture and to train a new generation of anthropologists to make better field studies.

Nevertheless, as I sit here with the light of my pressure lamp casting long shadows on the dark, quiet square, wondering what may happen in the next few hours, I also reflect that fieldwork is one of the most extraordinary tasks we set for young people. Even today it means a special kind of solitude among a people whose every word and gesture is, initially, unexpected and perhaps unintelligible. But beyond this, the fieldworker is required to do consciously something that the young child, filled with boundless energy and curiosity, does without conscious purpose —that is, learn about a whole world. But whereas the child learns as part of growing up and becomes what he learns, the anthropologist must learn the culture without embodying it, in order to become its accurate chronicler.

Whether one learns to receive a gift in both hands or with the right hand only, to touch the gift to one's forehead or to refuse it three times before accepting it, the task is always a double one. One must learn to do something correctly and not to become absorbed in the doing. One must learn what makes people angry but one must not feel insulted oneself. One must live all day in a maze of relationships without being caught in the maze. And above all, one must wait for events to reveal much that must be learned. A storm, an earthquake, a fire, a famine—these are extraordinary conditions that sharply reveal certain aspects of a people's conceptions of life and the universe. But the daily and the recurrent events that subtly shape people's lives are the ones on which the anthropologist must concentrate without being able to foresee what he can learn from them or when any particular event may occur. Equipped as well as possible with his growing knowledge of names and relationships, his experience of expectations and probable outcomes, the fieldworker records, learns—and waits. But it is always an active waiting, a readiness in which all his senses are alert to whatever may happen, expected or unexpected, in the next five minutes—or in an hour, a week, a month from now. The anthropological fieldworker must take a whole community, with all its transmitted tradition, into his mind and, to the extent that he is a whole person, see it whole.

And then my mind turns back to Manus. What is happening here is a kind of paradigm of something that is happening all over the world: grandparents and parents settle for the parts they themselves can play and what must be left to the comprehension of the children. The Manus have taken a direction no one could have foreseen thirty-seven years ago. Yet in the midst of change they are recognizably themselves. Fieldwork provides us with a record of the experiments mankind has made in creating and handing on tradition. Over time it also provides a record of what men can do and become.

Victor C. Uchendu

3. A Navajo Community*

> We badly need people from [other cultures] to come and study our
> American values and *vice versa*. . . . We have to see a value system from
> this point, that point, and the other point. (Kluckhohn, in Tax 1953:340)

Although anthropology is the science of man—the scientific study of
man, his works and his behavior—it remains, basically, the study of
"other cultures" by students from Western cultures. This is to say that
the non-Western world has been a traditional laboratory for Western
anthropologists.

This peculiar development in the history of our discipline has created
a characteristic theme in fieldwork. The problem of field entrée has re-
volved around how the Western anthropologist goes about neutralizing the
effects of the "cultural load" which he bears. As a white man, usually
working in a typical colonial setting, he is aware that he is a member of
a powerful "out-group" which commands authority and enjoys high status
and prestige. He tries to create for himself a different image of a white

* Reprinted from the book *A Handbook of Method in Cultural Anthropology*,
copyright © 1970 by Raoul Naroll and Ronald Cohen. Reprinted by permission of
Doubleday & Co., Inc. Permission of the author is also gratefully acknowledged.

Fieldwork among the Navajo Indians of New Mexico and Arizona was done between
July 1964 and June 1965. Grateful acknowledgment is made to the Rockefeller Foundation whose Fellowship and field grant made my graduate training in anthropology
possible. The Foundation is not to be understood as approving by virtue of its grant any
of the statements made or views expressed herein. I thank Professor B.F. Johnston for
his editorial assistance.

man who is neither an administrator, nor a missionary, nor a trader—
the three categories of white men who have influenced the lives of his
subjects. It is probably for this reason that some anthropologists advise
against any formal identification with political authorities. Malinowski's
injunction that the ethnographer must cut himself "off from the company of other white men [because] the native is not the natural companion for a white man" (1961:6–7)—an extreme prescription which is
not generally applicable to all field situations—was no doubt influenced
by this "fear of white man's power and authority." On the other hand
there are a few anthropologists who naively assume that they must "go
native" in order to achieve rapport, a point of view that is no longer
persuasive.

One critical factor which influences the kind of adjustment which an
ethnographer makes in the field is the fact that he is a stranger, an outsider. The "stranger status" is an asset as well as a liability. As Beattie
has noted, the importance of "stranger value" in fieldwork lies in the fact
that "often people talk more freely to an outsider, so long as he is not
too much of an outsider" (1964:87, 1965:18). The initial problem of
field entrée, therefore, revolves on how to make oneself "not too much of
an outsider." There is no general prescription for achieving this goal.
Methods adopted should be consistent with the subjects' definition of a
stranger's role—and this is not always clear to an ethnographer, hence
the initial blunders—and they should be as unobtrusive as they are informal.

The "stranger status" constitutes a major constraint in gaining field
entrée. The kind of constraint resulting from this status is more subtle in
covert cultures like the Navajo than in overt cultures like the Igbo. As
an Igbo anthropologist, I became quite aware of not only the environmental and cultural contrasts between the Navajo country and the Igbo
country but the contrasts in the attitudes of these two societies toward
strangers. In Igbo country, strangers are not ignored. They are questioned
as to their whereabouts, their intentions and designs. In the Navajo country, I was completely ignored. Though children were quietly curious about
my presence their parents gave the impression that I did not exist. I
initiated all the action. I greeted my Navajo contacts only to be made
aware that greeting does not command as much value in Navajo society
as it does in Igbo society; and that whatever joys are derived from greeting are shared among acquaintances and kinsmen rather than between
strangers and Navajo.

My initial contacts with Navajo, under many different settings, made
me painfully aware of three facts: First, that it is not good behavior to
stare at strangers or to "bother" them. Second, that the exchange of
greetings does not guarantee a stranger any hospitality, and that it is not
considered "poor upbringing" if a stranger does not exchange greetings

with casual acquaintances. Third, that as a stranger I was carrying a heavy "cultural load" which I must lighten if I would have any claim to the confidence of my subjects.

ETHNOGRAPHER'S CULTURAL LOAD

My experience among Navajo Indians convinces me that as fieldworkers, anthropologists are viewed first as bearers of this or that culture and that their role as fieldworkers or professional status as scientists emerges slowly. As culture-bearing animals, ethnographers carry "cultural loads." That is, we share the stereotypes with which our cultures are characterized by our subjects. The challenge posed by the "cultural load" which we bear is that we must find out what our stereotypes are if we are to adopt compensating roles which might neutralize their effects. Viewing the problem in a different perspective, we must try to find out the "content" of our "cultural load," that is the "image" of our culture which our subjects have and the attitudes which they associate with it.

My ethnic background must have been clear to the reader by the few allusions that I have made. I am an Igbo, which is a major ethnic grouping in Nigeria. I have described this culture, and my participation in it, in my book, *The Igbo of Southeast Nigeria* (1965). Because of the "social visibility" of my skin color, I could not play a covert role in the Navajo country, assuming it was desirable to do so. To most Navajo with whom I came into initial contact, I was just another Negro, a term infrequently used by this literally-oriented culture. The English-speaking Navajo refer to people of my race (Negroes) as "colored guys"; and the Navajo words *Nakaii lizhinii*—a term applied to my race, which means "Black Mexican"—indicate where the Navajo put me in their racial genealogy.

As part of my preparation for the field, I was interested in learning the Navajo image of my race and their general attitude toward outsiders. It was the opinion of my teachers that I could neutralize the "racial factor" by emphasizing my "African-ness" rather than my "Negro-ness," should this become an issue. For me this emphasis was a dilemma because I was not psychologically prepared to separate the two dimensions of my social personality. I turned to the literature on the Navajo and found it unrewarding. Two references only came to hand, and both were equally frightening. Adams' only reference to the Negroes in his Navajo community study was on the role of Negro women as sex objects for Navajo railway workers off-reservation. On this subject he writes:

> Especially frequent is the practice of making invidious comparisons between Navajo women and the Negro prostitutes to whom railroad workers have frequent recourse, Negro women being held up as a kind of standard of sexual desirability. Negroes are seldom thought of in any

other context at Shonto, and any mention of them is almost invariably an occasion for humor (1963:76–7).

The Franciscan Fathers, another source of data, are no more complimentary than Adams, though they provide a broader perspective for judging Navajo inter-ethnic and interracial attitudes. They asserted that

> for the Zuñi and Hopi, the Navajo cherish a sense of natural superiority in addition to a traditional contempt for the latter tribe. The American, though not equal to the Navajo in rank, is respected according to deportment, while the Mexican, with few exceptions, comes in for a considerable share of paternalism. Together with other tribes the Navajo share a genuine contempt for the Negro (1910:439).

I am calling the reader's attention to my "cultural load," not as a *post facto* rationalization of my field experience but to make him aware of my psychological problems and the concern of my teachers, who, though quite enthusiastic about the innovation of having an African anthropologist work among an American Indian group, also felt that mistakes which could expose me to physical danger must be avoided. Suffice it to say that my anxiety was unjustified, and that whatever may be the feelings of a few Navajo toward Negroes, the Navajo as a people do not seem to manifest any group hostility against Negroes because they are Negroes. In effect, it was my experience that the "racial factor" was not a major constraint in my gaining acceptance among the Navajo.

ETHNOGRAPHER'S CULTURAL ASSETS

It would be unfair to infer that I had no cultural assets. Although I was a stranger like any other white anthropologist might be, yet I was a "different kind of a stranger." The subject of my research—the pattern of migrant labor activities among the Navajo—called for an "official clearance" and a working relationship with officials and personnel of the Bureau of Indian Affairs. I could not have achieved my goals without this "official clearance" since I needed information from unpublished but useful documents and manuscripts which can only come from these officials. It was with these officials that I found my status as a "visiting foreign scholar" most helpful and fruitful.

My working relationship with the Bureau of Indian Affairs [B.I.A.] personnel was helped by two factors. First, the period of my fieldwork was free from any major "crises" between Navajo and the administration, and the question of being caught up in a web of administrative or political factions did not arise. Second, the head of the Public Health Service, Department of Indian Health, Navajo Agency [PHS-DIH], Window Rock, Arizona, was very anxious to learn what he could about the problems of Navajo migrant workers and he provided me with an unusual "umbrella effect" for any anthropologist.

After satisfying the Bureau of Indian Affairs officials about the legitimacy of my research interests, I used their institutions and channels of communication to gain an orientation into the Navajo country. My major interest, within the first month, was to "know the country," to find my way. I made a few personal contacts, and strengthened the bonds with my guides who filled the multiple roles of interpreters, informants, contact agents and teachers of appropriate "Navajo Ways." The trading posts, the Bureau of Indian Affairs schools, the Indian Hospital, the squaw dances and other ceremonials, and the Navajo Chapter meetings provided me with opportunities to make informal contacts, and especially served the purpose of "exposing" me to my subjects. When the weather permitted, I put on my African robes, to emphasize my "African-ness" as I had been advised. (But the windy weather which sweeps Navajo country in summer proved an enemy to my robes!) Although I seemed to have passed unnoticed in my robes at the initial contacts, it became clear from information reaching me and from the comments of those who became my Navajo friends, that my embroidered robes were commented upon as "items of beauty." The perennial question was: How much did it cost?

During this period of "exposure" the field personnel of the Indian Hospital, and the subagency personnel, Crownpoint, New Mexico, were used to extend my social contacts. The former allowed me to accompany them on their "home visits" and to "field clinics" and many of the patients we visited proved to be migrant families who later became good friends and willing informants. The subagency personnel initiated me into a series of Chapter meetings and allowed me to participate in some of the conferences in which migrant labor problems were discussed with Indian traders.

The important lesson which I learned during the first few months of my fieldwork is that progress in data accumulation is slow. This can be painful to a young anthropologist whose enthusiasm for "getting things moving" might lead to unnecessary frustrations. Every fieldworker has his "phase of frustration." In the Navajo country, this "phase" was for me the "period of exposure." I could not speak the language and therefore could not do much by myself. My guides would not keep regular appointments, and I would drive forty miles or more only to discover that they were gone. When we next met, my delinquent guide would simply grin and no explanation or excuse would be offered. But there are positive factors which help fieldwork among the Navajo. A fieldworker who takes advantage of these factors, can make much progress in his work.

FACTORS PROMOTING FIELDWORK AMONG NAVAJO

The Navajo have achieved ethnographic prominence through the works of many anthropologists. Fieldwork among them appears to be a continuous activity. The summer attracts many scholars—anthropologists, sociologists and psychiatrists—thanks to the foundation funds, the Department of Health, Education, and Welfare, and the National Science Foundation grants. The effect of these research activities on field entrée is that it has made Navajo aware of the existence of fieldworkers. They may resent their publication insofar as Navajo feel that they and their culture are misrepresented, but they know of the existence of people "who run around asking questions about old ways."

Navajo awareness of the existence of fieldworkers, even though their roles may be misunderstood, and considerable reservations may be expressed about the practical value of what they are doing, has two positive contributions to fieldwork and field entrée. First, the neophyte can be easily directed to the guides and interpreters who have established a partial specialization in helping ethnographers in their work. Second, these guide-interpreters know exactly which informants have the specialized knowledge which is helpful to the ethnographer, which informants are willing or unwilling to discuss which topics, and under what conditions. I chuckled with laughter when one of my guides advised that he would introduce me to my prospective informants as the friend of Professor Barnett. Although I had not met Barnett, yet my guide's ingenious suggestion worked quite successfully. The implication of this is that fruitful contacts which may improve rapport may be established by using scholars who are well known to informants, as referees. In my view, Navajo informants do not regard the ethnographer-informant relationship as a contract which terminates with the exchange of information. They tend to retain a vague feeling of warmth for ethnographers whom they know very well and this relationship can be exploited with great effect by a neophyte.

Although the Navajo society is particularly distrustful, and in fact fearful of strangers, including non-related Navajo, there are certain values in this culture which help field entrée. The non-hierarchical nature of the social structure makes it possible for an ethnographer to start work at any social level—the family, the leaders and men or women. It is not necessary to get a clearance from any traditional authority before one talks to informants. Data collection is essentially an individual bargain with an informant, who may volunteer it or may not. I was impressed with the fact that informants who do not want to volunteer a type of information will say so with little or no expression. There is little deliberate attempt to misinform the ethnographer. I met a few uncooperative medicine men; many were willing and cooperative; and others volunteered what information they had and referred me to medicine men who were more knowledgeable in other fields. I was quite impressed with the honesty of my most knowledgeable medicine man whose life history I recorded. When I requested him to tell me all the facts of his life which he could remember and enjoined on him to hide nothing, he grinned in reply: "We Navajo don't tell everything as long as we are alive. Only the dead tell everything. As long as I live, I must keep some information to protect myself." This sensible statement shows how far a Navajo biographer can go.

The character of Navajo social structure has another implication: it is the limited mediating role of the ethnographer's guide. Anybody who reads Whyte's *Street Corner Society* (1964) will be impressed with "Doc's" power and authority which he wielded to the advantage of his friend, the scientist. Very few anthropologists have been blessed with a "Doc," and ethnographers who work among Navajo Indians will not find a "Doc" because Navajo leaders do not wield much authority.

A frustrating experience I had in Lukachukai, a Navajo community in Arizona, demonstrates this position. I was living with a family which is well known to many anthropologists who have worked in this area. My host arranged a two-day *Blessing Way* sing for his son who was visiting from Houston, Texas, where he worked. This was a welcome addition to the *Yiebichie* and *Fire Dance* which attracted me to this part of Navajo country. We concluded an arrangement with the singer about my taping the chants, and it was with this understanding that my host wanted the sing two days earlier than planned so that I could keep my other commitments. At the last minute, the singer changed his mind. He would not let me run the tape after he had intoned the first chant. My host simply told me, as a matter-of-fact: "Hastiin, you people simply visit and leave. I don't have any other place to go. I live here with these people. I can't force him. It is his way. You can watch the ceremony and I will answer your questions later on."

The individualist-orientation of the Navajo is another positive factor that contributes to field entrée. I was aware of the criticisms of some Navajo medicine men by both their practicing colleagues and clients that the "sings" are becoming less effective as curative institutions because anthropologists have taken "souls" out of them. There are critics who blame the increasing "ineffectiveness" of some sings on the drinking habits of the medicine men and their inability to maintain traditional discipline as regards sex code and other religious observances. These criticisms are enough to make rapport with medicine men difficult. However, there are many medicine men who think that they must make their own decision and "help out" enthnographers who seek information. As Reichard notes, the Navajo insists upon self-reliance in certain decisions and "the individual is persuaded; he is not high pressured into a judgment contrary to his own" (1963:xxxix).

And although labels tend to be libels, I would suggest that the "pragmatic empiricism" of Navajo morality and their ethical code which Ladd characterizes as a "Hobbesian system modified by an Epicurean psychology and Spinozistic sociology" (1957:308) are relevant factors in gaining rapport in a field relationship where payment for information is an established tradition.

A major problem in fieldwork among Navajo is the maintenance of privacy. Kluckhohn noted that "under the right circumstances almost any Navajo will talk about witchcraft" (1944:14). He listed two such conditions: first, the confidence in the person receiving the information and the trust in him that he will not allow idle or malicious gossip to be spread; second, an ideal field setting in which the investigator and a single Navajo informant are involved. All fieldwork problems are not centered on witchcraft. In fact, I wonder whether an ethnographer can learn very much about witchcraft in his first field trip unless he is unusually lucky to be doing his work during a period of crises.

In a country like the Navajo where a one-room hogan is the characteristic dwelling unit, information which is considered "secret" may be difficult to gain in this setting. I found it necessary to do much of my interviewing in my car. With the few medicine men with whom I developed intimate friendly relations, we agreed that I would be bringing them to my house. This was no doubt time-consuming but it proved to be quite rewarding. I remember on one occasion when my medicine-man friend from Mariana Lake, New Mexico, lied to his son's wife that I was taking him to a sub-agency meeting at Crownpoint—a clear indication that he wanted to protect himself from gossips and from the charge that he was selling his knowledge to outsiders.

OTHER FIELD SITUATIONS

I have so far discussed some of the factors which affect field entrée in the Navajo country, especially the ways these factors affected me as an African anthropologist. We must now examine briefly a few of the many field situations which the nature of my investigation called for and the kinds of demands they made on me in my attempt to gain rapport. I indicated earlier that my focal research interest was on the pattern of agricultural labor migration. This problem called for two different field settings: reservation communities and off-reservation work areas. Although I worked in five different off-reservation work camps, located in two states, I will simplify my presentation by treating these as if they constituted a single field setting. I must warn the reader that what emerges from this is a "composite model," because I made different kinds of adjustments in each work area as the circumstances demanded.

ENTRÉE INTO STANDING ROCK

Standing Rock, New Mexico, is a typical Navajo community, one of the ninety-eight socio-political action units on the reservation. Like many Navajo communities, it is served by three major institutions—the trading post, a B.I.A. School and a Chapter house—each an agent of acculturation and a center for specialized activities.

I gained entrée into this community gradually. The first step in this direction was merely accidental—the fact being that though he lived in Crownpoint most of the year, a guide-interpreter who was most highly recommended to me came from this community. An ex-migrant worker himself, my guide had no difficulty understanding the kind of information I needed. His reputation as one of the few English-speaking Navajo who could "transform" the non-literal English language into a literal Navajo language was an asset in using him to interview the "old ones." Although it was not clear to me first why he took me to certain camps rather than to others, I lost no time in realizing that proximity of kinship guided his choice of informants. Working through the channels of kinship network which he could manipulate, my guide became the bridge between me and the Standing Rock community. I needed just one more guide to map the main kinship groupings in this community.

After a reconnaissance of a few communities in the Crownpoint sub-agency area, I decided to do more intensive work in Standing Rock, having found it quite representative. By this time, I had known the area for about five months. By an unusual coincidence this community had plans for a new census which it could not finance from its allocation from the Tribal Works Program. The Chapter officials asked my guide whether I could "help them out." This was a tempting offer which promised, not only a maximum of rapport, but a most unusual opportunity for me to visit all the homesteads, get all the information I needed, and provide a needed service for my community.

On December 26, 1964, the local Christmas for this community, I was formally introduced to Standing Rock residents. In a most democratic manner, they affirmed their willingness to cooperate by a standing vote. Although the work took about two months to complete—repeat visits, my guides' flexible working schedule, and the inaccessibility of a few camps during the winter were among the factors—I found this the most rewarding aspect of my Navajo experience. It provided a good example of how a fieldworker can achieve his own research goals through serving his community. It shows too that where the fieldworker's goals and the interest of his community are complementary, *reciprocity* becomes a very effective technique for achieving rapport.

ENTRÉE INTO WORK CAMPS

Fieldwork among Navajo workers in an off-reservation setting has its peculiar problems. The fieldworker must reassure the grower that he is not a spy for the Federal or the State Employment Agencies. He must contend with the Navajo suspicion of the "outsider" and their desire to be left alone. He must adapt his timing of formal interviews to suit the convenience of migrants who work long hours. He must be "sponsored" by a Navajo who understands what the fieldworker wants to do and who can explain this to other Navajo on demand.

The strategy I adopted in many off-reservation work camps was to ensure that the grower agreed to be indifferent to the ethnographer's presence, neither encouraging it nor actively discouraging it—and this is the best that a fieldworker in this situation can expect. As one grower in Phoenix, Arizona, put it, "We are in business, not in research. Our business is very competitive and it comes first before friendship. We cannot allow too many people bothering our 'hands' with questions." This forthright statement may not come from every grower but the sentiments embodied in it are shared by many growers. American agriculture is a big business, not a way of life. Harvest labor is critical and must be available at the right place and at the right time. The presence of an anthropologist may be a disturbing factor.

Showing interest in the migrants' children and working side by side with them on the farm—a direct contribution to the output of each migrant household—were among the many devices used to gain rapport in this setting. Especially among the young men, I discovered that I was not totally a stranger to them. Many had seen my photograph in an issue of the *Navaho Times;* others claimed that they enjoyed my radio talk from Gallup in which I discussed the similarities and the differences between the Igbo and the Navajo acculturation experiences; and for a few, my African robes had advertised me during the Gallup Indian ceremonies.

The younger Navajo workers felt that I shared a common bond of "colonial" culture with them. The frequent questions asked of me were how the white man treated Africans and whether Africans lived on reservations. My answer to the latter question drew not only laughter but serious doubt: The following is an excerpt of the conversation:

"Do you live on reservation?" one Navajo friend asked.

"No. It is the white man who lives on reservation," I answered.

"How did you do this?" another asked unbelievingly.

"The mosquito did it for us," I grinned in reply.

The fact that I bear not only a tribal culture but share a common colonial experience with Navajo provided a common basis for identification with them, minimized Navajo suspicions, aroused their curiosity about Africa and improved rapport. As bearers of tribal cultures we were able to "trade" some exotic information with each other. The Navajo recorded my Igbo folk songs, proverbs and riddles in exchange for their own songs and myths, and what was most important to me, they "helped me out" with the information I needed. It was my young English-speaking Navajo friends who helped to explain to the "old ones" what I was doing and who encouraged them to answer my questions. "We want you to pass your examination. We shall sure help you out with your questions so that you can write your book," were typical remarks.

SUMMARY

As an African anthropologist working among Navajo, I was quite conscious of my "stranger" status and I made no attempt to assume any covert roles. The kind of investigation that interested me and the circumstances under which it was carried out demanded rapport with the B.I.A. personnel and I found this association rewarding. Two important factors which helped entrée among the Navajo were kinship and friendship. My interpreters were drawn from the community in which they have a wide kinship network. They introduced me as a "friend" who needed help and this help was invariably given. Off the reservation, I found that friendship, based on a vague feeling of "colonial" experience, was helpful in gaining rapport with more acculturated Navajo. With their sponsorship, it was easier to gain the confidence of the less acculturated Navajo workers.

Fieldwork among the Navajo fails or succeeds with the kind of contacts an ethnographer is able to establish. The fieldworker or his guide must know the informants well in order to get any kind of information from them. This requires time, it requires patience; and for the reservation-based Navajo it requires an additional incentive—an informant fee. It is possible to gain the confidence of a few Navajo families during the first field trip to this country. I have good reasons to believe that I achieved this. Whether a fieldworker can achieve more than partial penetration into the life of a Navajo community is a proposition that needs demonstration. This writer did not; but this fact did not place any major constraint in the achievement of my research goal.

Part II

LANGUAGE AND SPEECH

INTRODUCTION

The study of linguistic phenomena has traditionally been a part of socio-cultural anthropology. Although linguistics as a discipline has a lengthy history of its own (indeed, it is far older than anthropology), there are many anthropologists who are more interested in verbal behavior than they are in any other aspect of the human experience. For many years, of course, this interest was as much practical as theoretical. Anthropologists, as we have seen, made their reputations at least in part by living for extended periods of time with people in all parts of the world. Many of these people spoke unrecorded languages. As a consequence, ethnographers could make valuable contributions to linguistics as well as take significant steps forward in their own efforts to conduct successful fieldwork "simply" by learning how to talk with the people with whom they were living.

But very early in the growth of modern anthropology, linguistically oriented anthropologists began probing some of the thorniest and most fascinating questions about the verbal dimension of the human experience. One of the more fascinating of these questions concerns the origin of "language." As is well known, it used to be fashionable to define humans as "tool-makers," but then it was discovered that all sorts of animals (from blue jays to chimpanzees) made tools. Then it became fashionable and apparently safe to define humans as "talkers." But now, as we see in Peter Farb's essay (Chapter 4), this may not be safe, either. In this stimulating presentation (from Farb's altogether fascinating book *Word Play*), numerous older theories and "experiments" pertaining to the origin and nature of language are summarized. Most of these are startling and amazing in many ways. For different reasons, the modern theories of the linguist Noam Chomsky (1957 and 1972) are no less startling. As Farb notes, Chomsky has suggested that humans have an innate *competence* to acquire language. Although nobody has ever indicated what particular structures in the human brain might be involved here, Chomsky and his followers are

55

willing to assert that humans must have it. They make this suggestion because they feel there is no other way to explain how children are able to learn to make sense out of the verbal behavior they hear as they are growing up since what they hear is often ungrammatical, fragmentary, and garbled. Without an innate "theory" of language, they could not learn to speak; in more technical terms, without competence there would be no *performance*. It must be stressed that competence is assumed to be innate and, consequently, the same for all humans everywhere, regardless of which particular language they "perform." All of these views are still being debated, especially in view of some more recent data about "language" learning in primates. As Farb tells us, several chimpanzees—Washoe and Sarah being the most prominent at the moment—have learned to communicate using hand signs. By these signs, they are able to communicate meaningfully with humans, using sentences having many of the characteristics of sentences "performed" by humans (including the critically important quality of novelty). This is surprising enough regardless of what theory of language we adopt, but if we assume, with Chomsky, that competence is a prerequisite for performance and that competence is innate or is built into the structure of the human brain, what does this behavior by Washoe and Sarah do for Chomsky's theory and for our view of "man as talker"? There would seem to be three possibilities. Either the chimpanzees are human, or the competence theory must be thrown out or modified, or what Washoe and Sarah are doing is not the equivalent of human speech. At the moment, the last possibility seems to be the most likely outcome of the inquiry. Time will tell.

Chomsky's theories about innate human linguistic competence are relevant to anthropology in other ways. One surprising twist which grows out of the logic of Chomsky's views is that "deep down" (so to "speak") the diverse ways people around the world behave linguistically are essentially the same in that they are all manifestations of the same underlying competence. The performances are different because humans are able to manipulate universal linguistic building blocks in different ways producing different performances (as different as a sentence of German and a sentence of Navajo). These manipulations are the essential processes of *generative grammar*. A generative grammar may be understood to consist of "rules" which generate novel, valid, meaningful sentences of a particular language. The job of the linguist, then, is to develop these rules or, more realistically, their logical equivalents. That is, a linguist works to develop rules which, if followed, would generate acceptable sentences in a particular language. Few linguists continue to assume, as some did at the outset, that these rules are the same as the psychophysical reality of the human mind. But in any case, the efforts to develop such rule systems or generative grammars have been remarkably successful.

This theoretical development in linguistics is relevant to anthropologists for many reasons. First and most fundamentally, meaningful verbal behavior is most certainly a class of "cultural acts." A theoretical development of importance for conducting research pertaining to one class of cultural acts ought to have relevance, it seems, for the study of other classes of cultural acts. Since anthropologists are obviously interested in cultural acts of a non-linguistic sort, many of them have adopted, at least by analogy, the theoretical perspectives emerging in linguistics. An illustration of the use of linguistic theory in an anthropological inquiry is provided by Robbins Burling in Chapter 5. In this essay, Burling tries to develop rules for the composition of households among the Garo of India which are analogous to grammatical rules. His analysis is informative for several reasons. First, he provides a compact summary of the nature of "grammar" in the modern sense of the word, and indicates how and why it should be possible to find rules of a similar sort in non-linguistic dimensions of human life. Second, he stresses that rules as developed by a linguist or an anthropologist are not assumed to have anything more than a logical equivalence to what goes on in the mind of the "native." And third, he stresses that his use of the linguistic strategy for doing an ethnographic description is only superficially different from what anthropologists have always done when describing a set of cultural acts. Not all anthropologists will agree with Burling's views, and it may well be that not all classes of cultural acts will lend themselves to this sort of analysis, but Burling's essay does provide more of a basis for optimism and interest than it does for skepticism and scorn, as some seem to think.

Many linguists and other social scientists are interested in the relationship between context and content in speech. It is an important area of research for many reasons, not the least of which is that (as Bateson and others have said) without context there would be no meaning and no communication. Some of the many issues in the field of "sociolinguistics" are illustrated vividly in the brief essay by Edith Folb in Chapter 6. In it, she discusses the distinctive verbal styles of Black Americans living in one part of Los Angeles. Among other things, the way language elements can be used to reinforce ethnic identity are illustrated by her data. We also get a glimpse of the way patterns of speech change, and the way speech styles can be used to convey notions of status and role within a group. As such, her analysis, and that of many others in this field, complements the work of Chomsky and his followers as they all work to understand the linguistic dimension of the human experience.

Peter Farb

4. Man the Talker*

Some twenty-five hundred years ago, Psamtik, an Egyptian pharaoh, desired to discover man's primordial tongue. He entrusted two infants to an isolated shepherd and ordered that they should never hear a word spoken in any language. When the children were returned to the pharaoh several years later, he thought he heard them utter *bekos,* which means "bread" in Phrygian, a language of Asia Minor. And so he honored Phrygian as man's "natural" language. Linguists today know that the story of the pharaoh's experiment must be apocryphal. No child is capable of speech until he has heard other human beings speak, and even two infants reared together cannot develop a language from scratch. Nor does any single "natural" language exist. A child growing up anywhere on earth will speak the tongue he hears in his speech community, regardless of the race, nationality, or language of his parents.

Every native speaker is amazingly creative in the various strategies of speech interaction, in word play and verbal dueling, in exploiting a language's total resources to create poetry and literature. Even a monosyllabic *yes*—spoken in a particular speech situation, with a certain tone of voice, and accompanied by an appropriate gesture—might constitute an original use of English. This sort of linguistic creativity is the birthright of every

* From *Word Play:* What Happens When People Talk (Chapter 11, pages 221–36), by Peter Farb. Copyright © 1973 by Peter Farb. Reprinted by permission of Alfred A. Knopf, Inc. and Jonathan Cape, Ltd.; permission of the author is also gratefully acknowledged.

human being on earth, no matter what language he speaks, the kind of community he lives in, or his degree of intelligence. As Edward Sapir pointed out, when it comes to language "Plato walks with the Macedonian swineherd, Confucius with the head-hunting savage of Assam."

And at a strictly grammatical level also, native speakers are unbelievably creative in language. Not every human being can play the violin, do calculus, jump high hurdles, or sail a canoe, no matter how excellent his teachers or how arduous his training—but every person constantly creates utterances never before spoken on earth. Incredible as it may seem at first thought, the sentence you just read possibly appeared in exactly this form for the first time in the history of the English language—and the same thing might be said about the sentence you are reading now. In fact, if conventional remarks—such as greetings, farewells, stock phrases like *thank you,* proverbs, clichés, and so forth—are disregarded, in theory all of a person's speech consists of sentences never before uttered.

A moment's reflection reveals why that may be so. Every language groups its vocabulary into a number of different classes such as nouns, verbs, adjectives, and so on. If English possessed a mere 1,000 nouns (such as *trees, children, horses*) and only 1,000 verbs (*grow, die, change*), the number of possible two-word sentences therefore would be 1,000 × 1,000, or one million. Of course, most of these sentences will be meaningless to a speaker today—yet at one time people thought *atoms split* was a meaningless utterance. The nouns, however, might also serve as the objects of these same verbs in three-word sentences. So with the same meager repertory of 1,000 nouns and 1,000 verbs capable of taking an object, the number of possible three-word sentences increases to 1,000 × 1,000 × 1,000, or one billion. These calculations, of course, are just for minimal sentences and an impoverished vocabulary. Most languages offer their speakers many times a thousand nouns and a thousand verbs, and in addition they possess other classes of words that function as adverbs, adjectives, articles, prepositions, and so on. Think, too, in terms of four-word, ten-word, even fifty-word sentences—and the number of possible grammatical combinations becomes astronomical. One linguist calculated that it would take 10,000,000,000,000 years (two thousand times the estimated age of the earth) to utter all the possible English sentences that use exactly twenty words. Therefore, it is improbable that any twenty-word sentence a person speaks was ever spoken previously—and the same thing would hold true, of course, for sentences of greater length, and for most shorter ones as well.

For a demonstration of just why the number of sentences that can be constructed in a language is, at least in theory, infinite, show twenty-five speakers of English a cartoon and ask them to describe in a single sentence what they see. Each of the twenty-five speakers will come up with a different sentence, perhaps examples similar to these:

I see a little boy entering a magic and practical-joke shop to buy something and not noticing that the owner, a practical joker himself, has laid
a booby trap for him.

The cartoon shows an innocent little kid, who I guess is entering a magic
shop because he wants to buy something, about to be captured in a trap
by the owner of the shop, who has a diabolical expression on his face.

It has been calculated that the vocabulary and the grammatical structures
used in only twenty-five such sentences about this cartoon might provide
the raw material for nearly twenty *billion* grammatical sentences—a number so great that about forty human life spans would be needed to speak
them, even at high speed. Obviously, no one could ever speak, read, or
hear in his lifetime more than the tiniest fraction of the possible sentences
in his language. That is why almost every sentence in this book—as well
as in all the books ever written or to be written—is possibly expressed in
its exact form for the first time.

This view of creativity in the grammatical apects of language is a very
recent one. It is part of the revolution in ideas about the structure of language that has taken place since 1957, when Noam Chomsky, of the
Massachusetts Institute of Technology, published his *Syntactic Structures*.
Since then Chomsky and others have put forth a theory of language that
bears little resemblance to the grammar most people learned in "grammar"
school. Not all linguists accept Chomsky's theories. But his position,
whether it is ultimately shown to be right or wrong, represents an influential school in theoretical linguistics today, one that other schools often
measure themselves against.

Chomsky believes that all human beings possess at birth an innate
capacity to acquire language. Such a capacity is biologically determined—
that is, it belongs to what is usually termed "human nature"—and it is
passed from parents to children as part of the offspring's biological inheritance. The innate capacity endows speakers with the general shape of
human language, but it is not detailed enough to dictate the precise tongue
each child will speak—which accounts for why different languages are
spoken in the world. Chomsky states that no one learns a language by
learning all of its possible sentences, since obviously that would require
countless lifetimes. For example, it is unlikely that any of the speakers who
saw the cartoon of the child entering the magic store ever encountered
such a bizarre situation before—yet none of the speakers had any difficulty
in constructing sentences about it. Nor would a linguist who wrote down
these twenty-five sentences ever have heard them previously—yet he had
no difficulty understanding them. So, instead of learning billions of sentences, a person unconsciously acquires a grammar that can generate an
infinite number of new sentences in his language.

Such a grammar is innately within the competence of any native speaker of a language. However, no speaker—not even Shakespeare, Dante, Plato, or the David of the Psalms—lives up to his theoretical competence. His actual performance in speaking a language is considerably different, and it consists of numerous errors, hesitations, repetitions, and so forth. Despite these very uneven performances that a child hears all around him, in only a few years—and before he even receives instruction in reading and writing in "grammar" school—he puts together for himself the theoretical rules for the language spoken in his community. Since most sentences that a child hears are not only unique but also filled with errors, how can he ever learn the grammar of his language? Chomsky's answer is that children are born with the capacity to learn only grammars that accord with the innate human blueprint. Children disregard performance errors because such errors result in sentences that could not be described by such a grammar. Strong evidence exists that native speakers of a language know intuitively whether a sentence is grammatical or not. They usually cannot specify exactly what is wrong, and very possibly they make the same mistakes in their own speech, but they know—unconsciously, not as a set of rules they learned in school—when a sentence is incorrect.

The human speaker—born with a capacity for language, infinitely creative in its use, capable of constructing novel utterances in unfamiliar speech situations—shares the globe with a variety of animals that whistle, shriek, squeak, bleat, hoot, coo, call, and howl. And so it has been assumed, ever since Aristotle first speculated about the matter, that human speech is only some superior kind of animal language. Alexander Graham Bell saw nothing odd about his attempts to teach a dog to speak by training it to growl at a steady rate while he manipulated its throat and jaws. The dog finally managed to produce a sequence of syllables which sounded somewhat like *ow ah oo gwah mah*—the closest it could come to "How are you, Grandma?" And Samuel Pepys, in his *Diary* entry for August 24, 1661, noted:

> by and by we are called to Sir W. Batten's to see the strange creature that Captain Holmes hath brought with him from Guiny; it is a great baboon [apparently not a baboon at all but rather a chimpanzee], but so much like a man in most things, that though they say there is a species of them, yet I cannot believe but that it is a monster got of a man and a she-baboon. I do believe that it already understands much English, and I am of the mind it might be taught to speak or make signs.

Other experimenters concluded that animals could not be taught human languages, but they saw no reason why they themselves should not learn to speak the way animals do. A few enthusiasts have even published dictionaries for various bird and animal languages—among them E.I. Du Pont de Nemours, the French-born founder of the American chemical firm, who in 1807 compiled dictionaries for the languages of such birds as crows and nightingales. These efforts are ludicrous because human speech is quite different from most animal communication. Between the bird's call to its mate and the human utterance *I love you* lie a few hundred million years of evolution, at least one whole day of Biblical Creation. St. Francis of Assisi, talking to the birds, may have had much to say to them, but they had nothing to discuss with him.

Human speech seemingly resembles animal calls in that it employs a small number of sounds, often no more than the number of sounds emitted by many species of birds and mammals. But, unlike animal calls, human sounds are combined to form a vast vocabulary, which in turn is structured into an infinite number of utterances. The number of different units of sound in each human language, such as the *m* in *man* or the *ou* in *house,* varies between about a dozen and a little more than five dozen. English recognizes about 45 units, Italian 27, Hawaiian 13. This range is not notably different from the separate units of sound emitted by many kinds of animals: prairie dog, 10; various species of monkeys, about 20; domestic chicken, 25; chimpanzee, 25; bottle-nosed dolphin, 28; fox, 36.

Chimpanzees, with their 25 units of sound, are incapable of speech, while Hawaiians, with only 13 units, possess a very expressive language. That is because the chimpanzee employs one unit of sound in social play, another when a juvenile is lost, a third when attacked, and so on—but two or more calls cannot be combined to generate additional messages. In contrast, the 13 sounds of Hawaiian can be combined to form 2,197 potential three-sound words, nearly five million six-sound words—and an astronomical number if the full repertory of 13 sounds is used to form longer words. In the same way, a speaker of English can select three units of sound out of his store of 45—such as the sounds represented in writing by *e, n,* and *d*—and then combine them into such meaningful words as *end, den,* and *Ned.* But the chimpanzee cannot combine the three units of sound that mean play, lost juvenile, and threat of attack to form some other message. Nor can the chimpanzee's call that means "Here is food" ever be changed to talk about the delicacies it consumed yesterday or its expectations about finding certain fruits tomorrow. Generation after generation, as far into the future as the chimpanzee survives as a species, it will use that call solely to indicate the immediate presence of "food."

Certain animals—most notably parrots, mynahs and other mimicking birds—can emit a wide repertory of sounds, and they also have an uncanny ability to combine them into longer utterances. Nevertheless, they do not exploit their abilities the way human beings do. A trained mynah bird can so unerringly repeat an English sentence that it is scarcely distinguishable on a tape recording from the same sentence spoken by a human being. Parrots also can duplicate human speech with awesome fidelity, and they have been taught vocabularies of more than a hundred words. A parrot can easily enough be trained to mimic the utterance *a pail of water* and also to mimic a variety of nouns such as *sand* and *milk*. But, for all its skill, the parrot will never substitute nouns for each other and on its own say *a pail of sand* or *a pail of milk*.

Even the most vocal animals are utterly monotonous in what they say in a given situation. The well-known nursery rhyme does not reveal what Jack said to Jill when they went up the hill to fetch a pail of water, and in fact no way exists to predict which of the tremendous number of strategies two people will select in such a speech situation. But everyone knows what a male songbird will say when another male enters its territory during the breeding season. It will emit a distinctive series of sounds that signify "Go away!" It cannot negotiate with the intruder, nor can it say, "I'm sorry that I must ask you to depart now, but I will be happy to make your acquaintance after the breeding season is concluded." The male defender of the territory is simply responding to the stimulus of an intruder at a certain time of the year by uttering a general statement about the existence of such a stimulus.

Specialists in animal behavior infer the "meaning" of animal sounds from the behavior of the animals at the time they emit the sounds, but it is safe to conclude that the sounds express only indefinable emotions. Individuals belonging to the same animal species emit approximately the same sounds to convey the same emotions. All expressions of pain uttered by any individuals of a monkey species are very much the same, but in the human species the sounds that a speaker uses to communicate his pain are quite arbitrary. A speaker of English says *ouch,* but a Spaniard says *ay* and a Nootka Indian *ishkatakh.* Jill might have emitted an animal-like cry of pain as she came tumbling down the hill—but, as a speaker of English, she also had the choice of saying *I hurt my head* or *Please take me to a doctor.* Even if Jill merely uttered the conventional word, *ouch,* which signifies pain in English, this sound is nevertheless considerably different from an animal's cry of pain. An animal's cry cannot be removed from its immediate context, but Jill's *ouch* can. She could, for example, tell someone the next day about her accident by saying *When I fell down the hill, I cried "ouch."* Or she could utter *ouch* in a completely different context, as when someone makes a feeble pun and she wishes to convey that her sensibilities, not her bones, have been wounded.

An animal, though, has no such choices. As Bertrand Russell remarked about a dog's ability to communicate, "No matter how eloquently a dog may bark, he cannot tell you that his parents were poor but honest." Despite the variety of sounds in the babel of the animal world, nonhuman calls are emotional responses to a very limited number of immediate stimuli. Every other kind of sound made by living things on the planet belongs to human speech alone.

The search for the genesis of speech in the lower animals has not uncovered a single species that can communicate with all the same features found in human speech. The most promising candidates in whom to search for the roots of human language would appear to be man's closest relatives, the apes and monkeys. Many species possess extensive repertories of calls concerned with emotional states, with interpersonal relationships inside the troop or with animals outside of it. The chimpanzee, in particular, has important attributes for learning: intelligence, sociability, and a strong attachment to human beings. The potential for language in chimpanzees seems so great that several attempts have been made to teach them to speak. All such experiments failed, even when the chimpanzees were reared in households on an equal basis with human children. The most successful of these attempts, which involved six years of painstaking attention by a psychologist and his family, resulted in a chimpanzee's learning to speak merely approximations of four English words.

It is now known to be fruitless to teach chimpanzees a spoken language because their vocal apparatus is considerably different from that of human beings. But about 1966 two psychologists at the University of Nevada, Allen and Beatrice Gardner, had the novel idea that chimpanzees might possess a capacity for language even though they lack an apparatus to speak it, a situation similar to that of deaf-mute human children. They decided to attempt to separate the chimpanzee's possible capacity for language from its proven inability to utter the sounds of the language. Since use of the hands is a prominent feature of chimpanzee behavior, the Gardners employed visual rather than vocal signals by teaching a chimpanzee the American Sign Language system that is used with deaf children in North America. The Gardners theorized that their infant female chimpanzee, Washoe, should see as much sign language as possible, since they knew that merely exposing a human child to speech triggered its language-learning capacity. They took great care to keep her isolated from all other chimpanzees and from most human beings as well. The Gardners always communicated with each other in sign language whenever Washoe was present, and they demanded that anyone in contact with her remain silent and use hand signals.

Their efforts were rewarded almost immediately. Washoe began to repeat the gestures she was taught and also those she noticed the Gardners using between themselves. She built up a vocabulary of thirty-four words in less than two years. Much more important, when she learned a new word she enlarged its application from the specific thing it labeled to an entire class of similar objects. For example, she first learned the sign for *hurt* in reference to scratches and bruises, but later she used the same sign to indicate stains, a decal on the back of a person's hand, and a human navel. And she was able to communicate about things that were not present, as when she heard a distant bark and immediately made the sign for *dog*.

Her proficiency soon went beyond the mere naming of things. She learned verbs and pronouns, and she invented combinations of signs which she used correctly in appropriate speech situations. She combined the signs for *open, food,* and *drink* when she wanted something from the refrigerator and the signs for *go* and *sweet* when she wanted to be taken to a raspberry bush. Before she had reached the age of six, she had a vocabulary of 150 signs which she could combine to describe situations entirely new to her. At this writing in early 1973, Washoe is living at the University of Oklahoma with a colony of chimpanzees who are also being trained in sign language. As yet, no sign-language communication has taken place between them. Whether or not Washoe will transmit the signs she has learned to her progeny will not be known until 1974 or 1975, when she becomes old enough to reproduce. She has, however, already demonstrated that she can at least spontaneously communicate with human children who know sign language—even though her status still remains that of an ape. One poignant illustration of that occurred when a mute girl and her parents came to visit the Gardners. Washoe spotted the child and eagerly rushed across the yard to play with her, excitedly giving the sign for *child.* But the human child, seeing a chimpanzee come bounding toward her, responded by tickling her ribs—the sign for *ape.*

Washoe has successfully bridged the barrier between human and non-human communication, although she required human help to do so. She progressed from uttering a small number of automatic cries, which referred only to immediate emotions or situations, to learning a language system in which elements could be combined to make further statements. Beyond any doubt, she has learned more of a language, although in visual terms, than any other nonhuman before her. Nevertheless, Washoe's achievement falls far short of the human child's. The fact that a human child at an equivalent stage of development has a vocabulary of thousands of words instead of only 150 is the least significant difference. More important, Washoe apparently does not understand the principles of grammar, as human children do by age three when they construct sentences according to the patterns offered by their languages. An English speaking child, for example, knows the difference between the subject-predicate-object pattern of *Baby going home* and the question pattern of *Is baby going home?*—but Washoe does not. When Washoe wants to be tickled, she signals any one of several combinations that have no reference at all to sentence structure: *you tickle, tickle you,* or *me tickle.*

The major deficiency in Washoe's accomplishment, though, concerns the relationship of language to human thought. Human beings conceive of their environment as interlocked objects, properties, and actions. A chair is not simply a kind of object, but rather it belongs to a particular category. Because it is inanimate, it can be broken—but it lacks animate characteristics, which means that it cannot drink milk. That is why *chair* can take a verb that refers to inanimate subjects, *break,* but not a verb that refers to animate things, *drink.* A child who unravels a simple statement like *The chair broke* thus must do more than decode a grammatical utterance. He must first master the subtle category of things that *break,* like *chairs* and also *machines* and *windowpanes.* Then he must distinguish the category of things that *break* from things that *tear,* like *paper* and *bed-sheets,* or things that *smash,* like *vases* and *cars.* The child must next interpret the influence on the chair of the verb *broke* out of all the possibilities that verb implies, such as that the breaking of a chair is conceptually different from breaking the bank at Monte Carlo or from waves breaking on a beach. To achieve all this, the child unconsciously unravels the sentence into parts that can be analyzed, and then puts the elements together again in a meaningful fashion. Nothing in Washoe's behavior indicates that she uses language in this metaphorical way, which is, after all, the very hallmark of the human mind.

About the time that the Gardners began their experiments with Washoe, David Premack, a psychologist at the University of California, started to teach a chimpanzee named Sarah to read and write by means of a code of variously shaped and colored pieces of plastic, each of which represented a "word." Within six years she had mastered a vocabulary of more than 130 different pieces of plastic; amazingly, she seemed able to understand the grammatical relationships between words which Washoe did not understand. She often makes correct choices between questions, between the concepts of "same" and "different," between the ideas of color and size. She has even shown that she can understand the complex grammatical structure of a compound sentence. When her trainers arranged plastic pieces to mean *Sarah, put the apple in the pail and the banana in the dish,* she responded by the appropriate actions. To do so, she needed to understand that *apple* and *pail* belonged together, but not *apple* and *dish.* Moreover, she had to know the grammatical function of *put,* that it referred to both the *apple* and the *banana*—and she had to interpret the sentence to mean that she was the one who was supposed to do all these things.

Despite Sarah's remarkable responses, serious doubts remain whether or not she has achieved language as human beings know it. Since she performs correctly only about 75 to 80 per cent of the time, the question arises whether or not she has truly internalized the rules of her language. She appears to handle language in somewhat the same way that trained pigeons are able to "play" Ping-Pong. The pigeons, of course, are not truly playing the game of Ping-Pong. They do not unconsciously know the rules of the game even though they go through the motions of it; they lack the desire to win, the satisfaction of a successful play, individual styles, the selection of one strategy in place of another at various stages of the game. Evidence for a lack of internalization is Sarah's failure to generate sentences on her own; she merely accepts those offered by her trainers for her to read and to reply to. A further question that must be raised is whether or not the "Clever Hans Phenomenon" is operative with Sarah. Since she performs better with some experimenters than with others, it is possible that she also is detecting nonverbal cues.

Both Sarah and Washoe had to be taught language by human beings, but the honeybee has on its own evolved a communication system that possesses most of the features of human language—although it does so in a trivial way. When a foraging honeybee locates a source of pollen or nectar, she brings a sample of her find to the hive and thereby informs the other workers about the kind of flowers to look for. She also tells them the exact distance to the source by the tempo of a dance she performs in the form of a figure eight. And the exact direction in which to fly (after, unbelievably, the dancer compensates for wind direction) is indicated by the angle of the dance path. The dance thus conveys two kinds of information: the distance from the hive to the food source and the direction based on the angle of the sun. The other workers use this information to fly unerringly to a source that is sometimes as far away as eight miles.

Strictly speaking, the bee dance meets most of the criteria for a language. It uses arbitrary symbols (the various movements of the dance); it combines them in apparently infinite ways to communicate about something remote in space and time (the food source which the forager recently discovered but can no longer see); and it constantly communicates about situations which the bees have never before experienced (each food source is a unique occurrence at a particular time and place). The bee dance, though, is severely limited as to what it can communicate. It always contains two, and exactly two, components: distance and direction. Some English sentences also contain only two components—such as *Birds fly*—but speakers of English are not forced to construct all their sentences out of a single noun and a single verb. If the other bees in the hive refuse to respond to the communication by the forager, she cannot express the message in any other way. She cannot ask the question *Why don't you fly to the food?* Nor can she issue the imperative *Fly out and forage!* She can only repeat her dance over and over again.

The topics that bees can communicate about—pollen and new locations for hives—are undoubtedly of endless fascination to them but of limited interest to almost all other living things. Bees cannot use their language to explain English grammar, but human beings can talk about the way bees communicate by dancing. Human language is unique in that it can be used as what linguists call a "metalanguage": It can state the rules of any communication system, including its own. In other words, only human language can talk about language. A speaker can discuss the dance of the bees or anything else that he cares to, even when it is foolish or a lie. Because human beings alone possess language, they can hurdle the barriers of time and space, have a history, speculate about the future, and create in myths beings that never existed and may never exist.

The study of animal communication reveals that human language is not simply a more complex example of a capacity that exists elsewhere in the living world. One animal or another may share a few features with human language, but it is clear that language is based on different principles alto-gether. So far as is known, people can speak because of their particular kind of vocal apparatus and their specific type of mental organization, not simply because of their higher degree of intelligence. No prototype for language has been found in the apes and monkeys, and no parrot or mynah bird has ever recombined the words it learned into novel utterances. In contrast, every human community in the world possesses a complete lan-guage system. Obviously, something happened in evolution to create Man the Talker. But what was it?

Since sentences do not leave anything equivalent to the fossils and pottery shards that allow anthropologists to trace the prehistory of man, linguists can only speculate about the origins of language. Theories have been advanced, have won adherents for a while, then later were shown to be fanciful—and given derisive baby-talk names. Because some of these the-ories occasionally reappear today in new guises, let me mention several of them as a guide to the wary.

The Bow-Wow Theory states that language arose when man imitated the sounds of nature by the use of onomatopoeic words like *cock-a-doodle-do, cuckoo, sneeze, splash,* and *mumble.* This theory has been thor-oughly discredited. It is now known that many onomatopoeic words are of recent, not ancient, origin and that some of them were not derived from natural sounds at all. But the most telling argument against the Bow-Wow Theory is that onomatopoeic words vary from language to language. If the human species had truly based its words on the sounds of nature, these words should be the same in all languages because of the obvious fact that a dog's bark is the same throughout the world. Yet the *bow-wow* heard by speakers of English sounds like *gua-gua* to Spaniards, *af-af* to Russians, and *wan-wan* to Japanese.

The Ding-Dong Theory dates back to Pythagoras and Plato and was long honored, but nowadays it has no support whatsoever. This theory claims a relationship between a word and its sense because everything in nature is supposed to give off a harmonic "ring," which man supposedly detected when he named objects. But the Ding-Dong Theory cannot explain what resonance a small four-footed animal gave off to make Englishmen call it a *dog* rather than any other arbitrary collection of vowels and con-sonants—and what different resonance it communicated to Frenchmen to make them call it a *chien* or to Japanese to make them call it an *inu.*

Still other explanations for the origin of language are the Pooh-Pooh Theory, which holds that speech originated with man's spontaneous ejacu-lations of derision, fear, and other emotions; the Yo-Heave-Ho Theory, which claims that language evolved from the grunts and groans evoked by heavy physical labor; the Sing-Song Theory, which placed the origin of speech in the love songs and the rhythmic chants of early man; and the Ha-Ha Theory, which states that language evolved out of spontaneous laughter. All these speculations have serious flaws, and none can withstand the close scrutiny of present knowledge about the structure of language and about the evolution of our species.

Lately, some anthropologists and linguists have speculated that language originated as a much more recent event than previously believed. Their evidence is largely circumstantial, but it is intriguing. It is based upon the slowness with which human culture evolved over millions of years until its sudden acceleration during the last Ice Age, between about 100,000 and 35,000 years ago. The forerunners of our species arose some five million years ago. Not until about three million years ago did they begin to make crude pebble tools—and they continued to make them in almost the same way, with only a few slight improvements, until the last Ice Age. Then a sudden burst in creativity occurred. This flowering of technology included the increasing diversity of design and materials—and, more important, the use of tools to make other tools by a variety of methods such as boring, scraping, cutting, and polishing. Of all the possible ways to account for this florescence of culture after millions of years of barely perceptible change, the most apparent is the rise of speech as we know it today (but no doubt building upon some earlier system of communication). One vital property of speech is that it can talk about the future; it can plan forward. The flowering of tool manufacture during the last Ice Age demanded just such forward planning, because the succession of different operations, one following the other in precise order, could be achieved only by involved discussions.

Every new discovery in animal behavior, human evolution, or human physiology provides the impetus for scholars to construct new theories about the origins of speech. We can expect that some linguists will continue to search back into the unrecorded past to discover the wellsprings of speech, even though most of them today despair of ever finding it. In fact, since 1866 the Linguistic Society of Paris has had a rule that the origin of language is one topic it would not discuss at its meetings. Speculations may be provocative, well reasoned, and based on available evidence—but they never can be demonstrated to be anything more than possibilities. Evidence about language goes back only as far as the earliest written documents, a mere five thousand years or so ago. But by that time languages were already fully developed and not significantly different in kind from those spoken today. . . .

Robbins Burling

5. Linguistics and Ethnographic Description*

INTRODUCTION

Anthropologists have long turned to linguistics for techniques by which they have hoped to solve their own problems—techniques for learning an exotic field language, for recording myths in an adequate transcription, for classifying languages so as to make inferences about migrations, for providing glottochronological dates—but I believe that the deepest influence of linguistics upon anthropology has not been to provide these specialized techniques but to suggest far more general viewpoints from which other aspects of culture than language alone might be considered. In whatever way we define culture, it is difficult to exclude language from the scope of our definition, and anthropologists and linguists share many assumptions about their respective subjects. Language, like culture, is seen as being perpetuated within a social group, as having continuity through time but also as undergoing continual change. Both language and culture are regarded as having "structure" but both are subject to diffusion (or borrowing).

* Reproduced by permission of the American Anthropological Association from the *American Anthropologist*, vol. 71 no. 5, 1969:817–27. Permission of the author is also gratefully acknowledged.

I am indebted to my colleague Roy A. Rappaport not only for the original suggestion that I organize my ideas on this subject for presentation to one of our classes, but also for numerous cogent ideas that emerged in our many subsequent discussions. Joseph Jorgensen has tried to help me untangle a few notions I had about the relationship between statistics and rules.

71

Anthropologists and linguists even share the term "informant" to describe the man from whom they learn, and for me this symbolizes the similarity of their approach. An "informant" is regarded as a collaborator, as a man who has an intelligence entirely comparable to the investigator's. The "subject" of some other social sciences always runs the risk of being mistaken for a rat. An informant does not share the subject's peril.

If language must be accepted as one aspect of culture, it is still, in some ways, a very special aspect. It can be argued that of all the many aspects of culture, language is the easiest to study and its description the easiest to formalize. To the extent that language is easier to study than the rest of culture, it may be strategic first to try out new viewpoints and theoretical approaches on language and then see whether these same approaches might also be applied elsewhere. The extension of linguistic approaches to other aspects of culture has in fact been a regular anthropological habit, and there is hardly a generalized theoretical viewpoint in anthropology without its rather direct analogue in linguistics. Just as some anthropologists have been interested in the synchronic structure of a society at a particular point in time, some linguists have been concerned to describe a language synchronically. Other anthropologists have been interested in the changes that culture undergoes through time, and other linguists have shared this interest with respect to language. In language as in the rest of culture, one can make a distinction between the cumulative evolution associated with long-term trends, and the fine scale evolution of shorter periods—those that can involve systematic changes without implying any accumulated complexity. Both in linguistics and in anthropology the relationship of the individual to his culture (or to his language) raises some rather complex issues, but practitioners of both fields frequently study their subject matter as if it were divorced from particular individuals, even if both must finally recognize that it is individual speakers and actors who carry their language and their culture and who exemplify in their behavior.

THE GOALS OF GRAMMAR

In the last decade linguists have suddenly become far more articulate than formerly in considering the goals and purposes of linguistic description. This development has been stimulated by Chomsky and his disciples, but it has by no means been confined to them. Anthropologists might benefit by trying to understand the attitude that linguists are taking toward the role of linguistic description, to see whether this attitude might have implications for anthropological endeavors in the way other linguistic attitudes so often have had.

In this paper I explore one way in which I believe linguistic viewpoints can clarify anthropological ideas. Specifically, I ask whether the writing of ethnographic descriptions, which I take to be one characteristic activity of anthropologists, might be illuminated by a clear understanding of the comparable task of the linguist: the writing of a grammatical description. So that my comparison between grammar and ethnography will be as unambiguous as possible, I must first discuss with some care just what a grammatical description amounts to. The following points seem to me to be the most important ones:

1. A grammar is a theory of how a language works. We can refine this by saying that a grammar is a theory that in some manner specifies what can be said in a particular language. Still more explicitly we might say that a grammar constitutes a device that distinguishes between those sequences of vocal noises that are allowable ("grammatical") in some particular language and other sequences that are not allowable ("ungrammatical").

2. It is important to note that a grammar does *not* specify what *is* said on any particular occasion, but only what *can* potentially be said. At any particular moment a great many things might be said, and linguists have had little or nothing to say about how the choice among the enormously large number of grammatical sequences is to be made. If linguistics is a predictive science, it can only be predictive in a much looser sense than that of predicting what somebody is actually going to say. Instead, linguists have usually been quite content if they could predict whether native speakers would accept or reject various sequences of noises. Since an enormous number of sequences will be accepted as grammatical, any explicit grammatical formulation must provide for these alternatives, but it cannot predict which of these many alternatives will actually be chosen at a particular time.

3. All linguists use some criteria of simplicity, though these are rarely clearly stated. Other things being equal, the grammatical description that covers the situation in a simple way is better than one that does the same job in a more complicated fashion. We must admit the enormous complexities of defining simplicity, but at the very least a grammar should be simpler than the full set of data for which it accounts. One might try to argue that the total list of possible sentences in a language would constitute a grammar of that language. To find out whether any particular sequence was grammatical we would simply have to check it against the list. If a sentence was found in the list it would be grammatical and so the list would do a job of specifying grammaticality, and this is what we ask a grammar to do. But no linguist would be satisfied with such a list, for he wants his description to be briefer or more parsimonious than the total list of possible sentences, and in general the simpler or briefer the description, the better it is judged to be. Any decent grammar, in other words, should provide for (generate) a larger amount of data than it contains itself.

4. A grammar accomplishes its task by a system of rules. These rules account for or "predict" back to the known data, but beyond this they also predict or "generate" new data that are not contained in the original body of information with which a linguist begins. Any body of data is limited in

quantity, but the rules a linguist formulates to account for these limited data are expected to have such generality that they will predict new grammatical sequences as well. This allows an investigator to check his formulation against empirical evidence, i.e., against the judgment of a native speaker as to whether or not the new sequences generated by his grammatical rules are in fact acceptable.

5. The rules of a grammar are justified by their predictive utility, not by the procedure used in working them out. Rules, to be sure, are constructed by a linguist on the basis of his knowledge, but in the final analysis it is not how he goes about finding the rules but whether or not they work that decides their status. Most linguists today have accepted the idea that the discovery procedures they use are ultimately irrelevant and they even tend to believe that the discovery of grammatical rules is, *in principle,* not capable of systematization. There is no algorithm for writing grammars. Of course, linguists develop skills, and they try to communicate these skills when teaching their students, but if a rule finally works and if it does account for data, it matters not one jot if it first came to the linguist in a trance. It is the ability of rules, acting together in the grammatical system, to generate grammatical sequences that is their justification, not the way in which they were discovered.

6. A difficult question remains open: just what is the locus of these grammatical rules? One can argue that the rules are simply devices, schemes, tricks, constructed by the linguist to do the job of accounting for acceptable sentences. It is easy, however, to begin speaking as if one were actually working out rules that are in the heads of speakers of the language and that have just been waiting to be discovered. In practice it seems to make very little difference what attitude a linguist takes. He can perform the same sort of operations and construct the same sort of rules whether he regards them simply as devices that work to generate sentences or whether he takes them more seriously as a real part of the language he is investigating. Linguistics has developed and will no doubt continue to develop without all linguists agreeing on this question.

I will return to these points later and I will argue that ethnographic descriptions have the same general characteristics, but first I wish to present some concrete ethnographic data so as to give some flesh to the abstract bones of my arguments.

GARO HOUSEHOLD COMPOSITION

I shall take as my data certain facts about household composition among the Garo of Assam, India.[1] I shall offer some rules that will account for the

---

[1] The data on Garo residence patterns was obtained in the field while I held a fellowship from the Ford Foundation between 1954 and 1956 and have been more fully presented in Burling 1963.

varied composition of these households, and I shall then ask whether the rules are in any way analogous to grammatical rules. I start with rather concrete data (analogous to linguistic texts), set out in the form of kinship diagrams that show the kinship ties binding the members of real households to one another (Figure 1). These are households that are, or were in 1956, "on the ground." The symbols used in the diagrams are conventional except that in a few diagrams I have used a curving dotted line to indicate a kinship relationship between coresident women through other relatives (always women) who do not actually live in the household in question.

In spite of the considerable diversity among households shown in the diagrams, inspection leads rather easily to a few generalizations. Most, though not quite all, households have at least one married couple, and a good many have two; but more than two couples is unusual. In a household with two married couples, the two wives are most often mother and daughter, or at least they are related to each other through women; and in only one example do two married sisters live together. More striking perhaps, no married son lives with either of his parents. A few men have two living wives, and the wives always seem to be related, occasionally as mother and daughter. The reader can easily add other statements of this sort, and if data on more households were available, they might be refined and extended, but they are not the kind of generalizations most anthropologists really like. They are statements of statistical probability, and they seem to leave out any real explanation for the presence of some kinds of households but the absence of others. I suspect that most anthropologists would be happier with a set of rules such as the following:

1. Marriage constitutes a particular relationship between a man and a woman, which among other things requires common residence.

2. Unmarried children reside with their mother and, when she is married, with her husband who is usually their father.

3. After marriage, one daughter must continue to live permanently with her parents. (It follows as a corollary from rules 1 and 3 that this girl's husband must move in with his wife and his parents-in-law.)

4. All other daughters may live temporarily with their parents after marriage (e.g., household 29) but within a year or so they establish a separate household.

5. Couples with no daughters will "adopt" a girl to act as a daughter. Adoptions are always made from among the close matrilineal kinsmen of the daughterless woman, and the ideal choice is her sister's daughter (households 6, 14, 16). (As is implied by this rule and by rule 3, the adopted daughter lives permanently with her adopted parents.)

6. A young mother who, whether through divorce, widowhood, or illegitimacy, has no husband may live with her parents or if her parents are dead with her sister (12, 29).

7. A widower may remarry and bring his new wife to live in the house

FIGURE 1

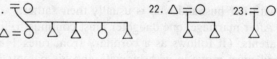

he had shared with his first wife and their children. If the new wife has unmarried children she will bring them along (3, 8, 28).

8. Widows may remain unmarried for a time and live only with their children (23); unless they marry a widower, their new husband must always be simultaneously married to or at least promised to a younger woman. (Garos rationalize this by saying that every man, at some time in his life, should have a "new" wife.) If a remarrying widow has a daughter, she is felt to be a suitable cowife for her mother's new husband (10, 27), otherwise a younger matrilineally related woman must be adopted as the widow's daughter to serve as her cowife (13, 20, 24). (The cowives are virtually always approximately a generation apart in age even if not real mother and daughter, for Garos feel that the women will quarrel less if they are not too close in age.)

9. A widow who has already acquired a resident son-in-law before she is widowed will not remarry, although she will henceforth be described slightly metaphorically as the "wife" of her son-in-law (1, 4, 5, 6, 16, 21, 24, 26).

10. Widowers who already have a resident son-in-law may remarry (3, 8, 18) but they do not always do so. Widowers without resident sons-in-law, virtually always remarry rapidly (28).

With one exception (30) the households shown in the diagram conform to the possibilities provided by these ten rules. I will return to this exceptional household later but first I will try to suggest how these rules can be regarded as similar to grammatical rules.

HOUSEHOLD COMPOSITION RULES

I must be very clear on one point: I do not regard the treatment of household composition given in the last section as deviating in any substantial way from general ethnographic practice. Except for setting my rules off with numbers and making an extra effort toward precision and parsimony, I mean to provide an entirely conventional description of some ethnographic phenomena. My purpose is *not* to suggest that we can give better ethnographic descriptions by following some sort of "linguistic technique" but merely to suggest that we may be able to get a clearer view of what we have been doing all along if we look at our conventional ethnographic practice from the same vantage point as linguists use for viewing their endeavors. To this extent only, I believe the nature of the rules for household composition can be clarified if they are seen in the light of the points already made about grammar rules:

1. The rules of household composition can be said to constitute a theory. They are a device that specifies the possible composition of a household, or more explicitly, they provide a means for distinguishing

between proper and improper assemblages of people who might live together.

2. The rules do *not* specify the composition of any particular household. Like grammatical rules, which specify the range of possible grammatical sentences without predicting any particular sentence, these composition rules specify the range of proper households, but do not predict any particular household. As in any sequence of grammatical rules, these rules of household composition contain alternatives that allow for a broad range of final results.

3. In some sense (a sense that need not be defined very closely) the rules of household composition are simpler than the data for which they provide. The rules are of limited length, but they will provide a very wide range of households. One can list these rules in less space and with greater parsimony than would be needed to list all the possible household types separately.

4. Households have been accounted for by a system of rules that predict back ("generate") the original data, but they also predict additional data in the form of other household types that were not included in the original sample. Just as one can use grammatical rules to generate new sentences that can then be tested against the judgment of a native speaker, so one can use these composition rules to generate new household types. These newly generated types could be tested against empirical data, either by checking on additional real households, or by testing their acceptance among informants to find out if they would be regarded as proper and reasonable hypothetical households even if they do not happen to be known to have occurred.

5. The composition rules cannot be justified by reference to any particular methodology used in working them out. They stand or fall entirely by their utility in accounting for the data. To be sure, it would be exceedingly difficult to work out these rules if one were limited to bare descriptions of particular households such as are available from the diagrams. As a practical matter it is easier to ask informants for their explanation and to try these out against the data. But the methods by which we work out the rules are, in the end, irrelevant; and if the rules an ethnographer comes up with can be used to "explain" the households that do exist and to suggest additional plausible household types, that is entirely sufficient to justify the rules.

6. Just as with grammatical rules, we are left with some difficult questions about the locus of the composition rules. Anthropologists, like linguists, seem to have been divided in their attitudes. Do we, as anthropologists, rest content with a system that simply accounts for our data? Or do we want to discover rules that the people themselves use, rules that in some way already exist in the culture independent of the analysis. I will return briefly to this problem later but must first consider some more

specific implications of the composition rules and point out a few ways in which they have particularly close parallels with grammatical rules.

ETHNOGRAPHIC PARALLELS TO LINGUISTIC DESCRIPTION

If one examines the composition rules closely, he will discover that in two cases households having the same composition can arise in two different ways. First, a simple nuclear family consisting of a single married couple and their children can come about either through the marriage of a girl who leaves her parents and establishes a new and separate household with her husband or through the survival of an in-living daughter and her husband and children after the time of her parents' death and after the departure of all her brothers and sisters at the time of their respective marriages. Second, a household consisting of a woman, her real or adopted daughter, and a man who is said to be the husband of both of them, can also arise in two ways. If a woman is widowed after her daughter has been married, Garos speak as if the son-in-law "inherits" his mother-in-law. They describe the son-in-law as being married to both women at once. A household with identical composition occurs when a woman is widowed before she acquires a resident son-in-law; for after she is remarried, she must take her real or adopted daughter as a second wife for her new husband.

The composition of the households is the same in these two cases, but their status in Garo society is different. Garos describe the surviving nuclear family as having quite different ties to related households than the newly established nuclear family, and these differences are symbolized in a number of ways that I need not give here in detail. Similarly, the two kinds of families in which a man is said to be married to both a mother and her daughter by a previous marriage are actually quite different. Among other things, if the husband is first married to the daughter and only later "inherits" the mother-in-law, he is not expected to engage in sexual relations with the older woman, although Garos use the usual terms for "husband" and "wife" to describe their relationship. If a man marries the older woman first, however, and then or subsequently acquires her daughter as his second wife, Garos do expect that he will engage in sexual relations with both women. Garos show nothing but approval if such a man should father children by both women.

These superficially identical but fundamentally distinct households can be compared, with some reason, to "structurally homonymous" sentences. The famous sentence "The shooting of the hunters was terrible" can mean either "It was bad that the hunters got shot," or "the aim of the hunters was poor." The superficial sentence can reflect two different derivational histories, and it is best to say that there are really two different sentences, produced by different sequences of rules which in the end culminate in homonymous forms. Similarly, by applying different sequences of composition rules, we can generate superficially identical households that for some purposes are not regarded as identical at all. Somewhat metaphorically, we might even describe these households as having "homonymous composition."

I have already pointed out that one of the households included in the diagram does not fit the rules as I have given them. This is household 30, in which a woman and her husband have moved in with the family of her sister's daughter, the intervening sister having died. Since the rules do not account for this very real household, the rules must seem imperfect and one's first impulse might be to modify or expand the rules until they can account for household 30 along with all the others. To do this, however, would require either a rule with extremely peculiar limitations (e.g., a married woman and her husband are allowed to move into her deceased sister's daughters family) or a rule of a more general character that would run the danger of simultaneously providing for a large number of other household types that never seem to occur (e.g., matrilineally related women may live together after marriage).

Neither of these alternatives by which the rules might be modified is at all attractive, but unless the rules are modified somehow, household 30 is left as an exception to them. But perhaps this is a realistic way to look at this household. Perhaps it simply does not conform to plausible rules, and in this way is comparable to an ungrammatical sentence. We know that people do utter ungrammatical sentences. When asked about them they may edit them out and confess that they spoke in a broken fashion that was not really correct. Similarly when I inquired about this rather deviant household, my informants admitted that it did not fit their conception of a proper household. People freely predicted that it would soon split up and that it certainly would not remain in its present form for long. Just as I was led to recognize "homonymous households," perhaps this deviant assemblage of people could be labeled "ungrammatical."

To characterize this household as ungrammatical is to assert something utterly different than simply to characterize it as statistically unusual or extreme. If one simply wanted to give a statistical summary of household composition, the data from this particular household would have to be fed into the statistical maw along with the data from all the other households. This one might prove to be very unusual in terms of certain statistical measures, but it could never, by such means alone, be characterized as "wrong." From the viewpoint of the composition rules, however, it can indeed be labeled "wrong." Here we have a difference between a set of rules, on the one hand, and a statistical summary, which adds up cases, finds averages, and charts frequencies, on the other. It is probably fair to say that most anthropologists, like most linguists, have been partial to descriptions by rules, which like my composition rules introduce few or no measures of probability for the occurrence of various alternatives. By contrast, both anthropologists and linguists have tended to dislike measures that involve counting proportions and reporting frequencies.

However, the rules I have given, like most ethnographic descriptions are surely deficient in some respects. The composition rules cannot tell us what percentage of households have two married couples or specify the average number of unmarried children per household or answer any number of other similar and reasonable questions that could nevertheless be readily determined from the same sort of data on households to which the rules apply. Analogously, conventional grammatical rules give us no means for summarizing or predicting the proportion of nouns to verbs in running discourse or of describing the relative frequency of bilabial stops.

A statistical summary and the usual description by rules tell us different things about our subject matter, but they are by no means irreconcilable. In particular it would seem promising to try to combine them by introducing some sort of probabilistic parameters into the sequence of rules for either grammar or household composition. One could specify the frequency with which each choice should be made at each point where the rules leave alternatives. For household composition we would have to specify such things as life expectancy, fertility, and divorce rate and then weave these into the composition rules. For grammar we would have to specify such things as the proportion of selections of transitive and intransitive verbs and frequency of application of negative and question transformations. If statements of probability were woven into a set of rules in a clever enough way, it might conceivably be possible to develop rules that would generate either sentences or households in which the proportions of word classes or of marriages would approximate the proportions found in the empirical data. Therefore, I see no incompatibility between a rule-based description and measures of probability. I simply feel it to be a fair generalization that whether explicitly or not, most anthropologists like most linguists have expressed their descriptions in a manner that can be seen as consisting of sets of rules, and they have rarely been strong on specifying the probability of their application.

CULTURALLY EXPLICIT RULES AND RULES OF AN OBSERVER

I have pointed out several close analogies between the grammatical description of sentences and the cultural description of household composition, but the differences between them should not be glossed over. Perhaps the greatest difference lies in the way in which an investigator works out the rules. I have no intention of compromising with my claim that the discovery procedures by which rules are worked out are ultimately irrelevant, but it cannot be denied that linguists and anthropologists have different habits of investigation, and these varying habits make it easy to *imagine* that they are following different principles. The contrast in our work habits lies in the differing ways linguists and anthropologists use informants, and I believe this depends in turn upon the different techniques by which everyone first learns his own culture.

I have pointed out that both anthropologists and linguists use the term "informant" to describe the person from whom they learn, but it must be admitted that they typically use their informants in rather different ways. The linguist characteristically uses an informant to elicit *examples* of behavior, while the anthropologist is more apt to elicit statements that *describe* behavior. The difference is not absolute. Sometimes linguists ask their informants for explanations of why they say the things they do, and anthropologists sometimes look at their informant's behavior and try to interpret it without relying upon the informant's own description, but by and large the difference is there. I believe that these differing methodologies rest upon and correspond to the differing ways in which all human beings learn their own culture. If presented with enough examples, a normal child will always learn to speak, and he need never be given any explicit instruction at all. As a result, when people do formulate explicit generalizations about their own language these generalizations are often rather wildly different from anything that a linguist would be willing to recognize as a valid description. Explicit grammatical generalizations have no real pedagogical use to the people of the culture, since language can be perpetuated without them or even in spite of them. If children can learn the grammar of their language without explicit instruction, the linguist should be able to do the same. What he needs for his work are examples of linguistic behavior from which he can make his own generalizations, and this is what a linguist looks for from his informants.

Children learn many other aspects of their culture with the help of explicit verbal instructions, or at least in a context in which activities are constantly discussed and described. Garos may never formulate rules of household composition quite as explicitly or concisely as I have done in this paper, but they do talk about household composition. When asked to describe appropriate behavior, or to consider alternative possibilities, they can articulate their own rules quite successfully. It may be unlikely that rules of behavior of this sort could be successfully passed from one generation to the next without at least some verbal formulation, whether this comes in the form of explicitly stated rules or less explicitly in descriptions and discussions of actual behavior. To the extent that a child requires a verbal context and verbal instruction to learn his own culture, an anthropologist would seem to be forced to rely upon similar sorts of verbal description. For this reason it is probably absolutely necessary for the cultural anthropologist, unlike the linguist, to elicit *statements about* behavior, from his informants. He cannot expect to rely entirely upon *examples of behavior* as a linguist can generally do. As a result of these contrasting uses of informants, the rules that an ethnologist formulates tend superficially to look much more like the rules that are explicitly known and used in the culture than do the rules worked out by a linguist. The natives do not need to be able to articulate anything about the grammatical rules of their language, but they can certainly articulate many statements that bear upon the rules of most other sorts of behavior.

I think it would be a mistake, however, to overstate this difference, and it is here, above all, that I find the linguistic analogy helpful in clarifying our ethnographic assumptions. If, in the end, it does not matter how we arrive at our rules, then whether we use an informant's explicit verbal statements to give us hints or extract the rules instead entirely from examples of observed behavior is a matter of no importance at all. What matters is whether or not our rules do somehow correspond to the data we seek to describe, and my rules for household composition, in the working out of which I was surely helped by informants' statements, have exactly the same formal status as a linguist's grammatical rules. In both cases we may have differences of opinion about whether the rules are simply convenient devices by which an observer can account for the data or are in some more important way a part of the language or the culture of the people that was waiting there to be discovered and that enters into the cognitive processes of the people. But the degree of correspondence between the rules of the observer and the explicit criteria that the natives themselves use has no more bearing upon the status of the rules than the procedures by which rules are worked out. This is simply to say that disconformity between the explicit rules of the native and the rules worked out by ethnographers will not lead us to reject our rules so long as the rules work (natives can be wrong about their own behavior) and by the same token agreement between the native's and the ethnographer's rules amounts to no confirmation of the latter.[2]

---

[2] In this connection, I believe that Marvin Harris's recent work (1968: Chapter 20, "Emics, Etics, and the New Ethnography"), which contrasts what he calls the "emic" and "etic" points of view, seems to me to unnecessarily polarize our alternatives. Claiming to go back to Pike's original definitions of "emic" and "etic" Harris bypasses whole schools of linguistics in which these terms came to be understood. In Harris's words:

> Emic statements refer to logico-empirical systems whose phenomenal distinctions or "things" are built up out of contrasts and discriminations significant, meaningful, real, accurate, or in some other fashion regarded as appropriate by the actors themselves [1968:571].

> Etic statements depend upon phenomenal distinctions judged appropriate by the community of scientific observer [1968:575].

By these definitions, the Bloomfieldian phoneme is not an "emic" unit, since the Bloomfieldians were firmly, even obstinately, opposed to any sort of mentalistic inter-

Of course it should still be an interesting empirical question to ask how closely the explicit rules of the people correspond to the rules of an ethnologist or linguist. I suspect that they will tend to be much closer to each other in some areas of culture (such as household composition) than in others (such as language). But this empirical question can never even be raised in a clear fashion unless the explicit rules that are formulated and articulated by the people themselves are first clearly differentiated from those other rules the ethnologist and linguist construct when they try to account for their respective fields of human behavior.

---

pretation of language. Furthermore not all of the anthropologists concerned with semantics whose work Harris dismisses as "emic" have been concerned with cognition. Lounsbury, for instance, has never made cognitive claims for his rules, and indeed he has not cared in the least whether or not his rules have any sort of cognitive status. By Harris's definition, therefore, Lounsbury's rules should not be called "emic." It is true, of course, that some of the generative grammarians have been making extensive claims for the innate or cognitive or psychological importance of their rules, but the accomplishments of linguistics hardly stand or fall upon these particular and by no means undisputed claims. By indifferently dismissing ethnosemantics, Lounsbury rules, and indeed much or all of linguistics, as "emic" and therefore as idealistic, Harris makes it difficult to salvage a non-idealistic but rule-based description, of any sort. Whatever Pike's original definition of "emic," most linguists and most anthropologists other than Harris would surely grant "emic" status to both the Bloomfieldian phoneme and to Lounsbury's rules. By the same token I think it not unreasonable, and in accordance with general usage, to call all ordinary grammatical rules and my rules of household composition "emic," because they represent theoretical statements, separated in certain respects from (and not algorithmically derivable from) the more directly observable "etic" data, such as households on the ground or sequences of noise, but at the same time the rules provide a means of interpreting and understanding the observable (and "etic") data of real households or real sentences. Of course it is silly to argue about the meaning of a word, but even if we decide that "emic" is not appropriate for such descriptions, it is still important to keep them distinct from the more directly observable "etic" phenomena, and Harris's simplistic bifurcation into idealist "emics" and material-ist "etics" is in danger of squeezing out the middle ground between them. The rules of household composition, the Bloomfieldian phoneme, grammatical rules, and Louns-bury's rules stand or fall on their ability to account for observable phenomena, though none may be directly observable themselves. Whether or not they are in any sense cognitively or psychologically real is in an entirely separate question.

Edith Folb

6. Rappin' in the Black Vernacular*

Scene I
   Speaker 1: Hey, baby, what it is?
   Speaker 2: What it was, brother, what it was.
   Speaker 1: What's it gonna be?
   Speaker 2: Say man, let's trip on down to L.I.Q. and get us some pluck.

Scene II
   Speaker 1: What's happenin', man? You steppin' . . .
   Speaker 2: Irvine done vamped on me and my partner. Whupped 'im up-side the head 'fore he could put in the wind. Shit, pig did 'im so bad, he like to off the brother.

Scene III
   Speaker 1: Man, that some fine stuff you mackin' on . . .
   Speaker 2: I hear ya, brother. 'Cept punk over there rankin' my play. Nigger runnin' off at the jibs 'bout his "new shot" and how it be decked out with lifts and some ole pimp rest and color bar. Chump better cool it, man, 'cause I'm gonna buy his ticket, *for sure!*

Three scenes from *Superfly?* Not quite. Just three conversations over-heard in Watts, California. A white English paraphrase might read as fol-

* From *Human Behavior,* August 1973. Copyright © 1973 *Human Behavior* Magazine; reprinted by permission. Permission of the author is also gratefully acknowledged.

lows. Scene I: Greetings are being exchanged between two friends. One suggests, "Let's go to the liquor store and get some wine." Scene II: A man flees from the police. He tells another of his escape and of his friend's probable fate at their hands—a beating he fears will end in his friend's death. Scene III: One young man watches his friend talk to a particularly attractive young woman and compliments him on his taste. The second acknowledges the compliment, but complains about a third male who is "muscling in" on his advances by trying to impress the girl with remarks about his supposed new car and all the special accessories it has. Angered by this move, the second male threatens to challenge the "bullshitter."

For most whites (and a number of blacks) the words and phrases of the black English vernacular (commonly called "slang" but which also includes "argot," "jive" and "hip" talk, Southernisms and the like) might as well be Greek. But they're not Greek: they are largely English words and phrases being redefined, sometimes reconstructed and rearranged, into new and graphic strings—something lovers of literature should recognize and appreciate. If you happen to be black, especially a young black male "running the streets" of Watts, the conversations need no translation. They are part and parcel of your life. Even if you are "coming up" in the ghettos of New York or Chicago, Philly or Oakland, you would understand most of what was being said. Whatever you didn't know, you could fill in from your own experience with scores of similar situations. Whether someone understands the vernacular vocabulary or not, it isn't difficult to see how much is "lost in translation." For one is trying to paraphrase, to capture somehow through conventional white English, the tempo and tenor of life in America's black ghettos.

The origins of what we know today as black slang are uncertain. William Grier and Price Cobbs, two black psychiatrists writing about the black experience in white America, have suggested that multiple meanings for words and phrases may very well date back to the earliest appearance of African slaves in this country. Brought to America from different tribes, purposely robbed of the bond of a common language (a move on the part of slave traders and owners to stifle conspiracy and possible revolt), not allowed to read or write English, seldom exposed to the spoken language of their masters, the slaves still managed to develop their own version of English—a "lingua franca" that not only allowed for communication with whites when it was necessary, but one that also "began to be used as a secret language among the slaves . . . with a particular emphasis on double meanings." It is well known among students of black history that the early spirituals were a means of passing coded information from slave to slave about happenings on other plantations, plans for revolt or escape and, not the least, expressions of hostility and hatred toward the white man. As one black writer put it, the vocabulary, with its double meanings and private expressions, was "created out of the will to survive on black terms."

With his move from the farm to the city, the black was brought face to face with a poverty and racism that were much more insidious than what he had left behind. The "will to survive on black terms" took many forms —legal and otherwise. Some engaged in sporadic and petty crime, others turned to more organized criminal activities and became pimps or prostitutes, drug pushers and users, confidence men, numbers runners, even "hit men." Many unlucky ones ended up in prison. Others managed to succeed in more socially acceptable ways—entertainment, athletics, religion. A handful "made it" in the professions. Still others, particularly females, contended with a dreary assortment of menial jobs or faced the humiliation of the welfare system. All of these worlds contributed something to the store of black vocabulary—all of them part of the tough fabric of ghetto life.

Perhaps the world that has left the greatest mark on the vernacular vocabulary is that of jazz. Robert Gold, in his excellent and well-documented account of the lexicon of jazz, points out the historical inseparability of this uniquely black music from the "strange amalgam that constitutes the language of the jazz world—the curious mixture of Negro folk expressions with the imagery of the new city life, and the blending of the two with the terms revolving about the music in which these newly freed people found . . . release."

Second only to the world of jazz as a contributor to black slang is the vast and diverse subculture popularly referred to as "the underworld," and its inevitable extension—the prison. "Argot," the specialized and often secret vocabulary of criminal and quasi-criminal professions, is not only the criminal's "working vocabulary," but his hostile, overt rejection of the dominant culture's values, as well as its language. Argot also serves to identify a criminal group as a *group,* and intensifies the participants' own values, attitudes and strategies at the expense of the larger culture. Much of the black vernacular vocabulary can be seen in this light—as a statement of linguistic and social identity and solidarity that thumbs its nose at white America.

Viewed from a historical and social perspective, the black vernacular vocabulary is nothing less than a collective statement, an oral history of black America—where it's been, what it's done, what it thinks and feels and what it has judged important enough to specially name or label. Though each black community, even each neighborhood, may use words and phrases known only to that group, though terms pass in and out of use or are taken over by mainstream America, though new expressions are continually being created and used, there still remains a large and stable pool of expressions that crosses the boundaries of both time and distance. Expressions like "pluck" (wine), "blood" (black person), "beast" (white person), "fronts" (suit of clothes), "gunny" (marijuana), "girl" (cocaine), "boys" (heroin), "to off someone" (to kill someone), "to go from the shoulders" (to fight), "to run off at the jibs" (to talk too much), "git-go" (beginning), "pootbutt" (inexperienced person, usually young), "to mack" (to pimp: to talk smoothly and persuasively to a woman with sex as the end) and literally hundreds more have been common currency among ghetto dwellers for some time, wherever they live in the urban United States.

Clarence Major, author of the *Dictionary of Afro-American Slang,* claims that most general American slang comes from the black vernacular. Certainly, vernacular expressions do escape from the ghetto and do find their way into mainstream American slang. A variety of cultural "intermediaries," who move in both black and white circles and share a vocabulary of common interest and circumstance, have passed black terms on to members of the larger culture. Also, the current flood of black literature, black movies and plays, black public rhetoric and commentary further serves to popularize the slang.

Yet, black vernacular vocabulary is clearly not intended for white ears. First, a good portion of the vocabulary is virtually inaccessible to mainstream white America. Few whites today have any contact with the black ghetto and those that do—the social worker, the police, the businessman or the antipoverty bureaucrat—are viewed with suspicion by ghetto people and are often the subject of hostile vernacular outpourings. Expressions like "honky," "peckerwood," "pig," "beast," "paddy" and "devil" are just a few of the store of pejoratives used by ghetto blacks to identify white "outsiders."

Second, vernacular usage, like any form of human behavior, undergoes continual change. This is true of most specialized subcultural vocabularies. Words are constantly being created and used to enhance one's image, to claim identification with a particular group, to meet new conditions and experiences of life and to replace expressions that have been coopted by the dominant culture. So, for every expression that escapes from the ghetto and becomes part of white usage, there are scores of new ones created to take its place. Even terms and phrases that have become part of white America's slang repertory have retained unmistakably "black" meanings. "Uptight," "to take care of business," "to do your (the) thing" or "to rip off someone" have decidedly sexual connotations for most ghetto blacks—despite what Madison Avenue and network news have read them to mean. Like the proverbial two-thirds of the iceberg submerged from view, the black vernacular vocabulary still remains a vast, uncharted territory for mainstream America.

Not too long ago, in the South Central Los Angeles ghetto, an antipoverty functionary was interviewing a young black man for a job. The interviewer asked the young man what he did. "Whatchu mean, *'what do I do?'* I fiend and I lean, I wheel and I deal, I cop and I blow—I be *me,* man!" The startled interviewer had no idea what the young man was talking about, no recognition that the question, "What do you do?" is the same as "Who are you?" to many ghetto blacks.

Thomas Kochman, who has written extensively about the differences between ghetto black and mainstream white communication, has noted that much of the miscommunication between the two groups results from the vast difference in their respective points of world view. Invariably, in mainstream society you are asked the question, "What do you do?" (One need only remember back to his last cocktail party encounter.) The measure of a man (and more recently of a woman) is inevitably evaluated in light of his status or occupation in the society. In black ghetto culture, where middle-class status, occupation or office still remain inaccessible and illusory, the mark of a person, particularly a male, is what he is, his "self" and the extensions of that self—his personality, the clothes he wears, the possessions he displays, the woman he claims as his own and, not the least, his ability to "rap." No one epitomizes these qualities more than the black pimp. As the Milners have pointed up in their recent book, *Black Players: the Secret World of the Black Pimp,* he is the consummate "rapper." It is his stock in trade. The pimp is still a great folk hero to many ghetto males, and his manner, his dress and his conversational style are widely emulated. He has "made it" through his wits, guile and verbal skills, and more often than not, at the expense of "whitey"—a fact that is not lost on ghetto blacks.

Because who you are (and often how well you survive) depends so heavily on how well you talk, verbal dexterity is highly valued in the ghetto. The oral tradition is still very strong in ghetto culture. Youths growing up in black communities play endless verbal games, much as their mainstream white counterparts play games of "war," "cops and robbers" or "cowboys and Indians." (It is hard to overlook the grim irony that the white child's "game" is very often the ghetto child's daily reality.) Black slang plays a prominent part in these activities. Even the names given the games are in the vernacular. For example, "playing [or "shooting"] the dozens" (variously called "sounding," "woofing," "screaming," "signifying," "joning," "cutting," "chopping" or "basing") is a popular, ritualized speech event in which would-be combatants exchange a variety of insults most often directed at an opponent's mother and less frequently at other near relatives. The "dozens" run the gamut from the quick one-liners— "Your mama's so fat, she needs wheels to turn the corner"; "Your mama's like a doorknob, everybody gets a turn"—to rhymed couplets—"I don't play the dozens, the dozens ain't my game/But the way I fucked your mama is a righteous shame"; "Iron is iron, and steel don't rust/But your mama's got a pussy like a Greyhound bus."

The "dozens," along with a variety of other verbal games, are literally "child's play." The more complex speech events in the ghetto are usually the province of male adults. One of the most intricate speech events (and one reserved for only the very best "rappers") is the "toast," or long, epic narrative. Though the story line and form of most traditional toasts are highly stylized and known to many members of the audience, each narrator adds his own touch and his own vernacular wording. Some time ago in Watts, I heard a local storyteller begin the well-known toast. "The Signifying Monkey," in his own unique way:

> Deep down in the jungle where the coconut grow
> Live a chili pimp monkey, you could tell by his clothes.
> Had a three-quarter piece with a belt in the back,
> Had a pair of thousand eyes and a pair of silk slacks.
> Yessiree, his fronts were pretty little things,
> Styling his apple hat and a big diamond ring.

Like the opening scenes, the meaning and impact of the "toast" are lost on most whites. For speech events, such as the "dozens" and the "toasts," are not only activities that hone and sharpen one's verbal skills, but ways of passing on attitudes, values and ghetto traditions.

Not everyone living in the ghetto uses vernacular vocabulary. Some do not understand very much of it, although virtually everyone is familiar with it and uses certain words and phrases in their daily dealings. Others understand the vocabulary, but choose not to use it. It depends on your lifestyle. Ulf Hannerz has pointed out in his study of community life in a Washington, D.C., ghetto neighborhood that living in the ghetto and being *of* the ghetto may be two different matters. If you're a "mainstreamer," that is a ghetto-dweller who sees himself or herself and is seen by others in the community as "respectable people" or "model citizens" (labels that refer more "to a lifestyle ideal than to socioeconomic status"), as Hannerz points out, you probably avoid vernacular usage, and furthermore you probably discourage your children from using it. If you're a "swinger," a member of a "street family" or a "street corner man," the chances are that you frequently express yourself in the vernacular.

During my work in South Central Los Angeles, I found that the vernacular vocabulary was viewed with double-edged feelings. Most of the young males I talked with regularly expressed themselves in the vernacular, but, at the same time, a number of them labeled it "bad English" or "trashy talk." Some even likened it to "cussin'" and avoided using it in front of their elders—particularly older female members of their families. Adult response was also mixed. Some saw it as "just the way I talk"; others dismissed it as "improper speech." Yet, even the most dedicated "mainstreamer" was quick to admit that slang was as much a part of ghetto life and culture as its "soulful" food or music or religion. Whether or not a ghetto-dweller condones or condemns the vernacular, it is still recognized to be part of the collective experience and identity of black people. As one elderly black woman put it: "That talk ain't much to my likin', but I ain't never been nowhere it ain't been talked, 'cept with white folks. And they don't rightly know much 'bout us black folks."

Who uses slang in the ghetto and who doesn't depends on sex as well as lifestyle. Men are the primary creators and users of the vocabulary. Though I have seen black women of all ages use the vernacular with great style and effect, it is still primarily a male institution. This is true of most nonstandard vocabulary use, whether it be black vernacular or more general American slang. But in ghetto culture, which is historically matrifocal, where a man feels compelled to fight for and establish his masculinity in the face of a white culture that continues to emasculate him, where the ability to "rap" hard and well is so intimately tied up with status and therefore one's manhood, mastery of the vernacular vocabulary takes on an even stronger male cast. The vocabulary is largely the language of the street and the activities and behavior that make up street culture. Though women participate in the street culture and may even be spectators at a variety of speech events, the street is still male turf.

Some 15 years ago, E. Franklin Frazier, the noted black sociologist, wrote a book called the *Black Bourgeoisie*. In it, he exposed the world of "make believe" created by the middle-class black in his attempt to escape from the dilemma of being a marginal man, rejected by the white culture on the one hand, rejecting his own cultural past on the other. In his effort to break with his "folk background," as Frazier called it, he abandoned many things, among them the black vernacular—its sounds, its phrasing and its vocabulary.

Today, matters are somewhat different. The middle-class black who has physically moved away from his beginnings or the middle-class black youth who has never known life in the ghetto do not automatically reject their roots in order to "make it" in the white world. Not all, of course, but many middle-class blacks display intense racial pride and a commitment to their people, their history and their institutions. The young, in particular, see their identity and vitality rooted in ghetto culture. It is not surprising today to hear affluent young blacks "rapping" with much of the same style and force as their ghetto peers. Being *of* the ghetto can be as much a state of mind as a matter of economics or geography, a psychological fact of life for many middle- and high-income blacks who, like their ghetto "brothers" and "sisters," experience the daily frustration and anger of coping with "Mr. Charlie" and his middle-America mentality that wants nothing more than to "keep them in their place." One militant student laid it out when he observed, "All the brothers and sisters have to be tough and stick together. To the 'Man' we're all niggers."

The human animal, along with his other unique characteristics, is a compulsive name-giver, a labeler of the events and persons, objects and emotions that bombard his senses. More often than not, he gives more names and more attention to those things that immediately touch his nerve endings. In the Eskimo vocabulary there are many terms for various kinds and conditions of snow—snow falling, snow on the ground, good-packed and bad-packed snow. Black vernacular vocabulary, like the Eskimo lexicon, reflects man's need—the black man's need—to take full note of his environment. The word is a powerful tool. And black America has wielded it with particular creativity and force.

Part III

EXCHANGE AND PRODUCTION

The various facets of the human experience discussed in this book are so closely interrelated that it is essentially arbitrary which one we start with. There is, consequently, a certain irony in the linear structure inherent in anthropology textbooks. With topic *A* followed by topic *B* and then *C*, some may be misled and conclude that the causal arrow is direct and linear (*A* causes *B* causes *C* and so forth) when in fact human lifeways are systemic (*A, B,* and *C* are mutually and complexly interrelated). Even though it is possible to begin discussing the human experience from almost any starting point, some are better than others. As it happens, several factors led to the development of the sequence ultimately used in this book. Since there are important reasons for introducing the topics in Parts III and IV at this point, these will be noted briefly.

The first two parts of the book have provided several of the more vital conceptual and methodological foundations anthropologists depend upon when assessing the human experience. Thus, we have seen the important role of fieldwork as the means par excellence for obtaining needed data; we have seen something of the central though dual role of the culture concept; and we have examined the critical matter of language—that capacity which is so distinctively human and which, as we come to understand it in particular, seems to offer so many valuable insights about human behavior in general.

By contrast, Parts III and IV pertain to two of the most fundamental adaptive processes of the human experience. First, if living organisms are to endure through any length of time, they obviously must be successful in getting food and other material necessities. The salience of environmental limitations and options is greater here than in any other dimension of human life. For humans, this part of the adaptive process involves exchange and production; few if any other aspects of the human experience are more

93

critical than these. Second, human infants and young sub-adults must, if they and the group are to survive, acquire the behavioral repertoires typical of adults. They must, in a word, be socialized (or "enculturated"); they must be made human in their own group's terms. This dimension of human social life is critical for many obvious reasons, not the least of which is that it is here that the variety of biogenetic materials and potentials a group is "presented with" is shaped, not into uniform molds, but into the variety of personalities (both "normal" and "abnormal") found in any society. Other features of a given sociocultural system take on new and clearer meanings when these fundamental adaptive processes have been considered first. Thus, we will consider the processes of exchange and production here and then will turn to socialization and personality in Part IV.

EXCHANGE

Of the three basic types of exchange, two—reciprocity and redistribution—are discussed in the first two selections in Part III. (The third— market exchange—will not be discussed here primarily because it is the one with which we are most familiar). In reciprocity exchange, labor and the fruits of that labor are exchanged on a reciprocal basis (hence the name). Although there are variations, there is generally an assumption that the exchange is more or less direct and immediate, so that each person involved can assume that an item exchanged today will be balanced (approximately) with the same or an essentially equivalent item in the near future. The relationships among family members in our own society can serve as an analogy to the process as it operates in whole societies.

Assuming a family consisting of a pair of adults and two offspring, we can expect that over the months and years (especially after the children are young sub-adults being socialized into adult roles), each member of the family *may* contribute various and equal labors and products to the family as a whole. Stated in so summary a fashion, we have what is obviously an ideal picture. We all know from personal experience that not everybody contributes the same amount of labor to the family unit. Some are more skilled at some tasks than others and, more importantly, some are simply willing to work harder than others. What happens in such situations? Undoubtedly we all have faced the angry parent who has said something like the following: "I have worked hard all day over a hot stove (or in a hot office), so the least you can do is take out the trash (or mow the grass)," or: "We have spent the best years of our lives working and slaving for you, so the least you can do is try and get higher grades in school." Exaggerations? Well, perhaps, but such statements illustrate several fundamental facts about reciprocity exchange.

First, there generally is no precise system for calculating or measuring the value of the labor or the products exchanged in a reciprocity system. (Only recently have we seen members of a family trying to put precise money-values on the things they do and produce.) But even though there are no such guidelines (and indeed, in many instances there are rather strong pressures against making such calculations), there are limits. They may not be very well defined, but at certain points it becomes legitimate to say, in effect, "O.K. I've been playing this reciprocity game for a long time and I've been assuming you have been, too. But it's been so long since you've reciprocated that I've come to the point where I must tell you what it should be assumed you already know—it is your turn to give me something in return for all that I've given you." Although illustrated in terms of relationships between individuals, these developments can characterize the relationship between groups, too.

A second feature of reciprocity illustrated in these statements (albeit rather subtly), is that the exchange process can best be balanced by the exchange of roughly similar things (I cook, you wash the dishes; I clean house, you mow the grass, and so on). In part, this also directs our attention to a third feature of reciprocity, namely that the process can be greatly distorted if not stopped altogether if one person (or group) gives so much that the receiving party cannot reasonably be expected to return a similar amount. Such gift-giving can introduce great tension into social relationships, especially if there is a hint (or even more than a hint) of pride, boastfulness, and a "see-if-you-can-match-that" attitude involved, as well. This particularly subtle and yet vital dimension of reciprocity exchange is vividly illustrated by Richard Lee in his essay on a gift-giving incident among the Bushmen (Chapter 7).

In rather sharp contrast to this sort of exchange is that known as redistributive exchange. Here, goods, labor, and other services are given to and, in effect, accumulated in a central place. After a period of time, the goods are redistributed to people once again, although very often on the basis of different principles than those which led to the accumulation of the goods. The example we are most familiar with is the paying of taxes and, so it is said, of receiving these valuables again in a different form. This kind of exchange, in contrast to reciprocity, is intimately linked to politics, with those responsible for receiving, storing, and then redistributing the valuables being important, powerful people ("big men"). Aspects of this type of exchange are illustrated in the essay by Harold Scheffler (Chapter 8).

Although Scheffler begins his essay by suggesting that the "big man" syndrome is the essence of politics in Melanesia and the essence of his presentation, it is instructive to emphasize that the subtitle of his article contains the phrase "political finance." Trade, politics, *kesa* shells, feasting, being a big man, redistributive exchange—these are collectively the essence of politics and economics. Although only hinted at in Scheffler's brief essay, the vital role of pigs in many Melanesian societies should be emphasized. A great deal of effort is required in order to raise pigs, so that when they get large and numerous enough, the task can become almost (if not literally) impossible. At this point, as well as on other special occasions, large feasts are held at which dozens or even hundreds of pigs may be slaughtered. As Scheffler notes, these feasts are the affairs of "big men" who validate their status and work to maintain it by engaging in the extensive preparations necessary to give such a feast. Broad trading networks, reinforced by the trade of *kesa* valuables (which are also used in more localized transactions such as in marriage payments), are of critical importance to the aspiring big man and to the society as a whole. In contrast to reciprocity, there is precise calculation, much boasting, a very overt "now-see-if-you-can-top-that" attitude, long delays between giving and receiving, and no built-in assumption that each is working for the benefit of all the others (although it can be shown that such systems do in fact produce benefits for whole regions of people).

PRODUCTION

Environment, mode of exchange, and the things produced are all closely related, and together these factors appear to have a rather pronounced impact on the shape of other aspects of life in human societies. This is illustrated in the essay by Fredrik Barth (Chapter 9). In it, he shows clearly how a group of pastoral nomads, the Basseri (who may be considered to be a special type of peasantry), accumulate capital and how this, in turn, influences the shape of Basseri social organization. Barth also describes the different types of capital goods, the variations in rights of ownership and use (e.g., grazing rights), and the nature of trading relationships between nomads and village dwellers. But most importantly, perhaps, the way the "shape" of Basseri capital influences the patterning of the stages through which a family grows and develops is clearly demonstrated. And we learn how social differentiation and political organization are pressed toward remarkable degrees of homogeneity, equality, and independence. And finally, the way pastoralism (and the attendant methods of capital accumulation and investment) requires attitudes of thrift and, paradoxically, of generosity and hospitality is vividly illustrated.

The concluding selection in Part III, T. G. McGee's essay on the paradox of peasants in cities, raises several fundamental questions, not the least of which is: "What is a peasant?" Few other questions within this branch of anthropology have drawn more attention and yet reached such inconclusive results. (McGee, it may be noted, is a geographer, and this may be a partial explanation for his success in finding a new way to approach this old question.) As McGee notes, virtually all definitions of "peasant society" and "peasant economy" begin with and stress the observation that peasants are rural, agricultural people. McGee rejects this starting point. As a consequence, he is forced to question the suggestions of others that there are peasants in cities *because* some who have moved there from rural areas have retained their rural values and lifestyles. Instead, he defines peasants in terms of their basic mode of production. Here he follows the lead of others (such as Chayanov 1966) and notes that peasants are neither capitalists nor socialists, but rather, they utilize a family based labor supply. Some may prefer adding criteria and indicators to this basic definition in order to differentiate peasant societies from other societies with production organized in family or lineage units (e.g., many hunting and gathering societies and some horticultural societies). But there are, I think, numerous advantages to this view of peasant society, and these are delineated in the second half of McGee's essay (Chapter 9).

Richard B. Lee

7. Eating Christmas in the Kalahari*

The !Kung Bushmen's knowledge of Christmas is thirdhand. The London Missionary Society brought the holiday to the southern Tswana tribes in the early nineteenth century. Later, native catechists spread the idea far and wide among the Bantu-speaking pastoralists, even in the remotest corners of the Kalahari Desert. The Bushmen's idea of the Christmas story, stripped to its essentials, is "praise the birth of white man's god-chief"; what keeps their interest in the holiday high is the Tswana-Herero custom of slaughtering an ox for his Bushmen neighbors as an annual goodwill gesture. Since the 1930s, part of the Bushmen's annual round of activities has included a December congregation at the cattle posts for trading, marriage brokering, and several days of trance-dance feasting at which the local Tswana headman is host.

As a social anthropologist working with !Kung Bushmen, I found that the Christmas ox custom suited my purposes. I had come to the Kalahari to study the hunting and gathering subsistence economy of the !Kung, and to accomplish this it was essential not to provide them with food, share my own food, or interfere in any way with their food-gathering activities. While liberal handouts of tobacco and medical supplies were appreciated, they were scarcely adequate to erase the glaring disparity in wealth between the anthropologist, who maintained a two-month inventory of canned

* Reprinted with permission from *Natural History* Magazine, December 1969. Copyright © The American Museum of Natural History 1969.

goods, and the Bushmen, who rarely had a day's supply of food on hand. My approach, while paying off in terms of data, left me open to frequent accusations of stinginess and hard-heartedness. By their lights, I was a miser.

The Christmas ox was to be my way of saying thank you for the cooperation of the past year; and since it was to be our last Christmas in the field, I determined to slaughter the largest, meatiest ox that money could buy, insuring that the feast and trance dance would be a success.

Through December I kept my eyes open at the wells as the cattle were brought down for watering. Several animals were offered, but none had quite the grossness that I had in mind. Then, ten days before the holiday, a Herero friend led an ox of astonishing size and mass up to our camp. It was solid black, stood five feet high at the shoulder, had a five-foot span of horns, and must have weighed 1,200 pounds on the hoof. Food consumption calculations are my specialty, and I quickly figured that bones and viscera aside, there was enough meat—at least four pounds—for every man, woman, and child of the 150 Bushmen in the vicinity of /ai/ai who were expected at the feast.

Having found the right animal at last, I paid the Herero £20 ($56) and asked him to keep the beast with his herd until Christmas day. The next morning word spread among the people that the big solid black one was the ox chosen by /ontah (my Bushman name; it means, roughly, "whitey") for the Christmas feast. That afternoon I received the first delegation. Ben!a, an outspoken sixty-year-old mother of five, came to the point slowly.

"Where were you planning to eat Christmas?"

"Right here at /ai/ai," I replied.

"Alone or with others?"

"I expect to invite all the people to eat Christmas with me."

"Eat what?"

"I have purchased Yehave's black ox, and I am going to slaughter and cook it."

"That's what we were told at the well but refused to believe it until we heard it from yourself."

"Well, it's the black one," I replied expansively, although wondering what she was driving at.

"Oh, no!" Ben!a groaned, turning to her group. "They were right." Turning back to me she asked, "Do you expect us to eat that bag of bones?"

"Bag of bones! It's the biggest ox at /ai/ai."

"Big, yes, but old. And thin. Everybody knows there's no meat on that old ox. What did you expect us to eat off it, the horns?"

Everybody chuckled at Ben!a's one-liner as they walked away, but all I could manage was a weak grin.

That evening it was the turn of the young men. They came to sit at our evening fire. /gaugo, about my age, spoke to me man-to-man.

"/ontah, you have always been square with us," he lied. "What has happened to change your heart? That sack of guts and bones of Yehave's will hardly feed one camp, let alone all the Bushmen around ai/ai/." And he proceeded to enumerate the seven camps in the /ai/ai vicinity, family by family. "Perhaps you have forgotten that we are not few, but many. Or are you too blind to tell the difference between a proper cow and an old wreck? That ox is thin to the point of death."

"Look, you guys," I retorted, "that is a beautiful animal, and I'm sure you will eat it with pleasure at Christmas."

"Of course we will eat it; it's food. But it won't fill us up to the point where we will have enough strength to dance. We will eat and go home to bed with stomachs rumbling."

That night as we turned in, I asked my wife, Nancy: "What did you think of the black ox?"

"It looked enormous to me. Why?"

"Well, about eight different people have told me I got gypped; that the ox is nothing but bones."

"What's the angle?" Nancy asked. "Did they have a better one to sell?"

"No, they just said that it was going to be a grim Christmas because there won't be enough meat to go around. Maybe I'll get an independent judge to look at the beast in the morning."

Bright and early, Halingisi, a Tswana cattle owner, appeared at our camp. But before I could ask him to give me his opinion on Yehave's black ox, he gave me the eye signal that indicated a confidential chat. We left the camp and sat down.

"/ontah, I'm surprised at you; you've lived here for three years and still haven't learned anything about cattle."

"But what else can a person do but choose the biggest, strongest animal one can find?" I retorted.

"Look, just because an animal is big doesn't mean that it has plenty of meat on it. The black one was a beauty when it was younger, but now it is thin to the point of death."

"Well I've already bought it. What can I do at this stage?"

"Bought it already? I thought you were just considering it. Well, you'll have to kill it and serve it, I suppose. But don't expect much of a dance to follow."

My spirits dropped rapidly. I could believe that Ben!a and /gaugo just might be putting me on about the black ox, but Halingisi seemed to be an impartial critic. I went around that day feeling as though I had bought a lemon of a used car.

In the afternoon it was Tomazo's turn. Tomazo is a fine hunter, a top trance performer (*see* "The Trance Cure of the !Kung Bushmen," *Natural History,* November 1967), and one of my most reliable informants. He approached the subject of the Christmas cow as part of my continuing Bushmen education.

"My friend, the way it is with us Bushmen," he began, "is that we love meat. And even more than that, we love fat. When we hunt we always search for the fat ones, the ones dripping with layers of white fat: fat that turns into a clear, thick oil in the cooking pot, fat the slides down your gullet, fills your stomach and gives you a roaring diarrhea," he rhapsodized.

"So, feeling as we do," he continued, "it gives us pain to be served such a scrawny thing as Yehave's black ox. It is big, yes, and no doubt its giant bones are good for soup, but fat is what we really crave and so we will eat Christmas this year with a heavy heart."

The prospect of a gloomy Christmas now had me worried, so I asked Tomazo what I could do about it.

"Look for a fat one, a young one . . . smaller, but fat. Fat enough to make us //gom ('evacuate the bowels'), then we will be happy."

My suspicions were aroused when Tomazo said that he happened to know of a young, fat, barren cow that the owner was willing to part with. Was Toma working on commission, I wondered? But I dispelled this unworthy thought when we approached the Herero owner of the cow in question and found that he had decided not to sell.

The scrawny wreck of a Christmas ox now became the talk of the /ai/ai water hole and was the first news told to the outlying groups as they began to come in from the bush for the feast. What finally convinced me that real trouble might be brewing was the visit from u !au, an old conservative with a reputation for fierceness. His nickname meant spear and referred to an incident thirty years ago in which he had speared a man to death. He had an intense manner; fixing me with his eyes, he said in clipped tones:

"I have only just heard about the black ox today, or else I would have come here earlier. /ontah, do you honestly think you can serve meat like that to people and avoid a fight?" He paused, letting the implications sink in. "I don't mean fight you, /ontah; you are a white man. I mean a fight between Bushmen. There are many fierce ones here, and with such a small quantity of meat to distribute, how can you give everybody a fair share? Someone is sure to accuse another of taking too much or hogging all the choice pieces. Then you will see what happens when some go hungry while others eat."

The possibility of at least a serious argument struck me as all too real. I had witnessed the tension that surrounds the distribution of meat from a kudu or gemsbok kill, and had documented many arguments that sprang up from a real or imagined slight in meat distribution. The owners of a kill may spend up to two hours arranging and rearranging the piles of meat under the gaze of a circle of recipients before handing them out. And I also knew that the Christmas feast at /ai/ai would be bringing together groups that had feuded in the past.

Convinced now of the gravity of the situation, I went in earnest to search for a second cow; but all my inquiries failed to turn one up.

The Christmas feast was evidently going to be a disaster, and the incessant complaints about the meagerness of tne ox had already taken the fun out of it for me. Moreover, 1 was getting bored with the wisecracks, and after losing my temper a few times, I resolved to serve the beast anyway. If the meat fell short, the hell with it. In the Bushmen idiom, I announced to all who would listen:

"I am a poor man and blind. If I have chosen one that is too old and too thin, we will eat it anyway and see if there is enough meat there to quiet the rumbling of our stomachs."

On hearing this speech, Ben!a offered me a rare word of comfort. "It's thin," she said philosophically, "but the bones will make a good soup."

At dawn Christmas morning, instinct told me to turn over the butchering and cooking to a friend and take off with Nancy to spend Christmas alone in the bush. But curiosity kept me from retreating. 1 wanted to see what such a scrawny ox looked like on butchering, and if there *was* going to be a fight, I wanted to catch every word of it. Anthropologists are incurable that way.

The great beast was driven up to our dancing ground, and a shot in the forehead dropped it in its tracks. Then, freshly cut branches were heaped around the fallen carcass to receive the meat. Ten men volunteered to help with the cutting. I asked /gaugo to make the breast bone cut. This cut, which begins the butchering process for most large game, offers easy access for removal of the viscera. But it also allows the hunter to spot-check the amount of fat on the animal. A fat game animal carries a white layer up to an inch thick on the chest, while in a thin one, the knife will quickly cut to bone. All eyes fixed on his hand as /gaugo, dwarfed by the great carcass, knelt to the breast. The first cut opened a pool of solid white in the black skin. The second and third cut widened and deepened the creamy white. Still no bone. It was pure fat; it must have been two inches thick.

"Hey /gau," I burst out, "that ox is loaded with fat. What's this about the ox being too thin to bother eating? Are you out of your mind?"

"Fat?" /gau shot back, "You call that fat? This wreck is thin, sick, dead!" And he broke out laughing. So did everyone else. They rolled on the ground, paralyzed with laughter. Everybody laughed except me; I was thinking.

I ran back to the tent and burst in just as Nancy was getting up. "Hey, the black ox. It's fat as hell! They were kidding about it being too thin to eat. It was a joke or something. A put-on. Everyone is really delighted with it!"

"Some joke," my wife replied. "It was so funny that you were ready to pack up and leave /ai/ai."

If it had indeed been a joke, it had been an extraordinarily convincing one, and tinged, I thought, with more than a touch of malice as many jokes are. Nevertheless, that it was a joke lifted my spirits considerably, and I returned to the butchering site where the shape of the ox was rapidly disappearing under the axes and knives of the butchers. The atmosphere had become festive. Grinning broadly, their arms covered with blood well past the elbow, men packed chunks of meat into the big cast-iron cooking pots, fifty pounds to the load, and muttered and chuckled all the while about the thinness and worthlessness of the animal and /ontah's poor judgment.

We danced and ate that ox two days and two nights; we cooked and distributed fourteen potfuls of meat and no one went home hungry and no fights broke out.

But the "joke" stayed in my mind. I had a growing feeling that something important had happened in my relationship with the Bushmen and that the clue lay in the meaning of the joke. Several days later, when most of the people had dispersed back to the bush camps, I raised the question with Hakekgose, a Tswana man who had grown up among the !Kung, married a !Kung girl, and who probably knew their culture better than any other non-Bushman.

"With us whites," I began, "Christmas is supposed to be the day of friendship and brotherly love. What I can't figure out is why the Bushmen went to such lengths to criticize and belittle the ox I had bought for the feast. The animal was perfectly good and their jokes and wisecracks practically ruined the holiday for me."

"So it really did bother you," said Hakekgose. "Well, that's the way they always talk. When I take my rifle and go hunting with them, if I miss, they laugh at me for the rest of the day. But even if I hit and bring one down, it's no better. To them, the kill is always too small or too old or too thin; and as we sit down the kill site to cook and eat the liver, they keep grumbling, even with their mouths full of meat. They say things like, 'Oh this is awful! What a worthless animal! Whatever made me think that this Tswana rascal could hunt!'"

"Is this the way outsiders are treated?" I asked.

"No, it is their custom; they talk that way to each other too. Go and ask them."

/gaugo had been one of the most enthusiastic in making me feel bad about the merit of the Christmas ox. I sought him out first.

"Why did you tell me the black ox was worthless, when you could see that it was loaded with fat and meat?"

"It is our way," he said smiling. "We always like to fool people about that. Say there is a Bushman who has been hunting. He must not come home and announce like a braggard, 'I have killed a big one in the bush!' He must first sit down in silence until I or someone else comes up to his fire and asks, 'What did you see today?' He replies quietly, 'Ah, I'm no good for hunting. I saw nothing at all [pause] just a little tiny one.' Then I smile to myself," /gaugo continued, "because I know he has killed something big.

"In the morning we make up a party of four or five people to cut up and carry the meat back to the camp. When we arrive at the kill we examine it and cry out, 'You mean to say you have dragged us all the way out here in order to make us cart home your pile of bones? Oh, if I had known it was this thin I wouldn't have come.' Another one pipes up, 'People, to think I gave up a nice day in the shade for this. At home we may be hungry but at least we have nice cool water to drink.' If the horns are big, someone says, 'Did you think that somehow you were going to boil down the horns for soup?'

"To all this you must respond in kind. 'I agree,' you say, 'this one is not worth the effort; let's just cook the liver for strength and leave the rest for the hyenas. It is not too late to hunt today and even a duiker or a steenbok would be better than this mess.'

"Then you set to work nevertheless; butcher the animal, carry the meat back to the camp and everyone eats," /gaugo concluded.

Things were beginning to make sense. Next, I went to Tomazo. He corroborated /gaugo's story of the obligatory insults over a kill and added a few details of his own.

"But," I asked, "why insult a man after he has gone to all that trouble to track and kill an animal and when he is going to share the meat with you so that your children will have something to eat?"

"Arrogance," was his cryptic answer.

"Arrogance?"

"Yes, when a young man kills much meat he comes to think of himself as a chief or a big man, and he thinks of the rest of us as his servants or inferiors. We can't accept this. We refuse one who boasts, for someday his pride will make him kill somebody. So we always speak of his meat as worthless. This way we cool his heart and make him gentle."

"But why didn't you tell me this before?" I asked Tomazo with some heat.

"Because you never asked me," said Tomazo, echoing the refrain that has come to haunt every field ethnographer.

The pieces now fell into place. I had known for a long time that in situations of social conflict with Bushmen I held all the cards. I was the only source of tobacco in a thousand square miles, and I was not incapable of cutting an individual off for noncooperation. Though my boycott never lasted longer than a few days, it was an indication of my strength. People resented my presence at the water hole, yet simultaneously dreaded my leaving. In short I was a perfect target for the charge of arrogance and for the Bushmen tactic of enforcing humility.

I had been taught an object lesson by the Bushmen; it had come from an unexpected corner and had hurt me in a vulnerable area. For the big black ox was to be the one totally generous, unstinting act of my year at /ai/ai, and I was quite unprepared for the reaction I received.

As I read it, their message was this: There are no totally generous acts. All "acts" have an element of calculation. One black ox slaughtered at Christmas does not wipe out a year of careful manipulation of gifts given to serve your own ends. After all, to kill an animal and share the meat with people is really no more than Bushmen do for each other every day and with far less fanfare.

In the end, I had to admire how the Bushmen had played out the farce —collectively straight-faced to the end. Curiously, the episode reminded me of the *Good Soldier Schweik* and his marvelous encounters with authority. Like Schweik, the Bushmen had retained a thoroughgoing skepticism of good intentions. Was it this independence of spirit, I wondered, that had kept them culturally viable in the face of generations of contact with more powerful societies, both black and white? The thought that the Bushmen were alive and well in the Kalahari was strangely comforting. Perhaps, armed with that independence and with their superb knowledge of their environment, they might yet survive the future.

Harold W. Scheffler

8. Big Men and Disks of Shell: Political Finance in Melanesia*

Melanesia, an ethnic region composed of islands in the Pacific Ocean northeast of Australia, was once thought to be an area of remarkable cultural uniformity, but now it is becoming known as an area of remarkable diversity. For instance, we can no longer refer to Melanesia as "the matrilineal sea." Instead we find there social forms that are frequently variations on such a well-known organizational theme as matrilineality, but which also include patrilineality and even cognatic or "bilateral" descent. Some of these forms are unique to Melanesia and provide interesting grist for the mills of anthropological theory. However, despite the variation in kinship structure, there remains a common organizational theme, the competition among "big men"—those who acquire prestige and power through the manipulation of the allegiances of other men. And it is this kind of activity that passes for politics in these societies.

Important in this political process is the control of basic resources, such as land, pigs, and other "valuables." The latter are often items processed from shell of various kinds, including those made from gold lip, cowrie, and bailer shell that are found throughout large areas of New Guinea. These shell valuables, like our dollars, have no intrinsic productive value but are of considerable symbolic significance. They are valuable, not in themselves, but for what men do with them, and their significance lies in the activities

* Reprinted with permission from *Natural History* Magazine, December 1965. Copyright © The American Museum of Natural History 1965.

through which they are acquired and subsequently redistributed. Dr. Bronislaw Malinowski, the noted ethnographer, tells us in *Argonauts of the Western Pacific* how the Trobriand Islanders give each *kula*—a necklace or armband of shell—a personal name and how men fondle them and treat them as pets. However, a recent reanalysis of the "*kula* ring"—a pattern of interisland trade in which *kula* valuables flow in one direction and goods of practical value in the other—has suggested that it is the political significance of these valuables that partly accounts for their importance. Perhaps more than Malinowski realized, the "big man" system of politics operates in the Trobriands, too, and *kula* exchange in its various forms is, or was at one time, an integral part of acquiring political eminence.

Although they vary widely in form and significance, shell valuables are common throughout Melanesia. The shells are processed, converted into valuables, and sometimes traded over long distances, as from the coastal areas to the remote highlands of New Guinea. In such instances, their value increases proportionately with the distance from their source of manufacture. Sometimes they function very much like money, that is, as a more or less universal standard of commercial exchange, but they are also frequently used in social contexts in which we would find monetary exchanges inappropriate. Bride price transactions are a notable case in point. There are few markets in Melanesia, and daily provisions are seldom bought and sold; thus, while shell valuables are, in a sense, monies, they are best thought of as limited-purpose monies.

The most-cherished and, until the twentieth century, the most politically significant valuable on the island of Choiseul, in the British Solomon Islands Protectorate, is called *kesa*. (Choiseul is known as Lauru by its inhabitants.) *Kesa* consists of sets of shell cylinders, probably giant clam, *Tridacna,* and each set usually consists of nine small tubes that are bound together in a single leaf package.

To the best of my knowledge *kesa* is yet to be described to the Western world, and other than the pieces I possess, I do not believe that there are any complete sets extant outside of Choiseul. Most other items of ethnographic interest on Choiseul have long since been carted off by passing curiosity seekers. Today *kesa* has lost most of its social utility because of the changes consequent to pacification and missionization since 1900. Yet, it still remains valuable in and of itself, and the few big men who own it will not part with it for any amount of money that may be offered.

When one asks a Choiseulese what *kesa* is made of, he is not able to say, for as far as he knows, humans had no part in its making. According to ancient tradition it was made and given to man by *bangara Laena,* a water god. Long ago, so goes the story, *Laena* thought to himself, "I am the god of Lauru, and I must make something important for Lauru, something that can be the 'mark' of the big men there." He thought of *kesa,* but the first two attempts at manufacture proved abortive. There were too many or too few pieces to each set, and he was not satisfied with his handiwork. He tried a third time and then produced *kesa* with nine pieces to a set, and this pleased him. He sent word to the men of Choiseul to erect a large house at a place called Nuatambu, on the north coast. Each of the six dialect areas was told to prepare a pig for presentation to *Laena* and then to come to Nuatambu to receive *kesa* and instruction in its use. (It was to become the custom that baked pig should always accompany the exchange of *kesa* in any transactions.)

When *Laena* brought the *kesa* ashore—he is said to have manufactured it in the ocean's depths—he placed the larger varieties in the rear of the house and the smaller and less valuable varieties in the front near the entrance. When he finished, the house was full. Then the people arrived in their canoes from all over Choiseul, and *Laena* said to them, "There is the *kesa,* help yourselves!" They presented their pigs to him and began to gather it up. The people from the Varisi, Taula, Bambatana, and Ririo areas, to the north and west, were quick. They entered the house first and gathered up the small *kesa* that completely blocked the front entrance. The Sengga and Kumboro people, from the southeast areas, were slow and had to go through the rear entrance. Thus they were able to collect the large *kesa.*

As the people helped themselves, they fought over possession of it. Each big man said to the other, "I will take plenty for myself alone," and as they snatched it from one another, much of it fell to the ground and was smashed. Now when one goes to Nuatambu, one can see hundreds of broken sherds of *kesa* strewn about on the beach.

Laena promised to come again and bring more *kesa.* He told the people to go home and await his message. But it was not long after that he became involved in a contest of strength with another god, *Nggola,* a snake, and lost his life by being baked in an earth oven. That is why, the story goes, that there is so little *kesa* today. Had it been brought ashore more than once there would have been plenty for everyone, but as it was, only the important men could have it, and so a man could acquire it only by diligent competition with other men.

A visitor to Choiseul will note that *kesa* looks suspiciously like fossilized shell, but he will have difficulty figuring out how it might have been made. There are other forms of shell valuables relatively common throughout the Solomons, such as large polished rings of clamshell. Some have reddish streaks running through one edge, giving them a higher value. These, called *ziku kesa* by the Choiseulese, are commonly known to have been made even in recent years by a process of pecking and rubbing the shells on sandstone or pumice and finally by drilling with fine sand and bamboo. It may be that *kesa* was made in a similar way, but one can only guess.

Informants assured me that it is true, as the story reports, that many frag-ments of *kesa* are to be found at Nuatambu, but I did not see the place and even if I had, I might not have known whether it was the manufacturing site or simply a place where much *kesa* was broken.

I saw only a few sets of *kesa*. Today, most men will disclaim possession of any lest someone try to borrow it, but at the same time they are so ambiguous in their replies to queries that one is not sure. On more intimate acquaintance they may offer to take one to see where it is hidden—to prove that they are truly big men. I saw more come to light in the occasional bride price transactions, but *kesa* "doing work" (used as money) is a rare sight today.

Kesa is all the same in form—nine thin-walled cylinders per set—but is widely variable in size, in quality and, therefore, in value. There appears to be no definite standard of value against which it has ever been com-pared. For instance, one of the few things it can purchase is pig, but the transaction depends upon the quality of the shell valuables, the quality and size of the pig, and even the quality of the interpersonal relations of the people involved. Recently, the Choiseul Council decided that the smallest *kesa,* which was once commonly used in transactions, is worth three pounds in Australian currency (about $6.75). Others are said to be worth up to ninety or more dollars, but this is an arbitrary evaluation. In the past, if one did not have *kesa,* one could substitute ten *ziku*—arm rings also made of clamshell. However, then as now, no one would trade ten *ziku,* or three Australian pounds, for one *kesa*. Thus these equivalences are purely utili-tarian—for substitution in transactions in which *kesa* is preferred.

The smaller variety of *kesa* is often termed *kesa zazu, kesa* that "works," or *kesa soka, kesa* for "exchanges." The larger variety is simply "large *kesa,*" which, in the past, was seldom used in transactions but was kept as security against attack or vengeance.

Working *kesa* comes in five sizes, each of which is valued at three times its "size" in Australian pounds. Thus *kesa potaka kavasi* ("worth four") is the equivalent of twelve Australian pounds (about $27.00). A set of *kesa potaka kameka* ("worth one") was presented to me when I left Choiseul in 1960 after a fifteen-month visit. In this set, each of the nine rings is approximately two and three-quarter inches wide and one and three-quarter to two inches long. They are approximately one-eighth inch thick at the center of the cylinder and taper to paper thinness at the edges. Each cylinder is known as one *mata,* or eye, and three *mata* make one *salaka,* a term for which there is no English equivalent. Each *salaka* is then bound together in a sago palm leaf, and the three *salaka* are tied together to make up a single triangular package known as one *kesa*. "One *kesa*" is thus a conveniently ambiguous term, for it may refer to a set "worth one" or to a single set of any size. (*Mata* and *salaka* are never used singly in transactions.)

The small *kesa* I have is about seventeen or eighteen inches tall when all nine *mata* are stacked edge on edge. The Choiseulese "stand up the *kesa*" in this way during transactions in which it must be examined meticulously for size and quality. The length of the set is then measured against a rod made from the midrib of a sago palm leaf that is placed inside the stack and that also prevents it from toppling over. Arranging the *kesa* to stand up on its own is no mean feat, and it may require several hours of patient manipulation of the uneven, jagged cylinder edges. Only old men are thought to have the necessary skills.

When the *kesa* is finally stacked, usually before an audience that offers advice about the process, the palm leaf rod is broken off even with the height of the *kesa* and then measured against the human arm. The smallest working *kesa* should reach approximately from the finger tips of an outstretched hand to about three inches below the inner crook of the elbow. The fifth and largest of this type should reach to the center of the biceps. It is obvious that these measurements vary from person to person, and the variation leaves room for debate as to the relative worth of particular sets. (Some men used to mark the lengths of the various *kesa* they had owned or were owed on the handles of their war clubs.) A set's value is also dependent in a vague and not readily calculable manner upon its condition as well as its size—again leaving room for debate about the equivalence of transactions.

Large *kesa* also comes in a variety of sizes, and some unusual and highly valued sets contain eight or ten rather than the usual nine cylinders. I recorded the names of some nine varieties whose values are said to range from sixteen pounds Australian to extremely valuable, and I once saw one reputed to be worth ten times the standard one *kesa,* or thirty pounds (about $68.00). When it was standing up, it was about the length of one's arm from shoulder to finger tips. The largest *kesa* seen by anyone I spoke with was said to be six feet long, with individual cylinders that measured from the tip of the thumb to the tip of the small finger over an outstretched hand (some eight to nine inches).

In addition to working *kesa* and large *kesa,* there are some sets that are exceptionally small. There is, for instance, *napukana,* somewhat smaller than the standard one *kesa,* which was used in the past only in peacemaking transactions and was said to bring a war to an unequivocal end. To accomplish peace the disputing parties would agree to exchange *kesa,* one side always using *napukana.*

Valuable as it was in Choiseul tradition, in terms of political as well as economic prestige, *kesa* was the object of much jealousy, envy, connivance, and thievery. Disputes over ownership, debts, or whatever, were among the principal sources of Choiseulese conflict until about 1920, and it was very important to keep the amount and hiding place of one's valuables as secret as possible. This secrecy helped prevent continual demands for loans from one's less fortunate relatives, and also made for a margin of uncertainty as to one's political potential. Successful men were those who were clever at getting and circulating *kesa,* but they also had to be able to convey the impression of wealth when they were temporarily indisposed.

As noted earlier, *kesa* may be called money only in a restricted sense because it is not and never was a universal medium of exchange. Indeed, such universal mediums are fairly rare in the primitive world. More often, valuables are of limited utility, and the range of situations in which they are useful is narrow. On Choiseul, *kesa* was traditionally too valuable to use in the myriad of minor transactions between kinsmen, who would give and receive assistance in any event. Reciprocation, not payment, was expected. Its most important uses were in bride price payments and in the formation of alliances between individuals or groups for purposes of vengeance. Although it was sometimes used to pay for a canoe or to purchase a pig for a feast, there was usually no such obvious material gain in the transaction. *Kesa* was also exchanged with other men through a process of competitive feast-giving and in a manner reminiscent, although not strictly comparable, with the well-known potlatches of the Indians of the American northwest coast.

These competitive feasts were called *kelo,* and although they are no longer given, they were once the outstanding public events of Choiseulese life. A big man might arrange several during the course of his career, and the most powerful men gave perhaps as many as ten or more. The feasts required the joint efforts of a large number of people—usually members of the big man's kin group and his followers. Assistance came, too, from outsiders who hoped to benefit from the occasions. The benefits received might be in kind, perhaps at a later date when the former helper turned principal party in another transaction. But a big man's followers usually rendered assistance for less tangible but equally important returns in the form of protection and security. This was a society without "law" in our more formal sense of the term, and in order to comprehend the sense of social life on Choiseul (and in Melanesia in general) we must note that a man could attain and maintain his political and economic interests only through other men and only by force or agreement. The obligations one managed to impose on others were an important form of capital. To protect life and property one either had to become a big man, or else secure the protection of one by helping him realize his ambitions.

Renown would accrue to a man who organized and executed gift exchanges, but these were not undertaken solely for profit in *kesa.* It was desirable to come out ahead, but in some forms of exchange it was the giving and the doing that counted most. Indeed, these transactions called *kelo* were important precisely because they "made one's name go out"; they demonstrated one's abilities as a manager of men and goods. Thus men were sometimes tempted to challenge others to a round of exchanges on a conventional but rather meaningless pretext. For instance, if Tanakesa's father died, one of his more remote, but friendly, kinsmen might challenge Tanakesa to a series of exchanges by offering to provision and direct the funeral feast. At a later feast, the kinsman would be presented with *kesa,* and he might follow with still another feast, returning part of the kesa. The amount returned would depend on whether he wished to continue competition and whether he knew Tanakesa would continue too.

These meaningless exchanges, or exchanges "without bottom" as the Choiseulese called them, were common enough before 1920, but the most significant *kesa* transactions grew out of contractual political alliances between big men. Let us suppose that Tanakesa, whose very name would mean "one who seeks after *kesa*," was a big man. He had to take revenge for any offenses against himself or become known as one who could be offended with impunity. The first thing he had to do was "size up" his opposition. If he felt they were weak in *kesa* or potential allies (remember that much of one's potential might be in the hidden form of debts owed to oneself by others, as well as in immediate possessions), he then sought revenge in one of two ways. He could arrange the assassination of the culprit or one of his kinsmen, or he could organize a raid upon the culprit's village in which many people would be sure to die. Which course he chose depended in large upon his reserves in *kesa* or upon the outstanding obligations of others to help him. Either way he would probably not have undertaken to carry out the revenge himself, but would have contracted another man or group to do it for him. In this way he could hold a feast and gift exchange to pay the agents the *kesa* that had been promised them. But the transaction did not end there. The agents were also obliged to give a feast at which they could return, again, either more or less *kesa*. (Returning more would have been a way of stating a claim for more *kesa* for the services that had been rendered.)

Seldom did exchanges go much further than two or three rounds, even though, ideally competitors should have wanted to exchange *kelo* until they were incapacitated through depletion of resources. Although they usually did not act in this way, they sometimes fostered the impression of having done so in order to postpone their own payment of debts or to implement collection from debtors. Such exchanges were not always so simple, and often there was a great deal of wrangling over debts and their payment. Also, kin groups often recruited more and more allies for the big man in a chainlike fashion and so organized large war parties. There then followed a "chain of *kelo,*" which usually meant a long postponement of final settlement of any dispute. What is more, it often led to quarrels among the big man's supporters.

This process of acquiring debts and credits gradually led the big man into a web of obligations that could act to constrain violent outbreaks as well as to provoke them. Groups and their leaders would often refrain from conflict in favor of a period of co-operation, and there could be periods of peace throughout an area. Thus, some aspects of interpersonal and inter-group hostilities helped to constrain conflict as well as to aggravate it.

Still, this way of life was an unstable one in many ways, and it was easily toppled by external as well as internal influences when European contact became intensive in the area toward the end of the nineteenth century. While the Choiseulese found satisfaction in competition and violence, they also found it in peace, and it was only in times of peace that men could meet the obligations incurred during conflict. Established in the 1890's, the British protectorate, with its firearms and superior forces, soon convinced the islanders that Europeans could play the game better than they could. In addition, the Christian missionaries who arrived early in the 1900s provided a rationale for peace in Christian dogma, and they credit much of their success to the islanders' desire for peace. Still another powerful force for change was the Melanesian attraction to European material goods, and it may well be that peace was accepted out of economic necessity. The islanders could get the goods they coveted only by engaging in the copra trade with Europeans, and settled internal conditions were essential to its development. In any event, the acceptance of peaceful conditions proved the undoing of much of the indigenous culture, and the Choiseulese have for some forty or more years been a peaceful oceanic peasantry completely dependent upon the copra trade for their mode of life. (In fact, intergroup violence is not permitted today by the protectorate courts and councils, nor is there any inclination toward it.)

Kesa, like the rest of the indigenous culture, has little meaning on Choiseul now, although men are more attached to it than, perhaps, to anything else in their past. Some Choiseulese accept responsibility for the demise of their former way of life, saying, "We killed it ourselves." Clearly the choices were not always theirs to make. Much that happened was quite beyond their ken or control, although without outside "assistance" they could not have done much to ease their internal conflicts.

Fredrik Barth

9. Capital, Investment, and the Social Structure of a Pastoral Nomad Group in South Persia*

In this essay, I shall present a summary analysis of some aspects of the pastoral nomad economy of the Basseri tribe of Fars, South Persia. I shall discuss the nature of pastoral capital and its implications for the social structure of the nomads, granted certain cultural premises current among the Basseri. In this discussion I shall draw on material collected in the field during the winter and spring of 1958.

The Basseri are a tribe of 15,000–20,000 pastoral nomads, divided residentially into camps of ten to fifty tents, who migrate between winter pastures in the steppes and deserts of southern Fars and summer pastures in the high mountains 300 miles farther north. A general picture of this tribe has been presented elsewhere (Barth 1961), and certain aspects of the prevailing system of land use and migration have been analyzed (Barth 1960). In general, the following description may be taken as representative of conditions among the pastoral nomads of the whole South Persian area, a population of about half-a-million nomads.

A pastoral nomadic subsistence is based on assets of two main kinds: domesticated animals, and grazing rights. The recognition by the sedentary

* Reprinted with permission of author and publisher from *Capital, Saving and Credit in Peasant Societies*, E.R. Firth and B.S. Yamey, eds., 1964 (pages 69–81), George Allen and Unwin, Ltd. and the Aldine Publishing Co., publishers.

authorities of traditional grazing rights vested in distinct tribes is basic to the pastoral adaptation in Fars. Such tribes mostly have centralized political organizations based on chiefs, as do the Basseri, and are further united into large confederacies, which were formerly integrated into the semi-feudal traditional organization of Persia, and which are still recognized by the authorities. The association of every tribe with a corporate estate in the form of shared grazing rights has important implications for the political forms developed in the area. But in this essay I shall concentrate on the internal organization of the tribe, particularly the structure of local camp units. Within camps, all members share equal access to *pastures*; so for my present purposes I shall concentrate my analysis on the other main form of asset, the *herds,* and try to show the connection between features of this form of capital, and the internal structure of camps and of the tribe.

CAPITAL FORM

Animals are individually owned private property, and a Basseri household makes its livelihood from the production of the animals owned by its members. A certain minimum of additional property is necessary in a nomadic adaptation, mainly a tent, bedding, saddlebags, ropes, and leather sacks for milk and water, all produced by household members, and clothes, shoes, cooking and eating utensils, obtained from the towns. The total value of such equipment is slight compared to that represented by the animals. Of them the most important producers are sheep, subsidiarily goats, while donkeys are necessary for transport. Every household also has a watchdog.

In South Persia in 1958, the market value of a live adult female sheep was around 80 Tomans (£4). Its product per annum was estimated at:

clarified butter	c. 25 T.
wool	20 T.
lamb: skin	15 T.
total	60 T. or £ 3.

In addition, there were the lambs' meat, buttermilk and curds, to which the nomads could not give a money value of any meaning since these products are not regularly marketed. The corresponding values for goats are somewhat lower, and there is no market for their hides. On the other hand, twinning is much more frequent among them. The main reason why some goats are kept in every herd, however, is to provide goathair for the production of tent cloth.

The productive capital on which the pastoral adaptation is based is thus a large herd of sheep and goats. Of these a 10 percent population of rams and he-goats is sufficient to ensure the fertility of the ewes and she-goats.

Certain features of this form of capital appear to have fundamental implications for the economic and social organization of the nomads:

a. Essentially all productive capital is in consumable form. The livestock may at any time be slaughtered and eaten; and thus the main productive asset of a household may be consumed without the necessity of conversion through a market.

b. A significant fraction of the income is in the form of capital gains. Lambs reach maturity in two years, and a female sheep is estimated by the Basseri to have a productive period of about seven years. To maintain the full capital value of the herd, about 15 percent of the lambs must be set aside each year to ensure replacement of stock; the remaining female lambs and a proportionate fraction of male lambs may be regarded as capital gains and give a possible capital increase rate of nearly 40 percent per annum. As in the case of point a., no market mechanism is necessary to effect a conversion form consumable product to productive capital.

c. There is a continual risk of total or partial loss of capital. Since all nomadic property is movable, total loss through robbery or warfare is a continual and real danger in the weakly administered areas frequented by the nomads. Furthermore various other disasters may strike the herd: accidents and predatory animals threaten the sheep, particularly when they stray from the main flock, so constant vigilance is required to keep the animals together and protect them; and at times epidemic disease, drought or famine may strike the herds, reducing the total animal population by as much as 50 percent.

d. The rate of income decreases with increased capital. This is mainly a consequence of the herding and management techniques known to the Basseri. Unassisted by dogs, a shepherd cannot control a flock larger than about 400 head; the man who owns more animals is forced to divide his flock and entrust other persons with shepherding duties. In fact, since shepherding is a strenuous and exacting occupation, owners of herds larger than about 200 animals already tend to hire a shepherd. A recognized consequence of this is somewhat less careful herding and more frequent losses, as well as a continual pilfering of the produce. The larger the total number of animals, the less effective is the owner's supervision of his shepherds, and the greater is the decrease in the rate of income. Standard shepherding contracts, especially the long-term ones in which there is no supervision, reflect these expectations in their stipulations:

(i) *dandune* contract: the shepherd pays 10–15 Tomans per animal per year and takes all produce. At the expiration of the contract period, he returns a flock of the same number and age composition as he originally received;

(ii) *nimei* contract: the shepherd pays 30 Tomans per animal per year for a period of 3–5 years. He takes all produce, and at the expiration of the contract returns half the herd as it stands, and keeps the other half (cf. Lambton 1953: 351 ff and Barth 1961).

In addition to these characteristics of the pastoral form of capital, certain other aspects of the economic situation of the Basseri should be described before discussing social implications, namely consumption patterns, borrowing, and investment.

A striking feature of the consumption patterns is the importance of agricultural produce to a nomad household. Wheat is the main staple; rice, dates, sugar and tea are also consumed in large quantities. Together with the considerable needs for cloth and clothing, various equipment, and luxuries, this implies a strong productive specialization and a dependence on market exchanges. A few family budgets in the nomad camp best known to me suggest an average rate of consumption in agricultural and industrial products to a value of more than 3,000 Tomans, or nearly £200, per annum per household of about six persons.

These products are paid for by the marketing of pastoral products, which only among the very poor is augmented by seasonal labour. Marketing and purchases usually take place through the medium of 'village friends'—small peddlers who live in predominantly agricultural villages where they sell industrial goods to the peasants, while supplying nomads with both agricultural and industrial produce. A nomad householder establishes a relation with such a village friend in every area where he spends a long period; during his time there he is provisioned by the peddler, and before his departure he usually settles the accumulated debt by delivery of butter, wool and hides. Though money is rarely used in these transactions, all values are estimated in terms of fluctuating current market prices.

Where the nomad does not have accumulated stores to cover his purchases, he is usually granted a half-year's or one year's credit. While such debts are usually paid for by villagers at a rate of 5 percent per month, nomads are rarely charged more than 20–30 percent per annum, and this is often waived when payment is made. Some nomads' debts run up to 4,000 to 5,000 Tomans.

Though this would appear to represent borrowing for current consumption, such credit serves in fact to conserve the productive asset represented by the herd: payment could be made by delivery of livestock, but by obtaining credit with security in the flock, this loss of productive animals is prevented. With a rate of income on mature sheep of nearly 100 percent per annum (value: 80 T., product: 60 T. plus various foodstuffs), such borrowing is clearly advantageous for the nomad even when full interest is charged; and nomads often succeed in recouping in the course of a year or two in spite of heavy indebtedness.

There are thus outside sources of credit available to members of a nomadic group; likewise, outside investments are open to them. There is, in Fars, an open market in land, and standard land tenancy contracts secure a considerable income for the absentee landowner (one sixth to two thirds of the crop, according to the quality of the land). However, there are difficulties in converting capital in herds into capital in land which partially prevent such investments. Animals may be freely sold, but the market for livestock is severely restricted. The strains of sheep owned by the nomads, though larger and more productive than those of the villagers, are less robust, and experience shows that only some 30 percent survive if kept in one locality through the whole year. Old sheep are of course sold for slaughter to the villages, but they fetch only a small price; animals for breeding and use can only be sold to other nomads. But since fellow nomads have very few sources of income other than their own herds, those who wish to increase their flocks by purchase have relatively limited means and represent only a very small market. The marketing of livestock is thus inevitably a rather slow process.

On the other hand, income from the sale of wool, butter and hides beyond what is required to pay for the household's consumption may freely be accumulated in the form of money, and can be invested in land. The advantages offered by this investment are security, in that the land cannot be lost through epidemics or the negligence of herdsmen, and the fact that income from land is in the form of the very agricultural products which a nomad household requires.

SOCIAL IMPLICATIONS

The above sketch of some relatively simple features of the economic situation of the Basseri pastoral nomads highlights factors of relevance to the economic choices faced by nomadic householders. I shall now try to show the social implications which they have for *a.* the family development cycle, *b.* processes which maintain social homogeneity within the nomad camp, and *c.* attitudes and practices with respect to saving and investment.

a. *Family development cycle.* A pastoral household requires flocks to subsist as an independent productive unit; among the Basseri at the time of my visit the nomads estimated that a herd of sixty adult sheep/goats was about the minimum required by an elementary family, while the average size of flock was at that time nearly 100 head. But a pastoral adaptation also implies certain labour requirements, and the tasks that are necessary are among the Basseri traditionally divided in such a way as to require the cooperation of at least three persons: a male head of the household, who loads the pack animals and directs the migration, erects the tent, fetches water and wood, and keeps most equipment in repair; a woman who does the cooking and housework, assists in packing and camping, and milks the flock; and a man who herds the animals, driving them to camp to be milked at about 12 a.m. and 5 p.m.

These capital and labour requirements define conditions which a family must satisfy if it is to live as an independent household. It is immediately apparent that an elementary family can only expect to satisfy these conditions with regard to labour force for a limited period of its natural development cycle, i.e., from the time the first son reaches the age of about eight to ten years, till the last son marries; and that it can obtain the necessary capital, if not on credit, then only through inheritance, i.e., normally at the dissolution of the parental household(s). Yet the value placed in Basseri culture on the elementary family as an independent household has called forth certain standardized adjustments, the forms and wider consequences of which may be analysed as social implications of pastoral capital forms and uses, granted the ideal of elementary family households.

The labour requirements of such small households are safeguarded among the Basseri by the formation of cooperative herding units of two to five tents. Since a single shepherd, as noted above, can control a herd of up to 400 head, several households can usually combine their flocks and still remain below this critical number, thus together requiring only one shepherd. Families which are short on personnel establish herding cooperation with families with several adolescent sons, thereby securing the additional labour assistance they need. The increased work involved in shepherding a flock say of 300 instead of 100 is negligible, and so the payments for this service are small: a household which supplies no herdsman for the flock of its cooperative herding unit generally gives the boys from the other tents who perform this duty one or two lambs a year and occasional small presents.

The capital requirements of a newly established family, on the other hand, are obtained by a different pattern, essentially a pattern of anticipatory inheritance. Only sons, subsidiarily collateral agnates or adopted sons, receive a share of their father's flock. This share they are given at the time of their marriage, thereby losing further claims on the estate. Each son receives at the time of his marriage the share which he would have received if his father had died at that moment, with no subsequent adjustments. An example will illustrate this: A man had 200 sheep when the eldest of his three sons married. He first paid the brideprice of 20 sheep, leaving 180; of this estate the groom received his rightful third, or 60 head, leaving 120 for the father and remaining two sons. If the father's flock subsequently increases to 200 again before the next son marries, that son will, assuming the same brideprice, receive 90 sheep at his marriage; and there is no attempt to correct the disparity between the 60 and the 90 sheep received respectively by the first and second son—because, the Basseri argue, his 60 sheep may meanwhile have grown to 600, or have been lost. The marriage of the last son is usually delayed until the parents are old, or one parent dies, so the son can become head of the new household in which the old parent(s) are permitted to live. If the son or only son reaches maturity while the father is still in his prime, the two often divide the flock 'as brothers' and separate.

In a culture where elementary families should live apart in separate tents, the capital forms and management patterns described above thus have clear social implications: certain technical patterns of herding cooperation and inheritance rules are developed, and these again have wider implications. Since the establishment of a household unit depends on the allocation to it of independent productive capital, the separation of men from their fathers and brothers is already completed when they marry— no vested economic or managerial interest ties them to their parental household. They are free to join whichever cooperative herding unit they wish, for personal or economic reasons—the practices prevent the formation of minimal or potential patrilineal nuclei on the basis of shared economic interests.

b.   *Social homogeneity.* The Basseri constitute a population of striking social homogeneity—apart from the unique position occupied by the quite small chiefly dynasty, which is based on a number of unique features such as private title to lands, political functions, and taxation rights. Nearly all Basseri commoners are independent small herd owners, and this homogeneity of the population has extensive implications for the political organization of the tribe. There is no effective hierarchy of authority in camps or sections, and groups of every size experience great difficulties when trying to reach corporate decisions, unless these are dictated by the tribal chief (cf. Barth 1960a). This basic social homogeneity may be analysed as the result of a number of processes, to a large extent implicit in the economic features I have outlined. I shall try to show (i) that these features are such as to inhibit the concentration of wealth, and thus the emergence of status differences based on wealth, and furthermore (ii) that they tend to encourage the elimination from the group of persons who deviate significantly in wealth from the average.

(i) A number of different factors tend to inhibit the accumulation of capital in the form of large herds. The continual risk of capital losses has been noted: epidemics, famines, and losses of young animals in case of late frost may all strike as sudden disasters and reduce the herd in a fashion which is unpredictable, and which thus the herd owner cannot anticipate in his stock management. All herds will thus experience intermittent setbacks, sometimes gross reductions.

While this control on herd growth strikes large and small flocks alike, other controls, implict in Basseri consumption patterns, have increased effects with growing herds. The household with larger herds not only increases its consumption of luxuries and of foodstuffs—that is lambs, as well as tea, sugar, rice, etc. With greater capital in herds, an increasing amount of the wealthy household's labour is also diverted from pastoral production and management to other pursuits: the men require greater leisure, and their efforts are taken up by training and tending horses, hunting, and political activity; the women weave and tie rugs (which are never marketed); and the increased weight of household belongings and larger tents requires more beasts of burden, including camels, which again means a need for a separate camel herder. All these activities and persons depend on the herd without significantly contributing to its care and production; their presence will serve as a brake on the rate of herd increase.

Greater wealth also generally leads to an earlier fragmentation of the household. The pattern of anticipatory inheritance noted above means that the marriage of sons effects a dispersal of the household's capital; furthermore, such a marriage is only possible if the son can be equipped with a share of animals sufficient to support his wife and himself—i.e., about fifty animals or more. The expected marriage age of men is in their twenties; among poor people it may be postponed till the man is as much as thirty-five to permit the necessary accumulation of capital. Wealthy people, on the other hand, have no reason for such delay; and pressure from the boy and the community at large assure a marriage age of eighteen to twenty for the sons of the large herd owners. In other words, within about twenty years of his own marriage, the dispersal of the successful herder's flock commences, giving only a brief period of accumulation for the wealthy, and nearly twice that time for the poorer and less successful. For the wealthy this means also an early loss of the cheap and dependable labour represented by adult, unmarried sons.

Finally, it is common for wealthy herd owners to contract plural marriages; they may after some years take a second, younger wife, and sometimes even a third and fourth. This means a significant increase in the size of household which must be supported by the flock, and the increased consumption will represent a drain on that flock. Furthermore, since plural marriage extends the herd owner's fertile period, it affects the distribution of wealth by inheritance. The elder sons will wish to be married at a time when their father's younger wife is still bearing children—this means that they will receive unduly large shares of their father's estate, since the shares of as–yet unborn half–brothers will not be deducted. In short, the effects of all these different and partly interconnected factors—accidental capital losses, differential consumption rates and the diversion of labour from pastoral production, accelerated division of household and capital, polygyny and increased family size without corresponding reduction of the inheritance shares of elder sons—these all act together to inhibit the concentration of wealth in the form of large herds.

(ii) These factors are not, however, completely effective checks on the accumulation of wealth. Even less are they an effective guarantee against impoverishment, though reduced consumption, postponement of the fragmentation caused by the marriage of sons, etc., will facilitate cases of rehabilitation, just as their obverse hampers accumulation. The homogeneity of the tribe with respect to wealth will not result from these processes alone. But there are other features of the economic situation which also tend to produce homogeneity, though by a different process:

there is a distinct tendency and clearly observable frequency of elimination from the tribe of households with unusually great and unusually small capital. This is possible because the Basseri, like other Persian nomads, are but a segment of a larger population where assimilation by sedentarization into peasant villages and urban centres is possible and frequent, and for different reasons sedentarization is the normal result of great capital accumulation, or capital losses.

Firstly in the case of accumulation: factors which tend to reduce the rate of income with increased size of herd have been noted. This means that while the risk of capital losses remains or increases, the increment to a large herd owner's income which results from the addition of further animals to his flocks decreases significantly. Consider, then, the possibilities of alternative investment. In nomadic activities they are nil; but the possibility of investment in agricultural land is always persent. I should emphasize that sedentarization is never regarded as an ideal among the nomads; they value their way of life more highly than life in a village. But the economic advantages of land purchase are palpable: the risk of capital loss is eliminated, the profits to an absentee landowner are large, and they are in the form of products useful in a nomadic household. There is thus no feeling that land purchase implies sedentarization—a small plot of land can be let out on tenancy contracts and is merely a source of economic security and useful products. The difficulty in such investment is to convert the capital in animals to money capital by which land may be purchased. As noted, this is a relatively slow process, unless the owner is willing to take a considerable loss; none the less, with some patience it may be done, and banking facilities are available in the towns for accumulating savings, though no credit is available to nomads for investment in land.

Once a piece of land has been bought, the wealthy herd owner's money income increases rapidly, since production in marketable goods such as wool, butter and hides continues while expenses for the purchase of agricultural produce are reduced or eliminated. If a herd owner continues to be successful, he will thus accumulate wealth more rapidly, with little promise of profit through further investment in herds, but increasingly in a form which may be directly invested in land. Furthermore, title to land is held in a sedentary legal system where sons upon their marriage have no rights to anticipatory inheritance—which makes it an attractive form of capital from the owner's point of view and prevents a premature dispersal of the wealth.

This gradual process of land accumulation was observed in the field in its various stages. Only towards the very end do informants see sedentarization as its natural end result: they have a house built on their property and become increasingly concerned with the need for management of house and land, they develop a taste for many comforts that can only be satisfied by sedentary residence, etc. Sudden stock losses at this stage seem to be a common precipitating factor which drives them into the village; and even when they are well established as petty landowners they generally erect their old tent in their compound, and reside in it in the summer months.

Cases of sedentarization through capital accumulation and land purchase are by the nature of things relatively rare, and my material for the above description consists mainly of a handful of life histories. Sedentarization through impoverishment, on the other hand, is a constant threat for many and has a high empirical frequency, of the order of one person in every three in the groups of my censuses. Here the process is very simple: accident, sickness or poor management of a small herd leads to losses, and thus to an annual production below what is required for the purchase of food and clothing. But the herd itself is a large food store, and hunger easily drives the nomad to invade this his only productive capital, reducing the pastoral output further, in a vicious circle. The only alternative is to seek additional sources of income. Since shepherding contracts are relatively few (because they are, as we have seen, unprofitable for the herd owner), such sources are mainly found in sedentary society: as seasonal labourer, shepherd for the village flocks, doing local transport with donkeys, etc. To be successful, these activities must give the nomad income both to support his household *and* to increase his flock (thereby constituting a market for rich herd owners who wish to buy land). But frequently such work for a village community disturbs the nomad's migratory cycle, and thus leads only to reduced pastoral production and further animal losses, which makes him all the more dependent on sedentary sources of income. The Basseri feel that once a household's flock falls significantly below the minimal level of sixty adult head, this downward spiral is pretty inevitable and quite rapid; and there is a steady flow of impoverished settlers from every South Persian tribe to the villages and towns of their area.

These features of capital form and management thus tend, in the wider economic situation of the Basseri, to maintain a general economic homogeneity among the nomads, both by inhibiting the concentration of pastoral wealth, and by a constant elimination through sedentarization of the top and the bottom of the economic spectrum. As a consequence, social differentiation based on, or accompanied by, economic differences becomes impossible; and the nomad population becomes characterized by a striking social homogeneity, consisting of independent, economically self-sufficient small herd owners.

c.   *Saving and investment.* A final implication of these features may be seen in attitudes and practices relating to saving, thrift, and capital accumulation. I have noted the fact that pastoral capital is in a directly consumable form and consists of animals with a short life span. This creates a situation where a certain minimum of thrift is necessary in capital management—the capital can only be maintained through a systematic policy of reserving lambs for the replacement of stock. Whereas in agriculture the distinction between produce and land is clearly apparent, among pastoralists nearly every instance of consumption threatens the productive capital itself, and must be considered and evaluated by the nomad. What is more, many of the factors involved are unknown. Disease may strike so that even a conservative policy of slaughter of lambs and yearlings still result in a reduction of stock. Milking practice is also a field of continual economic choice: not only the question of how many sheep should be left with lambs, but also how much sheep with lambs should be milked, and how much should be left to those lambs. In a good year, near-starvation of lambs gives a greater yield in butter to the nomad and does not appear to have great ill effects; on the other hand, if such lambs are subject to special strain or mild disease, they are lost in much higher frequency than are well-fed, robust lambs. In short, the management of pastoral capital requires a constant awareness of savings and investment policy; it breeds an attitude of continual and thrifty concern for the herd in its practitioners.

The Basseri are very aware of the economics involved in these choices, and discuss such policy at length within the household, though rarely in public, except in the form of gossip about third persons. The basic guiding principle which they adopt comes out in an almost obsessive desire to postpone every incident of consumption—to let each lamb gain weight one more day, or week, or season, to have one more lamb from an old sheep, to make a worn-out pair of shoes last till the next market town, or till arrival in the summer area, or till next spring equinox (the Persian New Year, when it is customary to put on new clothes).

Yet—or perhaps precisely as a correlate of these interests—hospitality is a highly valued virtue. The hospitable man is admired and people speak highly of him whether he is present or absent. Men seek his company and flock to his tent, though without importunity. By their own standards, then, most Basseri are miserly; and a few glaring examples are held up for public ridicule. Thus one of the largest herd owners in the group is popularly known as D.D.T. Khan because, they say, he is such a miser he eats his own lice.

But this failure in good manners (by Basseri canons) caricatured by some and prevalent in most need not be explained only in terms of the special habits of thrift developed as a result of pastoral life. There are also clear social reasons why a pattern of conspicuous consumption and hospitality is not only economically unwise, but also socially and politically unprofitable—in contrast to most of the local societies in the Middle East. These are found in the very features of social structure described in the previous section: the great economic and social homogeneity within Basseri camps. Where wealth differences are small, a policy of social aggrandizement through public consumption of wealth is bound to bring very limited returns. Nearly all the tents of a camp remain independent and self-supporting units; a hospitable man may gain influence in his camp through hospitality, but never to the extent of being able to dominate his camp fellows, or to expect economic support or advantage from them at a later date. On the contrary, the homogeneity itself is valued, and lampoons are sung about anyone who puts on airs and assumes an authoritative manner. For the Basseri commoner, there is little to gain by spendthriftness, and thus few inducements, but many controls, on the practice of hospitality.

CONCLUSION

The material presented in this brief paper can hardly be drawn together further, since the paper itself is already a summary of select features of the economic and social organization of a pastoral tribe which show a clear relation to certain features of sheep and goat herds as a form of capital. As noted in the introduction, other economic features (e.g., relating to pasture rights and the organization of migrations) have not been discussed, though they appear to have methodologically analogous implications for centralized authority and other features of the political organization of the tribe. In the present essay I have merely attempted to show how certain elementary characteristics of capital in the form of herds are related to a limited range of features of family organization, social homogeneity within camps, and common saving and consumption patterns— granted certain cultural values and conceptions held by the Basseri people. The characteristics of pastoral capital which I have discussed are, I believe, of a type familiar in conventional economic analysis, though here admittedly in a very elementary and rough form. What is interesting, and perhaps surprising, to a social anthropologist is the fact that it should be possible at all to show their social implications by a discussion involving relatively few 'cultural' facts—that the processes by which they are made relevant to social action and features of a local social system seem to implicate few of the other basic premises of Basseri culture. Admittedly, some of these premises are contained in the specific economic definitions and characterizations used; and it would seem a hopeless, and perhaps fundamentally impossible, task to state them all in a manner so that their implications would have the form of a deductive system. But it does seem possible to show how specific social forms are related as a product to simple constellations of determining factors, and thus how partial features of Basseri social structure are directly related to specific characteristics of pastoral capital and other economic facts.

T. G. McGee

10. Peasants in the Cities: A Paradox, a Paradox, a Most Ingenious Paradox*

The pedlars, whether carrying their wares around on a pole or setting up stalls along the street, have but small capital, make but a meagre profit, and do not earn enough to feed and clothe themselves. They are not much different in status from the poor peasants and likewise need a revolution that will change the existing state of affairs (Mao Tse-Tung 1926).

Any review of the voluminous body of literature on the concept of the peasantry leaves the reader with one central conviction[1]—there is much disagreement about who peasants are, but little disagreement that they are rural people. Perhaps this is best summed up by Redfield's description: "The peasant is a rural native whose long established order of life takes important account of the city" (Redfield 1953:31). Eric Wolf echoes such a formulation when he says, "We have spoken of peasants as rural cultivators; that is they raise crops and livestock in the countryside, not in greenhouses in the midst of cities, or in aspidistra boxes on the windowsill" (Wolf 1966:2). It is not difficult to cull similar statements from other writers on the subject of the peasantry.

* Reproduced by permission of the Society for Applied Anthropology from Human Organization, vol. 32 no. 2, 1973:135–42. Permission of the author is also gratefully acknowledged.

[1] It is beyond the scope of this paper to indicate any but the major contributions to this literature. See Redfield (1956), Nash (1966), Wolf (1966), Potter, Dias, and Foster (1967), and Franklin (1969).

The recent publication of a book with the title, *Peasants in the Cities. Readings in the Anthropology of Urbanization,* edited by William Mangin, appears to challenge this conventional interpretation of the peasants as rural people.[2] Hence the paradox—for if in truth peasants are rural people, how can they be urban? It emerges from Mangin's introduction that "peasants in the cities" are rural people who move to cities and bring with them peasant "ways of life" which persist in the city. Two quotations will illustrate the thrust of his arguments.

> Since all definitions of peasants involve contact with cities, we can say that peasants have been coming to cities since there have been peasants and cities. Rural people have been visiting and settling in cities for centuries retaining many patterns of behaviour, changing others (Mangin 1970:xiv).

> Without adopting a Redfield-Tonnies approach to societies as polar types with rural-sacred at one end and urban-secular at the other and without pushing the importance of peasants' characteristics in slums and ghettos, I think that many peasants in cities carry with them much of their rural culture and pass some of it on to their children. In the United States many of us are second and third generation peasants (Mangin 1970:xix-xx).

In these terms, Mangin's formulation of peasants in the cities is neither original nor remarkable. Surely it is not surprising that people moving from rural to urban areas take with them habits and behavior patterns learned in their previous place of residence. As Mangin admits, they are not likely to discard these attributes after a day's travel but rather to change and adapt them after residence in the city.

But this is not the basis for my disagreement with Mangin. Rather I believe that he has side-stepped the explanation of the existence of "urban peasants" by utilizing the concept of a persisting "rural culture" as his explanatory framework. In so doing, I would argue that Mangin's arguments are simply a masquerade of the increasingly criticized Redfield-Tonnies approach.[3] In fact, a major part of his introductory essay is concerned with an attack on the "limited-good" and "culture of poverty" concepts of the poor and peasants which stress their lack of mobility and resistance to change. Mangin points out quite correctly that there is increasing evidence to suggest that this situation does not pertain either in the city or the countryside, at least in Latin America. For instance, he says, "When rural people migrate to cities, however, the type of limited aspiration encountered in the closed community can be rarely continued for more than a generation" (Mangin 1970:xxviii). This statement certainly appears to at least partially contradict his earlier statements which

---

[2] Not all the papers in this volume follow the viewpoint of the editor. See Gould (1970:137–49).

[3] See Benet (1963), McGee (1964), Pahl (1966, 1967), and Lupri (1967).

have been cited. Basically it can be argued that this discussion of the "behavior" of peasants, while interesting, does little to aid the definitions of "urban peasants" for it stresses that the "behavior" of peasants, at least in Mangin's view, varies little between city and countryside. It is therefore difficult to see why Mangin utilizes the concept of "rural culture." Perhaps he could not escape from the definitions of the "rural character" of peasants, for if a peasant is defined on the basis of place of residence and the cluster of peasant characteristics which are assumed to be part of a rural place of residence, agricultural occupations, etc., how can peasants persist in the city? Well, they can still be peasants if they keep their "rural culture"!

The most powerful case that might be presented for retaining a term such as "urban peasants" is the widespread existence of "circulatory migration" in parts of Africa and the Pacific in which "wage earning," as Mayer comments, ". . . is a normal part of . . . peasant life . . ." (Mayer 1962:91). While I would not want to quarrel with Mayer's assertion that circulatory migrants may regard the process of acquiring wages in urban centers as a part of their peasant life, surely the point is, what they are while in residence in the city. If they are wage earners in factories, it is clear they constitute a part of the urban proletariat rather than the peasantry. If they work for wages on plantations, they are rural proletariat. While the continuance of circulatory migration over a long period of time raises some very important questions about the types of class structure which might emerge in these societies, this is an area of future research which Mangin's formulations only distort.[4]

In view of the growing body of anthropological research on cities, especially those of the Third World, I think it necessary to challenge Mangin's concept of "urban peasants" lest it resume its former influential and entrenched position in the literature of the social sciences. Thus, in the remainder of this paper, I wish to offer an analytical framework which offers an alternative conceptual framework for the understanding of "urban peasants." I seek therefore to polarize positions, initiate debate, and produce a more viable conceptual framework for the analysis of the Third World city.[5]

PEASANTS: AN INSTITUTIONAL DEFINITION

Analysis of research into the peasantry leaves one reasonably certain that there is least agreement about the universality of a definition for

---

[4] These arguments are further clouded by debate over the difference between tribal and peasant systems summarized by Dalton (1972), for "circulatory migration" appears to be far more common in countries with tribal societies. Thus, if one were to accept Mangin's formulation on this point, we would have urban tribesmen as well as urban peasants.

[5] Some of the points introduced in this discussion have been made before. For earlier statements, see Armstrong and McGee (1968) and McGee (1971a, 1971b).

"peasant culture," but considerable agreement exists about the economic features of peasant life, allowing for variations stemming from what Wolf has described as different "ecotypes." Thus, one finds in the work of Wolf (1966), Nash (1966), and Firth (1946) considerable agreement over economic features of the peasantry, but their concern is with peasants who live in the countryside not in the cities. To develop an economic definition of peasantry in the cities, one must see them as involved in a system of production distinct from either socialism or capitalism. Chayanov[6] was one of the earliest researchers to recognize this theory in the 1920s, and Franklin reached a similar conclusion in the 1960s quite independently. In Franklin's view (1962, 1965, 1969) one may delineate in theoretical terms three main systems of production—peasant, capitalist, and socialist—in which:

> ...the fundamental differentiator is the labour commitment of the enterprise. In the peasant economy the individual entrepreneur is committed to the utilisation of his total labour supply—that of his family, who may and do often find alternative or additional sources of employment. This accounts for the diversities of historical peasant societies, but if these sources are not available the chef d'entreprise must employ his kin...

> In the capitalist and socialist systems of production labour becomes a commodity to be hired and dismissed by the enterprise according to changes in the scale of organisation, degree of mechanisation, the level of market demand for products. It is for this reason especially, not so much because of the introduction of mechanisation and the factory system, that the capitalist system of production has been disruptive of traditional societies. It introduces to society a hitherto unheard of scale for the evaluation of the human individual (Franklin 1965:148–49).

The advantage of such a distinction between systems of production is that while it recognizes the fact that the majority of peasant enterprises may be family farms, it does not exclude the fact that peasant enterprises, such as family-organized industry or retailing, may exist in cities. This is what Franklin means when he says:

> The scheme ignores the agricultural-industrial division. At this level of generalisation the division has little importance. Agriculture is carried out under all three systems of production and so is manufacturing. Admittedly, in peasant-folk-traditional societies, agricultural activities predominate without excluding the appearance of a capitalistic system of production—but it is the systems, not the societies, which are our concern (Franklin 1965:148).

Franklin elaborates the features of the peasant system of production in much greater detail, and his evidence is convincing. In limiting his concep-

---

[6] See Chayanov (1966). This is the first English version of his work which was first published in Russian in 1925.

tion of the peasant enterprise to the family unit, he may not have gone far enough. I think it is possible to find other social institutions (age groups, village and tribal groups) who operate as units of production and are committed to the total use of labor (Bohannan 1955). There are some enterprises recorded in the studies of small Japanese factories where labor is hired according to the capitalist system of production although employees are not dismissed at times when rationally they should be (Abegglen 1958).

It must be stressed that this institutional definition of the peasant system does not exclude "culture" as a concept. Indeed, the argument that the "chef d'entreprise" is committed to the utilization of the total labor supply available in his family assumes "cultural attitudes." Nor does this definition of the "peasantry" imply that peasants will adopt or resist change because they are peasants. Indeed, it is perfectly possible for peasants to behave like capitalists, but much more difficult for capitalists to behave like peasants. However, the major advantage of such a schema is that it allows some definition and measurement of peasant activities in the city. This, it must be argued, is a basic prerequisite for the investigation of the "behavioral" aspects of the peasantry.

DELINEATING THE PEASANT SYSTEM
OF PRODUCTION IN THE CITY

The application of Franklin's conceptual scheme to the Third World cities requires an understanding of the economic structure of these cities. In this respect the most useful model is that which sees most cities of the Third World as consisting of two juxtaposed systems of production—one derived from capitalist forms of production, the other from the peasant system of production.[7] In essence, this was what Geertz (1963) delineated in his division between the "firm-centered economy" and the "bazaar economy" of Modjokuto, the Indonesian town that he studied in the 1950s. It also resembles the model of technological dualism proposed by Higgins (1956) and social dualism postulated by Boeke (1953). Where this model differs is in its emphasis upon the two systems of production as being subsystems which operate in an interlocking fashion within the city. As Santos has recently pointed out, these two subsystems are better described as "circuits," a word which better denotes the internal flows existing within the subsystems. This model accepts the subsystems as part of an interlocking, overall city economic structure. In fact, Santos divides the two circuits into what he terms "upper system" and "lower system." The economic activities of the "upper circuit" are banking, export trade, modern industry, modern services, wholesaling, and some forms of transport (shipping,

---

[7] It must be obvious that China, North Vietnam, and other socialist societies are excluded from this discussion; but they too have had their problems with the juxtaposition of socialism and peasant systems of production.

airlines). The lower system consists of noncapital intensive industry, services, and trading. There are, of course, intermediate types of activities, but these mixed forms do not invalidate the model of the two systems.

In addition to distinguishing between the economic activities of the two systems, it is also possible to distinguish between the populations linked to each circuit, although some of the population of one circuit may temporarily sell its labor power to the other sector. For instance, in Hong Kong it is not uncommon for hawkers to work periodically in factories to supplement their income. [There is, of course, considerable doubt as to where

TABLE 1

The Two-Circuit Urban Economy Characteristics

Characteristics	Upper Circuit	Lower Circuit
Technology	Capital-intensive	Labor-intensive
Organization	Bureaucratic	Generally family-organized
Capital	Abundant	Scarce
Hours of work	Regular	Irregular
Regular wages	Normal	Not required
Inventories	Large quantities and/or high quality	Small quantities; poor quality
Prices	Generally fixed	Generally negotiable between buyer seller
Credit	Banks and other institutions	Personal noninstitutional
Benefits	Reduced to unity, but important due to the volume of business (except luxury items)	Raised to unity, but small in relation to the volume of business
Relations with clientele	Impersonal and/or through documents	Direct; personal
Fixed costs	Important	Negligible
Publicity	Necessary	None
Reuse of goods	None; wasted	Frequent
Overhead capital	Indispensable	Not indispensable
Government aid	Important	None or almost none
Direct dependence on foreign countries	Great; outward-oriented activity	Small or none

Source: Adapted from Santos (1972).

those employed by governments of the Third World countries fit into such a model, particularly in countries such as Indonesia (Santos 1971).]

The main features of these two circuits are listed in Table 1 (slightly modified from Santos). These characteristics are obviously oversimplified, but they do form internally coherent constellations of economic activity which are measurable and distinct. From the point of view of this paper, it is clear that "urban peasants" are most clearly involved in the economic activities of the lower circuit and can be defined on the basis of their participation in this sector. This fact, of course, has been recognized by anthropologists, particularly those carrying out research on the distributive systems of the economies of developing countries. There is, however, considerable debate over the organization of the economic units which make up the distributive system. In societies where women play a major role in trading activity—including West Africa, the non-Hispanic Caribbean, and parts of mainland Latin America—Mintz has assembled a large body of evidence (Mintz 1971:247–69) to suggest that economic decisions by female traders are made independently of the male household head. For instance, he reports on a tendency for women traders in West Africa to invest their earnings in education to increase opportunities for their children. Of course, this does not mean that the female traders are uncommitted to the principle of total labor commitment, nor that they are not contributing to the household budget. Rather they are attempting to find opportunities for the commitment of their children to the "wage sector" or upper circuit of the city's economy.

There is also some confusion when several members of the same household operate within the same market. Thus, Geertz reports in his study of the *pasar* system in Modjokuto that

> A man and his brother, a son and his father, even a wife and her husband will commonly operate on their own at the bazaar and regard one another within that context with nearly as cold an eye as they would any other trader (Geertz 1963:31).

This would seem to suggest independent economic activity by the various members of the family, but it does not exclude per se the possibility of the appropriation of the individual earnings by the head of the household. Thus, as Geertz points out, a man who wishes to introduce his son to the *pasar* trading system will not always apprentice him but will simply give him goods to peddle. In addition, Dewey's study of *Peasant Marketing in Java* stresses the family basis of the trading units in discussing the difficulties of becoming a trader.

> For this reason, traders often come from families with marketing experience and have been trained by their elders. The average person aware of the risks and of his own inexperience is afraid to compete and hesitates to enter trade (Dewey 1962:39).

Other studies emphasize the social basis of the trading unit. Thus, Kaplan states categorically in his study of the Mexican market place:

> It is important to underscore the fact that all sellers in the market place represent households rather than firms and they behave as such (Kaplan 1965:87).

In many cities of Southeast Asia where much of the city's distributive sector is effectively in the hands of the overseas Chinese, there is ample evidence of the social basis of economic organization.[8] For instance, T'ien (1953) has described the social basis of retailing ownership and employment in Kuching and shows how the links of kinship and dialect are dominant factors in explaining concentration in the sale of particular goods, in the offering of services, and in various industries. Skinner (1957) has reported similar patterns among the Chinese of Bangkok, and this phenomenon is common throughout the economic organization of Chinese in Southeast Asia.

Research by the author among hawkers in Hong Kong[9] provides further evidence to distinguish "urban peasants." In this dynamic metropolis of Victoria-Kowloon, which had grown to almost 3.5 million persons by 1971, there has been a radical change in the economy from a rather sleepy entrepôt colonial port involved in the South China trade to a dynamic industrial society ranking among the world's major industrial producers (Hopkins 1971).

Despite these considerable economic changes in the last 20 years, the two systems of production described earlier continue to exist in the urban areas of Hong Kong, although the capitalist systems of production have steadily taken over more and more of the economic activity of the peasants' system of production. Thus large-scale factory production accounts for the major portion of industrial production within the colony, but this penetration by the capitalist system of production has been much less discernible in the distributive sectors of the cities' economy, particularly in retailing. Within this sector, the activities of street vendors selling foodstuffs, textiles, and clothing and offering various services are of major importance.

These hawkers have always been part of urban Hong Kong, but their numbers increased dramatically in the 1950s as a result of the influx of refugees from mainland China. Despite the rapid increase of employment opportunities in the capitalist sector (particularly industrial factories), their numbers seem also to have increased during the 1960s. It is exceptionally difficult to arrive at an accurate estimate of their numbers, but the most authoritative figure suggests an estimate somewhere between 50,000 and 60,000.[10] Approximately one third are located in the Hong Kong urban area, the remainder in Kowloon.

Hawkers are an essential part of the retailing structure of the Hong Kong urban area and, like their counterparts described by Geertz, they are clearly part of the peasant system of production. Data collected in a 1969 survey of 642 hawkers located in the urban areas of Hong Kong

---

[8] The literature on overseas Chinese is considerable; for a broad overview of their economic features, see Jeromin (1966) and Purcell (1965).

[9] This research has been funded by a grant from the Center of Asian Studies, University of Hong Kong.

[10] This estimate is based on unpublished data obtained by the Chinese University of Hong Kong in a survey of hawkers conducted in 1971.

Island (McGee 1970) provided information to support this assertion.[11] First, 88% of the hawker units were owned by some form of family ownership, mostly joint ownership between husband and wife. Secondly, the majority had a very small capital investment in stock—the majority falling below $2,100 (HK). Investment in equipment and business structures was minimal—baskets for carrying goods, Chinese scales, a cheap wooden stall. The majority of hawkers earned a monthly income below $600 (HK). Most of the selling was done by family members who often worked long and irregular hours. Regular wages were not, as a rule, paid. Goods were obtained from many sources, but once in the hawker's hands, prices were negotiable with customers who often tended to patronize the same hawker (particularly for raw foodstuffs and cooked food).

The personal characteristics of the hawkers showed a certain clustering of features. Almost 40% were over 40 years old. Some 61% had been hawking for more than ten years, and a small proportion had begun hawking in the last five years. Almost three-quarters of the hawkers had no education or had stopped at the primary level. Most hawkers lived close to their place of business, often within walking distance. Approximately one third had other jobs before becoming hawkers, many of them in the "upper circuit," particularly in factories. But for the majority, hawking had been a lifetime occupation. Some had inherited the hawker operation; others had become hawkers because friends or relatives were in the same occupation.

This highly generalized picture of the hawkers in Hong Kong suggests that they are involved in what Santos would label the "lower circuit" of the city's economy or, as I would call it, the "peasant system" of production. While there may be certain exceptions, the hawkers of Hong Kong appear to be most easily understood as individuals participating in a peasant system of production which persists in the city. This does not mean that they will always be "urban peasants," for as the capitalist system of production expands (supermarkets are moving into housing estates), the hawkers will gradually disappear. Already declining densities in some inner city areas are causing hawkers to choose alternative locations. In addition, there is growing pressure from the government to limit their activities.

Fortunately, defining the peasant systems of production in the manufacturing sector is not so complicated as in the distributive factor. This can be illustrated with respect to the industrial structure of Ibadan, Nigeria. Akinola suggests that one may divide the manufacturing industries of Ibadan into three groups—the traditional craft industries, the modern small-scale industries, and the modern large-scale industry. Traditional craft industries, such as spinning, weaving, and pottery, are characterized by small-scale, one-man or one-family operations requiring neither expen-

---

[11] The following statements concerning the Hong Kong hawkers are very brief. More information can be obtained from McGee (1970a and 1973, in preparation).

sive capital equipment nor power-driven machinery, are generally located in the worker's dwellings, and utilize craft skills passed from parents to children or within certain lineages "such that there are many compounds in Ibadan where nearly all members follow the same crafts" (Akinola 1964:117). Thus these craft industries would clearly fit into Franklin's definition. The second category, modern small-scale industry, is more difficult since Akinola remarks that:

> One striking difference between the traditional crafts and the modern small-scale industries is that, in the former case, the children of the craft family or compound are trained from their youth to take up the trade of their parents whereas in the latter, the apprentices and journeymen are not necessarily related by blood ties (Akinola 1964:117).

While such modern small-scale industries employ less than ten workers and have a low capital investment of below 50 pounds, they would appear to fit clearly into the capitalist system of production. The third category, modern large-scale industry, employs more than ten workers on a wage basis and fits into the latter category. Service industries, such as the repair of automobiles, appear to be characterized by forms of employment which range from peasant to capitalist. Such patterns of industrial activity would appear to be duplicated in the cities of most Third World countries.

CONCLUSION

In this brief review, I have attempted to suggest that there are other ways to delineate peasants of Third World cities than by utilizing the concept of the "rural culture" in the melting pot of the city. While there are problems associated with the definition of a "peasant system" of production, its advantages are that it is measurable cross-culturally; it is not confused by the definition of any rural-urban dichotomy; it does not assume preconceived "peasant behavior" patterns in reaction to change; and it does provide a useful framework for analyzing change in the cities. Mintz's (1971) perceptive observation that the intergenerational shift of female traders from independent employment to wage employment has produced significant differences in sex-role differentiation within families by actually limiting the freedom of the female recognizes the importance of the effect of the two different systems of production. Just as important is the role that the peasant system of production plays in labor absorption in the rapidly growing cities of the Third World.

It may be that all this argument boils down to is simply semantic confusion. A possible solution would be to cease using the term "peasants" in the city. What we have are populations living in many Third World cities who do not fit into either the traditional definition of "peasants," "proletariat," or "urban bourgeoisie," and who are characterized by their participation in the peasant system of production. A compromise answer, which seems satisfactory because it signifies a group clinging to a semantic grey zone, is to label this group a "proto-proletariat." This has the advantage of leaving the conventional definition of the "lumpen proletariat" to include the unemployed from the wage-earning sector, the seasonally unemployed from the "proletariat," and the unemployable.

In many Third World cities, the protoproletariat form a very large percentage of the cities' populations. Their numbers are constantly swollen by the influx of migrants and by natural increase. They are constantly depleted by the departure of members to the proletariat or their return to the peasantry. Viewed in such a way, the concept of the protoproletariat raises a whole range of research questions for the anthropologist. Does membership in the protoproletariat ease the process of assimilation for rural migrants? Do more migrants move into this sector than into proletariat employment? Does the protoproletariat sector offer a training ground for urban skills? What are the relationships between the protoproletariat and peasantry? Are the protoproletariat "conventional nontractable members of society," as Mangin would have us believe? There are, of course, many other possibilities, but I believe that the thrust of urban anthropology in the Third World should be directed at exploring such questions, rather than utilizing the rather limited concept of "rural culture." It would seem that peasants in cities are a paradox, but a paradox which can be resolved.

Part IV

SOCIALIZATION AND PERSONALITY

We have emphasized, with Geertz, that to be human means to acquire a particular "culture." In this sense, culture is something we learn, and much of this learning occurs in childhood. This process of acquiring a culture is sometimes referred to as "enculturation" or, more commonly, "socialization." This complex process is one of the key sources of behavioral variation within a society, in part because the biogenetic make-up of individuals is so varied and in part because parents and others who rear children do so in many different ways.

Nevertheless, there are patterns in the socialization process that bear emphasis. In particular, there is a relationship between socialization practices and the techno-economic dimensions of a given society. Some facets of this relationship are noted in the analysis of socialization by Herbert Barry, Margaret Bacon and Irvin Child in Chapter 11. In their article, which is based on what is known as the "hologeistic method" or the method of making comparisons within a large sample of societies from the whole world, they set out to delineate the nature and extent of sex differences in socialization. Of particular interest is whether or not differential rearing of the sexes is an arbitrary imposition and if it is not, then to discover the ways it is patterned. Their research leads them to suggest that such differences are not arbitrary but, rather, reflect adjustments to the reality of sex differences and to environmental pressures. At the same time, however, they argue that such patterns as emphasizing achievement training for boys and nurturant training for girls, while relevant to some contexts are not mandatory for all conceivable contexts.

The next selection in Part IV, Chapter 12, is in many ways a continuation on a much broader front of the issues raised by Barry, Bacon, and Child. It contains the concluding observations from a study by Robert Edgerton of the relationship between personality, on the one hand, and ecology and economic mode of life on the other. As such, it illustrates an important recent trend in the field of culture-and-personality or psychological anthropology—namely, an increasing interest in exploring the link between personality and the fundamental material conditions faced by a group of people. Sometimes these inquires have had strong neo-Freudian overtones, but generally the concern has been to consider whether ecological factors produce differences in individual values, attitudes and personalities (measured, for the most part, in non-Freudian terms). The basic form of this research has been to compare the values and personalities of people whose cultures are similar in most respects but who differ in ecology and economic mode. Of the many comparisons of this type that can be made, one of the most interesting is the comparison of farmers and pastoralists.

Anyone who has seen a few B-grade Hollywood "westerns" knows that pastoralists and farmers ("cattle ranchers" and "sod busters" in movie parlance) are very different people. Indeed, extensive experience from around the world supports the idea that pastoralists and farmers differ significantly in values, attitudes and personality. But still, the comparisons have often been vague and impressionistic, and even where this has not been a problem, the findings have been clouded by the uncontrolled presence of factors other than the variables of interest (ecology and economic mode). The study excerpted here, however, largely escapes these problems and is in fact notable for its general sophistication, both in analytical techniques and overall design.

In this study, Edgerton compares the attitudes, values, and personalities of people in four East African societies: the Pokot, Hehe, Kamba, and Sebei. These were selected for study for many reasons, one of the most salient being that in each there were (and still are) large numbers of both farmers and pastoralists. In a sense, then, there were eight groups being studied (Pokot farmers, Pokot pastoralists, Hehe farmers, Hehe pastoralists, and so on). This made it possible, among other things, to compare farmers and pastoralists while controlling (keeping constant) many of the other factors which might be seen as causing differences in values and personality. In addition, however, other useful comparisons could be made—e.g., Edgerton could compare Hehe farmers with Pokot farmers or Kamba farmers with Sebei pastoralists, or he could compare all pastoralists with all farmers, regardless of "tribe."

When making these comparisons, using personality and attitude data collected in interviews, a number of important patterns were discovered in the data. For example, if Edgerton wanted to predict how someone would respond to the interview, he could do this best by knowing the tribe to which the respondent belonged. Neither age, sex, extent of acculturation (exposure to non-local and especially to western cultures), *nor economic mode of life* were as useful in predicting a person's responses as was tribal affiliation. In other words, Edgerton found that a person's tribe or culture was "dominant over his economic mode of life" in determining his values, attitudes and personality (1971:272). Nevertheless, for Edgerton the central concern was to determine whether or not there were "consistent differences between pastoralists and farmers that could be attributed to ecological variation" (1971:272). The bulk of the book containing his findings in this regard demonstrates convincingly that there was such differences between farmers and pastoralists in all four societies. Thus, although the differences in most of the variables could be accounted for by variation in tribe, they could also safely be seen as evidence that there were fundamental differences in the values and personalities of farmers and pastoralists. These differences are reviewed in the excerpt from Edgerton's concluding chapter included here (Chapter 12).

Although environment, economic mode, sex and other factors have a great deal to do with the formation of personality, it is nevertheless true that there is great variation in the end product of the socialization process. One of the broader contrasts drawn from this variety is the distinction between "normal" and "abnormal" personalities. The title of the paper excerpted for Chapter 13 suggests that it is about religion, and it is; but more than this, it is about the problem of studying personality cross-culturally, and especially with the valid identification of "abnormal behavior requiring psychiatric rather than sociocultural analysis." Noting the classic relativistic stance about abnormality articulated long ago by Ruth Benedict, the author of this chapter, Melford Spiro, considers the behavior of Burmese monks.

He shows that by outward appearance, and judged by absolute standards, monks exhibit behavior which is symptomatic of "severe pathology." Moreover, when the responses made by monks to Rorschach ink blots are analyzed without considering the context, the symptoms of pathology are very strong. And, notes Spiro, these are trends which are only different in degree from the Burmese in general. Are we to conclude, therefore, that these monks have pathological personalities? The answer Spiro provides is, I think, very significant and deserves emphasis. Only if we assume that personality can be examined in isolation (*in vacuo*) can we conclude that Burmese monks have abnormal personalities. But as Spiro insists, personality does not exist in isolation and should not be examined as if it does; rather, it exists in a particular cultural context. In Burma, if not elsewhere, monasteries provide monks with culturally constituted defense mechanisms. Consequently, they are not left to create their own potentially pathological, individualized defense mechanisms. If a Burmese exhibited personality characteristics similar to those exhibited by monks but was not a monk (and did not have some other culturally appropriate role), then it is possible the individual would be "abnormal" in a pathological sense, but even then it would have to be determined whether such a personality resulted in psychological distortion and/or sociocultural impairment.

Herbert Barry III,
Margaret K. Bacon, and Irvin L. Child

11. A Cross-Cultural Survey of Some Sex Differences in Socialization*

In our society, certain differences may be observed between the typical personality characteristics of the two sexes. These sex differences in personality are generally believed to result in part from differences in the way boys and girls are reared. To the extent that personality differences between the sexes are thus of cultural rather than biological origin, they seem potentially susceptible to change. But how readily susceptible to change? In the differential rearing of the sexes does our society make an arbitrary imposition on an infinitely plastic biological base, or is this cultural imposition found uniformly in all societies as an adjustment to the real biological differences between the sexes? This paper reports one attempt to deal with this problem.

DATA AND PROCEDURES

The data used were ethnographic reports, available in the anthropological literature, about socialization practices of various cultures. One

---

* Reprinted by permission of authors and the American Psychological Association from *The Journal of Abnormal Psychology and Social Psychology* (now: *The Journal of Abnormal Psychology*), vol. 55 no. 3, 1957:327–32.

This research is part of a project for which financial support was provided by the Social Science Research Council and the Ford Foundation. We are greatly indebted to G. P. Murdock for supplying us with certain data, as indicated below, and to him and Thomas W. Maretzki for suggestions that have been used in this paper.

hundred and ten cultures, mostly nonliterate, were studied. They were selected primarily in terms of the existence of adequate ethnographic reports of socialization practices and secondarily so as to obtain a wide and reasonably balanced geographical distribution. Various aspects of socialization of infants and children were rated on a 7-point scale by two judges (Mrs. Bacon and Mr. Barry). Where the ethnographic reports permitted, separate ratings were made for the socialization of boys and girls. Each rating was indicated as either confident or doubtful; with still greater uncertainty, or with complete lack of evidence, the particular rating was of course not made at all. We shall restrict the report of sex difference ratings to cases in which both judges made a confident rating. Also omitted is the one instance where the two judges reported a sex difference in opposite directions, as it demonstrates only unreliability of judgment. The number of cultures that meet these criteria is much smaller than the total of 110; for the several variables to be considered, the number varies from 31 to 84.

The aspects of socialization on which ratings were made included:

1. Several criteria of attention and indulgence toward infants.
2. Strength of socialization from age 4 or 5 years until shortly before puberty, with respect to five systems of behavior; strength of socialization was defined as the combination of positive pressure (rewards for the behavior) plus negative pressure (punishments for lack of the behavior). The variables were:
   a. Responsibility or dutifulness training. (The data were such that training in the performance of chores in the productive or domestic economy was necessarily the principal source of information here; however, training in the performance of other duties was also taken into account when information was available.)
   b. Nurturance training, i.e., training the child to be nurturant or helpful toward younger siblings and other dependent people.
   c. Obedience training.
   d. Self-reliance training.
   e. Achievement training, i.e., training the child to orient his behavior toward standards of excellence in performance, and to seek to achieve as excellent a performance as possible.

Where the term "no sex difference" is used here, it may mean any of three things: a. the judge found separate evidence about the training of boys and girls on this particular variable, and judged it to be identical; b. the judge found a difference between the training of boys and girls, but not great enough for the sexes to be rated a whole point apart on a 7–point scale; c. the judge found evidence only about the training of "children" on this variable, the ethnographer not reporting separately about boys and girls.

SEX DIFFERENCES IN SOCIALIZATION

On the various aspects of attention and indulgence toward infants, the judges almost always agreed in finding no sex difference. Out of 96 cultures for which the ratings included the infancy period, 88 (92%) were rated with no sex difference by either judge for any of those variables. This result is consistent with the point sometimes made by anthropologists that "baby" generally is a single status undifferentiated by sex, even though "boy" and "girl" are distinct statuses.

On the variables of childhood socialization, on the other hand, a rating of no sex differences by both judges was much less common. This finding of no sex difference varied in frequency from 10% of the cultures for the achievement variable up to 62% of the cultures for the obedience variable, as shown in the last column of Table 1. Where a sex difference is reported, by either one or both judges, the difference tends strongly to be in a particular direction, as shown in the earlier columns of the same

TABLE 1

Ratings of Cultures for Sex Differences on Five Variables of Childhood Socialization Pressure

Variable	Number of Cultures	Both Judges Agree in Rating the Variable Higher in		One Judge Rates No Difference, One Rates the Variable Higher in		Percentage of Cultures with Evidence of Sex Difference in Direction of		
		Girls	Boys	Girls	Boys	Girls	Boys	Neither
Nurturance	33	17	0	10	0	82	0	18
Obedience	69	6	0	18	2	35	3	62
Responsibility	84	25	2	26	7	61	11	28
Achievement	31	0	17	1	10	3	87	10
Self-reliance	82	0	64	0	6	0	85	15

table. Pressure toward nurturance, obedience, and responsibility is most often stronger for girls, whereas pressure toward achievement and self-reliance is most often stronger for boys.

For nurturance and for self-reliance, all the sex differences are in the same direction. For achievement there is only one exception to the usual direction of difference, and for obedience only two; but for responsibility there are nine. What do these exceptions mean? We have reexamined all these cases. In most of them, only one judge had rated the sexes as differently treated (sometimes one judge, sometimes the other), and in the majority of these cases both judges were now inclined to agree that there was no convincing evidence of a real difference. There were exceptions, however, especially in cases where a more formal or systematic training of boys seemed to imply greater pressure on them toward responsibility. The most convincing cases were the Masai and Swazi, where both judges had originally agreed in rating responsibility pressures greater in boys than in girls. In comparing the five aspects of socialization we may conclude that responsibility shows by far the strongest evidence of real variation in the direction of sex difference, and obedience much the most frequently shows evidence of no sex difference at all.

In subsequent discussion we shall be assuming that the obtained sex differences in the socialization ratings reflect true sex differences in the cultural practices. We should consider here two other possible sources of these rated differences.

1. The ethnographers could have been biased in favor of seeing the same pattern of sex differences as in our culture. However, most anthropologists readily perceive and eagerly report novel and startling cultural features, so we may expect them to have reported unusual sex differences where they existed. The distinction between matrilineal and patrilineal, and between matrilocal and patrilocal cultures, given prominence in many ethnographic reports, shows an awareness of possible variations in the significance of sex differences from culture to culture.

2. The two judges could have expected to find in other cultures the sex roles which are familiar in our culture and inferred them from the material on the cultures. However, we have reported only confident ratings, and such a bias seems less likely here than for doubtful ratings. It might be argued, moreover, that bias has more opportunity in the cases ambiguous enough so that only one judge reported a sex difference, and less opportunity in the cases where the evidence is so clear that both judges agree. Yet in general, as may be seen in Table 1, the deviant cases are somewhat more frequent among the cultures where only one judge reported a sex difference.

The observed differences in the socialization of boys and girls are consistent with certain universal tendencies in the differentiation of adult sex role. In the economic sphere, men are more frequently allotted tasks that involve leaving home and engaging in activities where a high level of skill yields important returns; hunting is a prime example. Emphasis on training in self-reliance and acheivement for boys would function as preparation for such an economic role. Women, on the other hand, are more frequently allotted tasks at or near home that minister most immediately to the needs of others (such as cooking and water carrying); these activities have a nurturant character, and in their pursuit a responsible carrying out of established routines is likely to be more important than the development of an especially high order of skill. Thus training in nurturance, responsibility, and, less clearly, obedience, may contribute to preparation for this economic role. These consistencies with adult role go beyond the economic sphere, of course. Participation in warfare, as a male prerogative, calls for self-reliance and a high order of skill where survival or death is the immediate issue. The childbearing which is biologically assigned to women, and the child care which is socially assigned primarily to them, lead to nurturant behavior and often call for a more continuous responsibility than do the tasks carried out by men. Most of these distinctions in adult role are not inevitable, but the biological differences between the sexes strongly predispose the distinction of role, if made, to be in a uniform direction.[1]

The relevant biological sex differences are conspicuous in adulthood but generally not in childhood. If each generation were left entirely to its own devices, therefore, without even an older generation to copy, sex differences in role would presumably be almost absent in childhood and would have to be developed after puberty at the expense of considerable relearning on the part of one or both sexes. Hence, a pattern of child training which foreshadows adult differences can serve the useful function of minimizing what Benedict termed "discontinuities in cultural conditioning" (Benedict 1938:161-7).

The differences in socialization between the sexes in our society, then, are no arbitrary custom of our society, but a very widespread adaptation of culture to the biological substratum of human life.

VARIATIONS IN DEGREE OF SEX DIFFERENTIATION

While demonstrating near-universal tendencies in direction of difference between the socialization of boys and girls, our data do not show perfect uniformity. A study of the variations in our data may allow us to see some of the conditions which are associated with, and perhaps give rise to, a greater or smaller degree of this difference. For this purpose, we classified cultures as having relatively large or small sex difference by two different methods, one more inclusive and the other more selective. In both methods the ratings were at first considered separately for each of the five variables. A sex difference rating was made only if both judges made a rating on this variable and at least one judge's rating was confident.

In the more inclusive method the ratings were dichotomized, separately for each variable, as close as possible to the median into those showing a large and those showing a small sex difference. Thus, for each society a large or a small sex difference was recorded for each of the five variables on which a sex difference rating was available. A society was given an overall classification of large or small sex difference if it had a sex difference rating on at least three variables and if a majority of these ratings agreed in being large, or agreed in being small. This method permitted classification of a large number of cultures, but the grounds for classification were capricious in many cases, as a difference of only one point in

---

[1] For data and interpretations supporting various arguments of this paragraph, see Mead 1949, Murdock 1937, and Scheinfeld 1944.

the rating of a single variable might change the overall classification of sex difference for a culture from large to small.

In the more selective method, we again began by dichotomizing each variable as close as possible to the median; but a society was now classified as having a large or small sex difference on the variable only if it was at least one step away from the scores immediately adjacent to the median. Thus only the more decisive ratings of sex difference were used. A culture was classified as having an overall large or small sex difference only if it was given a sex difference rating which met this criterion on at least two variables, and only if all such ratings agreed in being large, or agreed in being small.

We then tested the relation of each of these dichotomies to 24 aspects of culture on which Murdock has categorized the customs of most of these societies[2] and which seemed of possible significance for sex differentiation. The aspects of culture covered include type of economy, residence pattern, marriage and incest rules, political integration, and social organization. For each aspect of culture, we grouped Murdock's categories to make a dichotomous contrast (sometimes omitting certain categories as irrelevant to the contrast). In the case of some aspects of culture, two or more separate contrasts were made (e.g., under form of marriage we contrasted monogamy with polygyny, and also contrasted sororal with nonsororal polygyny). For each of 40 comparisons thus formed, we prepared a 2 x 2 frequency table to determine [its] relation to each of our sex-difference dichotomies. A significant relation was found for six of these 40 aspects of culture with the more selective dichotomization of overall sex difference. In four of these comparisons, the relation to the more inclusive dichotomization was also significant. These relationships are all given in Table 2, in the form of phi coefficients, along with the outcome of testing significance by the use of χ^2 or Fisher's exact test. In trying to interpret these findings, we have also considered the nonsignificant correlations with other variables, looking for consistency and inconsistency with the general implications of the significant findings. We have arrived at the following formulation of results:

1. Large sex difference in socialization is associated with an economy that places a high premium on the superior strength, and superior development of motor skills requiring strength, which characterize the male. Four of the correlations reported in Table 2 clearly point to this generalization: the correlations of large sex difference with the hunting of large animals, with grain rather than root crops, with the keeping of large rather than small domestic animals, and with nomadic rather than sedentary residence. The correlation with the unimportance of fishing may also be consistent

---

[2] These data were supplied to us directly by Professor Murdock.

TABLE 2

Culture Variables Correlated with Large Sex Differences in Socialization, Separately for Two Types of Sample

Variable	More Selective Sample		More Inclusive Sample	
	Φ	N	Φ	N
Large animals are hunted	.48*	(34)	.28*	(72)
Grain rather than root crops are grown	.82†	(20)	.62†	(43)
Large or milking animals rather than small animals are kept	.65*	(19)	.43*	(35)
Fishing unimportant or absent	.42*	(31)	.19	(69)
Nomadic rather than sedentary residence	.61†	(34)	.15	(71)
Polygyny rather than monogamy	.51*	(28)	.38†	(64)

* $p < .05$.
† $p < .01$.
Note: The variables have been so phrased that all correlations are positive. The phi coefficient is shown, and in parentheses, the number of cases on which the comparison was based. Significance level was determined by χ^2, or Fisher's exact test where applicable, using in all cases a two-tailed test.

with this generalization, but the argument is not clear.[3] Other correlations consistent with the generalization, though not statistically significant, are with large game hunting rather than gathering, with the hunting of large game rather than small game, and with the general importance of all hunting and gathering.

2. Large sex difference in socialization appears to be correlated with customs that make for a large family group with high cooperative interaction. The only statistically significant correlation relevant here is that with polygyny rather than monogamy. This generalization is, however, supported by several substantial correlations that fall only a little short of being statistically significant. One of these is a correlation with sororal rather than nonsororal polygyny; Murdock and Whiting (1951) have presented indirect evidence that co-wives generally show smoother cooperative interaction if they are sisters. Correlations are also found with the pres-

---

[3] Looking (with the more inclusive sample) into the possibility that this correlation might result from the correlation between fishing and sedentary residence, a complicated interaction between these variables was found. The correlation of sex differentiation with absence of fishing is found only in nomadic societies, where fishing is likely to involve cooperative activity of the two sexes, and its absence is likely to mean dependence upon the male for large game hunting or herding large animals (whereas in sedentary societies the alternatives to fishing do not so uniformly require special emphasis on male strength). The correlation of sex differentiation with nomadism is found only in nonfishing societies; here nomadism is likely to imply large game hunting or herding large animals, whereas in fishing societies nomadism evidently implies no such special dependence upon male strength. Maximum sex differentiation is found in nomadic nonfishing societies (15 with large difference and only 2 with small) and minimum sex differentiation in nomadic fishing societies (2 with large difference and 7 with small difference). These findings further strengthen the argument for a conspicuous influence of the economy upon sex differentiation.

ence of either an extended or a polygynous family rather than the nuclear family only; with the presence of an extended family; and with the extreme contrast between maximal extension and no extension of the family. The generalization is also to some extent supported by small correlations with wide extension of incest taboos, if we may presume that an incest taboo makes for effective unthreatening cooperation within the extended family. The only possible exception to this generalization, among substantial correlations, is a near-significant correlation with an extended or polygynous family's occupying a cluster of dwellings rather than a single dwelling.[4]

In seeking to understand this second generalization, we feel that the degree of social isolation of the nuclear family may perhaps be the crucial underlying variable. To the extent that the nuclear family must stand alone, the man must be prepared to take the woman's role when she is absent or incapacitated, and vice versa. Thus the sex differentiation cannot afford to be too great. But to the extent that the nuclear family is steadily interdependent with other nuclear families, the female role in the household economy can be temporarily taken over by another woman, or the male role by another man, so that sharp differentiation of sex role is no handicap.

The first generalization, which concerns the economy, cannot be viewed as dealing with material completely independent of the ratings of socialization. The training of children in their economic role was often an important part of the data used in rating socialization variables, and would naturally vary according to the general economy of the society. We would stress, however, that we were by no means using the identical data on the two sides of our comparison; we were on the one hand judging data on the socialization of children and on the other hand using Murdock's judgments on the economy of the adult culture. In the case of the second generalization, it seems to us that there was little opportunity for information on family and social structure to have influenced the judges in making the socialization ratings.

Both of these generalizations contribute to understanding the social background of the relatively small difference in socialization of boys and girls which we believe characterizes our society at the present time. Our mechanized economy is perhaps less dependent than any previous economy

---

[4] We think the reverse of this correlation would be more consistent with our generalization here. But perhaps it may reasonably be argued that the various nuclear families composing an extended or polygynous family are less likely to develop antagonisms which hinder cooperation if they are able to maintain some physical separation. On the other hand, this variable may be more relevant to the first generalization than to the second. Occupation of a cluster of dwellings is highly correlated with presence of herding and with herding of large rather than small animals, and these economic variables in turn are correlated with large sex difference in socialization. Occupation of a cluster of dwellings is also correlated with polygyny rather than monogamy and shows no correlation with sororal versus nonsororal polygyny.

upon the superior average strength of the male. The nuclear family in our society is often so isolated that husband and wife must each be prepared at times to take over or help in the household tasks normally assigned to the other. It is also significant that the conditions favoring low sex differentiation appear to be more characteristic of the upper segments of our society, in socioeconomic and educational status, than of lower segments. This observation may be relevant to the tendency toward smaller sex differences in personality in higher status groups (cf. Terman and Miles 1936).

The increase in our society of conditions favoring small sex difference led some people to advocate a virtual elimination of sex differences in socialization. This course seems likely to be dysfunctional even in our society. Parsons, Bales, et al. (1955) argue that a differentiation of role similar to the universal pattern of sex difference is an important and perhaps inevitable development in any social group, such as the nuclear family. If we add to their argument the point that biological differences between the sexes make most appropriate the usual division of those roles between the sexes, we have compelling reasons to expect that the decrease in differentiation of adult sex role will not continue to the vanishing point. In our training of children, there may now be less differentiation in sex role than characterizes adult life—so little, indeed, as to provide inadequate preparation for adulthood. This state of affairs is likely to be especially true of formal education, which is more subject to conscious influence by an ideology than is informal socialization at home. With child training being more oriented toward the male than the female role in adulthood, many of the adjustment problems of women in our society today may be partly traced to conflicts growing out of inadequate childhood preparation for their adult role. This argument is nicely supported in extreme form by Spiro's analysis of sex roles in an Israeli kibbutz (Spiro 1956). The ideology of the founders of the kibbutz included the objective of greatly reducing differences in sex role. But the economy of the kibbutz is a largely nonmechanized one in which the superior average strength of men is badly needed in many jobs. The result is that, despite the ideology and many attempts to implement it, women continue to be assigned primarily to traditional "women's work," and the incompatibility between upbringing or ideology and adult role is an important source of conflict for women.

Note on regional distribution. There is marked variation among regions of the world in typical size of sex difference in socialization. In our sample, societies in North America and Africa tend to have large sex difference, and societies in Oceania to have small sex difference. Less confidently, because of the smaller number of cases, we can report a tendency toward small sex differences in Asia and South America as well. Since most of the variables with which we find the sex difference to be significantly correlated have a similar regional distribution, the question arises whether the correlations might better be ascribed to some quite different source having to do with large regional similarities, rather than to the functional dependence we have suggested. As a partial check, we have tried to determine whether the correlations we report in Table 2 tend also to be found strictly within regions. For each of the three regions for which we have sizable samples (North America, Africa, and Oceania) we have separately plotted 2 x 2 tables corresponding to each of the 6 relationships reported in Table 2. (We did this only for the more inclusive sample, since for the more selective sample the number of cases within a region would have been extremely small.) Out of the 18 correlations thus determined, 11 are positive and only 3 are negative (the other 4 being exactly zero). This result clearly suggests a general tendency for these correlations to hold true within regions as well as between regions, and may lend further support to our functional interpretation.

SUMMARY

A survey of certain aspects of socialization in 110 cultures shows that differentiation of the sexes is unimportant in infancy, but that in childhood there is, as in our society, a widespread pattern of greater pressure toward nurturance, obedience, and responsibility in girls, and toward self-reliance and achievement striving in boys. There are a few reversals of sex difference, and many instances of no detectable sex difference; these facts tend to confirm the cultural rather than directly biological nature of the differences. Cultures vary in the degree to which these differentiations are made; correlational analysis suggests some of the social conditions influencing these variations, and helps in understanding why our society has relatively small sex differentiation.

Robert B. Edgerton

12. Ecology and Personality: Conclusions to a Study of Farmers and Pastoralists in East Africa*

... Given ... that differences between farmers and pastoralists do exist, what conclusions can we reach about the nature of these differences? I have presented the basic data derived from observation and interview, I have offered tests of statistical significance, and I have made various inferences from these data. I shall now set down my general conclusions about farmers and pastoralists. In doing so, I shall follow my convictions as they are built up out of a long acquaintance with all of these data. I say this not to prepare the reader for my extravagant flights of interpretive fancy, but rather to explain why my conclusions may, at times, be either more or less conservative than the earlier statistical tests of significance might seem to warrant. At times, therefore, I shall be more conservative because it is sometimes possible with samples the size of ours to reject the null hypothesis with deceptive ease. As the psychologist David Bakan (1968) has

* Excerpted from *The Individual in Cultural Adaptation: A Study of Four East African Peoples,* by Robert B. Edgerton, 1971 (Chapter 11, "Conclusions," pages 271–94). Originally published by the University of California Press; reprinted by permission of The Regents of the University of California. Permission of the author to excerpt the original chapter in this way is gratefully acknowledged.

[Editor's note: In this excerpt from the concluding chapter of Edgerton's study, the general structure of which was summarized above, pages 140–41, the discussion begins with the author's general assessment of the attitude, values, and personality differences observed when comparing farmers and pastoralists in four East African societies.]

warned, P-values derived from tests on large samples can be comforting, and are often demanded by scientific audiences, but they can also provide a dangerous illusion of proof where an honest skepticism should more properly prevail. At other times, I may appear to go beyond the confidence levels of these data, as for example, when they do not reach the 1 percent or even 5 percent level, but *are* consistently in the expected direction. That is, in this the final analysis I shall rely not only upon my understanding of the magnitude of the differences between farmers and pastoralists, but also upon my sense of the consistencey, coherence, and emphasis of these differences.

Proceeding in this manner, I feel confident in saying that farmers and pastoralists can be distinguished by the attributes illustrated in the polar comparison shown in figure 1. This figure attempts to portray diagrammatically both the kinds and the emphases of the differences between farmers and pastoralists. Thus, the attitude closest to the farming pole (disrespect for authority) is the most characteristic farming variable. Also highly characteristic, but slightly less so, are these attributes: anxiety, conflict avoidance, emotional constraint, hatred, impulsive aggression, and indirect action. Somewhat more weakly related we find friends, then still more distant are insults, litigiousness, and fatalism. At the periphery, there are two final, quite weakly associated attributes: fear of poverty and jealousy of wealth.

At the pastoral pole, we find five fundamental attributes: affection, direct aggression, divination, independence, and self-control. Almost equally central in importance are those attributes: adultery, sexuality, guilt-shame, depression, and respect for authority. Somewhat more weakly related are fear, bravery, brutality, and concern with death. Farther toward the boundary of the pastoral pattern but still well within it are concern with wrongdoing, cooperation, industriousness, clan, and kinsmen.

Figure 1 is not meant to be a precise map of each attribute in m-dimensional space. It is simply an illustrative representation of all those attributes that I feel confident about as farming or pastoral characteristics. It is also an indication of the relative strength of association between these attributes. The closer a variable lies to either pole, the greater is my confidence that it serves to characterize that pole. As variables move toward the central area between poles, I become less confident about their farming or pastoral affiliation. Thus, if I were to follow out this illustration, I could place in the empty center portion of Figure 1 those variables that have *no* farming or pastoral affiliations.

Turning now to the nature of these attributes that best characterize farmers and pastoralists, I believe it possible to note differences in the extent to which each set of attributes is characterized by a dominant focus. It seems to me that the farming attributes consistently relate to a central

FIGURE 1
A Polar Comparison of Farmers and Pastoralists.

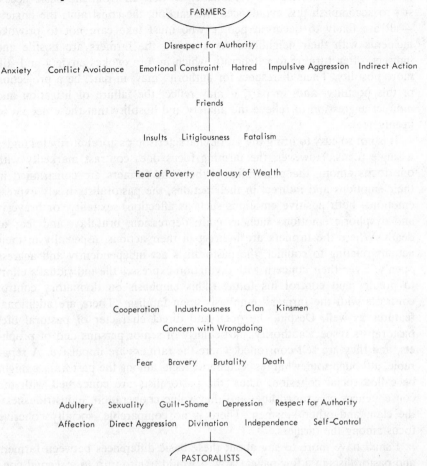

core, or theme, that might be called "interpersonal tension." For example, the farmers employ indirect action, featuring secrecy and caution; their emotions are constrained and they live with great anxiety. They not only show disrespect for authority, but the prevailing affect between people is hostility or hatred. They avoid conflict, engaging instead in litigation and witchcraft. Yet, their hostility, anxiety, and sensitivity to insults sometimes produce impulsive physical attack when open aggression does occur. There is remarkable coherence in this pattern. What is more, the pattern contains its own central dilemma, the necessity to avoid overt conflict. The need of farmers to avoid overt conflict in order to live together upon finite, scarce, and usually dwindling land resources was a basic expectation of this research project. I believe that farmers in these four tribes do attempt to avoid overt conflict, and I believe that the other attributes found here to characterize farmers can reasonably be derived from the basic necessity to accomplish this avoidance. The caution, the constraint, the anxiety —all are likely to occur in people who must take care not to provoke incidents with their neighbors. As a result, the farmers are hostile and indirect, often turning to witchcraft, which in turn evokes anxiety and still more hostility. Their disrespect for authority may, in part, be a projection of this hostility, and, in part, it may reflect the failure of litigation and indirect aggression to relieve the anxiety and hostility that these people so keenly feel.

It is not so easy to bring the set of characteristic pastoral attributes under a single focus. However, the farming focus does contrast markedly with one focus among the pastoralists. Where the farmers are constrained in their emotions and indirect in their actions, the pastoralists freely express emotions, both positive emotions such as affection, sexuality, or bravery, and dysphoric emotions such as guilt, depression, brutality, and fear of death. Where the farmers are indirect in their actions, especially in their actions relating to conflict, the pastoralists act independently and aggress openly. Even their concern with divination expresses the individual's effort to predict and control his future. This emphasis on divinatory control contrasts with the farmers' emphasis upon fatalism. There are additional features as well. Despite the open and direct character of pastoral life, pastoralists respect authority, particularly of senior persons and of prophets, and they are self-controlled where the farmers are impulsive. A separable, although somewhat less emphatic, focus among the pastoralists might be called social cohesion. Thus, the pastoralists are concerned with the consequences of wrongdoing, and they value cooperation, industriousness, the clan, and other kinsmen. There is no comparable, socially cohesive focus among the farmers.

I shall have more to say about these basic differences between farmers and pastoralists in a few pages. Now, I would like to turn to a second consideration. I have spoken of the focus of each set of characterizing attributes; it is also possible to speak of its "emphasis." Thus, we find that whereas the farming set of attributes was more tightly integrated around one central focus than were the pastoral attributes, the farming attributes are *less* emphatic. Aside from disrespect for authority, none of the farming attributes was extremely emphatic. The farming variables are coherent; but, taken separately, few are expressed frequently or emphatically enough to permit us great confidence in saying that they typify farmers. On the other hand, many of the pastoral attributes do have this force. They are expressed so frequently and emphatically that many of them can confidently be said to typify pastoralists in these four tribes. The following attributes all carry that degree of force: affection, direct aggression, independence, divination, self-control, adultery, sexuality, guilt-shame, depression, and respect for authority.

We might also compare the "level" of these farming and pastoral characteristics. The many variables that were considered throughout this research, including those that constitute this concluding farming-pastoral comparison, represent different levels of psychological and cultural abstraction. For example, many of these variables clearly represent values (e.g., the desirability or valuation of cattle); others are just as clearly psychological (e.g., anxiety). But most of these variables are more difficult to characterize because they reflect both cultural values and psychological orientations. To oversimplify a complex matter, we might refer to these "mixed" variables as attitudes.

Turning first to values, I would conclude that the characteristic farming variables are rarely expressed as values. Farmers do not say (or, I think, believe) that they *ought* to be anxious, to hate, to aggress impulsively, to disrespect authority, and so on. They do sometimes emphasize the desirability of avoiding conflict, but very seldom do they attach values to the other variables. Conversely, many of the characteristic pastoral variables are regularly expressed as values. All of these variables express pastoral values: direct aggression, independence, divination, self-control, sexuality, respect for authority, bravery, cooperation, industriousness, concern with the consequences of wrongdoing, clan, and kinsmen. On the other hand, both pastoral and farming variables are clearly psychological in that they represent emotions or cognitive orientations which are not normally conceptualized or easily verbalized. I would judge that the farmers and pastoralists are about equal in the psychological level of their characterizing attributes.

There is an important difference here. The pastoralists are characterized by attributes that are expressed as both cultural values and psychological orientations, but the farmers' attributes lack the support of cultural values. In this sense, the core of that which characterizes the farmers is covert, and as such it may exert great influence. Yet, without the corresponding support of values, it lacks cultural recognition and institutionalization as a *proper* way of thinking, feeling, or behaving. The pastoral core of attributes *has* such cultural institutionalization; it is both deeply built into the actors and strongly reinforced by values.

When we take the farming and pastoral cores of characteristic variables together and contrast them with the "cultural" cores (each tribe's distinctive variables . . .), another difference emerges. These distinctive cultural cores consistently reflect both basic psychological orientations and cultural values. In a few instances, only psychological attributes are expressed (the Hehe, impulsive aggression; the Kamba, need for affection; the Pokot, depression; the Sebei, anxiety); but the great majority of these variables combine both values *and* psychological attributes. Among the characteristic farming and pastoral variables, on the other hand, a far greater proportion are primarily psychological. I would judge, and of course any such judgment must be highly subjective, that of . . . twenty-six features listed [earlier] as distinctive cultural designata, only seven exist on the psychological level alone, without corresponding valuation. These seven include the four listed above plus these three Sebei distinctions: fear of death, fear of the malignant power of women, and jealousy and hostility. (This lack of value support for so much of what was distinctive of Sebei culture led me earlier to speak of the negative, uncommitted character of the Sebei.) In striking contrast, almost all of the farming designata and almost half of the characteristic pastoral variables are primarily or entirely psychological.

In summary, what is distinctive of pastoralists in all four of these societies is a common set of linked values, attitudes, and psychological orientations. Both farmers and pastoralists participate in the distinctive core of their tribe's culture, and in so doing they accept certain values. However, what is distinctive of farmers in these four societies is a nonvalued set of psychological dispositions, most of which are clearly expressive of tension, hostility, and conflict.[1]

To return now to the general question, what finally can be said about the fundamental differences between farmers and pastoralists? I must first make it clear that when I speak of such differences here, these differences, as before, are *relative*. That is, when I spoke earlier of the farmers being, for example, anxious, I meant that they were substantially more anxious than the pastoralists, not that the pastoralists were completely free of anxiety. Here, too, I am suggesting quantitative contrasts between farmers and pastoralists, not absolute differences.

At the most general level of comparison, I believe that farmers and pastoralists are differentiated on two dimensions: 1. open versus closed emotionality, and 2. direct versus indirect action. These dimensions— themes, perhaps—appear to me to find expression primarily as psychological sets, although they also serve as general orienting principles of the kind sometimes referred to as world view, or value orientation. However, I am far less concerned with the epistemological nature of these themes than I am with how many attitudes and behaviors can be subsumed under them and what predictive utility they might have. I believe that these two summative themes epitomize the differences between farmers and pastoral-

---

[1] If the negativism and hostility characterizing farmers were primarily produced by acculturation or deculturation, it is difficult to see why they should be so selective in their operation, leaving many strong values in place while eroding a few willy-nilly. As Walter Goldschmidt points out in his epilogue, an ecological explanation is a good deal more plausible.

ists and that these themes can account for many of the variables we have previously discussed.

To illustrate what I have in mind in these two dimensions of comparison, let me rephrase what we have already said about the emotionality of farmers. The emotions of farmers may well be strongly felt—indeed, there is every evidence that they are—but they are not openly expressed. Perhaps I should say that they are not readily revealed, for it seems that farmers are actively engaged in conscious concealment of their true feelings. At the same time that they may be unaware of certain emotions (we might presume the presence of certain ego-defense mechanisms), it is my impression that farmers tend to withhold emotional expression because of their calculation that it is in their best interest to do so. For the most part, farmers seem to succeed in closing off their emotions to others, for it is only now and then that suppressed feelings break through in impulsive, uncontrolled fashion. And when this happens, it brings socially disruptive consequences.

In strong contrast, the pastoralists display their feelings easily, openly, and seemingly "naturally." I assume that the emotions of pastoralists, like those of people anywhere, are subject to both conscious concealment and unconscious censorship; nevertheless, in comparison to farmers of the same tribe, pastoralists are remarkably expressive of a wide range of emotion. The good and the bad, the joyous and the sad, the soft and the harsh —all are expressed with far greater freedom. Perhaps because their feelings are so openly expressed, the pastoralists appear to lack those occasional impulsive lapses of control which occur among the farmers.

Similarly, farmers and pastoralists differ with regard to directness of action. The farmers are characteristically indirect. Not only do they avoid expression of their feelings, when they do speak and act, it is with a careful eye to obscuring their motives, to veiling their meanings, and to avoiding confrontation over any potentially contestable issue. Compared to farmers, pastoralists strongly value independent and direct action. They make decisions as individuals, openly pursue goals, and typically say and do what they wish—directly. They even aggress openly, abusing or assaulting an adversary, but usually doing so only when appropriate and within sublethal limits. Despite their open, direct, sometimes even brutal approach to other humans and animals, their actions are controlled. When farmers aggress, social cohesion is threatened; when pastoralists do so, social relations continue as before.

As I have argued earlier, there are a number of noteworthy differences between farmers and pastoralists, but these two themes, control of emotion and of action, are to me the most fundamental and the most reliable distinctions of all.

What, then, of the causes of these distinctions? Insofar as we may venture any conclusions regarding how differences between farmers and pastoralists may relate to ecology, we can most confidently begin by pointing to conflict as the pivotal concern. The farmers avoid direct conflict; the pastoralists accept it, sometimes even seek it. This difference is important, but it is a functional distinction, not truly an ecological one until we can specify the conditions that have led to it. Our expectations in this regard have been set forth by Walter Goldschmidt in his introduction to this volume, so I need not repeat them here. . . . We should recall that shortage of land appeared to be less efficient as a predictor of farming attributes than was shortage of cattle. Nevertheless, there is reason to conclude that scarcity of major economic resources, land or cattle, *does* relate to farming attitudes and psychological orientations. So, too, does the clustering of households: the closer households are clustered together, the greater is the expression of hatred and the concern with conflict avoidance. Both of these findings support our original expectations.

We anticipated that the pastoral set of distinctive attributes would be related, in large part, to an ecology that set demands, particularly upon a man, to be able, quickly and alone, to take action in order to defend himself and his assets, be these assets his wives, his children, or his herds. We are able to offer no conclusive support for this assumption, but I continue to find it plausible. We did find a strong linkage between the cooperative aspect of the pastoral response pattern and the need to manage water resources; it seems highly likely to me that the pastoral focus upon social cohesion is a direct reflection of this sort of ecological necessity.

But there is a still more basic dimension of the environment to be considered, and this dimension has heretofore been ignored. We had originally postulated that the relative mobility of each population would be a crucial environmental determinant of its members' attitudes, values, and personality. It was not possible to measure this environmental variable with any adequacy, . . . however, if I were now to select the one environmental variable that I believe would explain most about differences between farmers and pastoralists, it would be this one. I believe that Goldschmidt was correct in hypothesizing that farmers must avoid conflict because they cannot move away from it. They are tied to the land, and a neighbor, however angry, will remain a neighbor; given this fact of immobility, it becomes essential to avoid open conflict. The pastoral contrast can be dramatic. Ideally, when a pastoralist quarrels with someone, he can pick up stakes and move away with his family and his animals in tow, all with little difficulty. It is this ability to quarrel directly with, and then move away from, an adversary that so drastically alters the imperatives of social control and conflict avoidance among pastoralists.

Since this surmise is based upon ethnographic observations rather than upon systematic interview responses, and since it is offered as a suggestion for research rather than as a demonstrable finding, I can only illustrate the relevance of such differential mobility for questions of social conflict.

Pastoralists in these four tribes often told me that men who are angry should be allowed to fight, for if anger should not be dispelled, witchcraft would be the likely result. I.M. Lewis, writing of the pastoral Somali, reached a similar conclusion: ". . . where sorcery or witchcraft occur it is usually between people who, for one reason or another, are prevented from fighting" (1961:26). But I was also told by these pastoralists that if a fight were unusually serious or left "bad feelings," then the antagonists should move away from each other. I do not know how often combatants actually moved away from one another, but I do know that the option to move away was present and that it was often exercised.

I also know that other East African pastoral societies have recognized the relationship between mobility and the reduction of conflict. For example, Paul Spencer concluded this regarding the pastoral Samburu of Kenya: ". . . the constant need for migration and dispersal *inevitably* dampens local strains" (1965:207; italics mine). Spencer added this comment: "Moreover, if two people quarreled then they generally moved apart and kept apart throughout the remainder of my stay" (ibid:xxiv). As a paradigm example of this same phenomenon, I offer Philip Gulliver's account of the nomadic Turkana of Kenya (1966:165):

> Another factor leading to the dispersion of a house is the principle that where tensions exist between individuals, for whatever reason, it is best to relieve them by geographical separation, when, if they do not gradually die down, they will at least necessarily be reduced. . . . If two co-wives habitually quarrel, one of them will go to live in the other homestead of the same nuclear family; at another level, if two men quarrel and bad relations persist, then one or both will shift his homestead elsewhere. Such practical arrangements are not difficult in Turkanaland, where on the one hand each family maintains at least two homesteads, and on the other where mobility is high.

Such "practical" arrangements *are* difficult for farmers, and therein lies a major ecological difference between the life conditions of farmers and pastoralists.

Throughout this book, and in Walter Goldschmidt's epilogue, various alternatives to our ecological position have been considered: differential acculturation, deculturation, vagaries of history, and the like. I mention here another alternative, the possibility of selective migration. Might it not be, as some of my academic colleagues have seriously suggested, that the distinctive pastoral response pattern is a product of selective migration from the hills to the plains by those men and women who were already more independent, aggressive, culturally committed, and so forth? Although the histories of these four tribal areas are poorly known, all evidence indicates that no such migration took place. Past migration patterns were different in all four areas, but none conformed to this putative pattern. Recent migration from the hills to the plains is far from being extensive, and when it does occur, primarily involves land-poor men or young relatives of the rich, not necessarily those with "pastoral" attributes. There is, in short, no evidence whatever to support the idea that the distinctive pastoral-farming differences are the result of past or present selective migration.

But even were we to assume that just such migration took place, or continues to take place, our ecological thesis would in no way be weakened. On the contrary, our position would be just as compelling because such migrants would neither leave their farming areas nor survive in pastoral ones, unless their attitudes, values, and psychological attributes were favored by the pastoral way of life. In a selective migration position, ecology remains sovereign, rendering farming conditions less congenial for these people, and pastoral life more so. Since the facts do not permit us to sustain our thesis by referring to fables about selective migration, however, we have relied upon a more conventional ecological explanation. . . .

ECOLOGY AND THE INDIVIDUAL

This final chapter has compared farmers and pastoralists in terms of those attributes that most fundamentally yet reliably characterize them. It has also considered some general problems that we faced in this study. Before offering a final evaluation of the findings of this research, I would like to make an important point about the problems that were encountered. These problems have been discussed throughout this volume, so I shall only mention them here. I have in mind the fact that we were not able to locate communities that fitted our ideal pastoral or farming types; instead, our communities were at best approximations of the ideal ecological forms our expectations called for. What is more, within each of the four tribes, there was not only an exchange of information between the pastoral and farming communities, but sometimes there was an exchange of persons as well. In addition, as this chapter has pointed out, we had difficulties in our control over the length of time that each community had existed, as well as in the number of communities in our sample. I return to these difficulties here because their combined effect was to *reduce* the magnitude of the differences that we found between farmers and pastoralists. Our procedures of data collection and analysis did nothing to compensate for this reduction. For example, we sampled respondents on a probability basis: we did not interview only those persons who were most intensively engaged in a pastoral or farming mode of life. Similarly, the analysis of the data attempted to treat the statistical differences between populations quite conservatively, choosing for the most part to err on the side of overlooking rather than enhancing any small differences that might exist.

As a result, the differences that were found to characterize farmers and pastoralists become quite impressive. These differences (open versus closed emotions, direct versus indirect action, social cohesion versus social negativism) seem to be both general and fundamental, general in the sense of including several specific differences, and fundamental in the importance of these differences for an understanding of pastoral and farming life. For example, one is tempted to think of the pastoralists as extraverts with well-developed social consciences and the farmers as angry and fearful introverts. I mention this analogy because many of the basic farming-pastoral differences can be accounted for by this extravert-introvert comparison, but also to point up the fact that the contrasts between the two ecological types are on a similar level of generality.

To summarize, our primary goal was to discover relevant differences in attitudes, values, and personality characteristics between farmers and pastoralists. I believe the differences that we found are valid ones and that they serve effectively to distinguish persons in these two ecological types.

Our second, and more difficult goal, was to relate these human differences to environmental differences. When we attempted to tie particular differences in these personal characteristics to particular features of the environmental and the situational aspects of the two life-modes, we found that we could not demonstrate specific sets of relationships. The relationships we uncovered were at best suggestive. This difficulty may derive from some of the inadequacies of the experimental situation or from our inability to scale some of the more important variables. Another viewpoint is possible, however, namely, that the several environmental and situational features combine as a system, and the attributes of behavior and personality we have found to be relevant to the two modes of economy relate to this generalized system, rather than to this or that specific feature of it.

I believe we can conclude, therefore, that farmers and pastoralists live in significantly differential milieux and that each milieu makes different demands on its human inhabitants and subjects them to different kinds of constraints. As a result, the individual is pressed toward the kind of behavior and attitudes appropriate to the milieu in which he finds himself, and with time he not only takes on attitudes and values that are appropriate to it but some aspects of his personality too come into conformity with that milieu. Individuals of course, vary in their adaptive capacity: some undoubtedly adapt very rapidly to a new environment, perhaps because of their flexibility of character, perhaps because they find it congenial. In other instances, or in other aspects of behavior more recalcitrant to change, the process may be a matter of generations.

But the essential fact is this: we have found significant differences in values, attitudes, and personality attributes where we expected to find them, and of the kind we expected to find, despite the short time span involved and the limited social distance between the communities of farmers and pastoralists, and, we add once more, despite the imperfections of the natural laboratory in which we were testing these ideas. These differences reflect the ecological conditions in which the two types of economy operate. They therefore contribute to an understanding of the processes of cultural adaptation.

Melford E. Spiro

13. Religious Systems as Culturally Constituted Defense Mechanisms*

Since the range of beliefs, values, and rituals related to supernatural beliefs and events is enormous, it is obvious, as Durkheim observed long ago, that no belief, value, or ritual is intrinsically identifiable as "religious." Since the "religious," on the contrary, is a quality capable of being attached to almost any instance of these three dimensions of religious systems, the latter, to use a modern idiom, are in large measure projective systems. It is this characteristic of religion that poses a problem which has long confronted its students, and which comprises the problem of this paper: If religious systems are indeed projective in character, how can we be sure that religious behavior is not abnormal behavior, requiring psychiatric, rather than sociocultural, analysis?

Anthropology, as is well known, has adopted a fairly uniform stance with respect to the cross-cultural variability which characterizes notions of the good, the true, and the beautiful. This stance, so far as the normal-abnormal distinction is concerned, was given classic expression by Benedict (1934), who maintained that judgments concerning abnormality are necessarily relative to intracultural standards. What is judged to be abnormal in one cultural setting may be properly characterized as normal in other cultural settings. . . .

[In particular, it may be argued] that briefs and rituals which char-

* Excerpted with permission of Macmillan Publishing Co., Inc., from *Context and Meaning in Cultural Anthropology,* Melford E. Spiro, ed. (pages 100–13). Copyright © 1968 by The Free Press, A Division of Macmillan Publishing Co., Inc. Permission of the author to excerpt the original article in this way is gratefully acknowledged.

acterize the behavior of religious actors in non-Western societies, although phenotypically identical with beliefs and behavior which may characterize abnormal individuals in our society, are not necessarily (or even usually) abnormal when sanctioned or prescribed by the religious systems of the former societies and taught to the actors as part of their cultural heritage. There are a number of reasons for this conclusion. *a.* The religious actor acquires his beliefs and rituals, as he acquires other aspects of his cultural heritage, through the usual techniques of instruction and imitation. Hence these beliefs and rituals are expressions, rather than distortions, of (his culturally constituted) reality. They are consistent with, rather than obstacles to, social and cultural functioning. Psychotic beliefs and behavior, on the contrary, are devised by the actor himself, as an attempt to reduce the painful tension induced by inner conflict. This attempt is necessarily based on his private distortion of (culturally constituted) reality, resulting in serious impairment of his social and/or cultural functioning. *b.* Since religious beliefs and practices are derived from tradition, they are frequently compulsory; but since they are not created by the actor himself to defend against forbidden or shameful impulses, they are not compulsive. Psychotic beliefs and practices, on the contrary, are not compulsory— indeed they are usually prohibited—but as attempts to reduce tension, they are compulsive. *c.* Although not devised by the actor to resolve conflict, religious beliefs and ritual may be used for that end. When so used they may not only resolve conflict, but as "culturally constituted defenses" (Spiro 1961:472–97) they are consistent with, rather than distortions of, reality; they comprise culturally sanctioned, rather than culturally prohibited, behavior; they protect the individual and his society from the disruptive consequences both of his shameful and/or forbidden needs and of his private defensive maneuvers. Conflict may also be resolved by psychotic beliefs and practices; but these idiosyncratic resolutions produce those psychological distortions and sociocultural impairments which, as I have argued, are properly characterized as abnormal. I should like to examine these propositions in the context of one empirical situation—Burmese Buddhist monasticism.

BURMESE MONASTICISM[1]

In Burma, one of the centers of Theravada Buddhism, the monastic vocation is the most venerated of all patterns of life. Almost every village contains at least one monastery with at least one resident monk. The monk, in theory at least, lives an exclusively otherworldly existence. His monastery is outside the village gates, and his interaction with the layman is confined

[1] Materials in this section are based on field work carried out during 1961–62; I am grateful to the National Science Foundation for a research fellowship which made the research possible.

to occasional ritual situations. The monk is prohibited from engaging in any form of physical labor, including any economic activity. All of his wants are attended to by the laymen, who provide his daily meals, his robes, and other necessities. Except for teaching young children, the monk's official responsibilities to the laymen are restricted to chanting of "prayers" at funerals and to public recitation of the Buddhist precepts on the "Sabbath" and other sacred days. His primary responsibility is to himself and to his attempt to attain nirvana. The latter goal is achieved through the study of Scripture and through various techniques of Buddhist meditation. These activities are believed to be instrumental to the attainment of Release from the round of rebirths because they lead to ultimate comprehension of the true characteristics of existence, viz., impermanence, suffering, and the absence of an ego. This comprehension, in turn, is believed to lead to the severance of all desire for, and cathexis of, the world. With the destruction of desire or "clinging" (*tanha*), the basis for rebirth is destroyed. Nirvana, whatever else it may be, is the cessation of rebirth.

The true monk, then, is completely absorbed in his own "salvation." Although living in a state of absolute dependence on the laymen, he has withdrawn both physically and psychologically from the physical and social world, and even—in states of trance (*dhyānas*)—from his own self. This extreme withdrawal from reality is similar to that withdrawal behavior which, in our society, would be taken as symptomatic of severe pathology, most certainly schizoid, if not schizophrenic. Is the Burmese monk to be similarly characterized? Such a judgment, in my opinion, would be grossly in error. Phenotypically, the behavior of the monk and that of the schizoid or schizophrenic patient may be very similar. Genotypically and functionally, however, they are importantly dissimilar. All of the criteria suggested in the previous section for assessing pathology are applicable to the schizophrenic; none is applicable to the monk.

In the case of the schizophrenic the actor resolves his inner conflict by constructing private fantasy and action systems; in the case of the monk, however, the actor uses culturally constituted fantasy and action systems (Buddhism) to resolve his inner conflicts. This difference not only provides the primary basis for a differential diagnosis of monk and schizophrenic, but it also provides, parenthetically, an important insight into the nature of religion. Culturally constituted religious behavior not only is not a symptom of pathology but, on the contrary, it serves to preclude the outbreak of pathology. The schizophrenic and the Burmese monk, alike, are characterized initially by pathogenic conflict, and schizophrenia and monasticism may each be interpreted as a means for resolving conflict. But this is where the similarity ends. Although schizophrenia and monasticism are both symptomatic of pathogenic conflict, the former represents a pathological, whereas the latter represents a nonpathological, resolution of the conflict. Let us examine these claims.

An analysis of monastic personality, based on the Rorschach records of a sample of Burmese Buddhist monks, and without reference to their (monastic) behavioral environment, would surely lead to a diagnosis of severe pathology. Dr. James Steele (1963), who has analyzed these records, finds the following "pathological" features, among others: 1. a very high degree of "defensiveness"; 2. "pathologically regressed" expression of aggressive and oral drives; 3. cautious avoidance of "emotionally laden" situations as a means of obviating the necessity for handling affect, for which there are no adequate resources; 4. a "hypochondriacal self-preoccupation" and "erotic self-cathexis," instead of a cathexis of others; 5. latent homosexuality; 6. above-average fear of female- or mother-figures.

One of the significant characteristics of the Rorschach protocols of these monks, according to Steele, is their similarity to the records of Burmese laymen. It is not that the monastic records do not differ from those of the laymen; but the difference is one of degree, not of kind. Monks differ from laymen, not because they have different problems, but because they have more of the same problems. The monk, in other words, is a Burman *in extremis.* Burmese laymen (like Burmese monks) are constricted, ruminative, defensive, anxious about females, distrustful of others, and, perhaps, latently homosexual. The monks differ from the laymen only in that, for all these characteristics, they are *more so.* Monks are *more* constricted, *more* ruminative, *more* . . . , etc. For other characteristics, however, monks are *less so.* Compared to laymen, monks are ". . . less phallic, less self-confident, less striving, and less impulsive." In summary, Burmese monks not only appear to have "more of the basic problems" which characterize Burmans in general, but they also seem to be characterized by a "more constricted adjustment." It is the latter feature, still quoting Steele, which makes them "less accessible to social interaction with the protection that this provides."

This picture of the Burmese monks is surely a picture of pathology. Are we to conclude then—holding in abeyance a specific psychiatric diagnosis, and assuming that the Rorschach test is a reliable instrument—that these monks are abnormal? If personality existed in a social and cultural vacuum, the answer would be an unqualified "yes." Acute psychological conflicts and attendant intrapersonal tensions are marked. That these conflicts have produced defensive distortions of various kinds—perceptual, cognitive, affective—is clearly indicated. That social impairment is a most likely consequence of these conflicts, tensions, and distortions can hardly be doubted. In brief, if personality existed *in vacuo* one would probably conclude that Burmese monks resolve their conflicts in a manner which issues in severe pathology (perhaps paranoid schizophrenia).

But the proviso, "if personality existed *in vacuo,*" is crucial. Although Steele's analysis of their Rorschach records is remarkably similar to my clinical impressions of these monks, impressions derived from intensive participant-observation in a score of monasteries, and from personal interviews with more than twenty-five monks—thus providing a dramatic test of the reliability of the instrument and of Steele's skill in its use—I did not ever feel that these monks, with but one exception, were pathological or, specifically, schizophrenic. Nor is this a paradox. The psychological analysis (based on Rorschachs and clinical impressions) provides a set of statements concerning the emotional problems of the subjects; it also provides, to a somewhat lesser extent, a picture of their idiosyncratic defenses, i.e., of those defenses which the subjects have constructed for themselves, in an attempt to resolve their problems. That these defenses are hardly adequate to the task is obvious from the Rorschach analysis. Left exclusively to their own inner resources many of these subjects would have become, I believe, genuine psychotics.

But personality does not exist *in vacuo,* and Burmese males, characterized by the problems described, are not confronted with the necessity of solving these problems by means of their own resources. In addition to their private resources, they are able to utilize a powerful cultural resource for their solution, i.e., they can solve their problems by recruitment to the monastic order. By utilizing the role-set prescribed for this institution as a culturally constituted defense, Burmese monks can resolve their conflicts with a minimum of distortion. Since, moreover, the performance of the roles comprising this role-set satisfies their prohibited and/or shameful needs and reduces their painful fears and anxieties, these potentially disruptive psychological variables, rather than provoking socially disruptive behavior, provide the motivational basis for the persistence of the most highly valued institution—monasticism—in Burmese society. As a culturally constituted defense, the monastic institution resolves the inner conflicts of Burmese males, by allowing them to gratify their drives and reduce their anxieties in a disguised—and therefore socially acceptable—manner, one which precludes psychotic distortion, on the one hand, and criminal "acting-out," on the other. Hence, the monk is protected from mental illness and/or social punishment; society is protected from the disruptive consequences of antisocial behavior; and the key institution of Burmese culture—Buddhist monasticism—is provided with a most powerful motivational basis. Space permits only a brief examination of these assertions.

The monastic rules which interdict *all* labor, and those Buddhist norms which guarantee that the laity provide monks with *all* their wants, combine to satisfy the monk's "regressed oral drives." The monastic life, moreover, makes no demands, either social or psychological, which might render the monk's weak "phallic-orientation," his low degree of "striving and impulsivity," and his lack of "self-confidence" nonviable modes of adjustment. Quite the contrary, the physical isolation of the monastery, and the monastic norms proscribing social participation, preclude the stimulation of "disruptive affect." At the same time, the monk's "self-preoccupation" and "erotic self-cathexis" is wonderfully expressed and institutionalized in the prescribed techniques of Buddhist meditation. Latent "homosexual" needs can be satisfied in the exclusively male setting in which the monks live. Finally, the strong interdiction on interaction with females provides little opportunity for encounters with them and for the consequent fear attendant upon such encounters. Buddhist monasticism, then, is a highly efficient means for coping with the psychological problems of many Burmese men. The differences between a monastic and a psychotic resolution of these problems are instructive.

1. In general the genesis of the psychotic's conflict is idiosyncratic, while the genesis of the monk's problem is rooted in modal features of his society. That is, the source of the monk's conflict—which we cannot discuss here— is to be found in culturally constituted experiences which the monk shares with many other members of his social group. The monk differs from other Burmans in one of three ways: his potentially pathogenic experiences are more intense than those of other males; other Burmans utilize alternative, non-Buddhist, institutions for the resolution of equally intense problems; still others (a minority) develop idiosyncratic methods of conflict-resolution (in extreme cases, these take the form of mental illness or criminal behavior).

2. The psychotic resolves his problems by means of idiosyncratic, private, defenses; the monk resolves his problems in an institutionalized manner, by utilizing elements of his religious heritage as a culturally constituted defense. The difference between these two types of defense accounts for the following differences between the psychotic patient, on the one hand, and the normal monk, on the other.

3. The behavior of the psychotic is incompatible with any normal social role within his society, and inconsistent with important cultural norms of the larger society. The psychotic is *psychologically incapable* of performing social roles or of complying with those cultural norms which he violates. The behavior of the monk, on the other hand, is entirely appropriate to— indeed, it is the enactment of—a most important and honorific social role. The monk may be psychologically incapable of performing nonmonastic roles, but he is ideally suited for performing the monastic role.

4. As a corollary of the above, the behavior of the psychotic is bizarre in the eyes of, and disapproved by, his fellows. The behavior of the monk is not only approved by the other members of his society, but it is most highly valued.

5. Following from the last point, the behavior of the psychotic alienates him psychologically from his fellows. The behavior of the monk, on the contrary, though isolating him physically from his group, serves to integrate him psychologically into the group; for in his behavior he expresses the most cherished values of Burmese culture.

6. The world view constructed by the psychotic represents a dramatic distortion of reality, as the latter is structured by the world view of his culture; and the cognitions and perceptions that are derived from his idiosyncratic world view are highly distorted, relative to the behavioral environment in which expected social interaction of his society takes place. The world view of the monk, on the other hand, rather than being constructed from his private fantasies, is taught to him as an integral part of the cultural heritage of his society. The private world view of the monk corresponds to the public world view of his society; his world view, in brief, is a culturally constituted world view. The Buddhist world view, of course, may be false, a distortion of reality, relative to the world view of modern science; but it is true, relative to the knowledge available to Burmese society. True or false, however, the monk's cognitions and perceptions are consistent with, rather than distortions of, reality, as the latter is structured by the world view and behavioral environment of his society. The perceptions and cognitions, the fantasies and emotions experienced by the monk in the course of Buddhist meditation and concentration may never be experienced by other Burmans—because the latter do not meditate or concentrate—but they are experiences consistent with the conception of reality which all Burmans hold, and they are vouchsafed to any Burman who is prepared to enter into these spiritual disciplines.

7. The psychotic sustains social relationships neither with the normal members of his society, nor with other psychotics. Psychotics, in short, do not participate in the society of which they are members, nor do they comprise a social group, distinct from the larger society, but nevertheless viable for its constituent members. Burmese monks, on the other hand, although socially isolated from Burmese society, are yet psychologically part of it. Moreover, although the monk may find difficulty in participating in the larger society, and in forming social relationships within it, he does enter into social relationships with other members of the monastic order. Monks are members of increasingly larger concentric groups, beginning with other members of the local monastery and extending to the entire order of monks. In short, while psychotics comprise a typological class, the monks constitute a social group. The psychotic cannot live as a member of a social group, even if it be but a subgroup of the larger society.

8. Finally, and as a corollary of the last point, the behavior of the psychotic is anomic; it violates many of the rules of his society. The monk, on the other hand, not only exemplifies the rules of Burmese society, but he must, in addition, comply with the 227 rules of the monastic order (as outlined in the *Vinaya*). Should he violate these rules, he is expelled from the order as a charlatan, regardless of whatever wondrous visions he is alleged to have had, or miraculous powers he is supposed to possess.

In summary, then, a psychiatrically diagnosed psychotic is not only incapable of participating in his own society, he is incapable of participating in any society. An American psychotic would function no better in a Buddhist monastery than in an American city. A Buddhist monk, to be sure, while not capable of functioning in every cultural environment, functions very well indeed within *his* cultural environment. This is hardly surprising, since the latter environment is so structured that it satisfies his needs and resolves his conflicts. That he cannot function in a radically different environment does not render him "sick," nor his adjustment precarious. Typically, differential sets of human needs are differentially satisfied in different types of cultural milieux. It is doubtful if the typical Burmese peasant could adjust to an American urban environment, or a typical American to a Buddhist monastery. For neither is the new environment capable of satisfying the needs and resolving the conflicts which were produced by the old.

SUMMARY AND CONCLUSIONS

Burmese monks, as Rorschach data and clinical observations agree, are characterized by serious emotional conflicts. Their religious heritage, however, provides them with institutionalized means for resolving conflicts, and, moreover, for resolving them in a manner which satisfies none of the five criteria suggested in the first section of this chapter as panhuman indices of abnormality (psychological distortions and sociocultural impairments).* Employing the monastic system as a culturally constituted defense obviates the necessity for Burmese males to erect private defenses which, necessarily, would lead to one or more of these distortions and impairments. Monasticism, in short, has important psychological functions for individual actors. By the same token, however, the psychological problems of these actors have the important cultural function of helping to perpetuate the monastic system; that is, these conflicts are not only resolved by means of the monastic system, but they provide the motivational basis for recruitment to the monastery and, hence, for the persistence of the system. The existence of the monastic system, moreover, not only permits the resolution of emotional conflict (the latent psychological function of the monastery), but by serving this function it reduces the probability of the occurrence of other, nonsanctioned means by which these conflicts might be expressed and resolved (latent social function of the monastery). If this culturally

---

* [Editor's note: Spiro's discussion of these indices is not included in this excerpt. Briefly, they are: 1. *cognitive distortion*—when "a demonstrably false belief is held to be true"; 2. *perceptual distortion*—when "stimuli are perceived to be other than what they are"; 3. *affective distortion*—"any emotional behavior which, relative to the stimulus condition, is characterized by hyper– or hypoaffectivity"; 4. *social impairment*—when "any condition of the actor precludes the performance of social roles"; and 5. *cultural impairment*—when "any condition of the actor precludes compliance with cultural norms and rules."]

constituted defense were not available for the resolution of conflict, the consequent persistence of tension might lead to defenses of a psychotic nature, psychosomatic disorders of various kinds, or many types of anti-social, i.e., criminal behavior. I would suggest that a study of Burmese crime, including dacoity and insurgency—both of which are, and have been, endemic in Burma—would reveal that a large percentage of dacoits and insurgents are recruited from the ranks of those for whom the monastic life is not (for reasons still to be determined) a psychologically viable means for resolving emotional conflict.[2]

The monastic system, in short, not only serves the important personal function of precluding psychotic breakdown, but it also serves the important social function of allowing potentially disruptive, antisocial drives to be channeled into culturally approved (institutional) behavior. Since the monastery, moreover—for reasons beyond the scope of this paper—is the most integrative institution in Burmese society, the social function of psychological conflict, when resolved in this fashion, cannot be overestimated.

If the foregoing analysis is correct, then—to return to the more general problem of this paper—abnormal behavior can be expected to appear under one of three conditions: 1. when emotional conflict is idiosyncratic, so that cultural means are not available as potential bases for culturally constituted defense mechanisms; 2. when emotional conflict is modal, and cultural means are available for conflict resolution, but these means have been inadequately taught or inadequately learned; 3. when, under conditions of rapid social change, culturally constituted defense mechanisms are unavailable, either because older institutions have been discarded or because the new situation creates a new set of conflicts. These three conditions, however, are necessary, but not sufficient, conditions for abnormal behavior. Although emotional conflict is potentially pathogenic, it need not produce pathology. Emotional conflict issues in pathology only if it is not resolved, or if it is resolved in a manner which is characterized by psychological distortion and/or sociocultural impairment. The latter resolutions are characteristic of neurotic and psychotic resolutions.

But neurosis and psychosis are not the only means for resolving conflict. Other private defense mechanisms may be constructed which are perceptually, cognitively, and affectively consistent with the behavioral environment of the actors, and which, moreover, constitute no obstacle to adequate sociocultural functioning. Finally, there is a third category of defense mechanisms—culturally constituted defenses—which are not only not dis-

---

[2] This generalization excludes those—and I have met them—for whom insurgency and dacoity are romantic, adventurous activities to be given up when the adventure palls. It also excludes those whose emotional conflicts are idiosyncratic, rather than culturally patterned, and for which there are no cultural institutions by which conflict can be resolved.

ruptive of, but rather serve to perpetuate, the sociocultural system. Conflict, in short, may indeed produce pathological defenses; but it may also produce normal defenses, either private or culturally constituted.

In most traditional societies, where religious beliefs and practices continue to carry conviction, religion is the cultural system *par excellence* by means of which conflict-resolution is achieved. In such societies, in which religious behavior is appropriate to, rather than disruptive of, the behavioral environment of the actors, and in which a religious world view is consistent with, rather than a distortion of, "reality," religion serves as a highly efficient culturally constituted defense mechanism.

Part V

FAMILY AND KINSHIP

If the last two parts may be said to have been concerned with two of the more basic processes of human adaptation, then the next three parts taken together may be seen as presenting an overview of the ways humans organize themselves socially. In using the word "organize," even though it has dynamic connotations, we risk conjuring up its more static images. In part this is because people tend to see their society as something which "has" structures (e.g., governments, social classes, lineages, secret societies, and so forth) which are enduring "institutions." As with many things, there are advantages to such a perspective of the patterns of behavior in human societies, but there are also advantages to seeing these institutions as dynamic, processual emergents from the countless individual decisions made by all the people in any society. Both vantage points provide valuable insights and the selections in this and the next two parts provide both views.

FAMILY

Whether or not the family is a "universal" depends upon how one defines the family (as is the case for all other "universals"). But by any of several definitions it is fair to say that virtually every society has some form of family. Those instances where there appear to be no families are generally cases where the institution has been lost (sometimes voluntarily, sometimes not) and not instances where such an institution failed to develop.

The discussion by Kathleen Gough in Chapter 14 of the origin and function of the family presents a number of vital issues pertaining fundamentally to our effort to understand the family but also pertaining to our effort to understand the roles of men and women in contemporary contexts. She begins her inquiry by considering the nature of primate societies in general and by drawing upon the fossil record of human evolution. From these

175

considerations, and from inferences made from contemporary hunting and gathering societies, Gough makes several observations about the function (and by implication, albeit indirectly, the origin) of the family and especially of the role of women in it. She notes that the record gives us no evidence of a "feminist Golden Age" or of matriarchical societies, but she also insists, as do all anthropologists, that this "does not mean that women and men have never had relations that were dignified and creative for both sexes. Nor does it mean that the sexes cannot be equal in the future, or that the sexual division of labor cannot be abolished." Views to the contrary, she suggests, are an outgrowth of our male dominated society. Perhaps, but they may also be another example of the widespread tendency people exhibit for making unwarranted projections from the past into the future. In either case, the future status of the family and of women would seem to be an open, not a closed, issue.

As all societies appear to have some form of family, so also does it appear that they all have some regulations about who can have sexual relationships with whom. Not only are there regulations, but there are strong punishments which potentially at least may be meted out to those who deviate from them. In the vast majority of cases, these so-called "incest taboos" pertain to sexual relationships between parents and offspring and between siblings. Several basic questions have been asked about these prohibitions, although no answer has received the unqualified support of even a sizable majority of anthropologists. The questions are about the origins and functions of these restrictions. In general, the answers seem to be one or another of two kinds. One suggests that these rules and prohibitions emerged in an evolutionary process (like most other rules), with societies that had such rules enjoying an adaptive advantage over those without them. These include some presumed genetic advantages (in the form of reductions in the number of malformed offspring) as well as social ones (e.g., forcing the exchange of women for marriage, thus increasing the number of groups with which productive interaction was possible). These views are not necessarily wrong, but they certainly do not explain the whole story, and some versions of these answers have very serious problems. For example, the genetic advantages of nonincestuous mating are not completely unequivocal, and the advantages of marrying outside the family do not account adequately for the rules against having sex within the family. Also, most of these views rest upon an assumption, often hidden, that humans have a strong (some would say innate) desire to copulate with parents and siblings (Freud's analysis, for example, depends upon such an assumption).

There are, however, several theories which do not build upon these assumptions. The most elaborate and well-known of these is that of Westermarck. Rather than assuming humans are strongly attracted to such behavior, his theory suggests that they are uninterested in having sex with those they live with in a family context. In a word, Westermarck's theory suggests that "familiarity breeds contempt (for breeding)." The essay by Arthur Wolf in Chapter 15 presents data from Taiwan which bears upon Westermarck's hypothesis. As Wolf stresses, these data do not give final confirmation to this hypothesis, but they are consistent with the main elements of it. To express the implications of Westermarck's hypothesis and Wolf's data in a rather different way, it would appear the widespread (if not universal) rules against incest no more justify the assumption that humans have a natural desire for sex with closely related individuals than the widespread (if not universal) rules against murder justify the assumption that humans have a natural desire to commit this act.

The societies of the world provide us with a wide variety of practices included within the term "marriage." Many individuals in our society are currently exhibiting quite a bit of creativity in this part of the human experience. Although there are only a few letters appearing in Ann Landers' columns about the problems young (and not-so-young) people are encountering as they embark upon these relatively unfamiliar paths, there are quite a few to be found in other parts of the world where different but comparable explorations are underway. Some of these are analyzed by Gustav Jahoda in Chapter 16.

Several main themes are developed in his essay, including the fundamental question about social change and the loss of norms by which people may judge their behavior. Does rapid social change produce anomie or the condition of being normless? Are there conflicts between traditional norms, as for example in regard to marriage, and the new norms being introduced to many parts of the world (including West Africa)? At the most general level, these questions are difficult to answer, but at the level of the concerns of specific individuals, as expressed in letters to advice columns, the answer would appear to be a qualified "yes." That is, there are certainly norms in these areas of rapid change; the problem is there are too many and they are not always compatible.

A second major theme in Jahoda's essay has to do with the kinds of problems young people seem to write about to the newspapers and magazines he sampled. Although the data are not without their potential biases, it is noteworthy that many of the problems are not that unfamiliar to us—dealing with family opposition to marriage plans, and handling the complexities introduced into a relationship when individuals vary greatly in ethnic background, age, level of education and the like. There are problems, however, which are not so familiar to our experiences—the role of parents in picking a spouse, basic questions about "love," and problems associated with taking the initiative in establishing a relationship with another person. In the final analysis, it would appear that whatever the place and however rapid the change, we may expect the advice columnists of the world will always have marital problems to solve.

KINSHIP

There are few other dimensions of the human experience which have been as elaborately assessed by anthropologists as kinship. Indeed, there are so many distinct and complex issues in this area that it is not possible to represent them in even three or four brief selections, let alone one. So it must be stressed that the essay by Thomas Beidelman is not presented as an overview of the field. His fascinating analysis is presented for different reasons. From the viewpoint of most beginning students of anthropology (not to mention quite a few advanced members of the profession), kinship is the most esoteric subject of the discipline. It is not surprising that Americans find this subject a bit anachronistic, for kinship itself is virtually an anachronism in our society. And while it is easily and often said that kinship is of great importance to the vast majority of the world's peoples, most anthropological discussions of this subject hardly provide much in the way of support for this contention. Unlike other topics in anthropology, one gets the impression it is possible to discuss kinship only with complex diagrams, bizarre terminologies of incredible length, and, ironically, by leaving out people!

Lineage structures, terminological systems, interpersonal relationships— all tend to be presented in the driest way possible. Beidelman's essay in Chapter 17, however, is notable in part because it so clearly is outside this trend. Not coincidentally, the essay is an analysis of a folktale. One major function of such tales, of course, is to use fantasy to instruct people about reality; the tale of hyena and rabbit certainly does that. In it, the implications of a matrilineal social system are shown with a realism that is too often absent in other accounts. Here, also, the importance of the basic conflict posed by the fact that men have authority but women forge the links between kinsmen is clearly presented. We can empathize with the dual role of women—as sisters and as mothers, and the conflict such a dual role can lead to is easily understood. And the implications of the death of a senior member of a kin group—an event which introduces new sources for conflict, segmentation and for shifts in the balance of power— can be fully appreciated. This is what kinship is really all about. It is real people working out day-to-day relationships with, whether we like it or not, all those hard to remember terms and those difficult to follow relationships very clearly in their minds. The trick is to get them into ours.

Finally, we may note that it is sometimes suggested that all of the basic issues discussed by the authors of the articles in Part V stem, ultimately from two very basic facts of life—that human reproduction is sexual and that the resulting offspring are so immature at birth that they require extended care before they can survive "on their own." While these well known facts of life are indisputably true, they most certainly do not in and of themselves account for the observed behavior of humans as it pertains to these facts. For as others have noted, such facts are only the beginning of what it is to be human. Indeed, being human is fundamentally being more than "natural"; it is, in a word, being "cultural." Faced with these basic facts of life, other organisms have simply lived by them; humans build upon them. Humans do not do the minimum necessary in order to survive; in a sense, they do the maximum. This is nowhere more clearly demonstrated than in the areas of family and kinship.

Kathleen Gough

14. The Origin of the Family*

Knowledge of how the family arose is interesting to women because it tells us how we differ from prehumans, what our past has been, and what the biological and cultural limitations from which we are now emerging have been. It shows us how generations of male scholars have distorted or overinterpreted evidence to bolster beliefs in the inferiority of women's mental processes—for which there is no foundation in fact. Knowing about early families is also important to correct the reverse bias among some feminist writers, who hold that there have been "matriarchal" societies where women were dominant over men. For this, too, there is no evidence.

The trouble with discussing the origin of the family is that no one really knows. It is not known *when* the family originated, although it was probably between 2 million and 100,000 years ago. It is not known whether it developed once or in separate times and places. It is not known whether some kind of family came before, with, or after the origin of language. Since language is the accepted criterion of humanness, this means that we do not even know whether our ancestors acquired the basics of family life before or after they were "human." The chances are that language and the family developed together over a long period, but the evidence is sketchy.

Although we can only speculate about the origin of the family, it is

* Reprinted with permission of author and publisher from *Up From Under* Magazine, vol. 1 no. 3, 1971:47–52. A somewhat longer and more technical version of this article appeared in the *Journal of Marriage and the Family*, November 1971.

better to speculate with than without evidence. The evidence comes from three sources. One is the social and physical lives of nonhuman primates— especially the New and Old World monkeys and, still more, the great apes, humanity's closest relatives. The second source is the tools and home sites of prehumans and prehistoric humans. The third is the family lives of hunters and gatherers of wild food who have been studied in modern times.

None of these sources tells the whole story, but together they give valuable clues.

WHAT IS THE FAMILY?

Some kind of family exists in all known human societies, although it is not found in every segment or class of all societies. Greek and American slaves, for example, were prevented from forming legal families, and their social families were often disrupted by sale, forced labor, or the sexual demands of the master. Even so, the family has always been an ideal which most people attained when they could.

The family implies several things: 1. Rules forbid sexual relations and marriage between close relatives. 2. The men and women of a family cooperate through a division of labor based on their sex; this varies in different societies in rigidity and in the tasks performed, but in no human society has it ever been entirely absent. Child care and household tasks tend to be done by women; war, hunting, and government by men. 3. Marriage exists as a socially recognized, durable, though not necessarily lifelong, relationship between individual men and women. From it springs social fatherhood, some kind of special bond between a man and the children of his wife. This bond of *social* fatherhood is universal even among people who do not know about the male role in reproduction, or where, for various reasons, it is not clear who the physiological father of a particular infant is. 4. Men in general have higher status and an authority over the women of their families, although older women may have influence or even some authority over younger men. This is contrary to the belief of some feminists that there have existed societies where women had paramount authority over men, either in the home or in society at large. But it does not mean that women and men have never had relations that were dignified and creative for both sexes. Nor does it mean that the sexes cannot be equal in the future, or that the sexual division of labor cannot be abolished. I believe that it can and must be. But we don't have to believe myths of a feminist Golden Age in order to plain for this in the future.

(It is true that in those few societies where group-membership and inheritance are passed down through the mother, women tend to have greater independence than in societies where these are passed through the father. Such societies are called "matrilineal." An example of how they work is that you would take the name of your mother rather than that of your father. Women are especially independent in those matrilineal tribal societies where the men come to live in the homes or villages of their wives —called "matrilocal" societies. But even here, the ultimate leadership of households, lineages, and local groups is with the men. In some other matrilineal societies, the men live separately from their wives, in different families. But then women and children fall under the authority of male relatives—their oldest brother, their mothers' brothers, or even their grown-up sons.)

PRIMATE SOCIETIES

A number of well-known anthropologists have argued that various attitudes and customs often found in human societies are instinctual rather than culturally learned, and come from our primate heritage. They include among these hierarchies of ranking among men, male political power over women, the greater sexual self-restraint, fidelity, and submissiveness of women, and the greater tendency of men to form friendships with one another, as opposed to women's tendencies to cling to a man. I cannot accept these conclusions and think they stem from the male dominance of our own society. A "scientific" argument which states that all such features of female inferiority are instinctive is obviously a powerful weapon in maintaining male dominance in the traditional family. But in fact these features do *not* exist among all nonhuman primates, and certainly not in some of those most closely related to humans. Chimpanzees have little male dominance and male hierarchy and both males and females are sexually indiscriminate. Gibbons have a kind of fidelity for both sexes and almost no male dominance or hierarchy. Howler monkeys are sexually indiscriminate and lack male hierarchies or dominance.

The fact is that among nonhuman primates male dominance and male hierarchies seem to be adaptations to particular environments, though some have eventually become genetically established through natural selection. Among humans, however, these features are present in very variable degrees and are almost certainly learned, not inherited at all. Among nonhuman primates there are fairly general differences between those that live mainly in trees and those that live largely in the ground. Where defense is important, among ground dwellers, males are much larger and stronger than females, exert dominance over females, and are strictly organized in hierarchical relation to one another. Among tree dwellers, where defense is less important, there is much less difference in size between male and female, less or no male dominance, a less obvious male hierarchy, and greater sexual indiscriminance.

As among chimpanzees, the difference in size between males and females among humans is small. Chimpanzees live in forest or semi-forest habitats. They build individual nests to sleep in, sometimes on the ground but usually in trees. They flee into trees from danger. Chimpanzees go mainly on all fours, but sometimes on two feet, and can use and make simple tools. Males are dominant, but not very dominant, over females. The hierarchy among males is unstable, and males often move between groups, which vary in size from two to fifty individuals. Food is vegetarian, supplemented with worms, grubs, or occasional small animals. A mother and her young form the only stable unit. Sexual relations are largely indiscriminate, but nearby males defend young animals from danger. The chances are that our prehuman ancestors—whose lives provide the second clue to the origin of the family—had a social life similar to the chimpanzees'.

HUMAN EVOLUTION

From the fossil record we know that apes ancestral to humans, gorillas, and chimpanzees roamed widely in Asia, Europe, and Africa some 12 to 28 million years ago. Toward the end of that period (the Miocene) a species appeared in North India and East Africa which seems to be the direct ancestor of modern humans. Called Ramapithecus, members of this species were small like gibbons, walked upright on two feet, had human rather than ape corner teeth, and therefore probably used hands rather than teeth to tear their food. From that time on, evolution toward humanness must have gone through various phases until the emergence of modern *homo sapiens* about 70,000 years ago.

In the Miocene period, before Ramapithecus appeared, there were several periods in which, over large areas, the climate became drier and subtropical forests dwindled or disappeared. A standard reconstruction of events, which I accept, is that groups of apes, probably in Africa, had to come down from the trees and adapt to life on the ground. Probably over millions of years, they developed specialized feet for walking. Thus freed, the hands came to be used not only (as among apes) for grasping and tearing, but for carrying objects such as weapons or infants (who had previously clung to their mothers' body hair).

Drought, and the spread of indigestible grasses on the open savannahs, forced the early ground dwellers to become active hunters rather than simply to forage for small, sick, or dead animals that came their way. Hunting and tool use involved group cooperation and helped foster the growth of language. Language meant greatly increased foresight, memory, planning, and division of tasks—in short, the capacity for human thought.

With the change to hunting, group territories became much larger. Apes travel only a few thousand feet daily; hunters, several miles. But because their infants were helpless, nursing women could hunt only small game or gather vegetarian produce close to home. This then produced the sexual division of labor on which the human family has since been founded. Out of the sexual division of labor came, for the first time, home life as well as group cooperation. Female apes nest with and provide foraged food for their infants, but adult apes do not cooperate with each other in food getting or nest building. They build new nests each night wherever they may happen to be. With the development of a hunting and gathering economy, it became necessary to have a headquarters or home. Men could bring several days' supply of meat there; women and children could meet men there after the day's hunting, and could bring their vegetable produce.

Later, fire came into use for protection against wild animals, for lighting, and eventually for cooking. The hearth then provided the focus and symbol of home. With the development of cookery, some humans—chiefly women, and perhaps some children and old men—began to spend more time preparing food so that people needed to spend less time chewing and tearing.

The change to humanness brought two bodily changes that affected birth and child care. These were width of pelvis and head size. Walking upright produced a narrower pelvis to hold the guts in position; and, as language developed, brains grew much bigger in relation to body size. Because of this, humans are born at an earlier stage of growth than apes. They are helpless longer and require longer and more total care. This caused early women to concentrate more fully on child care and less on defense than do female apes.

Language made possible not only a division and cooperation in labor but also all forms of tradition, rules, morality, and cultural learning. Rules banning sex relations among close relatives must have come very early. Precisely how or why they developed is unknown, but they had at least two useful functions: they helped to maintain the family as a cooperative unit by outlawing competition for mates within it, and they created bonds *between* families, or even between separate bands, and so provided a basis for wider cooperation in the struggle for livelihood and the expansion of knowledge. Although the evidence of dates is disputable, I think that this type of family life—built around tool use, the use of language, cooking, and a sexual division of labor—must have been established sometime between 500,000 and 200,000 years ago.

HUNTERS AND GATHERERS

Societies based on hunting and gathering were widespread about 15,000 to 10,000 years ago—after the ice ages but before the invention of farming and the domestication of animals. This period makes up 99 percent of human history. We have learned about these societies from studying the few similar ones that exist today. Though by no means "primeval," the hunters of recent times do offer clues to the types of families found among early hunters.

Modern hunters live in forest, mountain, arctic, or desert areas where farming is impractical. They include the Eskimo, many Canadian and South American Indian groups, the forest BaMbuti (pygmies), and the desert Bushmen of Southern Africa, the Kadar of South India, the Veddah of Ceylon, and the Andaman Islanders of the Indian Ocean. About 175 hunting and gathering cultures in Oceania, Asia, Africa, and America have been described by various anthropologists in fair detail.

In spite of their varied environments, hunters share certain features of social life. They live in bands of about 20 to 200 people, the majority having fewer than 50. Bands are divided into families, which in some seasons may forage along. Hunters have simple but ingenious technologies. Bows and arrows, spears, needles, skin clothing, and temporary leaf or wood shelters are common. Most hunters do some fishing. The band forages and hunts in a large territory and usually moves camp often.

Social life is egalitarian. There is no centralized government based on force. Except for religious shamans or magicians, the division of labor is based only on sex and age. Everyone who can works. Resources are owned communally and tools and personal possessions are exchanged freely. Band leadership goes to whichever man has the intelligence, courage, and foresight to command the respect of his fellows. Intelligent older women are also looked up to.

Within each household, the men, women, and children divide the work to be done and pool their produce. Where hunting and fishing are not entirely limited to men, they are chiefly men's jobs. Gathering of wild plants, fruits, and nuts is women's work. Men monopolize fighting, although interband warfare is rare. Women, more than men, care for children and shelters and do most of the cooking. In different societies men, women, or both may build homes or make tools, ornaments, and clothing. Girls help the women and boys play at hunting or hunt small game. The men of a whole band or of some smaller cluster of households sometimes cooperate in hunting or fishing and divide their spoils. Women of nearby families may go gathering together.

Family cooperation varies among hunters as it does in other kinds of societies. About half or more of known hunting societies are made up mostly of nuclear families (father, mother, and children), with some polygynous families (a man, two or more wives, and children) among them. About a third of hunting societies have what are called "stem-family" households—that is, older parents live together with one married child and grandchildren, while other married children live separately. Large extended families containing several married brothers (or several married sisters), their wives or husbands, and children, can be found in a few hunting societies, but these larger households did not become common until the rise of agriculture. Hunting societies also have few households composed of a widow or divorcee and her children. This is understandable, for neither men nor women can survive long without the work and produce of the other sex, and marriage is the way to obtain them.

With marriage, monogamy is the normal *practice* for most hunters, but it is not the normal *rule*. Only a few prohibit marriage to more than one person. The most common type of polygynous marriage is a man and two sisters or other closely related women. When someone dies it is common for a sister or brother to replace him or her in marriage.

Many hunting societies hold that the wives of brothers or other close kinsmen are in some senses wives of the group. They can be called on in emergencies or if one of them is ill. Many hunting societies have special times for sexual license between men and women of a local group who are not married to each other, such as the "lights out" games of Eskimos sharing a communal snow-house. In other situations, an Eskimo wife will spend the night with a chance guest of her husband's. This is expected as normal hospitality. Although often punished, adultery tends to be common in hunting societies, and few if any of them forbid divorce or the remarriage of divorcees and widows.

The reason for all this seems to be that marriage and sexual restrictions are practical arrangements among hunters designed mainly to serve economic and survival needs. In these societies, some kind of rather stable pairing best accomplishes the division of labor and cooperation of men and women and the care of children. Beyond the immediate family, either a larger family group or the whole band has other, less intensive, kinds of cooperative activities. Therefore, the husbands and wives of individuals within that group can be summoned to stand in for each other if need arises. In the case of Eskimo wife-lending, the extreme climate and the need for lone wandering in search of game dictate high standards of hospitality. This evidently becomes extended to sexual sharing.

THE POSITION OF WOMEN

Even in hunting societies it seems that women are always in some sense the "second sex," with greater or lesser subordination to men. This varies. Eskimo and Australian aboriginal women are far more subordinate than women among some forest people.

I think that women in hunting societies have greater power when they actually produce raw materials than when they mainly process meat or other supplies provided by men. The former situation is likelier to exist where gathering is important and where hunting is small scale than where it extends over a large territory.

In hunting societies, however, women are less subordinated in certain crucial respects than they are in all or most of the early states, or even in some modern industrial countries. These include men's ability to deny women sex or to force it upon them; to command or exploit their labor; to control or rob them of their children; to confine them physically and prevent their movement; to sell or exchange them for other objects of value; to cramp their creativeness; or to keep education and culture from them.

The power of men to exploit women systematically springs from the existence of accumulated wealth, and linked with that, from the rise of a centralized government (the state). Among hunters things are simple. There is only the family, and beyond it the band. With the domestication of plants and animals, the economy becomes more productive. Tribes form, combining several thousand people loosely organized into large kin groups such as clans and lineages, each composed of a number of related families. With still further development of the productive forces the society throws up a central political leadership, together with craft specialization and trade, and so the chiefdom emerges. But this, too, is structured through ranked allegiances and marriage ties between kin groups, and the chief does not have supreme power over the whole society. Eventually, however, with the development of stable, irrigated farm sites and other kinds of valuable property, the state arises. (This first happened between five and six thousand years ago.) In the state, there is a central government and a professional army, and there are economic classes—some of which own the land and control other people, while others have no property and must work for masters. With the rise of the state, most of the new positions of power in the army, the police, or the government were filled by men, partly because men already controlled the weapons and did the fighting, and partly because freedom from child care allowed men to enter specialized political and economic roles. Within the state, men of the propertied classes gained new powers to control the labor and persons both of other men and of women, while the men of all classes became vested with powers of guardianship and custody over the women and children of their own families, since the family became a legal unit—a kind of minor branch—of the state. The position of women reached its lowest ebb in the large agricultural states, where there were such customs as female foot-binding in China, the burning of widows in India, or witch burning in Europe and North America. There were also the kind of male possessiveness and exclusiveness regarding women that lead to such institutions as savage punishments or death for female adultery, the jealous guarding of female chastity and virginity, the denial of divorce to women, and female slavery, and male control over female labor and produce. These kinds of male power are shadowy or absent among hunters.

To the extent that men do have power over women in hunting societies, it seems to spring from the male monopoly of heavy weapons, from the particular division of labor between the sexes, or from both. Although men seldom use weapons against women, they *possess* them (or possess superior weapons) in addition to their physical strength. This does give men an ultimate control of force. When old people or babies must be killed for the survival of others, it is usually men who do the killing. The killing of babies—rather common among hunters, who must limit the mouths to feed —is more often female infanticide than male. Because men hunt they seem to have a greater need to organize in groups than do women. Perhaps because of this, in about 60 percent of hunting societies men choose which band to live in (often, their fathers'), and women move with their husbands. This gives a man advantages over his wife in terms of familiarity and loyalties, for the wife is often a stranger. In 16 to 17 percent of hunting societies, however, men move to the households of their wives, while in 15 to 17 percent either sex may move in with the other on marriage.

Probably because of male cooperation in defense and hunting, men are more prominent in band councils and leadership, in medicine and magic, and in public rituals designed to increase game, to ward off sickness, or to initiate boys into manhood. Women do, however, often take part in band councils—they are not excluded from leadership as in many farming states. Some women are respected as wise leaders, story tellers, doctors, or magicians, or are feared as witches. Women have their own ceremonies of fertility, birth, and healing from which men are often excluded.

In some societies, although men control the most sacred objects, women are believed to have discovered them. Among the Congo Pygmies, for example, religion centers about a beneficent spirit, the Animal of the Forest. It is represented by wooden trumpets that are owned and played by men when hunting is bad, someone falls ill, or death occurs. Their possession and use are hidden from the women. Yet the men believe that women originally owned the trumpet and that it was also a woman who stole the sacred camp-fires from the chimpanzees or from the forest spirit. When a woman has been infertile for several years, a special ceremony is held. Women lead in songs and an old woman kicks apart the campfires. Temporary female dominance seems to be thought necessary to restore fertility.

Because two thirds of modern hunting societies are patrilocal (the women go to live with their husbands in the husband's band) some male anthropologists have concluded that all hunting societies were patrilocal until the recent period of European contact. It seems just as likely, however, that among the *earliest* hunters men went to live with their wives. Among apes and monkeys it is almost always males who leave a troop or are driven out. Females stay closer to their mothers and their original sites; males move about, attaching themselves to females where they are able. The removal of the wife to the husband's home or band may have been a relatively late development in hunting societies where there was extensive hunting of large animals. Later still, after the domestication of plants and animals, men often moved to their wives' homes in societies where female gardening was important, but women moved to their husbands' homes where the herding of large animals predominated. With the invention of plough agriculture after 4,000 B.C., men came to control agriculture, and in most of the great farming states women moved to their husbands' homes and families were strongly male dominated.

CONCLUSIONS

The family is a human institution, not found in its totality in any pre-human species. It required language, planning, cooperation, self-control, foresight, and cultural learning, and probably developed along with these.

The family was made desirable by the early human combination of prolonged child care with the need for hunting with weapons over large areas. The sexual division of labor on which it was based grew out of a prehuman division between male defense and female child care. But among humans this division became for the first time crucial for food production and so laid the basis for future economic specialization and cooperation.

Together with tool use and language, the family was no doubt the most significant invention of the human revolution. All three required reflective thought, which above all accounts for the vast superiority in consciousness that separates humans from apes.

The family provided the framework for all pre-state society. In groping for the survival of their species and the flowering of their knowledge, human beings learned to control their sexual desires and to suppress their individual selfishness, aggression, and competition. The other side of this self-control was an increased capacity for love—not only the love of a mother for her child, which is seen among apes, but of male for female in enduring relationships, and of each sex for ever widening groups of people. Civilization would have been impossible without the initial self-control of incest prohibitions and the generosity and moral orderliness of primitive family life.

From the start, women have been subordinate to men in certain key areas of status, mobility, and public leadership. But before the agricultural revolution, and even for several thousand years after, this inequality was based mainly on the fact that women had to bear and nurse their children while men had to hunt and fight. It was largely a matter of survival rather than of human-made cultural impositions. From this springs the impressions we receive of dignity, freedom, and mutual respect between men and women in primitive hunting societies.

The past of the family does not limit its future. Although the family probably emerged with humanity, neither the family itself nor particular family forms are genetically determined. The sexual division of labor—until recently universal—need not and should not survive in industrial society. Prolonged child care will cease to be a woman's main role in life when artificial birth control, spaced births, bottle feeding, and communal nurseries will allow it to be shared by men. We now have the technology to make these things reality. Recent technological advances also remove most of the heavy work for which women are less well equipped than men.

The family was essential to the dawn of civilization, allowing a vast leap forward in cooperation, knowledge, love, and creativeness. But today, rather than enhancing women, confining them in their homes with small families artificially limits these human capacities. It may be that the human gift for personal love will make some form of voluntary, individual, long-term sexual relationships and companionship, and individual devotion between parents and children, continue indefinitely, side by side with public responsibility for domestic tasks and for the care and upbringing of children. There is no need to legislate personal relations out of existence. But neither need we fear a social life in which the family as a legal unit is no more.

Arthur B. Wolf

15. Childhood Association and Sexual Attraction: A Further Test of the Westermarck Hypothesis*

In the view of most social theorists, the incest taboo is imposed on man for the sake of society. It is generally agreed that this taboo is necessary, but many reasons have been given to explain why. Edward Westermarck's suggestion to the contrary was widely criticized by his contemporaries and rarely receives favorable mention in more recent discussions of the subject. Not much more than supposition was needed to convict Westermarck of folly. With the exception of questionable evidence presented by psychoanalysts, the case against his hypothesis rests on Sir James Frazer's insistence that "the law only forbids men to do what their instincts incline them to do" (1910[4]:97). This criticism was quoted, as Westermarck himself wryly noted, "with much appreciation by Dr. Freud" (1922[2]: 203) and is obviously the source of Leslie White's claim that "Westermarck's thesis . . . is not in accord with the facts in the first place and would still be inadequate if it were. Propinquity does not annihilate sexual desire, and if it did there would be no need for stringent prohibitions" (1948:420).

The reason for this ready acceptance of Frazer's critique of Westermarck is obvious. In explaining the incest taboo as the social means of achieving the advantages of mating and marrying outside of the family, anthropologists have had to assume that men are naturally inclined to mate and

* Reproduced by permission of the American Anthropological Association from the *American Anthropologist*, vol. 72 no. 3, 1970:503–15. Permission of the author is also gratefully acknowledged.

marry within the family. If intimate childhood association were sufficient to preclude sexual interest, as Westermarck hypothesized, the incest taboo would not be necessary to obtain the biological advantages of out-breeding. Mankind would not have been faced with those momentous choices pictured so vividly by White and Claude Lévi-Strauss. They would not have had to choose "between biological families living in juxtaposition and endeavoring to remain closed, self-perpetuating units, overridden by their fears, hatreds, and ignorances, and the systematic establishment, through the incest prohibition, of links of intermarriage between them," the condition of "a true human society" (Lévi-Strauss 1960:278). The tide that has run so long against Westermarck is drawn by the assumption that "the emergence of human society required some suppression, rather than a direct expression, of man's primate nature" (Sahlins 1960:77).

This tide has at last begun to turn. We now know that the social life of subhuman primates is not characterized by "selfishness, indiscriminate sexuality, dominance and brute competition" (Sahlins 1960:86). The chimpanzees observed in the Yerkes Laboratories engage in purposive cooperation and often evince "a capacity—or weakness—for developing a nondestructive interest in others" (Hebb and Thompson 1968:744). Recent field studies of Japanese and rhesus macaques show that the young males of the species do not commonly choose to mate with their mothers (Imanishi 1961; Kaufman 1965; Tokuda 1961–62; Sade 1968). The purpose of this paper is to provide another example challenging the view that man's behavior in society is largely a creation of society. The data reported continue but do not conclude an argument initiated in an article published in this journal in 1966. They do not explain the incest taboo and do not tell us why childhood association and sexual attraction are antithetical; they only suggest that there is "a remarkable absence of erotic feelings between persons living very closely together from childhood" (Westermarck 1922[2]:vi).

The locale of my first study was a small Chinese village in northern Taiwan. It is situated near the town of Shulin on the west bank of the Tamsui River. Twelve miles upstream, on the edge of the central mountain range, is an old riverport known as Sanhsia, the commercial center of the area included in my second study. The native residents of both communities are Hokkien-speaking Chinese whose ancestors migrated to Taiwan from southern Fukien in the seventeenth and eighteenth centuries. Because of their common origins and frequent intermarriage, the people of the entire area, from Shulin at one end of the valley to Sanhsia at the other, support the same institutions and share similar expectations about the nature of family life. There is therefore no need to repeat here the background information provided in my two previous papers. I simply remind the reader that customary law in this area of China recognizes two distinct forms of virilocal marriage. One I term the major form of marriage: the bride enters her husband's home as a young adult, often not meeting the groom until the day of the wedding. The other I call the minor form of marriage: the bride is taken into her future husband's household in infancy or early childhood and raised as a member of his family. These two forms of marriage provide a unique opportunity to test the Westermarck hypothesis. The major form of marriage forges a conjugal bond between strangers; the minor form unites a couple whose experience of one another is as intimate as brother and sister.

In comparing reactions to these two forms of marriage we must always keep in mind the changes that have overcome this area of Taiwan in recent years. When Taiwan was ceded to Japan in 1895 as one consequence of the first Sino-Japanese War, life along the southern edges of the Taipei basin was as conservative as anywhere in China. Camphor and tea from the hills around Shulin and Sanhsia were poled down the Tamsui River to Taipei, where they were transshipped to foreign markets, but the foreigners and the influences they brought to China did not move upstream into the rural areas of the basin. The early years of the Japanese occupation did little to change this pattern. Although the new colonial government quickly extended police control into the villages and registered the land and the population, these changes did not challenge the authority of Chinese custom or create pressure for change. The full impact of the Japanese presence did not reach the rural areas until twenty years later when the government completed an improved transportation network and established schools in the villages and rural towns. Until that time people living outside of the city earned their livelihoods in agriculture or by means of small family businesses; they now sought employment in the coal mines opened along the edge of the basin and in new industries like the Hsulin winery. A few of the more fortunate graduated from local schools and then sought further education and employment in the city.

It was not long before these new opportunities began to have an effect on family life. Young married couples continued to live with their parents, as they do even today, but the internal structure of the family changed. Whereas young people had previously deferred to their parents in all important decisions, including decisions about their own marriages, they now began to demand more of a voice in family affairs, particularly the right to some influence in the choice of husbands and wives. The basis of their demand was economic. If a young man's parents tried to force him into an unsatisfactory marriage, he could leave the family and support himself by a job in the mines or in the city. The threat of desertion was usually enough to make the parents acquiesce. While the changes brought about by the Japanese occupation freed young people from a dependence on their parents, it did not free the parents from a dependence on their children. The new government did not offer pensions or open homes for the aged. Without children to support him in his old age a man was no better off in 1930 than he would have been in 1830.

One of the first consequences of this change of authority in the family was a sharp decline in the frequency of the minor form of marriage. In the first two decades of this century the minor form of marriage accounted for nearly half of all virilocal marriages; by the end of the Japanese occupation the proportion of minor marriages had dropped to less than ten percent of the total. This change was not a result of parents deciding that the minor form of marriage was no longer so advantageous as it had once been, but was rather a direct result of emancipated young people refusing to marry a childhood associate. This is evident in the fact that the frequency of this form of marriage began to decline a decade before the rate of female adoption (Wolf 1966:886). Parents continued to adopt girls to raise as wives for their sons until it became apparent that young people could no longer be forced to consummate these arrangements. Even today a few families raise girls in the hope of somehow persuading a son to marry in the minor fashion. They are always disappointed. One old man who had adopted a wife for his favorite grandson told me that he wanted them to marry "because that girl has always been very good to me, but I don't know whether they will or not. You just can't tell young people what to do anymore."

Were degree of childhood association the only difference between the two forms of marriage, this refusal of young people to marry a childhood associate would go a long way toward proving Westermarck's contention. But unfortunately this is not the only difference between the two forms of marriage. As I have pointed out in previous papers, the major form of marriage has advantages that might incline young people to prefer it to the minor form (1966:887–8; 1968:866–7). It is the right and proper way to marry, the prestigious way to take a wife, and it provides the new couple with a dowry and the advantages of dependable affinal ties. Anthropologists who are inclined to look for sociological explanations will immediately see that young people's dislike of the minor form of marriage may be motivated by practical rather than personal concerns. They may be seeking prestige and practical advantage rather than trying to avoid sexual intercourse with a childhood associate.

This explanation of the decline of the minor form of marriage sounds reasonable, probably because prestige and practical advantage are such common goals of human behavior. When I first encountered the problem, it did not occur to me to look for any other explanation, but talking to people about their attitude toward the minor form of marriage convinced me that this was a mistake. Chinese villagers, regardless of education, are articulate, socially sophisticated people; they understand many of the intricacies of their own society and are capable of verbalizing their insights. They can discuss at length the advantages and disadvantages of marrying a mother's brother's daughter and are well aware of the sociological consequences of the major and minor forms of marriage (Wolf 1968:871). They enjoy talking about the social calculations involved in deciding the appropriate value of wedding and funeral gifts. If young people objected to the minor form of marriage because it is less prestigeful and entails certain practical disadvantages, I think they would say so. But of the many people I have talked to, not one has given me these reasons for not wanting to marry in this fashion. Asked why they do not want to marry a childhood associate, most informants blush and become inarticulate. All they say is that "it's embarrassing" or "uninteresting" or "difficult because people who are raised together know one another's hearts too well." They obviously are not thinking of the relative prestige of the two forms of marriage, the size of the dowry, or the value of affinal alliances.

These reactions give me confidence in the Westermarck hypothesis, but they will not do as proof of the hypothesis. The evidence rests too heavily on my impressions of the people I am studying. A better way of determining the relative importance of personal and practical concerns is to compare the conjugal relationships created by the two forms of marriage. If the resistance to the minor form of marriage is motivated by practical considerations, a couple raised together should be no less satisfied with one another than those who first meet as young adults. They may resent having their best interests sacrificed by their parents, but this is not likely to disrupt permanently their relations as husband and wife. If, on the other hand, the source of the resistance is a sexual aversion rooted in childhood association, it should persist and permanently mar the conjugal relationship. Couples raised together should be less intimate and more prone to marital discord than those brought together by the major form of marriage.

The problem becomes one of assessing the quality of the marital relationship. The ideal measure would be frequency of sexual intercourse and degree of sexual satisfaction, but it is difficult to obtain that kind of information in any society and next to impossible in China. Willing as they are to talk about the money a relative wastes on prostitutes and winehouse girls or the possibility that a neighbor is not his son's genitor, few Chinese will discuss the sexual act itself, and I doubt that any would be willing to talk about his experience with his own spouse. There is no point in even asking. Because the Chinese kinship system views the parent-child relationship as pivotal, the conjugal relationship is ideally distant and unemotional. Husband and wife must avoid displaying any sign of personal intimacy outside of the privacy of their own bedroom. Under these conditions couples who enjoyed the most blissful of relations would probably deny any interest in one another.

The only alternative is to look for the effects of marital dissatisfaction on other aspects of behavior. In my first study I made use of village gossip to identify men who commonly seek the company of prostitutes or neglect their wives in favor of mistresses. As one would expect if childhood association promotes sexual aversion, the majority of these men had married in the minor fashion (Wolf 1966:889–90). The problem I faced in returning to Taiwan last year was how to replicate this finding with a larger sample. Although I have since had occasion to doubt the wisdom of my choice, I decided to rely on the information available in the household registration records. Initiated by the Japanese at the turn of the century and maintained by the present Chinese government, these remarkable records contain a complete history of the composition of every family on the island. I made two predictions that could be tested by an examination of these materials. Assuming a weakening of the conjugal bond as a result of sexual aversion, I predicted a higher divorce rate among minor marriages than among major marriages. And assuming a tendency for couples subject to an aversion to avoid sexual relations for long periods of time, I also predicted a lower birth rate.

By the time this test of the hypothesis was formulated, I was already living in Sanhsia and had made the acquaintance of the officials in charge of the local household registration office. I therefore decided to use these records for a preliminary test and chose for this purpose two of the districts into which Sanhsia Chen is divided. The two districts are located at the foot of the central mountain range on opposite sides of one of the tributaries of the Tamsui River. The district on one side of the stream includes four small hamlets, each clustered about a lineage hall; the district on the opposite side contains one large village with a number of small shops and a new temple. The majority of the men of both districts are descended from the ancestors enshrined in one or another of the four lineage halls; all but a few earn their livings as farmers, coal miners, laborers, or through a small family business. The differences between the wealthiest families and the poorest are too slight to support elaborate social distinctions. A local saying has it that the wealthy mix sweet potatoes with their rice while the poor mix rice with their sweet potatoes.

To avoid the complicating effects of social change I limited my sample to marriages contracted between 1900 and 1925. Since birth rates on Taiwan were rising at the same time that the frequency of minor marriages was declining, inclusion of marriages recorded after 1925 would produce an entirely spurious correlation between form of marriage and birth rates. There is also a danger that social change intensified the dissatisfaction of young people forced to marry a childhood associate. Those parents who insisted on the minor form of marriage after some had capitulated probably had to use exceptional means to see the arrangements consummated. If we included in our sample marriages contracted during the transitional period, the result would likely be a spuriously high rate of divorce among the minor marriages. As the reader can see by examining the information given in Table 1, the present sample avoids both these pitfalls. The relative frequency of major and minor marriages remains constant throughout the twenty-five-year period. Any differences we find between the two forms of marriage cannot be traced to rising birth rates or the resentment of young people who were allowed no choice in marriage after choice had

TABLE 1

Married Women by Type of Marriage and Year of Marriage

Year of Marriage	Minor Marriage	Major Marriage	Total by Year
1900–1905	26	38	64
1906–1910	17	31	48
1911–1915	22	34	56
1916–1920	29	34	63
1921–1925	38	34	72
Totals	132	171	303

become a possibility. The absence of a decline in the proportion of minor marriages argues that parents managed to preserve their traditional authority until sometime after 1925.

I also decided to limit my sample to marriages contracted by the end of the bride's twenty-fifth year. Since all second marriages are necessarily of the major form, this was done to keep the ages of the two halves of my sample roughly comparable. Even with this limitation the average age of women married in the major fashion is nearly two years older than the average age of those married in the minor fashion. Since this difference could affect both birth and divorce rates, it is important to note that these effects work against rather than for the hypothesis. If we find that minor marriages produce more divorces and fewer children, it is clearly not a consequence of the bride's youth. Women who marry earlier have more time to get a divorce and more time to bear children. This effect of the earlier age at which minor marriages are contracted may be offset by the bride's being too young to bear children and too much of a child to consider

TABLE 2

Married Women by Type of Marriage and Age at Marriage

Age at Marriage	Minor Marriage	Major Marriage	Total by Age at Marriage
13	1	2	3
14	7	4	11
15	27	11	38
16	23	20	43
17	31	34	65
18	18	26	44
19	11	24	35
20	6	16	22
21	3	9	12
22	5	9	14
23		7	7
24		4	4
25		5	5
Totals	132	171	303
Average age	16.8 years	18.4 years	17.8 years

divorce. The important point is that the evidence presented in Table 2 suggests that there is little danger of our accepting the Westermarck hypothesis for the wrong reason.

The data reported in this paper were compiled for me by clerks in the household registration office. I spent my own time conducting a general ethnographic survey but naturally took advantage of every opportunity to inquire about reactions to the minor form of marriage. The stories and anecdotes I was given confirm the impressions formed during my first field study. There are at least five men in the town of Sanhsia who live with mistresses and are reputed to visit their wives and children only at the New Year. All five married a childhood associate. The most interesting aspect of these cases is the apparent lack of jealousy on the part of the two men whose wives responded to this treatment by taking lovers. Whereas the average Chinese husband would be outraged by a wife's infidelity, their neighbors claim that these two men "just don't care what their wives do." In one case the husband and his mistress and the wife and her lover live next door to one another in the same compound without any apparent friction. Perhaps the aversion that precludes interest in one another also precludes jealousy.

Consummation of a marriage of the minor type usually takes place on the eve of the lunar New Year. After locking up their doors and windows to exclude the malignant influences of a dying season, the family sits down to a large meal. It is usually at this meal that the head of the family tells his son and daughter that they are henceforth husband and wife. Whenever the opportunity offered, I asked my informants to describe the couple's reaction. One old man told me that he had to stand outside of the door of their room with a stick to keep the newlyweds from running away; another man's adopted daughter did run away to her natal family and refused to return until her father beat her; a third informant who had arranged minor marriages for both of his sons described their reactions this way: "I had to threaten them with my cane to make them go in there, and then I had to stand there with my cane to make them stay." These are exceptional rather than typical cases, but as evidence they carry a special weight. Most of the people I talked to had heard of at least one instance of a father's beating his son and adopted daughter to make them occupy the same bedroom. When I asked whether they had ever heard of this happening in the case of a major marriage, they just laughed.

But the new information I collected in the course of these interviews was not all encouraging. While it did confirm my confidence in the Westermarck hypothesis, it also raised doubts about my choice of a test of the hypothesis. Women whose husbands desert them to live with a mistress often take lovers or seek occasional sexual satisfaction with a neighbor. The problem is that the children are almost always registered as the husband's offspring. Even when the wife is loyal to a husband who prefers another woman, the registered children are not always the wife's progeny.

One of the men who is reputed to visit home only once a year has registered three of his mistress's children as his wife's. A real difference in the number of children produced by the two kinds of marriage may be concealed by a combination of extramarital relations and falsification of the household registers.

My doubts about the test I had proposed were further aroused just by living again in a Chinese community. In the central room of every house, arranged on shelves generation by generation, are the family's ancestral tablets, mute but forceful reminders of every man's duty to perpetuate a line of descent. There must be heirs and descendants to inherit the family property and carry on the rites of ancestor worship. If there are no heirs to inherit, the work of many lifetimes is wasted; without descendants, the deceased members of the line are doomed to wander the world as hungry, homeless ghosts. Westermarck urged his readers to "not forget that a lack of desire, and even a positive feeling of aversion, may in certain circumstances be overcome" (1922[2]:201). He appears to have been thinking of situations in which there is no other opportunity for sexual gratification, but obviously the Chinese concern with perpetuating a line of descent would have the same effect. This concern may overcome and thereby conceal an aversion aroused by intimate childhood association.

There is also cause to worry about my use of divorce rates as a measure of marital dissatisfaction. No matter how dissatisfied a young couple may be with one another, for whatever reason, they cannot obtain a divorce easily. Divorce, like marriage, is under parental authority. Parents have the right to forbid a divorce that is not in the best interests of the family, and they also have the right to divorce a son's wife, with or without his consent. Because a major marriage requires payment of a bride price and expensive wedding feasts, it is rare for parents to initiate divorce proceedings. But it is not uncommon for parents to use their authority to prevent a divorce. By threatening to desert the family or by actually running away for a few months, young people sometimes persuade their parents to allow them to separate, but more often than not parental authority prevails. I know of a number of marriages in both Shulin and Sanhsia that would have ended in divorce if the couple's parents had not objected.

The role parents play with respect to divorce is relevant because it may introduce a bias against the Westermarck hypothesis. For reasons I have already discussed in detail elsewhere, a girl who is raised by her husband's family makes a better daughter-in-law than a girl who joins the family as a young adult (Wolf 1968:868–70). This is one of the reasons so many families choose to raise their sons' wives. Thus there is a possibility that parents will exert more pressure to preserve a minor marriage than a major one. The relative frequency with which the two forms of marriage end in divorce may not reflect relative marital satisfaction. Although the girl's early arrival in the minor form of marriage may preclude a close relationship with her husband, the problem may not be evident in divorce rates because of the girl's more satisfactory relationship with her husband's parents. Divorce may even be more common in the major form of marriage, not because of weaker conjugal ties, but because the husband's parents are more likely to be dissatisfied with their daughter-in-law.

These questions about the validity of my measures point up an important ambiguity in Westermarck's thesis. If the result of intimate childhood association is something as strong as "a positive aversion," the consequences of such association might be evident in birth and divorce rates despite contaminating circumstances. But if the consequences are only a mild distaste, as Westermarck suggests when he speaks of "an indifference," the effects of childhood association may be masked by other factors. My problem was to decide what conclusion to reach if the information from the household registers did not bear out my predictions. I could not argue that the failure to find any difference between the two forms of marriage indicates a mild aversion, but neither could I conclude that Westermarck's hypothesis is mistaken. The information I was collecting while the household registration data were being compiled argues that the minor form of marriage does create marital dissatisfaction and sexual avoidance.

I was beginning to look for another way to test the hypothesis when a young man who is known in the area as a petty racketeer and a confidence man asked me for a job. Because of his ties with people on whom my welcome in the community depended, I could not refuse his proposal, but at first I was at a loss as to how to make use of his talents. He suggested the answer when he told me a long, humorous story about his father's many escapades with prostitutes and winehouse girls. Here was a man who was charming, articulate, and completely without inhibition. He commanded respect because of his connections with important people, but his own reputation would not prevent free and easily conversation. Perhaps he could get people to talk about the adulterous affairs of their friends and neighbors. Our goal would be to identify those women who commonly sought sexual gratification outside of marriage. This would give me another way of testing the Westermarck hypothesis and would also allow me to correct some of the errors in the household registers.

After discussing the project with several of my friends and informal advisors, I decided to concentrate our attention on two men, one in each of the two districts from which my sample was drawn. These men are old enough to have known all of the women in the sample in their youth and are attuned to local gossip because they are often called upon to act as mediators and go-betweens. In outlining the nature of the project to my new assistant, who had had previous dealings of one kind or another with both men, I emphasized the need to explain the "scientific" nature of our interest. To credit my assistant's good manners, he listened politely; to credit his good sense, he ignored everything I said. He was a much better fieldworker than I will ever be. His first step was to invite one of our potential informants to my house for dinner. After we had eaten and toasted one another repeatedly, he initiated a joking conversation about prostitution and adultery. He always began by pointing out how common they are in the United States and Western Europe, illustrating his point with any table or chart that happened to be lying handy on my desk. "Look," he would say, pointing to an appropriate number in a table reporting crude death rates for selected prefectures, "this is the United States. More than a third of all the women in the United States sleep with other men. And look at this; this is France. In France almost all the women have lovers." At the end of this spiel came a question: "What about around here? Does this kind of thing ever happen here?" By this time our informant was usually impatient to contribute his favorite stories to the conversation; if he wasn't, or if he was still discreet about mentioning names, my assistant went on to his own family tree, explaining with gusto his own origin. "You know my father isn't really my father; he lived with another woman and my mother lived with a man from Yingke. And my grandmother was the same way." The result was that by the next time we got together, our informant was talking freely about the sex lives of his friends and relatives. We asked three questions about each woman in our sample: "Do you know this woman? Have you ever heard of her sleeping with other men? Do you think all her children are her husband's offspring?"

The reader will wonder about the accuracy of gossip concerning events that took place fifty years ago. I have no way of knowing how accurate it is, but I do not think the time factor is important. In the small communities in which my subjects and informants live, what people say about one another is not easily forgotten. In this world gossip is more than malicious talk; it is a part of a person's social identity, no more likely to be forgotten than the person himself. The gossip may be partially mistaken, consisting more of accusation than of fact, but even this does not disqualify it as evidence. There is no stereotype of women who marry in the minor fashion that contrasts their sexual behavior with that of women who marry in the major fashion. Whatever error occurs in the anwers we were given is random with respect to the hypothesis we are testing. If we do not find the predicted difference between the two forms of marriage, it may be because the error is great or because the hypothesis is wrong. But if we do find the predicted difference, it can be taken as evidence. Critics may be able to account for the difference in another way, but they cannot discount it. Random error does not produce significant differences.

We can now turn to the results of these various attempts to test the Westermarck hypothesis. Consider first the prediction that the minor form of marriage will end in divorce more often than the major form of marriage. As can be seen in the information reported in Table 3, my worries about the use of this measure of marital dissatisfaction were unfounded. There are clear and striking differences between the two forms of marriage. The one case in which a major marriage ended in divorce is one of those rare exceptions that does not detract from the rule. The woman in question had worked in Taipei as a prostitute for several years before her marriage. According to one of the couple's former neighbors, her husband was forced to divorce her "because she kept going back to work."

Table 3 also reports eight cases of permanent separation. This is part of the information collected by means of my unsolicited but invaluable assistant. We discovered two marriages that ended when the wife ran away to live with another man, another terminated by the wife's taking up a life of prostitution, and five others in which the husband permanently deserted his wife. Two of these five men ran away with local girls and are now living in mainland China. Although none of those marriages is registered as having ended in divorce, they can be taken as equivalent to divorce for our purposes. That seven of the eight are minor marriages makes the evidence in favor of the Westermarck hypothesis overwhelming. Perhaps

TABLE 3

Number and Percent of Marriages Ending in Divorce or Separation

	Minor Marriage	Major Marriage
Total number of marriages	132	171
Number ending in divorce	25	1
Number of permanent separations	7	1
Percent ending in divorce or separation	24.2	1.2

these couples felt the same as the Somerset Maugham character who couldn't imagine Byron's taking an interest in his sister. "Of course she was only his half-sister, but just as habit kills love I should have thought habit would prevent its arising. When two persons have known one another all their lives and lived together in close contact I can't imagine how or why that sudden spark should flash that results in love" (Maugham 1934: 787–8).

Of the 303 women in my sample, 286 were known to one or the other of my two informants. They claim that sixty of these women had sexual relations with other men while their husbands were alive. Some of those affairs were brief and involved only one other man, but for some of the women adultery was a way of life. One is said to have slept with "more than a hundred different men." "They used to come here all the way from Yingke and Sanhsia to sleep with that woman." Another woman "couldn't see men at home because her parents-in-law were very strict, but if you gave her ten cents she'd meet you anywhere you wanted." The most interesting case is that of a girl who avoided sexual relations with her "brother" by feeding him a potion concocted with juice extracted from pomegranate roots. This is said to have made the husband impotent. "After that she slept with dozens of other men. I don't know what was so different about that woman's bones; she just couldn't do without a man."

The relative frequency of adultery in the two forms of marriage is reported in Table 4. The sharp difference between the two strongly suggests a need for extramarital sexual gratification on the part of women who marry a childhood associate. That this is due to a distaste for sexual relations with their husbands is evident in my informants' characterization of the conjugal relationship. About a third of the way through the interviews one of the informants insisted that a couple's four children were all the offspring of one or another of the wife's several lovers. When I asked him how he could be so sure, he answered, "Because she has never slept with her husband." After this I was careful to inquire about each woman's relations with her husband as well as her relations with other men. By the time the interviews were completed, twelve couples had been identified as

TABLE 4
Number and Percent of Married Women Involved in Adultery*

	Minor Marriage	Major Marriage
Total number of women	127	159
Number involved in adultery	42	18
Percent involved in adultery	33.1	11.3

* Five minor marriages and twelve major marriages were dropped for lack of information.

having never engaged in sexual intercourse despite years of marriage. All twelve couples had been raised together. My informants say the reason for this remarkable abstinence is "embarrassment," but this is obviously only a euphemism for some more intense emotion. The example of those couples who meet for the first time on the day of their wedding argues that people can be embarrassed without being inhibited.

Although it is not at all unlikely that adultery is a common cause of divorce, the fact is that the twenty-six registered divorces in our sample include only six of the sixty cases of adultery. This is important because it says that our two tests of the Westermarck hypothesis are independent. The hypothesis is confirmed not only by the two tests but also by two independent sets of data. The significance of this can be seen in Table 5, which combines the two sets of data into one overall measure of marital dissatisfaction. We now find evidence of dissatisfaction in nearly half of all the minor marriages as against only ten percent of the major marriages. The reader will not need statistical assurances to convince him that a difference of this magnitude is not likely to be due to chance.

TABLE 5

Number and Percent of Marriages Ending in Divorce
and/or Involving Adultery by Wife

	Minor Marriage	Major Marriage
Total number of marriages	132	171
Number involving divorce and/or adultery	61	18
Percent involving divorce and/or adultery	46.2	10.5

By the time the data from the household registers were complete, I had all but given up the idea of using birth rates as a measure of conjugal sexuality. The Chinese concern with perpetuating a line of descent, the errors in the household registers, and the simple fact that birth rates are, at best, only a crude index of frequency of sexual intercourse had all combined to discourage me. One could only hope to find the predicted relationship if couples raised together avoided one another for periods of a year or more at a time. But again my pessimism was unfounded. Contrary to my expectations, but in line with my prediction, minor marriages do produce fewer children, far fewer than major marriages. The evidence is reported in Table 6. The intervals in this table are calculated separately for each woman; the first interval begins at the date of marriage. When a marriage is terminated by death or divorce the case is dropped from this and all subsequent intervals. If, for example, a woman marries and bears two children in the first five years, these two children are included in the average of the first interval. If the woman then bears a third child in the sixth year of marriage but gets a divorce in the seventh year, this child and the case are not included in the averages of the remaining intervals. The method is imperfect, but it is the best that can be managed with a small sample.

The averages reported in Table 6 are based on the number of registered births. We have seen that some of these children are really the offspring of a mistress or children whose registered father is not their genitor. The information provided by my two informants allows us to correct at least

TABLE 6

Average Number of Children as Taken from Household Registration Records

Years of Marriage (in five-year intervals)	Minor Marriage	Major Marriage
1st	1.27	1.81
2nd	1.19	1.62
3rd	1.12	1.54
4th	1.06	1.23
5th	0.54	0.75

TABLE 7
Average Number of Children as Corrected by Informants

Years of Marriage (in five-year intervals)	Minor Marriage	Major Marriage
1st	1.06	1.74
2nd	1.01	1.55
3rd	0.97	1.51
4th	0.94	1.21
5th	0.49	0.75

the more obvious of these errors. We can discount children who were conceived while the husband was living with another woman in another part of the island, children who are known to be the progeny of one of the husband's mistresses, and the children of women who are said to have never slept with their husbands. The corrected averages, shown in Table 7, provide striking, indeed surprising, confirmation of the assumptions made in my original prediction. Throughout the first twenty-five years of marriage, minor marriages produce thirty percent fewer children than major marriages.

By now all but the most skeptical readers will be willing to concede the existence of substantial differences between the conjugal relationships created by the major and minor forms of marriage. But they will ask, with good reason, whether there are other differences between the two forms of marriage that could produce these results. We must at least consider the fact that the girl who marries in the minor fashion is adopted. Although demographers have not as yet identified psychological factors that affect fertility, this is not to say they do not exist (Noyes and Chapnick 1964). Perhaps the trauma of adoption decreases a woman's chances of bearing children. The experience of being raised as an adopted daughter may also be relevant. Adopted daughters are often mistreated by their foster parents and are always expected to carry a heavier burden of household labors than the family's own daughters (Wolf 1968:871). Women who were raised as adopted daughters claim that they did not eat as well as the family's own children. This experience might also affect their ability to bear children and could even make it more difficult for them to adjust to marriage.

Because the desire to economize is one reason for choosing to raise a son's wife, minor marriages are probably more common among the poor than among the wealthy. Women who marry a childhood associate may be less fertile because they have to work harder on a less satisfactory diet. And if families choosing the major and minor forms of marriage do differ in wealth, they may also represent different strata of the society. While social status cannot vary greatly in communities composed largely of farmers and laborers, there may be some variation, a difference between what some Americans call "good families" and "poor families." Perhaps divorce and adultery are more common among minor marriages because of the kind of family that chooses this type of marriage. The very fact that they choose to raise a son's wife indicates that these families are somewhat less concerned about prestige and public opinion than many of their neighbors.

There are reasonable replies to all of these objections, but fortunately my case does not have to rest on reason alone. The women in the sample who married in the major fashion include forty-two who were raised as adopted daughters. A few of them came from families who decided against the minor marriage after having made the necessary arrangements. The majority are women whose intended husbands died before they were old enough to marry. Their foster parents then had no choice but to allow them to marry out in the major fashion. Because the Chinese always look for a daughter-in-law among families of approximately the same social status, we can safely assume that these forty-two major marriages are drawn from the same social strata as the minor marriages in the sample. And since all of these women were raised as adopted daughters, a comparison of the two is the ideal way to test for the effects of social status and the experience of adoption. The only difference between them is that one group of women married childhood associates while the other married strangers met for the first time the day of the wedding.

Consider first the evidence on divorce and adultery. The one major marriage that ended in divorce did involve a woman raised as an adopted daughter, but this is an exceptional exception. The reader will remember that the woman was a prostitute before marriage. Her neighbors claim she became a prostitute to avoid marrying her foster brother. That marital dissatisfaction is not often the lot of the adopted daughters who marry in the major fashion is evident in Table 8. The likelihood of divorce or adultery among these women is only a fifth of what it is among adopted daughters who married a childhood associate. This is almost exactly the

TABLE 8
Number and Percent of Marriages by Adopted Daughters Ending in Divorce and/or Involving Adultery by Wife

	Minor Marriage	Major Marriage
Total number of marriages	132	42
Number ending in divorce	25	1
Number ending in adultery	42	4
Percent involving divorce and/or adultery	46.2	9.5

TABLE 9

Average Number of Children by Adopted Daughters as Taken from Household Registration Records

Years of Marriage (in five-year intervals)	Minor Marriage	Major Marriage
1st	1.27	1.78
2nd	1.19	1.77
3rd	1.12	1.76
4th	1.06	1.31
5th	0.54	0.90

magnitude of the difference we found in comparing all major and minor marriages.

Major marriages involving an adopted daughter also produce more children than minor marriages. Table 9 reports the average number of registered children for the two groups; Table 10 includes the corrections made by my two informants. Again the difference between adopted daughters who marry in the major and minor fashions is almost exactly the same as the difference between all major and minor marriages. Although adopted daughters do experience trauma and deprivation and may represent a lower stratum of society, this is not the reason they bear fewer children, divorce their husbands, and sleep with other men. There is no evidence of unusual marital dissatisfaction as long as they marry a stranger; problems arise only when they are forced to marry a childhood associate.

This paper begins a story that is still years away from its concluding paragraphs. When I found the results of my first search of the household registers so encouraging, I decided to copy the complete records for Shulin Chen and Sanhsia Chen, an area with a present population of approximately 80,000 persons. An analysis of these records will take at least five years and perhaps as long as ten. The goal of this project is to retest the propositions presented in this paper and at the same time to specify the vague term "intimate and prolonged childhood association."

TABLE 10

Average Number of Children by Adopted Daughters as Corrected by Informants

Years of Marriage (in five-year intervals)	Minor Marriage	Major Marriage
1st	1.06	1.73
2nd	1.01	1.73
3rd	0.97	1.76
4th	0.94	1.31
5th	0.49	0.90

The household registers tell us when the parties to a minor marriage are brought into association and also the composition of the family in which they are raised. My hope is that this variation in the degree and quality of the association will allow me to isolate the conditions that produce lower birth rates and higher divorce rates. Raised like brother and sister, the parties to a minor marriage may come to think of themselves as brother and sister. They may be reluctant to marry because brother and sister never marry. Identifying the precise conditions that make some couples more averse to marrying than others will eliminate this alternative explanation and allow a more general formulation of the Westermarck hypothesis.

I began this paper by quoting questions raised by Westermarck's critics. It is appropriate to conclude by noting his response. When Frazer and then Freud criticized Westermarck for failing to recognize that the incest taboo is necessary, the law itself being sufficient evidence of man's inclination to commit the forbidden act, he replied: "The law expresses the general feelings of the community and punishes acts that shock them; but it does not tell us whether an inclination to commit the forbidden act is felt by many or by few" (1922[2]:203–4). Whether the feelings expressed by the incest taboo reflect an uncomplicated aversion, as Westermarck believed, or an anxiety created in reaction to strong desire, as Freud suggested on one occasion, or some other emotional consequence of family life remains to be determined. The only conclusion justified by the data presented in this paper is that there is some aspect of childhood association sufficient to preclude or inhibit sexual desire. This suggests that the taboo is not a response to the needs of the social order, instituted to suppress private motives, but that it is instead an expression of these motives, a formal statement of the feelings of the community, socially unnecessary but psychologically inevitable.

Gustav Jahoda

16. Love, Marriage, and Social Change: Letters to the Advice Column of a West African Newspaper*

The effects of major changes in the social system on the mental state of individuals have been the subject of a recent controversy. Miss Ward (1956), in a paper discussing the significance of an alleged increase in the number of witch-finding cults in Ashanti, argued that this can be taken as evidence of a widespread rise in the general level of anxiety resulting from rapid structural changes. In a subsequent rejoinder Goody (1957) challenged not only the view that such cults have in fact become more numerous, but also the underlying assumption, shared by many social scientists, that rapid social change produces an emotional malaise in the people caught up in it.

Without entering into the details of this dispute, a few comments may be justified as serving to introduce the present topic. Goody was clearly right in pointing out that we have no means of assessing comparative happiness or misery, so that statements about an *overall* increase in malaise are necessarily always speculative. One can also sympathize with his attack on the idea that rapid social change leads to anomie (normlessness), although it is doubtful whether many sociologists would really believe this; the problem here is probably at least partly of a semantic nature. Even if one rejects the notion of a drift towards anomie, it does not affect the likelihood that *conflicting norms* will exist side by side during the transition phase, so that individuals may lack a firm guide for their conduct in various

---

* Reprinted with permission of author and the International African Institute from *Africa* 29 (2), 1959:177–89.

situations. Or again, as a consequence of social changes people will tend to adopt new goals, which may be difficult to achieve, and this is liable to generate anxiety and discontent. There are certainly many ways in which social change can make life more difficult for some people, and these are worthy of study in their own right: one does not have to be able to balance them against the unquestioned gains in terms of personal security or material welfare with which social change can often be credited. The present study, carried out in Ghana, was part of a wider attempt to gain information both about the transformations of attitudes and norms, and the accompanying stresses.

In his discussion of the use of personal documents in anthropology, Kluckhohn (1945:105) refers to letters to the press as one of the 'yet unexploited research resources' on acculturation. In the present study an effort was made to secure all letters addressed to the advice column of a newspaper with a national circulation in Ghana (then still the Gold Coast) during a period of about three months at the beginning of 1955. Owing to the haphazard method of storage, and the fact that many of the letters were not dated, there is a certain overlap with earlier and later months. This means that the number of letters cannot be related to specified units of time, but there is no reason to suppose that it introduces any systematic distortion as regards content.

At the outset it may be well to evaluate this kind of material, and in particular to indicate its limitations. There is first the question of the motives for writing a letter; generally one may expect two main ones, namely the need to get outside help with a personal problem, and the wish to appear in print. In practice these cannot be easily disentangled, though it is possible to eliminate those letters which contain merely statements of fact or opinion. The bulk of the letters unmistakably relates to definite personal problems, freely and spontaneously described in the writers' own words.

It is clear, however, that for a variety of reasons the range of problems included in the letters cannot be considered as typical, both in character and frequency, for people in the society as a whole. Obviously only literates are likely to write letters to the press, and even if one makes a very generous estimate these can hardly have constituted much more than about one-quarter of the population aged 16 and over. Furthermore, there are a number of other institutions and agencies, modern and traditional, which people can and do approach with their troubles; among these would be doctors, social welfare agencies, ministers of religion, native doctors and herbalists, and finally some persons and organizations intermediate between the traditional and the modern.[1]

---

[1] The intermediate type is a characteristic product of social change, embodying a blend of western religious and occult notions with traditional indigenous beliefs.

Lastly, while editorial screening does not enter directly, the policy guiding the selection of letters for publication will influence the kind that are being sent in. The emphasis in the present case, undoubtedly patterned on British women's magazines, is on love, courtship, and marriage, and this is the salient theme of the letters.

Before presenting the actual problems, something has to be said about the social characteristics of the letter-writers. It is one of the drawbacks of this sort of research that one has to be content with such information as the writers choose to give about themselves. The temptation to put forward plausible inferences will not always be resisted, but in Table 1 below only information directly contained in the documents is listed.

In spite of this limitation a few trends emerge quite clearly from the table. First, the bulk of the letters came from unmarried young men; from

TABLE 1
Social Background of Writers

		Ages		Education			Occupations					Place of origin	
No.	*Numbers Given*	*Median*	*Range*	*Elementary Only*	*Secondary or Teacher Training*	*Other Post-Elementary*	*Clerical or Teaching*	*Trading*	*Artisan*	*Unemployed*	*Full-Time Education*	*Large Town*	*Other*
Men (unmarried) .	251	185	22	16–31	13	27	6	20	9	6	3	22	123	100
Men (married) ...	35	19	28	21–35	?	?	?	1	?	?	?	?	15	15
Men (not known) .	40	17	20	18–25	5	2	?	6	1	1	1	7	14	16
Women (unmarried) .	33	24	18½	16–24	3	1	1	7	?	?	?	2	15	12
Women (married) .	4	3	21	21–45	?	?	?	?	?	?	?	?	1	3
Totals	363	248	21	16–45	21	30	7	34	10	7	4	31	168	146

internal evidence it is very likely that most of the 40 men whose marital status is not definitely known also belong to this category; if one adds them to the previous total this accounts for nearly 90 percent of all letters. It may be noted that this is almost exactly the reverse of the position in Britain as set out by Greenland (1957). One important cause of this is probably the higher literacy rate among men; in 1952, for instance, nearly three times as many boys as girls were enrolled in all types of educational institutions, and in earlier years the discrepancy was far greater.

Almost two thirds specified their age, hence one may feel confident that the typical seeker for advice is in his or her late 'teens or early twenties. This is confirmed by the high proportion (among those who mention what they are doing) still undergoing full-time education.

The other reliable piece of information concerns the places from which the letters were sent. Over half of them originated from the four largest towns (Accra, Kumasi, Sekondi-Takoradi, and Cape Coast), whose combined population in 1948 represented only 7 percent of the country's total. Owing to the concentration of literates in the large towns this is, of course, not unexpected.

With education and jobs one is on far more precarious ground. Only some 16 and 24 percent respectively provide any details, and one cannot be sure how representative they are. An impressionistic judgment, based on style of writing as well as other indirect clues, suggests that rather more than half the writers had received an education beyond the elementary level. As far as jobs are concerned, clerical and teaching ones clearly predominate; in addition there seems to be a fair sprinkling of men in minor technical government posts. In view of the subsequent discussion of the nature of their problems it is important to stress that nearly all people in such occupations are, by virtue of their conditions of employment, liable to be transferred from one part of the country to another.

The analysis will concentrate on the largest single category, i.e., unmarried young men; problems of married men will be outlined insofar as they help to throw additional light on those of unmarried ones.

UNMARRIED YOUNG MEN

Their letters were subdivided according to the predominant causal factors, as viewed from a sociological standpoint. The most important of these were the persistence of traditional mores, and the influence of new patterns of living.

Persistence of Traditional Mores

1. *Marriages arranged by parents or relatives.* There were 20 cases of this kind. In 15 a young man's parents or relatives wanted to force him to marry a girl of their choice, to whom he objected. Four of these girls were explicitly stated to be illiterate, but the actual proportion was probably a good deal higher. The remaining 5 letters describe a situation in which the young man wanted to marry a girl, whose parents were exerting pressure for her to enter another marriage they had already arranged regardless of her wishes. Here is a summary of a letter illustrating the former problem:

> A young man aged 22, from internal evidence an Ashanti, has an uncle who took the responsibility of helping him with his education and assisted him whenever he was in any financial embarrassment. After he had held a job for a year, the uncle considered that he was almost ready for marriage and offered him one of his daughters, an illiterate then aged 10. The young man already has a girl friend who is educated, but does not hail from his town. The uncle, on the other hand, is anxious that he should not marry a 'stranger'. He does not wish to marry an illiterate

girl, yet at the same time is afraid to reject the offer of his uncle, who helped him in the past and on whom he might perhaps have to depend in the future.

This letter shows the nature of the dilemma very clearly. In a matrilineal society like Ashanti, the mother's brother stands in a very special relationship to his sister's son, who inherits his property. The good uncle creates an obligation on the part of his nephew by his generosity; moreover, cross-cousin marriage is traditionally favoured, and the rejection of his uncle's offer would constitute a grave hurt and insult. Similar situations do of course arise vis-à-vis parents and other relatives.

2. *Family opposition to projected marriages.* There were 52 letters focused on this theme: in 27 the opposition came from the man's side, in 21 from the girl's and in the remaining 4 from both sides. The distribution of such grounds for opposition as were given is to be found in Table 2.

TABLE 2
Reasons for Opposition

	Number
Traditional reasons	
"Stranger"	11
Prohibited kin	6
Total	17
New kinds of reason	
Disturbs studies	1
"Scholarship"	1
Political feud	1
Girl illiterate	1
Total	4
Not applicable	
Boy too young	1
Woman a widow	2
Family quarrel	1
Total	4

The traditional reasons, which clearly predominate, require some explanation. The term 'stranger' may refer to someone from outside the home town[2] (3 cases), someone belonging to a different tribe (6 cases), or a national of another West African country (2 cases). An example of the first kind is outlined below:

---

[2] The word 'village' does not form part of the ordinary vocabulary and all places, irrespective of size, are called 'towns'; this usage will also be adopted here.

This young man's mother objected to his marrying a girl who, though from within the district, was not from his town. He commented that the Creator could not have intended any such restrictions, and emphasis ought to be only on 'love and understanding'.

After elaborating somewhat upon this theme, the writer ended with two revealing questions:

1. 'Would it be better if I marry such a girl?'
2. 'If so, then what can I tell my mother just to [make her] understand the word "love and understanding in marriage"?'

Although he uses a universalist argument derived from Christian teaching, he is in fact plagued by grave doubts as to whether he ought to marry the 'stranger' of his choice in the face of his mother's objection. And if the advice is to marry her, he appeals for help in conveying to his mother a conception obviously quite foreign to her, namely that what matters most in marriage is the harmonious personal relationship of the partners.

The next example concerns tribal differences.

The writer, who comes from a poor Ga family, met a Fante girl from a well-to-do background at secondary school. The girl agreed to marry him, but his father said he would 'never allow any of his sons to marry anyone who is not a Ga born'.

Owing to variations in customs, marriages across tribal boundaries may involve complications, so that parental opposition in such instances cannot always be put down just to deep-rooted conservatism. This applies especially where one tribe is patrilineal and the other matrilineal, with the associated son-versus-nephew inheritance, which was referred to several times. Nevertheless, there is evidence that inter-tribal marriages are becoming increasingly prevalent in the larger urban centres.[3]

The other traditional reason for families withholding their consent was that the marriage would contravene rules about prohibited degrees of kinship. None of those mentioned related to direct blood relationships, and would thus not constitute reasonable objections in European eyes; and to the extent that the young men have adopted a western outlook, they are equally unacceptable to them.

The 'new' kinds of reasons can be dealt with more summarily. The first, disturbance of studies, is self-explanatory as a ground for postponing marriage. 'Scholarship' has nothing to do with learning, but is an expression coined to characterize the relationship between a man and a woman by analogy with that of a student to the government: it refers to a relationship in which the woman has a higher position and/or greater wealth than the

---

[3] Busia (1950:29) reported that in Sekondi-Takoradi nearly one-third of the marriages in his sample were inter-tribal.

man, and does in fact keep him. In the present instance the girl's parents opposed the union because her status in the teaching profession was senior to his, so that her salary was also higher.

The political feud divided, on the one hand, a family enthusiastic in their support for the CPP, and on the other a family devoted with equal fervour to the opposition party.

The last case is that of a man wanting to marry an illiterate girl, who found that his educated family were greatly disappointed by his choice. Their disapproval has made him rather uneasy, so that he is evidently seeking for outside support. Here we have what amounts to a complete reversal of the earlier problems, and one closely akin to that of the son of a western bourgeois family who wishes to marry an unskilled factory girl. It seems likely that, as social differentiation along western lines proceeds, this type of problem will become more common, while the incidence of the ones described earlier will decline.

Influence of New Patterns of Living

1. *Threatened or broken relationships.* Two kinds of difficulty are included under this heading: first, the man states that his girl has ceased to care for him, and asks how he can win her back (24 letters); second, a rival has appeared with whom the girl has started 'playing,' the question being what can be done about it (35 letters). In over half the cases of both types it was specifically stated that a more or less prolonged separation had occurred, of which details are given below.

Gone to work elsewhere, transferred: 11 men and 2 girls.
Went to school or college: 3 men and 5 girls.
Met at school or college and separated after leaving: 8.
Unspecified separations: 3 men and 1 girl.

These problems are to a large extent a consequence of the high degree of geographical mobility among the literate section of the population, brought about by social changes. Such enforced absences are liable to make the heart grow less fond, in spite of the exchange of letters that was frequently mentioned. In such circumstances one or other of the couple may look elsewhere for consolation—the present letters can, of course, tell only one side of the story.

Some additional features emerge from the cases where another man came into the picture. Seven of the writers stated that their girl had intercourse with the other man, and in 4 more pregnancy had resulted. It is of interest to note that 1 in 5 of the rivals was actually a friend of the writer. This is no coincidence, for a friend often acts as a go-between in love affairs; he cannot always be relied upon to remain detached, especially when friction has already arisen. Here is a summary of a typical instance:

> A young man of 23 had a quarrel with his girl. He called in a friend 'to
> settle the case between them'. The outcome was that the friend stayed
> with the girl, and as the writer somewhat naïvely elaborated 'I hope you
> know what happens when a man and woman sleep in the same room
> till the next day'. On the following morning the friend came to say that
> the girl still did not want to resume their former relationship. The writer,
> who heard what had happened, did not know what to do next.

Finally, in several cases not involving separation there were direct or
indirect indications that the man who had stolen the girl's affections was
of higher socio-economic status; e.g., 'he is holding a European post'[4] or
he was said to be 'a man of wealth—carful and fridgful'.

2. *Multiple entanglements.* The issue here may be regarded as complementary to the one just discussed, with similar causal factors. A schematic
presentation would run something like this: a man travels around, entering into liaisons with girls at two or more stations, in addition sometimes
to a girl at his home town; or again, his girl may go away for further education or to another work place. Pregnancies frequently occur (5 single,
3 double, 1 multiple). The man is then faced with a conflict situation:
sometimes he wants to know which one he ought to marry, or keep up
relations with (which one out of two in 8 cases, out of three in 2 cases);
alternatively, if he has a definite preference, the question becomes one of
finding means of getting rid of the others (4 cases). The remaining 6 do
not fit clearly into the scheme; none referred to any transfers or separations, but in 3 of them the writer lived in a large city, whose size and
anonymity permit the same basic pattern. The others were variations on
the theme in which the different girls knew each other, or were about to
collide.

An example of the problem first outlined will be given.

> A 23-year-old clerk writes about his wife-to-be, who is being trained as
> a telephone operator: 'I love this girl to the bottom of my heart'. How-
> ever, as she lives far away, he unfortunately made two other girls preg-
> nant and consequently is 'perplexed mentally'. He asks: 'What can I do
> to repel . . . these two girls . . . and get hold of my own darling as my
> ever and one wife?'

One means whereby dilemmas of this sort might be resolved would be
polygyny, which was in fact referred to in the present context. In 5 cases
this was only to reject it with varying degrees of vehemence, largely on the
ground of what one called 'my nautral distastes'. Two more objected
mainly because of the expense and only one man, in a very special situation, was seriously toying with the idea: both his girl friends came together
and announced their intention to marry him.

3. *Approach to girls and romantic love.* In presenting the problems

---

[4] i.e., one of the higher administrative posts formerly reserved for Europeans.

grouped under this heading the main types will be listed with brief examples.

    a. How can I get a girl friend? How does one approach a girl? (15 letters)

        'I am a boy of 19 years of age. As I don't have any girls as my friend, which step should I take to get one?'

        'I often meet a girl near the bus stop. This girl I love very much, but the first steps I should take to approach her is now my difficulty.'

    b. Complaints of feeling shy and nervous about girls (5 letters)

        '. . . several times I have been attracted by nice girls,, but always I have been beaten by nervousness. When in the 'teens I masturbated. Do you think this shyness of mine could be [the result of this]?'

It should be explained that this reference to masturbation was the only one of its kind, otherwise, the letter was typical.

    c. How does one choose a good wife? (5 letters)

        '. . . I cannot make my choice at all because [I] cannot distinguish between a good and a bad girl, and aged woman and a young woman . . . the old women . . . are all racing or scrambling for young men by "pan-cacking", "lip-sticking" and painting of nails.'

    d. Does she really love me? (10 letters)

        'I wonder if she is really in love with me. Please, how can I know that she has fallen for me?'

        'Is she a true lover?'

        'How can I be sure she will love me more than ever?'

        'Is this love really from Heaven?'

What is noteworthy about many of these problems is their resemblance to those experienced by young people in western societies. Types *a., b.,* and *c.* stem largely from comparative social isolation, either due to the impersonal atmosphere of life in a city as contrasted with a village, or to being a stranger in a small town. In such circumstances the establishment of relations with the opposite sex requires the exercise of individual initiative, which some people find harder than others. In the small village community, where nearly everybody has some sort of contact with everybody else, and where relatives have a hand in the choice of a marriage partner, such difficulties will be almost entirely absent.

The boy who worries about the effects of masturbation probably derived this idea from imported popular magazines and books. The same source[5]

---

[5] In a reading survey carried out under the direction of the author it was found that popular books and magazines on psychology and etiquette are widely read; women's journals and such publications as 'True Romances' enjoy a considerable circulation. Cf. Kimble (1956).

no doubt also contributes to foster the notion of romantic love, but they are perhaps outweighed by the long-term influence of certain facets of Christian teaching and, more recently, the cinema.

In connexion with the concept of romantic love a certain caution is advisable. From the fact that the phrasing employed is familiar, one is apt to jump to the conclusion that the referent, i.e., the emotional bond, is identical with that in western societies. While it is not possible to make any dogmatic pronouncements in such an elusive sphere, there are indications that matters may not be so simple. In the first place the frequent request for reassurance, for some sign that the love is really 'true', suggests that many young people are in fact groping for the full meaning of what is symbolized by the word 'love', for some criterion by which they could judge that it is really there. Secondly, in the West the concept of romantic love carries the connotation of exclusiveness; the usage frequently exemplified in the letters shows that this is not necessarily true of the writers. Thus it appears that although western influences have given a wide currency to the language of romantic love, its actual content of meaning remains circumscribed by the existing matrix of social values, which can alter only gradually.

Other Problems of Love and Marriage

This is a residual category of 65 letters that do not fit into any of the preceding ones. The largest single subdivision consists of questions as to how a marriage the writer had originally envisaged could be avoided or postponed. The main reasons given were that they felt too young or poor (5), that the girl was illiterate (2), or that she did not come up to expectations in some other way (6).

Next is a large and very mixed bag of problems, whose variety will be illustrated by outlining the essential elements of a few chosen at random:

> His girl brings two others for breakfast every day, which ruins him financially. His girl is too jealous. His girl refuses to come and see him in his room. He would like to get love letters from girls abroad. His girl gets too many 'offers' from other men. His school-girl friend washed his clothes and the head teacher confiscated them.

There are, in addition, some letters whose theme is more directly relevant in the present context, and these will be treated in more detail.

> A young man of 21 fell in love with a girl while they both attended secondary school. The relationship lasted for three years, when the girl's parents sent her to Britain for further education. Although she writes regularly, he is anxious about the future and wonders if she will still care for him after her return, 'I being just a junior clerk in one of the

local firms. And if she does, am I worthy of her hand in marriage if she comes back a "been-to"?'

The increasing importance of status differences is also brought out in another letter where a young man expresses himself bitterly about the attitude of his girl who is better educated than himself. Forthcoming in private, she hates to be seen in his company. As he somewhat ambiguously put it 'In the night she is a "devil", during the day she is an "angel" '.

In another letter a young unestablished government servant, who plans to marry a teacher, is worried because his work is not stationary and he is required to have a Christian wedding, which is far more expensive than the customary rite.[6] Again, a man would like to marry a divorced woman, yet fears that this may be contrary to the teaching of the Bible.

Finally three letters are worthy of special note, each being the only one of its kind. The first is phrased in terms strongly suggesting that the writer is a homosexual; he asks how one can get men friends, and complains that girls gossip about him and call him names. Nothing seems to be known about the incidence of such deviants in West Africa, but it is generally held to be very low. It is therefore of interest that a case should occur in such a small sample.

The second letter is from a man about to be married, who is afraid that he might be what he calls 'impotent', though it is evident from the context that he really means 'infertile'. This is contrary to the widely held assumption, at least until the opposite is established in any particular case, that infertility is the fault of the woman.

The last letter is from a young man who says that he cannot bring himself to kiss his girl, because her breath is so bad. The interest here lies not so much in the topic of halitosis with its usual accompaniment ('I can't tell her about her breath'), but in the reference to kissing. For this is not an indigenous practice, being in fact strongly disapproved of by older people as immoral. There was one other mention of kissing among the letters, which similarly implied that it was common. In this respect, therefore, western sexual mores seem to have been adopted, and one may suspect that films are largely responsible.

Other Observations and Summary of Problem Types

A great deal of incidental information may be gleaned from the content of the letters, and some of this is valuable in providing further pointers to the general picture.

The ages of 89 of the girls or women concerned were mentioned; these range from 12 to 45, with a mode of 18. In 79 cases it was possible to compute the age-differences: at one extreme the woman was 15 years older,

---

[6] Cf. Busia (1950:41). This is a very commmon and widely debated problem.

at the other the girl 10 years younger; the general tendency was for the man to be 2 or 3 years older (respective mode and median).

In 42 letters the place where boy met girl was stated: in 23 cases it was their home town, for the rest elsewhere; and 22 of the meetings occurred in schools or colleges.

There were 14 young men who mentioned gifts and/or remittances to their girl, and 10 more referred to reciprocal gifts; in three cases the man assumed financial responsibility for the schooling of the girl to whom he was engaged.

Although physical relations were explicitly said to have taken place in only 18 letters, the numerous oblique references to intercourse indicate that it is the norm rather than the exception. One has, of course, to add the 27 cases where the girl's pregnancy was reported. In this connexion it should be explained that the quotation under the heading of 'multiple entanglements,' where pregnancy was apt to produce special difficulties, may have been somewhat misleading as regards the usual attitudes to such an event. It appears to have been greeted mostly with pleasure and pride, a fact reflecting the persistence of procreation as a predominant value even among educated Africans. A more representative extract would be the following:

> 'Very fortunately enough my Darling conceived . . . My Darling was fed, clothed and cared by me until she delivered and the daughter and the mother are under my care.'

Like many other descriptions of this kind, it showed not only the acceptance of an obligation to look after the mother with her child, but also to marry her according to custom. In cases where attempts are made to evade this obligation, one will mostly find that special circumstances are operating; e.g., paternity may be in doubt, or more than one girl has become pregnant.

In concluding this section on unmarried young men, the frequency of the different types of problems for which they sought advice and help is listed below (percentages rounded to the nearest whole number):

	Percent
Threatened or broken relationships	24
Family opposition to marriage	21
Approach to girls and romantic love	14
Marriages arranged by parents or relatives	8
Multiple entanglements	8
Miscellaneous other	26

MARRIED MEN

The purpose of the majority of their letters was to ask what could be done about some defect of character in the wife. It was sometimes possible to infer that differences in education and social background may have had something to do with the lack of marital harmony. In several cases the circumstances were quite explicitly set out, and these will be briefly considered.

First, there were those marriages which had taken place in opposition to the wishes of the family, usually because the girl was a 'stranger'. In one case there was no offspring from such a union, in another the child was born with a harelip. Anything of this kind was seized upon as showing that the marriage was an ill-fated one—the men clearly had not succeeded in overcoming the conflict experienced as a result of marrying in the face of parental disapproval.

Second, there was the more common problem of those who had been pushed or driven into marrying illiterate girls. In view of the importance of this topic one of the most articulate of these letters, which brings out most of the difficulties of such a situation, is reproduced in full.

'I am 28 years old. I am married to an illiterate girl for the past three years. The marriage was arranged by my parents without my consent. My parents and the girl's parents are close friends. The girl was sent to me but I had not the courage to refuse her, fearing that the refusal would anger my father and also cast a blur on his friendship with the girl's parent. Again, I learnt that my father had spent much money on the girl on my behalf, so I decided to give her a trial. Fortunately for her our first mating resulted in pregnancy and we have now got a nice baby girl of whom I am very proud. But the girl is not the ideal wife I dreamt of in my college days. I have tried hard to bring her to the standard required of her, but she is still unprogressive. I feel shy to bring my friends to my house because no one likes to wash his dirty linen in public. The nature of my work is such that I spend most of the days of each month outside my home and I am entertaining the fear that my children will be ill-bred because the girl herself lacks training. However, she is honest and economical, but I feel she is not the right type of girl I ought to have married.

Recently I have fallen in love with an educated girl who I am sure is the girl I have been looking for. But polygamy is the first thing I detest. I am afraid of losing the confidence of my parents by putting away my wife and marrying the girl of my own choice. This is a hard nut for me to break. I don't in the least feel happy in my wife's company at all. I am a public-spirited fellow, but when I ask my wife to accompany me to a social gathering or church she always puts up a lame excuse and refuses to go.

What shall I do in this instance to be happy?'

The picture emerging from this and the other letters is a pathetic one: two people thrown together who soon realize their incompatibility, without an easy way out. Some marriages with illiterate girls undoubtedly turn out more successful than this; nevertheless, the unwillingness to marry illiterates voiced by many of the young men appears amply justified.[7]

Lastly it may be mentioned that only 4 of the letters were written by polygynous husbands, one of these being an attempt to defend and justify his having three wives in view of what 'gossipers' say. This fits in with the tenor of the material as a whole, which suggests that opinion is moving against polygyny as an institution.

Conclusions

An attempt will now be made to offer a broader perspective on the various aspects of social change, insofar as they are liable to give rise to the problems considered. The grouping of causal factors is inevitably to some extent arbitrary, as most of them are closely interrelated.

Geographical mobility and urban life. Both of these widen the potential range of contact with members of the opposite sex. At the same time this means that a person is more often thrown back on his own resources in establishing relations, which creates difficulties for shy and diffident people. Attachments are also liable to spring up between men and women of different tribal as well as social and educational backgrounds, and a proposed marriage across such barriers may lead to friction in the respective families.

Frequent movement for reasons of education or work tend to make for instability of relationships, occasioning distress to those who have been abandoned. Simultaneous friendships and/or engagements often land people in a net of incompatible obligations from which they are incapable of disentangling themselves.

Adoption of western norms, values and criteria of status. The main element in the present context is the taking over of the notion of romantic love, and of marriage as a partnership of like-minded individuals. A corollary to this is the rejection of traditional restrictions on the selection of a marriage partner, i.e., from outside a prescribed range of classificatory kinship and within the tribe. A relatively minor problem here is the difficulty experienced by some young people in recognizing the presence, especially in their partner, of the intense emotional bond which is regarded as the essential prerequisite of a satisfactory relationship. The consequences are much more far-reaching when the dictates of love clash with the wishes of the family of origin; this often results in the most acute anxiety. Even where

---

[7] The previous attitude of the men is probably the crucial variable. By no means all young men who have had some schooling prefer literate wives. It is reckoned by some that a wife with education is too great a financial liability, and they would rather have an illiterate who earns money by trading. For a more detailed discussion of this issue, cf. Jahoda (1958).

the idea of romantic love is not in the foreground, and the family leaves a man free to choose his wife, this new freedom may itself produce a state of uncertainty and doubt if he is not sure what he is looking for.

In this connexion reference should be made to the effect of the emergence of a status system of the western type, for this erects new kinds of barriers. As social differences become more pronounced, there are increasing hazards for matches in which there is a great disparity in terms of education and/or material wealth. The trouble is that many young people, brought together by their families, are of comparable status within the traditional system; and their incompatibility is revealed only when they live together in sections of society that no longer form an integral part of that system. The typical case is of course that of the educated young man who marries an illiterate wife, but other variants have been described in this paper. It is likely that assortative mating along western lines will in the long run operate cumulatively in building up a new class structure.

Differential rates of change of norms and values. It is implicit in much of what has been said that the underlying cause of many of the problems is not just social change as such, but rather the fact that the reorientation it brings about is not uniform; it affects the older generation far less than the younger people. This greatly exacerbates the divergence in outlook between successive generations which is found in varying degrees in all societies. Moreover, the ties of kinship, which are rooted in the old cosmology, have always been extremely close and powerful in West Africa; and the feelings of respect and dependence towards the family of origin have not weakened in proportion to the acceptance of new norms in other spheres. Youths or girls may have their own ideas about the kind of marriage partner they want, yet at the same time they are frequently not able or willing to ignore the pressures or objections of their elders who remain attached to traditional standards. Severing of the ties which bind them to the kin group is not only difficult because it runs counter to deeply entrenched sentiments, but would also be risky in practice in a society where as yet no safety net is provided by the welfare state. Even educated Africans derive comfort and security from the knowledge that they can confidently look forward to help from their kin if they should happen to fall upon evil days; it requires a very independent cast of mind to be able to cut oneself loose under such circumstances. Therefore it becomes necessary to tread an uneasy middle path between following the time-honoured customs as expected by one's elders and pursuing one's own goals and aspirations.

A large proportion of the letters consists of cases where there has been failure to reconcile the conflicting demands, and they are of three main types: first, family pressure has been disregarded, with consequent doubt, remorse or anxiety; second, having given way to family pressure, the result is unhappiness and chafing against the yoke; the most common outcome (and this above all leads to the writing of a letter) was a paralysing feeling of indecision, an inability to act.

There is, of course, no intention of suggesting that the whole of the younger generation is necessarily thus afflicted. The responses to such problems are always a matter of degree, depending on individual differences. No doubt many young people are either sufficiently tough-minded to do what they want irrespective of their family's wishes, or pliant enough to adjust themselves to these wishes without undue mental anguish. Furthermore, many families will tend to show an increasing readiness to compromise, and with the spread of literacy the more rigid of the older norms are likely to lose ground at an ever-increasing rate. Thus in time the conditions giving rise to the particular kinds of problem described will probably cease to exist. The material analysed indicates, however, that during the present period of transition the incidence of conflict and anxiety associated with social change is by no means negligible.

Thomas O. Beidelman

17. Hyena and Rabbit: A Kaguru Representation of Matrilineal Relations*

I

One purpose of this paper is to present a tale which serves as an interesting illustration of certain problems in Kaguru society. In the first part of this paper, I present this tale in a free English translation with a few notes in explanation of certain details in the story. In the second part I discuss the significance of this tale as a means by which one may gain insight into certain important problems in one African matrilineal society.

II

THE TALE OF HYENA AND RABBIT

Once there was a great famine in the land. Rabbit and his uncle[1] Hyena got together in order to discuss how they could manage until the famine ended at the coming harvest. When they met, Rabbit said to his uncle Hyena, 'Uncle, this is a great famine. What do you think we should do

* Reprinted with permission of author and the International African Institute from *Africa* 31 (1), 1961:61–74. A Chikaguru text included with the original article has been omitted and the introduction has been revised slightly because of this. Both of these changes have been made with the permission of the author and Institute.

This study is based on field work carried out in northern Kilosa District, Tanganyika, during 1957–8 under a Ford Foundation grant administered by the University of Illinois.

[1] Mother's brother.

until things get better? Let us sell[2] our mothers. If we keep them, there will be too many of us to get enough to eat.'

Hyena said, 'I think it is better if we kill our mothers. Then we can peddle their flesh in order to get wealth for buying food for our households.'

Rabbit grudgingly agreed to this suggestion. He said to Hyena, 'This is good advice. When shall we kill them? My mother is far away. Shall we start with yours?'

Hyena agreed. He said, 'Whichever one is present, that one we shall kill.'

So they went to Hyena's place, and when they got there, they caught the old woman, the mother of Hyena. Here and there she rushed, crying in vain until she was stabbed. The flayed meat was put in a basket and the two started off to peddle the meat until it was all sold. Then Rabbit began to feel upset and could not bear to kill his mother on account of the famine. So he lay low for many days. The time for Rabbit to kill his mother came and he was very upset. For this reason he hit upon the idea of going hunting and by good fortune he killed a bushbuck in a trap. He was able to flay this in a hurry and then took it to Hyena's. He said, 'Uncle, are you there?'

Hyena replied, 'I am here, sir![3] Why?'

Rabbit said, 'The old woman is ready. The meat is here.'

Hyena answered, 'Hee! Hee! Hee! That is what you've been putting off doing. Now our famine is ended.'

They passed around with their meat until they had none left. But the famine continued in the land. They didn't have anything to eat.

Every evening Rabbit went off to the place where he had hidden his mother so that Hyena should not know that she was still alive. That was where Rabbit was eating. But Hyena was really hit by hunger. To whom could he go to eat? He didn't have any mother left.

One day Hyena asked, 'You, Uncle,[4] where are you eating? Why aren't you getting thin the way I am?'

---

[2] Sell her into domestic slavery. In the past elder Kaguru sometimes secured wealth or paid heavy fines by selling the junior members of their matrilineage. These persons were usually redeemed later by payments by their matrilineage. Such persons were usually sold to other Kaguru and were not sent out of their local area. However, sometimes buyers of such persons sold them to third parties such as Arab slavers. Domestic slaves furnished labour for their masters. Slave women were the most desired. While the children of free women belonged to the matrilineages of their mothers, the children of slave women were entirely subject to their fathers and were quasi-members of their fathers' matrilineages.

[3] The term *mugosi* is translated as 'sir'. It is a form of polite address used to males (kin and non-kin) who are held in high respect. Hyena evidently expects that Rabbit has arrived to fulfil his obligations. See the next footnote.

[4] Among the Kaguru, mother's brother (*bulai* or *kolodyo*) and sister's son (*mwihwa*) terms are sometimes used in reverse of their normal order. A mother's brother is a person who aids a sister's son, but such aid is reciprocal. When such terms are used in reverse order, a sister's son is reminded of his duties to repay the kindness and care of his mother's brother. In this case, Hyena is reminding his well-fed sister's son that food should be shared, since Hyena gave Rabbit a share when he (Hyena) had some.

Rabbit said, 'I have no place to eat. I am like this no matter how bad a famine there may be.'

Many more days passed and Hyena became unconscious. After a few more days he died. Then Rabbit went to the cave where he had hidden his mother. He called out, 'Old woman, Hyena is no more. He is dead. You are free!' Then Rabbit stayed peacefully with his mother for many happy years.

III

The Kaguru are sedentary Bantu cultivators living in east-central [Tanzania] and are organized into approximately 100 matrilineal clans which are each composed of many matrilineages. Before colonial rule and the introduction of a hierarchy of chiefs, the Kaguru had no centralized political system. The cluster of settlements in each series of valleys or ridges formed its own politically autonomous group. Local groups tended to be built up upon the matrilineages of the clan which had gained dominance in an area. The need to maintain fairly large groups for self-protection from the raids of neighbours kept Kaguru settlements far larger than they are today and encouraged far more lineal solidarity than at present. In this period local matrilineages and their affinal connexions constituted the largest stable social and political groups.

The details of Kaguru clan and village organization are not directly relevant to the problems of this paper.[5] The problems presented here concern the different relations between men and women within Kaguru matrilineages. They derive from certain features common to matrilineal systems, viz. the relations between men who hold authority and women who serve to link such men with one another.

In the tale of Rabbit and Hyena the four characters are all members of one matrilineage. They are: two males, Rabbit and his mother's brother, Hyena; and two females, the mothers of Rabbit and of Hyena:

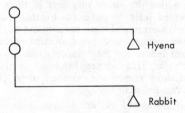

The tale describes relations between these four persons during a time of extreme difficulty. The Kaguru face constant problems in their social and

---

[5] For a description of Kaguru social organization, see Beidelman, 'Witchcraft in Ukaguru', in a symposium on African witchcraft, eds. J. Middleton and E. Winter, Kegan, Paul, London [1963].

physical environment. In the past they suffered not only from raids for women and livestock but also from famine. Today most of their difficulties are confined to raising resources for marriage, fines, education, medical expenses, and litigation. The problem of serious famine is only an extreme and traditional example of the many difficulties which beset all Kaguru and which encourage members of a Kaguru matrilineage to support one another. While such difficulties usually encourage cooperation and solidarity between the members of a matrilineage, if these difficulties are very serious they may sometimes formally separate certain matrilineal kin who are already potentially divided in their loyalties. It is often through such disputes that new matrilineages are formed.

The four individuals in this tale comprise a short-hand model of a Kaguru matrilineage. Each represents an entire category of persons.[6] Let us first consider the two males. Hyena is Rabbit's mother's brother (*bulai* or *kolodyo*[7]) and Rabbit owes him obedience and respect. Rabbit's disobedience to Hyena rests upon the assumption that Hyena does not deserve such authority and respect if he is found to be motivated merely by selfish reasons. If such authority is severely abused, a man may refuse to obey his mother's brother and may sever kinship ties with him.

The authority and power of men within a matrilineage depend upon reciprocation of aid and support between men and their sisters' sons. In their earlier years sisters' sons may depend upon mothers' brothers for economic and political aid and may have few resources of their own. But as these young men mature and establish their own households, they are able to repay the benefits they received from their seniors. The power of such lineage leaders and the solidarity and continuity of a matrilineage depend upon this. In the tale, this reciprocity may be seen in the Kaguru practice of reversed usage of kinship terms on occasions in which a senior

---

[6] Rabbit represents all junior males within a matrilineage, i.e., (in a lineage diagram) all males of ego's generation. Hyena represents all senior adult males within a matrilineage, i.e., all males within ego's mother's generation.

The tale presents the members of a matrilineage in a social vacuum. The positions of fathers and affines are ignored. Wealth, political power, and other factors also determine men's power and the number of kin whom they can control, but these factors also are neglected.

The affines of Hyena and Rabbit are not mentioned in this tale. I suggest that this is because Kaguru consciously think of the tale as an illustration of only one problem: the conflict of loyalties within a matrilineage.

There is a potential conflict between women's obligations to their brothers and to their husbands. Kaguru women sometimes obtain advantages by playing off these two groups of males against each other. Although the tale neglects this aspect, in real life Rabbit's mother would probably seek support and protection from her husband against any unjust demands from her brother.

[7] Kaguru informants insisted that *bulai* and *kolodyo* may be used interchangeably. The word *kolodyo* derives from *lukolo* (root), a Kaguru term for a clan or a matrilineage. *Kolodyo* means 'head of a *lukolo*'. The term *bulai* is the term more frequently used in address.

male desires repayment and aid from a junior, e.g., a man calls his sister's son 'mother's brother', to remind him of his obligations.

Kaguru relations of authority within the matrilineage involve almost exclusively persons of the same generation or of proximate generations. Within generations men have authority over their sisters, and elder siblings have authority over their juniors; between generations men have authority over the children of their sisters.

Now let us consider the two females. These are Hyena's mother and her daughter, Rabbit's mother. These two females link the two males within the matrilineage.

The names of these women are not given in the tale. Kaguru usually refer to women by teknonyms. Women owe their social position to their relations to men. When they are young, they are spoken of as the daughters of their fathers; after they bear sons, they are spoken of as the mothers of their children, especially their sons. A woman with no children does not reach full social maturity.

The roles of Kaguru women as intermediaries depend in Kaguru eyes upon their exclusion from formal authority. Because of this exclusion, Kaguru describe women as 'disinterested and unbiased', having at heart the best interests of all the men and women born into their matrilineage. Women may have strong feelings concerning their various relatives, but ideally they should not be concerned with power in the way that men are. Instead, they should be concerned with the solidarity of the entire group and with maintaining goodwill and cooperation between the various persons whom they link.

Kaguru women sometimes serve as mediators in disputes. Although they possess no formal authority, they may be appealed to as moral authorities and go-betweens for men. Their security and influence derive from this intermediary and supposedly neutral position between persons with formal authority. Let me give three examples of this: 1. A man may fail to obtain the cooperation he demands from his sister's son. He may appeal to his sister to urge her son to obey him. If she is reluctant to do this, her brother may appeal to their mother to persuade his sister in this. 2. A youth may require aid for his education or for paying a fine. He may ask his mother to urge her brother to help him. If this woman fails she may appeal to her mother, who may ask the man to grant his sister's pleas. 3. In the past, women often served as custodians of wealth. Several men within a matrilineage may disagree as to how to divide such wealth. If they are siblings by one mother, they may deposit the wealth with her or perhaps with one of their sisters. In this way, it is available to all men if they need, but none of them has exclusive control over it. This refers not only to wealth from inheritance but also to wealth obtained from brideprice.

Kaguru men are linked by women through women's dual roles as mothers and as sisters. Such a system works so long as women feel equally the demands and obligations entailed by both these roles, i.e., the demands of both their children and their brothers. However, it is quite clear that in certain severe disputes a woman may be called upon to choose between two men, i.e., between her son and her brother or her mother's brother. Kaguru invariably assign primacy to the mother–child relationship, and in any dispute in which such a choice is demanded women support their children and reject their brothers or mothers' brothers.

Here are two such situations:

1. Shortly after Yohanna's daughter, Margareti, was married, she became pregnant by her secret lover. This was her cousin, Yohanna's sister's son, Musa. Her husband returned Margareti to her father, Yohanna, and demanded that Yohanna return the brideprice. Yohanna refused, insisting that this was a matter between the husband and the offending youth. Yohanna said, 'I only gave you a wife; I am not responsible for who sleeps with her.' Musa's father had died and therefore the youth insisted

that his uncle Yohanna was responsible for him. The youth's mother, Yohanna's sister, supported this. They both demanded that Yohanna refund the brideprice. Yohanna insisted that Musa should himself repay the money since he was the trouble-maker. Yohanna's sister angrily left her brother's settlement, even though they had previously been quite close. (Their parents were dead.) The sister said she was going to seek witchcraft against Yohanna and later became renowned for her powers in exorcizing spirit-possessed women. When she died, Yohanna attended her funeral but many bitter words were exchanged between him and her sons. Later, when Yohanna became ill and died, his sons blamed the witchcraft of Yohanna's sister's children. They said that these children had inherited witchcraft from their mother.[8]

2. Madikuli and her son Musegu lived in the village of her brother, Chadibwa. Musegu was caught having sexual intercourse with Chadibwa's wife. Adultery is an offence meriting a fine, but adultery with a mother's brother's wife was traditionally a very serious offence sometimes punished by death. Today government law treats this as any other type of adultery

---

[8] See Beidelman, 'Witchcraft in Ukaguru', in a symposium on African witchcraft, eds. J. Middleton and E. Winter, Kegan Paul, London [1963].

and it is settled by a fine. Musegu paid a very large fine, but Chadibwa said that he did not want the youth in his village any longer. Musegu went to his mother (his father is dead) and asked her to intercede for him. Chadibwa told Madikuli that if she stood by her son, he would know that she had supported the youth's adultery. He told her that she must throw her son out. Madikuli refused and continued to defend her son. Chadibwa tried to drive his sister and her son from his village. The Kaguru court urged Chadibwa to allow the two to remain. Chadibwa adamantly refused and the woman and her son left.

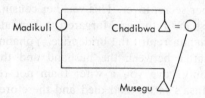

In our tale two males within a matrilineage meet to decide how to cope with a difficult situation. Rabbit suggests that they pawn the women of their matrilineage in order to obtain resources. This was a fairly common practice in the past. Such women could be retrieved later by the payment of certain fees. Men within a lineage obtain wealth and other advantages in brideprice, fines, and alliances by the manipulation of women. Selling women into slavery is an extreme example of such manipulation.

Hyena rejects the idea of pawning the women and suggests that they be killed. But this would dispose of the women irretrievably, and with this the matrilineage would be doomed to extinction.[9] The junior male, Rabbit, accepts this decision, but the tale implies that this is due to Rabbit being an obedient sister's son: the text states that Rabbit grudgingly (*nheifo-nheifo*) agreed. Although Rabbit is more properly called *Sungula* (the word for rabbit), in this and the following situations he is referred to as *Chibuga*. *Chibuga* means 'a small creature' and this term is used whenever Rabbit commits an act which is wrong but which is done at the order of his mother's brother, Hyena. The name *Chibuga* emphasizes Rabbit's junior status as a sister's son and Rabbit's obligation to submit to his senior, Hyena. Thus the onus for the crime falls solely upon Hyena.

Kaguru males are expected to obey their mothers' brothers even though some of their duties may appear odious, for such duties are said to be for the good of the entire matrilineage. However, the suggestion to kill these females is clearly not for the good of the matrilineage, since it involves the annihilation of its generative half. The act which Hyena tells Rabbit to do is in direct conflict with Rabbit's obligations to his own mother. This

---

[9] In the tale there are only two women within the matrilineage. If Rabbit had a sister, the problem of extinction would not be raised.

is also the case with Hyena, but in the tale Hyena appears utterly aberrant and quite pleased to commit such a heinous crime.

Within a Kaguru matrilineage there is a conflict between the chain of authority of males and these males' obligations and sentiments towards females. Both are necessary for the working of the Kaguru system, but Hyena has chosen to give priority to his own aims. He includes Rabbit in his plan and therefore sets the males against the females within the matrilineage. Hyena uses the females of his matrilineage in a way not only harmful to them individually but harmful to the lineage as well.

The conduct of Hyena and of Rabbit is sharply contrasted in the tale. Hyena kills his own mother. This is the most wicked act which Kaguru can imagine. But Hyena also tries to persuade Rabbit to commit a similar crime. Rabbit's intended victim is Hyena's sister. In a sense Hyena is therefore trebly guilty. His offences are matricide, intended sororicide, and evil influence on his nephew. By a ruse Rabbit avoids killing his own mother, but does not prevent Hyena from killing his (Hyena's) mother, Rabbit's maternal grandmother.

It may be asked why Rabbit agrees to the death of his maternal grandmother. Kaguru do not conceive of authority or great respect towards alternate generations. Authority, both jural and moral, is vested chiefly in the first ascending generation. Kin of alternate generations are equivalent and their relations are essentially informal, non-authoritarian, and at times even of a highly jocular character. The respect for and protection of Hyena's mother are essentially the responsibility of Hyena and it is Hyena's abnegation of this responsibility upon which the entire plot depends. Even though Rabbit may have aided Hyena, this was done by Rabbit in his role as *Chibuga* (small creature), the junior member following his mother's brother.[10]

However, Rabbit has a far more important reason for acceding to this crime. In a sense Rabbit may even secretly desire his maternal grandmother's death. So long as this old woman lives, there are very strong sanctions for solidarity between all her lineal descendants and Hyena remains in relatively secure power. Upon her death the process of lineage segmentation may begin and Rabbit may hope to assume some power himself, even while Hyena still lives.

Let us suppose that Hyena's mother has several daughters besides Rabbit's mother.[11] The descendants of these various females form potential

---

[10] Rabbit can place responsibility for Hyena's mother's death upon Hyena. Rabbit cannot easily do this with his own mother. The Kaguru insist that obligations to one's own mother outweigh all other social obligations.

[11] In the tale no such sisters appear. Nor are we told that Rabbit has sisters. However, one may presume that so long as Rabbit's mother lives it is possible she may bear such offspring. In Rabbit's eyes perhaps the greatest value of his mother is that she may provide him with sisters.

lineage segments united under one common living ancestress, Hyena's mother. Hyena has jural authority over these persons and uses the mediative influence of his mother and sisters to exert his power. When Hyena's mother dies, there is no longer a living link between these various groups. She may still be appealed to as a dead spirit, but this is far from being as effective as she was in life. Hyena remains the titular head of the group, but he will have more difficulty than before in exerting his power. Males in each lineage segment are always attempting to exert their own interests. A mother of one of these males sees herself occupying a position analogous to that of Hyena's mother and she may encourage her son in his claims for independence.

Rabbit gains by Hyena's crime so that one might say that he has proved to be even craftier than Hyena. Kaguru freely admit that a man may look forward to the death of his mother's brother since he wishes to assume power himself. In this tale the crime of Hyena (we shall see that he is a witch) makes his death not only convenient to Rabbit but morally right as well.

Kaguru speak of the struggle for power between men within a matrilineage, but they seem to avoid discussing the fact not only that men gain power from the deaths of mothers' brothers whom they replace but that they gain by the deaths of certain females as well. In fact, it would seem that the deaths of these females are even more important prerequisites to obtaining power or independence than are the deaths of males. The death of an elderly female linking many descendants constitutes the structural weakness which may lead to segmentation.

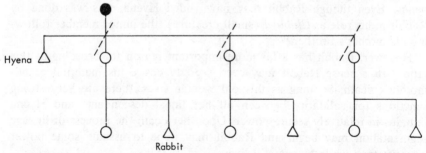

Once this murder has been accomplished, the entire moral and structural situation within the matrilineage vastly alters. Rabbit need obey or aid Hyena no longer since Hyena has shown himself to be a wicked relative. With the death of Hyena's mother, the senior female linking Rabbit's mother and Hyena is gone, and Hyena's control over Rabbit's mother and thus over Rabbit has decreased. In the tale Hyena presents the murders of his own mother and of Rabbit's mother as inextricably linked. An antisocial act against one female involves the other, and if Hyena becomes motherless while Rabbit does not, Rabbit's position within the matrilineage is strengthened at Hyena's expense.

In all the cases I encountered in which Kaguru siblings severed social relations by disowning each other, by accusation of witchcraft, or by grave insult, the mother uniting such siblings was dead. This does not mean that such siblings automatically break their relations when their mother dies. But there is a greater likelihood than before that future quarrels may become irreconcilable.

After the murder of his grandmother, Rabbit neglects his responsibilities to Hyena. Not only does Rabbit avoid the evil act which Hyena has urged, but he does not help starving Hyena when he is asked to do so. Hyena asks why Rabbit is still fat and apparently not suffering from starvation. He addresses Rabbit not as 'sister's child' (*mwihwa*) but as 'mother's brother' (*bulai*). Rabbit offers no assistance and Hyena dies.

The fates of Hyena and Rabbit affirm the Kaguru social and moral order. Hyena has no mother to care for him and he has forfeited the aid of his sister's child by his crime. He therefore starves to death. Rabbit has protected his mother and her care enables him to survive the peril of the famine. When I asked Kaguru if this tale had a moral, they replied that the moral was obvious: You may have many mother's brothers but you have only one mother and her well-being is essential to your own.

IV

A final set of motifs remain to be explained. These are: 1. the use of these particular animals, Rabbit and Hyena, to illustrate this tale; 2. the extreme violence of Hyena's behaviour, viz. murdering his mother rather than merely pawning her, and selling her flesh, presumably for cannibalistic purposes.

These motifs are explicable in terms of Kaguru beliefs in witchcraft which are inextricably associated with Kaguru concepts of anti-social behaviour (Beidelman, op. cit.).

Kaguru tend to interpret most anti-social behaviour, especially the failure to meet obligations towards kin, as witchcraft. A person of any age or sex may be a witch. While some witches have medicine for their power, really dangerous ones are considered inherently evil and able to work much of their harm by sheer ill will. A witch is said to work at night, to delight in injuring others, to devour human beings, and to travel through the air clinging to the belly of a hyena. Witches tend to have moral and physical attributes which are the reverse of those desirable in normal human beings. The most terrible of all witchcraft acts are associated with the suspected murder of lineal relatives and/or incestuous relations with such kin. Kaguru say that all real witches are incestuous and cannibalistic, and that these habits show how inhuman witches really are.

It may be possible to interpret certain portions of this tale in a Freudian manner in order to find indications of incest. I am not competent to carry out such analysis, but I offer one example of such sexual symbolization.

Hyena stabbing his mother may be interpreted as symbolic sexual intercourse with her. The Kaguru themselves clearly recognize such symbols and incorporate them into their songs and jokes. One of the best known initiation songs taught to boys and girls goes: Youngster, don't go outside early or you will meet a rhinoceros with a horn; it will be stabbing and cutting and they [sic] will be showing their parts (of the body) which are red. Young Kaguru are taught that the real meaning of this riddle-song is: A young person should not leave his or her bachelor-hut too early and enter a parent's hut or he will surprise his parents having sexual intercourse (a forbidden sight).

The characters of Rabbit and Hyena are sharply contrasted in Kaguru belief. A rabbit is usually seen as a somewhat playful, clever, and sympathetic creature—although Kaguru also enjoy eating rabbits. On the other hand, a hyena is considered to be the epitome of all that is objectionable and unclean. The hyena is a sly creature, but Kaguru also say that a hyena is not so sly as he thinks he is, for a hyena is often bettered at his own game. In addition to being a 'duped trickster', the hyena is invariably associated with witchcraft and thus with all that is anti-social and immoral in Kaguru life. It is quite clear that these two sets of characteristics fit the two protagonists in the tale.

The existence of two different species of animals within one matrilineage is analogous to the potential existence of two different types of Kaguru within one matrilineage. There are moral Kaguru and there are anti-social, immoral Kaguru, i.e., witches. The witch is quite alien to normal Kaguru, even though they may all be of the same matrilineage. Some of the most vehement accusations of witchcraft occur between members of the same matrilineage. Although Kaguru believe that witchcraft is inherited matrilineally, they admit that not all members of a matrilineage need be witches because one member is: sometimes this characteristic fails to be transmitted 'in the blood'.[12] A witch's inhuman tastes for human flesh and for incest mark such a person as a species apart.

Hyena shows himself to be the epitome of a Kaguru witch, i.e., an extremely anti-social and socially unmanageable person. Murdering his mother and peddling her flesh may be interpreted as extreme examples of what any anti-social and uncooperative behaviour is considered to be. Kaguru sometimes describe selfish, witch-like behaviour as 'devouring and murdering others'.[13]

---

[12] Kaguru say that they are related to their mothers by blood, to their fathers by bone and the solid parts of the body.

[13] As I have shown in my paper on Kaguru witchcraft, an economically or politically powerful person is often unmanageable by his subordinates and he is frequently suspected of witchcraft because of this. Among the Kaguru it is often the affluent and the powerful who can afford to act in an anti-social manner. Therefore we should not be surprised to find that in this tale the witch-like person is Hyena, the superior person within the matrilineage.

In the past a Kaguru suspected of witchcraft was killed if he or she was found guilty by ordeal. Today suspects cannot be dealt with so easily, although witchcraft accusations and suspicions are still very prevalent. At best, a Kaguru may practise counter-witchcraft or he may avoid a suspected witch. The fate of Hyena is therefore an idealization which may give comfort to some Kaguru: Hyena's witchcraft leads to his own destruction. Most Kaguru regret that the witches whom they suspect are about them are never punished.

V

In the tale of Rabbit and Hyena a social problem of great concern to the Kaguru is presented in simple and relatively innocuous form. The problem is that of conflict and division within a matrilineage, the most important social unit in Kaguru society. It is therefore not surprising that Kaguru consider the offenders in such cases to be witches, i.e., the most wicked and inhuman persons they can imagine. Ideally such persons' anti-social behaviour should lead to their own destruction—even though in life it seems to many Kaguru that such acts go unpunished.

These conflicts are inevitable. But it is important that, when they do occur, 1. the persons considered guilty of causing such conflicts should be punished, and 2. when loyalties conflict, the proper choice between them should be made.

The Kaguru are keenly aware of the conflict between the interests of male authority and its potentially selfish abuse, and of the obligations of children towards their mothers. The interests of men are seen as ultimately divisive outside the context of the women who link them with one another. A dead man may be replaced in his authority by another, often by his sister's son. A man has no lineal offspring, but a woman has and her death leaves an irreparable gap in the position of mediator between the potential lineage segments formed by her offspring. Furthermore, each woman's death represents the loss of a genitrix for her lineage and thus a threat to its perpetuation. Men have no such importance. If choice between allegiance to men and to women must be made (and Kaguru insist that such situations are to be avoided if at all possible), Kaguru invariably endorse the obligations to a mother, without whom the matrilineal system has no meaning.

Part VI

DIFFERENTIATION AND INEQUALITY

As we noted in the general introduction, Locke laid the foundation for Jefferson's assertion that "all men are created equal." As a premise about individual political rights, this is acceptable, but as a comment about individual biophysical endowment, this most certainly is not true. Indeed, if anything, the striking fact about individuals is how many ways they differ. All societies contain individuals of many different ages, shapes, and sizes. People differ in strength, stamina, general intelligence, particular types of intelligence, health, and so forth. The combinations of such factors produce individuals of endless variety. We use the term "differentiation" to refer to such variety. The word is essentially neutral and contrasts with a different but related term—inequality.

Conventionally, the word "inequality" as it applies to people implies that individuals or groups so described are not "merely" different, they are different in rank and power. When such inequality is relatively stable and backed by publicly recognized beliefs and values, we may say that the inequality is structured and that the society is stratified. Social stratification is, then, structured inequality. It is not possible to say for certain that all societies are stratified; in all probability they are not. But most societies are stratified to some degree, and it is the degree of stratification that is the critical matter. Indeed, it is so critical that some would limit the word "stratified" to those situations where the inequality is structured in such a way that some people do not have direct control over the basic tools and other resources needed for survival.

Of the many issues that pertain to differentiation and inequality, three of the more basic ones are discussed in the three selections in Part VI. The first has to do with the concept of role; the second directs our attention to rites of transition; and the third focuses on the complex issues of social stratification in pre-industrial society.

239

Next to individuals, one of the most important units of analysis is the social role or role relationship. The term "role" is borrowed from the theater and although recently added to the technical vocabulary of social science, is an old notion (Shakespeare's line "All the world's a stage, and all the men and women merely players" being one of the more famous expressions of this idea). In Chapter 18, Lincoln Keiser analyzes the roles and role relationships he found in the Vice Lord Nation, a large federation of street-corner groups in Chicago, thus providing a clear illustration of the principal characteristics of roles and role relationships. Three major points about roles may be noted here: 1. each role is only a facet of an individual's social identity; 2. roles are mobilized during social interaction —in a way, we could say that it is not whole individuals who interact, it is roles; and 3. roles and, as a consequence, role relationships are defined in terms of expected and appropriate behavior. Within any society, there are many roles and any individual may be expected to perform several of these each day, shifting from one to another with, usually, a great deal of ease. As an exercise, and as a way of gaining an understanding of both the strengths and weaknesses of the role concept, the reader may wish to try and list all the roles and role relationships he or she performs during a single day. How does this list compare with lists made by others? What are the implications of the differences?

Although there are many gradations of age, people in most societies are differentiated according to a fairly small number of age categories. Sometimes people within an age category form a group—that is, an interacting, organized unit. Probably no other age-based distinction is more fundamental than that of "adult/non-adult." In our society, at least until recently, a person became an adult—that is acquired privileges associated with adulthood—at many different times. For example, consider the laws in your state, especially as they stood approximately twenty years ago, regarding the right to own property, get married without the consent of a parent, to join or be inducted into the military, to have a permit to drive a car, carry a gun, go fishing, to vote, to be sent to prison rather than a "detention home," to pay full fare on buses, at the cinema, to drink "hard" liquor, and so on. In general, these "privileges" all come at different ages. In a world-wide perspective, such a complex pattern is rare. Most societies establish certain points at which a person ceases to be a child and becomes an adult—in all respects. Often these transition points are marked by elaborate initiation rituals, some involving a great deal of pain for the initiate.

In the brief essay by Jane Goodale (Chapter 19), we learn about a less painful transition rite (or rite of passage) which is carried out by the Tiwi of Australia. It is the "yam ceremony" and it takes six years for an initiate to be graduated as an adult. Today, however, there are no new initiates because the young people of Tiwi society are establishing themselves as adults by other means. But for the participating graduates, the instructional songs that are sung relay important information about how to be an adult. For traditional Tiwi men, this is more than being married and being economically self-sufficient. It is also having the knowledge and skills necessary to participate successfully in the complex social and political affairs of life and to be able to create linguistically sophisticated songs about these events at a yam ceremony.

In the essay by Wayne Suttles in Chapter 20, we see one of the earlier and more basic discussions of an issue that is still a very lively one nearly twenty years later (e.g., see the recent and hotly debated analysis by Ruyle 1973). This issue is whether or not there were "classes" within any of the Northwest Coast Indian societies. In our terms, the Coast Salish and the other ethnic groups of the Northwest Coast are stratified, but this does not tell us whether they did or did not have classes or whether or not there was much mobility between them. Suttles argues from historical data and contemporary observations to the effect that there are classes among the Coast Salish, the group with which he has lived and worked over a period of many years. Although discussed at greater length in his other publications, Suttles notes that the resource base of the Coast Salish people is abundant compared to other Northwest Coast groups. Since there is a great deal of evidence supporting a correlation between size of population, extent of resource base, and extent of stratification, it is possible to explain the existence of classes among the Coast Salish and their possible absence elsewhere at least partly in these terms. However, Suttles also stresses that the differential control of resources, in the case of the Coast Salish at least, does not account completely for the existence of a "lower class." Rather, other factors such as knowledge of spirits and "advice" (really knowledge of moral precepts and of one's own family history, as well as that of others) are relevant. "High class" people know these things; "low class" people do not. Also noted in Suttles' discussion is the role of "potlatching" in the status drives of individuals. Such efforts are very similar to the feast-giving activities of Melanesian "big men" and they offer some of the same ecological advantages (e.g., effectively distributing resources over larger areas and thus easing the strain caused by variations in the food supply—particularly salmon).

R. Lincoln Keiser

18. The Vice Lord Social System—Roles*

An important part of the pattern in Vice Lord social life is comprised of what can be called social roles. In our study of Vice Lord roles we shall use a theoretical framework to help organize and bring sense to the data. Dr. Allen Hoben has written a concise explanation of the role concept in a community study guide for Peace Corps volunteers. Part of this will form a section of our framework, and that portion of his work is included here.

Hoben identifies three general aspects of social roles:

> First, there are in any society a number of well-defined and publicly recognized social personalities or identities. Father, son, teacher, pupil, employer, and employee are examples of social identities in our own society. It should be stressed that these are not different kinds of people, but different social identities. The same individual is called upon to assume different identities in different situations.
>
> Second, in any society only in certain social identities can people interact with one another. There are very definite rules of combination—a sort of grammar of possible social interaction. For example, father-son, father-daughter, husband-wife, teacher-pupil, and employer-employee are grammatical combinations of social identities in our own society. Father-pupil, employer-son, daughter-teacher, and son-wife are not. A single

* Reprinted with permission of author and publisher from *The Vice Lords: Warriors of the Streets,* by R. Lincoln Keiser 1969 (Chapter 4, "The Social System—Roles," pages 37–48); Holt, Rinehart and Winston, Inc., publisher.

social identity (father or professor) may have a grammatical relationship with several other identities (father-son, father-daughter, or professor-student, professor-professor, professor-chairman of department).

Third, there are in any society, for each grammatically possible combination of social identities, agreed-upon rules concerning appropriate modes of interaction. This means, for example, that father and son, teacher and pupil, employer and employee are aware of the behavior they expect from one another [Hoben 5–6:n.d.].

If we focus on the third aspect—the "agreed-upon rules concerning appropriate modes of interaction"—differences in kinds of rules are found:

1. There are formal rights and duties limiting the behavior of individuals in identity relationships. A Vice Lord who assumes a particular identity expects certain rights, and owes certain duties to the Vice Lord who assumes the alter identity in the relationship. If either party fails to fulfill his duties, sanctions are imposed.
2. There are modes of behavior that are considered proper between individuals in social relationships. These we can call social etiquette.
3. There are modes of behavior that signal which identities are being assumed.

The final point in our framework concerns role distribution. If the distribution of roles in relation to social contexts is studied, important differences in contextualization are found. While Vice Lords assume some identities in a few contexts, there are, in contrast, other identities that are assumed in a wide range of social contexts.

VICE LORD–VICE LORD

The role Vice Lord–Vice Lord is found in a wide range of social contexts. Whether hanging on the corner, drinking wine, or gang fighting, individuals in the club often assume the identity Vice Lord in relationships with each other. There are a certain set of rights and duties that regulate behavior between individuals assuming this identity. When my informants discussed the way Vice Lords should behave toward one another, the idea of mutual help was a constantly recurring theme. As one person put it, "We may get to arguing and then humbug [fight], but soon as it's over we buy a drink, and we back together. See, the way we see this thing, we all out to help each other . . . really."

Mutual help can be divided into two kinds—help with regard to material things, and aid in fighting and other dangerous activities such as strong-arming. Vice Lords state that members of the club should help each other in any kind of dangerous activity. If a Vice Lord is jumped on by members of another club, all other Vice Lords present should help, regardless of personal risk. Also, if a Vice Lord asks another to help in hustling, he should not turn down the request. When I asked if most Vice Lords actually do usually give physical help to each other, the answer was an emphatic "yes." For example, I asked one Vice Lord what one should do if he saw another Lord getting jumped on. The answer was, "Help him! You not supposed to do this, you going to do this! You a Lord . . . Lords don't fear nothing but God and death. I never seen a Lord cop out [chicken out]— not a true Lord." When pressed, however, some informants admitted that not all Vice Lords act in this manner. Those who don't, however, are strongly sanctioned. A person who does not fulfill the obligations of physical support is derisively referred to as a "punk," or a "chump." According to one informant, if one is judged a punk, other Vice Lords will refuse to have anything to do with him: "They say he's a punk—tell him to go on away from them; tell him to go home; tell him to stop hanging with them." Another Vice Lord stated that a person would actually be physically sanctioned if he "punked out": "Most of the time when a fellow punks out they wait until the person get out of the hospital, get his side of the story, see did the dude really punk out. If the guy say he punked out on him they usually jump on him . . . or take him in Cobra territory and put him out."

It should be pointed out, however, that the obligation of physical support is similar to the commandment "Thou shalt not kill." Although this commandment is supported by sanctions, there are certain circumstances when it can be broken with impunity. Sanctions are not imposed for killing in self-defense, or during a war. Similarly, sanctions are not always imposed on Vice Lords who do not give physical aid to other Vice Lords. For example, if a small group of Vice Lords is attacked by a much larger enemy force, it is felt that one Vice Lord should run and get help rather than stay and help the others. Also if a Vice Lord sees another member being beaten up by an enemy group, he can try to get a weapon before helping in the fight. Even if he returns with his weapon after the fight is finished he will not normally be sanctioned for punking out. There are also situations where a Vice Lord's obligations to help other Vice Lords in hustling activities is put aside. For example, at 3:00 A.M. one morning two drunk Vice Lords came to the house of Doughbelly and yelled in his window asking him to help them hold up somebody. Because of the noise they created Doughbelly's mother told him he could no longer live in her house. He became enraged at the two drunk Lords for getting him "thrown out," and told them he would not help them, and further, if he saw them again he would kill them. It was never suggested publicly that Doughbelly had punked out for refusing to help in this situation, and no sanctions were imposed.

Since there are sanctions imposed for failing to fulfill the obligations of physical support, it seems clear that these are part of the rights and duties of the Vice Lord–Vice Lord role. A Vice Lord has the duty to give physical support to other Vice Lords and the right to physical support from other Vice Lords. This set of rights and duties, however, can be tempered by particular circumstances.

The rights and duties of mutual help regarding material things presents a more complicated picture. Although Vice Lords say they should lend money and clothes, share food, and should not try to "beat" (con) each other out of their possessions, many individuals admit that most do not usually act in this way. In fact when I asked if Vice Lords usually do give material help, the answer was often hoots of laughter. In my observations I found that Vice Lords frequently tried to beat each other out of things, and saw many cases where individuals refused to lend things to other Vice Lords. There were no group sanctions imposed for failing to live up to this ideal, and when questioned, my informants stated that it was the responsibility of the individual who felt he was wronged to take what action he felt necessary. Can it be said that mutual help with regard to material things is not important in the Vice Lord–Vice Lord role? I don't think so. It is generally felt that individuals who refuse to live up to the ideal of mutual help should not deny the validity of the ideal. Further, there are situations when most Vice Lords usually will extend material help to other members of the club. If they are convinced that a member is really in need, then he usually will be helped. An individual may have been thrown out of his home by angry parents and have to fend for himself on the streets, or he may have recently returned from jail with no money and nowhere to live. In such cases other Vice Lords usually give whatever help they can. I observed an instance where material help was given to a Vice Lord in need. A set had been planned by the 15th Street Lords. Throughout the prior week, the set was a constant topic of conversation. The clothes that were going to be worn and the girls that were going to be present were repeatedly discussed. The evening of the set I met a group of 15th Street Lords at the house of Tex, the 15th Street's president. Everyone was dressed and ready for the set except Old Dude. Old Dude was one of the least important members of the 15th Street Lords. He was thought by everyone to be "light upstairs" (not too intelligent), and he did not have a rep for gang fighting. His family was extremely poor, even by ghetto standards, and his mother gave all her attention to another brother. One of the fellows asked Old Dude, "Say man, why you ain't dressed for the set?"

"I ain't got no pants. It's my own fault. I knew about the set all week, but I just ain't got no pants."

Tex said, "Damn Jack! You should've asked us. You a Lord—we take care of you." Tex then asked his mother to press one of his extra pairs of pants, and another of the fellows went home to get a clean shirt for Old Dude to wear.

It is interesting that in this context Vice Lords sanction individuals who will not help a club member in need. Such a person is referred to as "stingy" and becomes the topic of derogatory conversation. Certainly anyone with leadership aspirations could not afford to be classified as stingy. From this we can conclude that material help is a binding obligation when it is thought an individual is in real need.

Looking now at the rights and duties regarding mutual help, a clearer picture emerges. Mutual help, both material and physical, is a binding obligation when Vice Lords feel real need is involved. If a Vice Lord is jumped on by members of an enemy club, he is in danger of serious physical injury. When a Vice Lord has nowhere to live and nothing to eat, he is also in need. The obligations of mutual help become binding in such situations. We can now better understand why Vice Lords feel that even when an individual is not in real need, it is still necessary to uphold the value of mutual help. Life in the ghetto poses many risks; the rights and obligations of the Vice Lord–Vice Lord role provide a kind of social insurance. No one knows when he may find it necessary to bring into play the obligations of mutual help. Thus the ultimate legitimacy of such obligations must be jealously guarded. Publicly denying that these obligations are legitimate would threaten the well-being of all Vice Lords. Therefore, it is felt that individuals should not deny the legitimacy of a request for help, although the request does not always have to be granted.

There are certain forms in the interactive behavior of individuals who assume the Vice Lord identity that can be called social etiquette. Standardized greetings are one example. When individuals pass one another on the street there are two greetings that are used. In some cases the right hand is raised to the side, the hand balled into a fist, and the arm raised and lowered two or three times. In other instances the club name is yelled out as a greeting.

Upholding the legitimacy of the obligations of mutual help is also a part of Vice Lord social etiquette. For example, if a Vice Lord were asked to loan money to another member and answered, "No man! I ain't your daddy. I ain't going to give you nothing!" this would be a breach of good manners, that is, it would go against social etiquette. It would also be interpreted as a hostile act—a signal not only that he was refusing to assume the identity Vice Lord vis-à-vis the asker but also that he was assuming an identity as a protagonist. The individual who asked for the money would then have the legitimate right to retaliate by starting a fight, that is, public opinion would support his starting a fight. In contrast, if the person asked for the loan couched his refusal in the form of an excuse, and in a friendly tone, this would constitute proper social etiquette. It would not be interpreted as a hostile act, and public opinion would not support the asker if he started a fight. I observed an instance that provides a good example.

A meeting of the Nation had just occurred, and groups of Vice Lords were standing around talking. I was with Goliath, my major informant, and a few other Vice Lords. While we were talking, Tico walked up and said to Goliath, "Hey man, give me a quarter. I get paid Tuesday, and I'll take care of you then, but I got to get me some jive [wine] tonight." Goliath answered, "Yeah man, I'll take care of you," and turned around and started talking to another Vice Lord who was standing with us. After a few minutes Tico again asked Goliath for the money. "Damn Jack, what about the quarter?" Goliath answered, "Yeah, I'll turn you on." This continued for a short time—Goliath kept assuring Tico he was going to give him a quarter, but made no move to actually do so. Finally he reached into his pocket, pulled out some change, and began counting it intently: "Let's see, I need forty cents for a Polish [sausage], twenty-five for a . . ."

"Shit man, we Vice Lords. We supposed to be brothers. Come on, Jack, I gotta get me a taste."

"I'll take care of you. You know that. Now I need forty for a Polish, twenty-five for carfare, fifty to get my baby some milk . . . shit! I'm fifteen cents short. Say man, can you loan me fifteen cents?" Tico shook his head, and walked away in disgust.

I should note that Goliath did not need 15¢—he had $10 in his wallet —but this was used as an excuse rather than denying that he should loan the quarter. Goliath was, therefore, observing the proper social forms of the Vice Lord–Vice Lord role. (Incidentally, Tico did not need the quarter. I saw him later that evening with $2.)

STREET MAN–STREET MAN

Another role that is found in a wide range of contexts is what I call the Street Man–Street Man role. The social identity Street Man is one that all male Blacks living in the ghetto assume at various times. Vice Lords often assume this identity in their relationship both with other members and those who do not belong to the club. The essential element in the Street Man–Street Man role is manipulation. It is expected that persons who assume the Street Man identity will try to manipulate (or, as Vice Lords say, "beat") each other out of as much as possible. This manipulation, however, has certain bounds set to it. An example will illustrate.

While driving down 16th Street, Cochise was hit by a woman who had gone through a red light. She did not have insurance, but agreed to pay $40 for damages. After two weeks she still had not paid Cochise, and he decided to get the money himself. He asked Jesse, another Vice Lord, to accompany him and help out in case of any trouble. Jesse was to get a share of whatever was collected in return for his help. Jesse and Cochise broke into the woman's house and took a television set, radio, and toaster. Cochise kept the toaster and radio. Jesse got the television set, but gave Cochise $20 so that each would have a fair share. Later Cochise and Jesse were on the corner of 16th and Lawndale discussing what had happened. Cochise mentioned that he was going to take the radio home and then try to sell it the next day. Jesse said, "No man, don't do that. The Man liable to come in your house, and if he find the radio he'll bust [arrest] you. Now I know an old building, ain't nobody in there. You can leave it there."

Later, when I mentioned this incident to Goliath he laughed and said, "You know why Jesse said that?" I said, "No."

"Well, if Cochise took that radio home, Jesse couldn't go in his house and get it, but if he put it in that old building then Jesse'd sneak back at night and get the radio hisself."

In this instance Jesse was attempting to manipulate Cochise in order to beat him out of the radio. According to the expectations of the Street Man–Street Man role it was acceptable for Jesse to attempt this. However, there are limits to the ways it could be done. If Cochise had taken the radio home, it would not have been acceptable for Jesse to have taken it from there. Stealing from the home of a close acquaintance is considered wrong behavior by Vice Lords, and few individuals would have much to do with a person known to act in this way. On the other hand, if Jesse could have talked Cochise into leaving the radio in an abandoned building, he would have been free to go back and get it for himself. Successfully manipulating others is called "whupping the game." If Jesse had been successful in whupping the game on Cochise, his prestige with other Vice Lords would have increased. It is now possible to isolate at least one of the rights and duties of the Street Man–Street Man role. Individuals who assume the identity Street Man have the right to expect others in the alter identity will follow the rules which set limits to manipulation, and have the duty to follow these rules themselves. The sanction of public opinion supports this right and duty.

The social etiquette of the Street Man–Street Man role consists of greetings, farewells, and forms of ongoing social interaction. These are two greetings that are generally used. An individual may say either "How you doing?" or "What's happening?" Sometimes "man" or "Jack" is placed at the end of the greeting—for example, "What's happening, Jack?" The person who begins the exchange has the option to choose the greeting he wishes. When one of these greetings is used to initiate a social exchange, the other is usually the response. To terminate a social episode most individuals say simply, "Later."

A form of behavior that is a part of ongoing social interaction is hand slapping. In hand slapping a person puts his hand out with the palm up, and another person touches the open palm with his own hand or arm. Although this might seem somewhat similar in outward form to shaking hands, as we shall see, it has radically different social significance. (Vice Lords do not usually shake hands like most middle-class Americans.)

A hand-slapping exchange can begin in two ways. In some cases during the course of a social episode an individual puts his hand out with the palm raised. The proper response is to touch the raised palm with a hand or arm. Other times a hand-slapping exchange is initiated by a person raising his hand with the palm down. The proper response is to put out the hand with the palm raised. The first individual then slaps the outraised palm. In the first kind of hand-slapping exchange there are several kinds of responses to an outraised palm that are considered proper. Some, but not all, of these have different social significance. A person can respond to an outraised palm by slapping it with his own palm either up or down. This has no particular social significance. Touching the outraised palm with the arm or elbow is also a possible response. Further, an individual can vary the intensity of his slap. These last two differences—touching the palm with an arm or elbow rather than the hand and varying the intensity of the slap—do have significance.

In general, when a hand-slapping episode occurs during social interaction it emphasizes agreement between the two parties. If an individual has said something, or done something he thinks particularly noteworthy, he will put out his hand to be slapped. By slapping it, the alter in the relationship signals agreement. Varying the intensity of the slap response indicates varying degrees of agreement. A Vice Lord may say, "Five Lords can whup fifty Cobras!" and then put out his hand, palm up. Another club member responds by slapping the palm hard, thus indicating strong agreement. The first Vice Lord might then say, "I can whup ten Cobras myself!" and again put out his hand. This time, however, the second individual may respond with a much lighter slap. This indicates that he does not emphatically agree with the statement. If he barely touches the outraised palm with a flick motion of the wrist he indicates disparagement. However, if he touches the outraised palm with his arm or elbow this shows that he respects the person, but does not feel his statement is either particularly true, or else particularly important. If the second individual raises his hand before the first puts out his hand, this not only emphasizes agreement, but also expresses esteem.

It is considered a serious breach of social etiquette to purposely ignore the initial moves of a hand-slapping episode. I was told that to do so is a serious insult. While I observed several instances in which Vice Lords indicated disparagement by lightly touching an outraised hand with a flick of the wrist, I never saw anyone refuse to respond at all in some appropriate way.

VICE LORD–ENEMY

The social identity, Vice Lord, has a grammatical relationship with the identity I call Enemy. An individual who is a member of the Vice Lords can assume either the identity Street Man or Vice Lord in social interaction with males who are not members of the club. If he assumes the Street Man identity, the grammatically proper identity for the alter to assume is also Street Man. However, if he assumes the Vice Lord identity, then the alter is automatically defined as an Enemy. Both parties in such a relationship have an initial option as to which identity they will choose, but if either chooses the identity which defines the situation as one of enmity, then the other must choose the grammatically matching one. In other words, if the individual who is not a member of the Vice Lords assumes the identity Street Man, then the person who is a Vice Lord has an option. He can assume either the identity Street Man, or that of Vice Lord. If he assumes the latter, then the first individual must act as Enemy. In contrast, if the first individual assumes the Enemy identity rather than that of Street Man, then the second person must assume the identity Vice Lord.

Although there is insufficient information to discuss the Vice Lord–Enemy role in terms of rights and duties and social etitquette, I did find both behavioral expectations between individuals interacting in this role and regularized forms of behavior that signal the assumption of the identities in question. There are two kinds of behavior that are expected in situations of enmity. Vice Lords call these "whuffing," and humbugging. Whuffing is the exchanging of insults and challenges to fight, while humbugging is actual fighting. Not all situations of enmity end in humbugging. Individuals who assume the identities Vice Lord and Enemy, respectively, can play out their social interaction solely in terms of whuffing.

People who intend to assume the identities which define a social situation as one of enmity do not signal this simply by initiating physical violence. There are certain verbal formulas which indicate a person is assuming the enmity identities. One of the most common is to demand a sum of money—for example, "Hey man, gimme a dime!" When put like this, it is not an actual request for money. If a dime were given, then a demand for more money would be made until finally the individual would have to refuse. Refusing the demand is the cue that the alter is assuming the grammatically matching identity of enmity, and from there the relationship can be played out in term of whuffing or humbugging.

Another formula for signaling the assumption of an enmity identity is to start an argument. Individuals often argue in the course of social interaction, and these arguments do not always signal enmity. However, when an individual starts a violent argument over something that is considered extremely inconsequential, it does function as such a signal. For example, an individual may be talking about the kind of clothes he likes the best. If another person begins to vehemently argue with him, it is a sign that he is assuming an enmity identity. Of course it is not always clear whether an argument is "consequential" or not, and there are other subtle cues which also indicate if an identity of enmity is being assumed. My informants, however, could not verbalize about these. They said, "Man, you just *know* . . . that's all." Unfortunately, during the time of my fieldwork I was not able to make a systematic study of these subtle cues. Possibly, they consist of such things as facial expressions and certain qualities and tones in the voice. Not all people are as adept at appropriately responding to such cues

as others. Being adept at responding properly is one of the things that constitutes "knowing what's happening," or, as Cupid puts it . . . , "knowing
how to live on the streets."

LEADER–FOLLOWER

There are several named leadership identities that are assumed in a few
social contexts. We have already discussed these . . . , and it is not necessary to deal with them in detail here. However, in order to be eligible for
these identities—for example, President, War Counselor—one must be what
Vice Lords call a "Leader." We can, therefore, discuss a Leader identity
without necessarily specifying a formal political position. Vice Lords define
a Leader as a person who has followers. To a person outside the world of
the fighting clubs this may seem overly simplistic, but what defines one as
a Leader or Follower is self-evident only to Vice Lords. There are several
reasons for this. Leadership is highly contextualized—that is, there are few
contexts when an individual's identity as Leader emerges. Further, the same
person may assume identities of both Leader and Follower at different
times.

A few definitions would help clarify the discussion. A Leader is one
who exercises power. Power is the ability to get others to do one's will.
The exercise of leadership is thus the exercise of power. Among Vice Lords
a person is recognized as a Leader when he has the ability to get others
to do his will. In some societies power is often a function of force. Individuals exercise leadership through the use, or threat of use, of physical or
mystical force. This fits the popular conception of the gang leader. Among
Vice Lords, however, power is not based on force. A Leader exercises
power through what we can call influence. Vice Lords follow others because
they like them, or respect them, or because they think they will gain something by doing so, but not because they fear them.

What are the contexts in which the Leader and Follower identities are
relevant? There are two kinds of contexts when people assume Leader and
Follower identities—that is, there are two kinds of contexts in which power
is exerted. The first kind includes situations that demand physical action.
Some obvious examples are: gangbanging, wolf packing, and hustling. An
example from the 15th Street Lords provides a good illustration. I had
met Tex, the President of the 15th Street Lords, several times before I
found out how important a person he was. Observing Tex riding in a car,
hanging on the corner, or drinking wine, there was no clue that he was a
person with power. He was not particularly assertive, and when demands
were made of him, he usually complied. If there was an argument over
who was going to sit by the window while we were riding, Tex usually lost.
If there was an argument over who was going to buy cigarettes, Tex usually
lost. At a party one evening a group of 15th Street Lords stole a large sum

of money from an individual who was not a member of the club. When Tex tried to get them to return the money, he was completely ignored. Then one evening there was a fight between a 15th Street Lord and a member of the Cobras. Everyone expected the Cobras would attack 15th Street territory. In this situation Tex's identity as a Leader became relevant. He immediately took charge of planning for the defense of the territory. Not only were his orders obeyed without question but individuals sought him out to ask what they should do.

I observed other instances which also demonstrated the pattern. Crow was one of the top Leaders in the Nation. Next to Cave Man, he was considered to be the most influential Vice Lord. I was on the corner of 16th and Lawndale one night with Pico talking to Crow. There had been an outbreak of fighting between the Lords and the Roman Saints that evening, and it was expected that the Roman Saints would attack 16th and Lawndale. Pico suggested that he lead a group of Lords into Roman Saint territory, but Crow felt he should stay and help protect the corner. Pico did not even put up an argument, but simply said, "Yeah man, I guess you're right." Another time I was riding with Pico down Lawndale. We pulled up to a corner where there was a group of Lords. Crow was standing in the group, and Pico wanted to talk to him. Pico yelled out the window, "Hey Crow, you skinny mother fucker, get your ass over here!" Crow smiled and said, "What's happening man?" and walked over to the car.

These two examples help us better understand how Vice Lord leadership works. Both Tex and Crow assumed the identity Leader in the gang-fight context, but at other times assumed different identities. The casual onlooker observing their behavior at these other times might think they were not Leaders. He would be wrong. Both Tex's and Crow's failure to exert power in these situations was unrelated to their identities as Leaders since these were social contexts where the Leader–Follower role was irrelevant.

The second kind of context in which leadership identities are relevant are those defined by public decision making. Some decisions which affect the club are made during discussions between Vice Lords while hanging on a corner or in an alley. Usually, however, public decision-making takes place during club meetings. These meetings form an arena for leadership competition and demonstrations of power. A major objective of individuals who either are recognized Leaders or have leadership aspirations is to prove they have power—that is, to demonstrate that others will follow them. Many times the particular decision under discussion is secondary to this objective. For example, Cave Man had long been president of the Nation. During the summer of 1966, however, a group of the Senior Lords met and decided it would be best for the club if someone else took over. Cave Man agreed to step down and let Lonzo be the new president. At this time the executive board was instituted. Cave Man was not even given a place on the board, but was relegated to the formal position of a regular member.

However, Cave still had considerable power, and lost little time in demonstrating it to the new officers. A group of social workers and clergymen from the West Side contacted Lonzo, the new president, to request permission to attend a meeting. They desired to get Vice Lord participation in a project. Several board members told them their request would be submitted to the club, but that the board would support it. When the meeting began, it was evident there was considerable opposition to this group. Cave Man had been hired by the YMCA to help control gang fighting, and had worked in close cooperation,with a social worker who was part of this group. At the meeting, however, he was the loudest voice in the opposition. He said, "What have them social workers ever done for us? Shit man, we don't want them in here!" Cave Man became the rallying point for the opposition, and was able to marshall enough support so that the group was not allowed in the meeting.

After the formal part of a meeting it is cutomary for Vice Lords to congregate on 16th and Lawndale to drink, sing, and recount past exploits. After this particular meeting, Cave Man called out to Vice Lords who were standing around in small groups:

> Come on! We're going to tear up this West Side! We're going to tear down all these signs! [Someone had painted "Black Power" on several buildings.] We're going back to the old days! We're going to gangbang! Those Cobras and Roman Saints, they ain't shit! We're going to run 'em out of the West Side! Vice Lord! Vice Lord! Terrifying, terrific Vice Lords! This whole West Side belongs to the Vice Lords! Come on, let's go!

With that, Cave started out for 16th and Lawndale, and about 25 other Vice Lords fell in behind echoing his yells and shouts.

Cave Man's actions, both during the formal meeting and immediately after, can be understood in terms of the way Vice Lord leadership operates. He opposed allowing the YMCA worker to attend the meeting even though he was getting money from the YMCA and had in the past closely cooperated with this same person. He stated that social workers had never done anything for the club, but he had been instrumental in getting Vice Lords to cooperate with YMCA programs. For some time he had been working to limit gang fighting, but after the meeting called for a resumption of gang wars. All this makes sense if we look at Cave Man's position at this time. He needed to demonstrate that while he was no longer a formal officer, he was still a Leader—that is, a person with power. He needed to show that others would still follow him. An important segment of the new officers had tacitly agreed to letting the outsiders attend the meeting, but many members were against it. This gave Cave Man his opportunity. By mobilizing the resistance and successfully opposing the new officers he convincingly demonstrated his power to everyone. His later behavior is also understandable in these terms. Arriving at 16th and Lawndale in full view, at the head of a large group, further emphasized Cave Man's ability to gather a following. I do not believe he seriously intended to lead Vice Lords in a new gang war. He simply used an appeal to gang fighting values that are seldom, if ever, publicly questioned to gather a following and validate his identity as a Leader. After Cave Man reached 16th and Lawndale at the head of this group, he made no further move toward initiating gang fighting.

Some Vice Lords who are considered Leaders sometimes assume Follower identities in certain situations. There is a formal hierarchy of leadership positions that partially accounts for this. For example, the president of the Nation is thought to be a higher position than president of a branch. Therefore, the president of the Nation assumes the identity Leader in certain situations, while presidents of branches are Followers. The *de facto* distribution of power, however, fits only partially with the formal hierarchy of political positions. The incident just discussed involving Cave Man provides a good example. Bat Man was a Leader and vice president of the 15th Street Lords. In the meeting of the Nation he opposed allowing the social workers to attend. Cave Man, even though he had no formal political position at this time, assumed the identity Leader in the meeting and Bat Man, who was a vice president, assumed that of his Follower. After the meeting, Bat Man joined the group that followed Cave Man to 16th and Lawndale.

The composition of a Leader's following changes in various situations. One time a Leader may join the following of another Leader (and bring his own following with him), but another time oppose that same Leader. Thus Vice Lords never know ahead of time exactly who will be allied and opposed in any particular instance. In other words, the strength of an individual's power is subject to constant fluctuation. We can now better understand why situations in which public decisions are made are contexts for the exercise of power. Power is based on the number of one's followers, but a Leader's following is constantly changing, and the exact extent of a person's power is not usually known. In situations where public decisions are made, however, lines of opposition are drawn, and power becomes crystallized. In the decision-making process individuals make the choice whether to assume a Leader or Follower identity. Those who choose the latter make the further choice as to whose following they will join. Through these choices power is actualized, and claims to the Leader identity are validated. . . .

Jane C. Goodale

19. Qualifications for Adulthood*

In 1912 Sir Baldwin Spencer, a professor of biology at the University of Melbourne, visited Melville Island, in the Timor Sea. There he observed a Tiwi tribal ceremony in which a number of young boys and girls participated in the ritual preparations of a species of yam the Tiwi called *Kulama*. Spencer wrote of this ceremony, "initation of young men [and women] on Melville Island is intimately associated with what is known as a yam ceremony." This statement is particularly noteworthy, for, in 1954, when I visited the Tiwi for the first time and witnessed the annual *Kulama* ceremony, no initiates took part. The ceremony, however, was still being performed with no significant changes in the complex ritual procedures that Spencer had described more than forty years before.

That the *Kulama* ceremony can and does take place without initiates does not mean that Spencer was wrong to consider it an important part of initiation into adult life. It does mean that many of the new generation of Tiwi believe that such participation cannot prepare them adequately for a way of life that has been radically changed by contact with Western culture during the past fifty years.

In order to understand what this ceremony means to those who still perform it, one must first understand what the Tiwi consider to be adulthood. The Tiwi, now about a thousand in number, have lived for untold

* Reprinted with permission from *Natural History* Magazine, April 1963. Copyright © The American Museum of Natural History 1963.

centuries on Melville and Bathurst Islands, which are situated thirty miles north of Darwin, the capital city of Australia's Northern Territory. The islands and surrounding waters are well supplied with food, and fresh water is plentiful. Economically and technically the Tiwi have been remarkably conservative. They came to the islands as hunters and gatherers of wild food, using crude chipped stone axes, digging sticks, simple wooden spears, and hunting dogs, and found that little else was needed to exploit the natural resources and to provide themselves with a stable, varied, and adequate diet. With the exception of the wallaby, the land animals of the two islands were small and nocturnal and could simply be collected during the day with little physical effort or skill. The few skills that were necessary were identifying tracks to find game and chopping out or digging up the sleeping animals. Young boys and girls were taught these techniques, since there was no essential sexual division of labor in food-collecting. Boys, however, received additional instruction in spear-fishing and birding, while girls were taught more intensively to locate and identify edible plants. The children, as a result, were generally independent economically in their early teens, by which time the girls were already married. Young males contributed to their parents' larder and to other households, but did not marry and acquire households until they were more than thirty years old. Even now, this late marriage age obtains in theory, but not always in practice.

Thus, to the Tiwi, economic independence and/or marriage did not alone signify adulthood. The Tiwi adult was intellectually, rather than physiologically, a mature individual who was expected to join actively in the non-economic affairs of the community. An adult was also expected to be almost entirely responsible for his own health, wealth, and future prospects. This included attaining success in hunting and in war and, for the men, in wife-collecting. If an adult became ill or was injured or, as a Tiwi would say, was unlucky in the pursuit of life's benefits, he alone was responsible for not behaving as an adult should.

The annual *Kulama* ceremony, held by each community in April at the end of the rainy season, was a most important event to insure individual success. Although a collective, community ceremony, its benefits accrued only to individual participants, and then only to those who had followed the complex procedures correctly. Thus it was vitally important to every Tiwi individual, male or female, to receive instruction in the *Kulama* ritual before being considered a fully adult member of the tribe. The instruction period lasted six years, during which the initiates, among other requirements, had to participate actively in six *Kulama* rituals. Following this training, the individuals were considered responsible adults by other members of the tribe, but only through continued participation in the ritual could that condition be maintained.

Today the ritual is still performed by those who believe in it, and it will probably continue until the last initiated Tiwi dies, or until the underlying meaning is totally lost and is replaced by ideas of how to be successful that have their origins in Western thought.

The ceremony itself takes three days to complete and centers on the preparation of a toxic variety of yam, the *Kulama*. To make this yam edible, it must first be soaked. It is then baked, mashed, and again soaked for a time in fresh water. Even after the poisons have been removed by this elaborate process, an extremely bitter taste remains. The Tiwi say they never eat the yam except at the conclusion of the *Kulama* ceremony. Those who believe in the ritual say the yam has tremendous power for causing good or evil, and thus one must handle the yam carefully during the preparation, speak to it softly, sing to it at times, and always treat it with respect. The individual absorbs the power of the yam by touching it, by rubbing the body with it, and finally by eating it. All these steps are ritualized. Special digging sticks are made, and, contrary to the usual practice of having the women gather plants, only men are allowed to dig the yam. A special dance area, or ceremonial ring, is cleared on the ground and a special cooking fire is built in its center. On each of the three ceremonial days the participants paint themselves in specified ways with ocher. During the evening of each day, while the yams are soaking or cooking, the male participants, singly or together, walk slowly counterclockwise around the ceremonial fire, beating sticks together as an accompaniment to specially composed songs. At times the wives, who remain outside the ring, sing with the men, or they may join their husbands in traditional dances that imitate various aspects of the natural world around them.

The songs are a vital part of the ritual. They must be newly composed for the occasion and may relate to any event or abstract idea the composer chooses. The songs often deal with injustices the singer has experienced in the past year, about which he wishes to register an "official" complaint:

> "There was a funeral,
> You went first, I came after.
> Old people came in first,
> I was late because I had a *Kulama*.
> Why didn't you wait for me?"
>   or
> "When Dory have baby girl
> The old man said, 'That's for you.'
> Dory, my mother-in-law, she burns me.
> Dory doesn't know the old people way.
> I would like to kill her."

Others may be in the nature of news reports, in which the listeners are informed of anything interesting that may have happened to the singer during the preceding year. For instance, the composer of the following song had just returned from Brisbane, where he and a group of eight other aborigines had performed dances in honor of Queen Elizabeth's 1954 visit to Australia:

> "The Queen was talking in England,
> 'I would like to see a blackfellow dance.'
> When I was in Brisbane, the Queen said,
> 'I would like to meet a black boy!'
> And I went up.
> King Philip, he had a good look at me.
> He was watching a lot as I danced.
> I was singing into a loud-speaker."

Some songs are historic in nature, retelling an event that must be kept alive according to the traditions of the tribe. One such composition recalls the Japanese attack on Darwin during World War II:

> "An enemy plane flies low over Melville Island.
> The men on the ground, at the word 'Standby,'
> Shoot it down with a cannon."

The children of the singer are often song subjects. This first example describes how the children behaved in one of their father's dreams.

> "My children have gone to the other side
>   of the island.
> But they must come back as they are hard up
>   for tobacco.
> My children have now come back.
> I know this for they have taken the tobacco
>   which I have held in my hand."
>   or
> "My children will wear clothes and shoes.
> They will go to school and learn to write."

All the songs have the same chanting tune, which is associated with the *Kulama* ceremony, and the composer must fit his words to the set meter of the chant. In many cases this requires using archaic words that are no longer a part of Tiwi speech. Poetic license in pronunciation and syllabification often occurs. The Tiwi have high regard for the linguistic ability needed to become a good Tiwi composer and singer, and instruction in the art of song composition and delivery is given to the initiates. Each initiate must perform in the *Kulama* before he can be considered a "graduate." According to my Tiwi informants, this requirement is the hardest of all, and it is also the reason for there being no set age for initiation. The old people are said to watch the young, and when the observers consider them mature enough, they swoop down upon their choices "like chicken hawks, without warning"—as the Tiwi say—and start the initiates along the path to adulthood.

As far as I know, the *Kulama* ceremony has no parallel elsewhere in Australia. And there are many interesting questions that come to mind concerning the origin of the *Kulama* as it exists today. For instance, why is instruction in the preparation of a poisonous yam that is not part of the daily diet considered so important for initiation into adulthood? What is the origin of the idea that a yam has power over good and evil, and health and sickness? Why is such prominence accorded a yam in what is principally a hunting and gathering society?

Any answers to these questions must be highly speculative, for the origin of the ceremony and its development lie in the unrecorded history of the Tiwi. However, I believe the following statements may well be valid.

Instruction in the natural resources of the land was considered vital to becoming an adult. Because the *Kulama* yam is poisonous and is not widely distributed, it was never part of the regular diet, but it could be used in economic emergencies if properly prepared. Instruction in its preparation was therefore extremely important as a potential survival measure. However, since the Tiwi live in a favorable environment, it is highly probable that such emergencies were very rare, so it was considered expedient to hold annual instruction periods. Because knowledge of the technique had to be made meaningful to the initiates, the lifesaving qualities of this famine food were explained as health-giving powers. A ceremony accompanied by song and dance was certainly a dramatic and effective means of impressing the initiates in preparation methods. The ritual served another purpose as well: because traveling is so difficult during the rainy season, each household is isolated from the others. The *Kulama* ritual follows this period, and it is natural to expect a reunion to be an occasion to exchange news, settle differences, and tell stories or sing songs that keep traditions alive.

Much harder to account for is the Tiwi idea of adulthood. That every adult is solely responsible for his own health and wealth, and that success in life depends entirely on personal behavior and industry, are ideals strangely similar to those that underlie the American way of life, despite the great gulf between the aboriginal culture and our own. But it is not at all surprising that the Tiwi have a great sympathy for much of Western civilization. Many hold the same views as the *Kulama* singer quoted earlier in this article who saw his children wearing clothes and shoes and going to school to learn to write, for this is the Tiwi's contemporaneous idea of success in a way of life introduced to them only a few short years ago.

Early in the summer of 1962 I revisited the Tiwi for two weeks. Although I knew that the Tiwi desired schooling and training in European ways of life and would seize any such opportunity afforded them, I was hardly prepared for the tremendous changes that had taken place during the eight years that had elapsed since my first visit.

Three months after the *Kulama* ceremony of 1954, a government school was opened. Now all the Tiwi children go to school, and some who have finished the six-year program in the government school have received subsequent training as teaching or nursing assistants. Some others have had "on-the-job" training in various activities connected with a large-scale forestry project that has been started on Melville Island. In fact, all the able-bodied Tiwi men and women are currently employed, and their tasks bear little or no relation to their old life in the bush.

It is perhaps significant—but to me not at all surprising—that I did not hear a single real complaint from the Tiwi regarding their new manner of living. They seem to like it and are anticipating bigger and better things (in the Western sense) for their children. Hunting has become a week-end diversion and the children receive little or no real instruction in that traditional skill.

Some aspects of Tiwi life are slow to die, however. Most of the old taboos, the observance of which was considered necessary in the past in order to insure health and wealth, are still observed, although at least one teenager expressed doubt that the taboos had any actual effect on the outcome of one's life. Western medicine and public health practices are fast replacing belief in the *Kulama*. During the past eight years only three men have begun the six years of training for *Kulama* initiation, and some of the older men no longer participate in the ceremony. However, as long as even a small number of Tiwi believe in the *Kulama,* the ritual will survive, but I doubt that it will for long.

Wayne Suttles

20. Private Knowledge, Morality, and Social Classes among the Coast Salish*

An exchange of views in a recent issue of the *American Anthropologist* shows that social stratification on the Northwest Coast is still a live issue. The principal question is whether Northwest Coast society had, apart from slaves, distinct social classes of nobles and commoners or merely a single class of freemen within which there were only ranked individuals. The recent exchange began with Ray's suggestion that Boas neglected the culture of the lower class among the Northwest Coast tribes. Lowie countered that if Drucker's analysis is right, there were only ranked individuals and no social classes, and hence no lower class to neglect. Ray then returned with quotations from several ethnographers who reported social classes and has promised us an analysis of the whole body of published Northwest Coast ethnography, which will demonstrate the existence of a lower class. Since this exchange, Codere has presented an analysis of some of Boas's Kwakiutl material, which seems to support Drucker's and Lowie's position—that there was no distinguishable lower class among the Kwakiutl (Ray 1955; Lowie 1956; Ray 1956; Codere 1957).

One of the bases of disagreement may be simply a difference in terms

* Reproduced by permission of the American Anthropological Association from the *American Anthropologist,* vol. 60 no. 3, 1958:497–507. The author's permission and particularly his informative "postscript" and his suggestions for updating the Salish orthography, are acknowledged with appreciation.

An abridged version of this paper was read at the 55th Meeting of the American Anthropological Association held at Santa Monica, December 1956.

or in emphasis on different factors in a definition of "class."[1] But another basis for disagreement may lie in real differences among the various Northwest Coast societies.

In this paper I will deal with a small segment of the Northwest Coast— the area of the Coast Salish of Northern Puget Sound, the Strait of Juan de Fuca, and Southern Georgia Strait.[2] My purposes are: 1. to call attention to evidence for the existence of a distinct, though probably relatively small, lower class; 2. to postulate a relationship between class and certain Coast Salish beliefs about morality; and 3. to suggest the possibility that the Coast Salish theory of morality and the absence of any very developed system of ranked individual positions may have allowed for a sharper definition of social classes among the Coast Salish than among the supposedly more rank-obsessed Kwakiutl.

When we enquire among the Coast Salish about social classes we are likely to encounter a paradox. We find among our informants a strong feeling that social classes did indeed exist in the past. Informant after informant will tell us that there were high-class people and low-class people. Yet if we ask for an identification of the descendants of former low-class people, our informants are likely to say they do not know or refuse to talk about the matter. Later, after we establish good relations with an informant, he will probably tell us that while he is of high-class descent, certain other families are of low-class descent. When we go to members of these other families, we may be told that our new informants' families are of high-class origin but certain other families, including that of our first informant, are really of low-class descent.

This is what happened to me on the Lummi Reservation. Two persons, each associated with one of the two leading lineages, told a story accounting for a low-class origin for the other lineage. One story was an account of a known ancestor of the lineage in question; the other story was really a local adaptation of a widespread folktale. Both stories, however, demonstrated the prior residence of the narrator's lineage, the former slave or serf-like status of the other lineage at some other place, and the generosity of the teller's lineage in allowing the other to settle at Lummi. Both informants agreed, as did others, in ascribing a still lower status to the family of a pair of slaves who had been freed in the 1860's.

---

[1] For the purposes of this paper, I can best follow Codere in accepting Goldschmidt's minimal definition of a social class as "a segment of the community, the members of which show a common social position in a hierarchical ranking" and his characterization of the true class-organized society as "one in which the hierarchy of prestige and status is divisible into groups each with its own social, economic, attitudinal and cultural characteristics, and each having differential degrees of power in community decisions." "Such groups," he writes, "would be socially separate and their members would readily identify" (Goldschmidt 1950:491–2; Codere 1957:473)

[2] I have done fieldwork in this area at various times since 1946. This work has been supported successively by the University of Washington, a Wenner-Gren Predoctoral Fellowship, and the University of British Columbia.

This situation, which could undoubtedly be encountered in many Coast Salish communities, suggests that except for the former slaves, social class was more a myth than a reality. Perhaps the accusation of lower-class ancestry is merely part of the gossip that all families enjoy relating about all others and which enables each to make claims of superior status, none of which has any more validity than another.

But there is other evidence for the reality of social classes in the past. The best evidence comes from descriptions of village structure and intervillage relations. We encounter again and again descriptions of villages in which there was a division of residence between upper-class and lower-class people. In some villages, households of lower-class people were at one end or on one side of the village. In other villages, the lower-class people were somewhat separate and often in an exposed position where an enemy might strike first. Then we are also told of villages set quite apart but in a serf-like status as vassals of high-class villages or villages with high-class inhabitants.

Barnett (1955:19, 30) reports that the Saanich village at Brentwood Bay and the Sechelt village had an upper-class section in the center and lower-class sections at the ends. I was told that the old Semiahmoo village on Tongue Spit consisted of two rows of houses, one facing outward and the other facing inward; the outer row was occupied by upper-class people and the inner row by low-class people. Gunther (1927:183–4, 261) reports lower-class settlements on exposed spits among the Klallam, and Barnett (1955:23) reports the same thing at Nanoose and possibly Chemainus. I was told that the principal Skagit village at Snakelum Point consisted of a great stockade enclosing a long house divided into three segments, each with its own named group of high-class people; outside the stockade were "camps" of low-class people who served as "scouts" and were not allowed inside the stockade. Haeberlin and Gunther (1930:15, 58) report a separate lower-class village, also unprotected, for the Snohomish. I was told of lower-class villages at Warm Beach on Port Susan, possibly vassal to the Stillaguamish or the Snohomish; at Greenbank on Whidbey Island, possibly vassal to the Skagit; and on Dugualla Bay, Whidbey Island, vassal to the Swinomish. According to an informant, the Dugualla people had to bring fuel to the Swinomish during the coldest part of the winter. Boas (1894:455), Hill-Tout (1902:407–8) and Jenness (1955:86) report that the Coquitlam on the Lower Fraser were vassals of the Kwantlen. And while Barnett reports that the Nanoose had a divided village, Jenness' and some of my own informants regarded the Nanoose as wholly lower class. They were the group with which the Coquitlam could marry, said one. One informant told of a tradition of open conflict between the lower- and upper-class segments of a village at Oak Harbor on Whidbey Island, and something similar was hinted at for a Songish village.

This is only a rough outline of the data on residence. There is no question in my mind about the existence of a lower class in this area. Its existence is also indicated by some data on marriages and inherited privileges, and it is reflected in the native terms used.

A person of high status was called *si²ε'm²*. This term is often translated as "chief," but it is clear that the whole institution of chieftainship as it now exists developed after European contact. *Si²ε'm²* meant and still means simply "Sir" or "Madam" in address and "gentleman" or "lady" in reference. One could speak of the *si²ε'm²* of a house, if it had one clearly recognized leader, perhaps the man who had organized the building; but not all houses had such leaders. One could also say *the si²ε'm²* of the village, but the title did not imply a political office. If there was *a si²ε'm²*, he was probably the wealthiest man, the leader in the potlatch. Leadership in other matters was apt to be in the hands of others, depending upon their special abilities. The plural, *sii²ε'm²*, is usually translated "high-class people."

People who are not "high class" are referred to by terms which are translated as "poor people," "nothing people," or "low-class people." According to one old man, the most polite term is *səsəla'yŏən*, the diminutive plural of "younger sibling." The term used in the Lkungeneng (Straits) and Halkomelem languages for the people of a vassal village is *st'ɛšəm*: their status is clearly distinguished from that of *sk'ʷə'yəs,* "slave." Slaves were private property, captured or purchased; vassals were simply in a low status as a group destined to serve other villages.

Thus it appears that Coast Salish society was in fact stratified. In addition to slaves, there were at least an upper-class and a lower-class. The proportions of upper- to lower-class people in each community probably varied, just as the spatial relationship between the two groups varied. But in the area as a whole, the vassal tribes were relatively few and the villages said to have lower-class sections were in the minority. It is difficult to get information on the subject but I believe the evidence strongly suggests that, taken as a whole, the upper class considerably outnumbered the lower class.

I suggest that the structure of native society was not that of a pyramid. There was no apex of nobles, medium-sized middle class, and broad base of commoners. Instead, native society had more the shape of an inverted pear. The greater number of people belonged to an upper- or respectable class, from which leaders of various sorts emerged on various occasions. Mobility within this group was fairly free. A smaller number of people belonged to a lower-class, upon which the upper-class imposed its will and which it treated with contempt. Movement from this lower-class into the upper-class was probably difficult. A still smaller group of slaves lived with their masters, who were always of the upper-class.

The principle of ranking individuals or groups in a numbered series seems to have been poorly developed among these tribes; it finds its most significant expression among the Nootka and Kwakiutl in seating and receiving order at potlatching. Among these Coast Salish tribes, there were two kinds of gatherings at which gifts were given: the *sX̌ɛ'šən* (from *X̌ɛ'šən,* to invite), an intrahousehold or intravillage gathering at which one person as host shared an unexpected surplus of food; and the *sX̌ɛ'nəq* (from *X̌ɛnəq,* to potlatch), an intervillage gathering at which the household or village as host gave away wealth. The second of these was the potlatch proper. The reason for giving away wealth at a potlatch was to pay guests from other communities to witness a change in the status of some member of the potlatcher's family. Such changes were life crises marked by the use of inherited privileges, or merely transfer of the privileges themselves, as in the bestowal of an ancestral name. While such changes might be marked by intragroup gatherings, the larger gathering was preferable. And while one man might lead in organizing the potlatch, it was more typically an occasion when the several leaders ($sii^2\epsilon'm^2$) of a household or village pooled their life crises, name-givings, and so forth, for a joint endeavor vis-à-vis other households and/or villages. At such an occasion, each of the hosts might have his own list of guests to whom he owed gifts from previous potlatches. Whenever gifts are given to individuals there must of course be an order of giving, but it is my strong impression that there was no permanent receiving order among these Coast Salish tribes; each host had an ad hoc order based on his own debts and his own evaluations of persons.[3]

If we ask what gave a man high status, we are apt to find different persons emphasizing different attributes, but generally we hear first that a man must be of good birth and must be wealthy. Being of good family, of high birth, and so forth, is sometimes put negatively as "having no black marks against one"—that is, having no taint of slave ancestry, low-class ancestry, or disgraceful conduct in the family. High-class people were those who had good family trees, with a stock of good hereditary names and a few other hereditary rights.

Wealth was of course important. A man had to have wealth to give away when taking or bestowing an hereditary name or exercising some other hereditary right. But wealth was itself only the product of and the proof of possession of more important things. In some cases, wealth came from the possession of hereditary rights, as in the case of a Songish or

---

[3] W. W. Elmendorf has indicated (personal communication) that there is evidence for a series of ranked individuals among the Twana and the Klallam, but that they constituted only a small part of the society. My position here is not that this principle is totally absent from the area but that it is relatively unimportant, and that such series, if they existed at all among some groups, were quite unstable. Among the tribes I have worked with I have not heard any accounts of conflict over position within a series; I would expect to hear such stories if the principle were of any great importance.

Lummi reef-net owner; but even then, the man not only owned the right to use a net at a certain place but also usually possessed the special practical and ritual knowledge necessary for its successful operation. This knowledge was acquired from other persons, usually older kinsmen. Other kinds of ritual knowledge were a source of wealth to persons who functioned as ritualists at life crises.

But many of the activities that led to the accumulation of wealth were due, in Coast Salish theory, to the possession of spirit power. The shaman, the warrior, the gambler, the hunter, the carpenter, all persons likely to accumulate wealth, were successful in doing so, it was thought, because they had guardian spirits which made them a shaman or a warrior or a gambler. In theory, spirits could be obtained by anyone—anyone, that is, who had the courage and endurance to fast and bathe and seek a spirit vision. Of course, some families knew better than others how to train their children for spirit questing, and the location of the best places for encountering certain spirits. But poor-boy-meets-spirit-and-makes-good stories are numerous and some of them are told of actual people, so we may assume that a man without inherited fishing sites and without ritual knowledge could also become wealthy and attain high status. Over a period of several generations there was probably a good deal of social mobility. The leaders were at various times fishermen, hunters, warriors, doctors, gamblers, ritualists—men who owed their material wealth to the possession of various types of incorporeal property.

One other possession theoretically necessary to upper-class status was a sort of private or guarded knowledge; in the Straits (Lkungeneng) language this was called *snəp,* usually translated "advice." Advice consisted of genealogies and family traditions revealing family greatness, gossip about other families demonstrating how inferior they are, instruction in practical matters such as how to quest for the right kind of guardian spirit, secret signals for indicating that someone is of lower-class descent, and a good deal of solid moral training.

If we ask what accounts for the status of a low-class person, we will probably be told that low-class people are those who don't have anything and don't know anything. One informant, who often returned to this subject, said repeatedly that low-class people were people who had "lost their history," who "had no advice" (*ə' wənə snə'ps*). High-class people preserved the knowledge of their own heritage and valued it, and possessed a knowledge of good conduct. Low-class people were those who, through their own or their forebears' misfortune or foolishness, had lost their links with the past and their knowledge of good conduct.

The moral training contained in "advice" included such warnings as "don't lie," "don't steal," "be polite to your elders," and so on. Such injunctions are presented as knowledge restricted to us few truly high-class families. It is hard for an outsider to believe that it was not generally known that one should not lie, steal, or throw rocks at his grandmother, but this was the Coast Salish fiction.

It is important to note that morality among the Coast Salish had little if any relationship to supernaturalism. Its sanctions were social, not supernatural. Children were not told that the supernatural would punish them if they misbehaved. And since there was no organized government, they could not be told that a policeman would come for them. What they were told was that if they misbehaved, they would be called "low-class." In a society that stressed private property as the Coast Salish did, it must have been very effective to present moral training as private property, in the context of secret knowledge on the gaining of wealth and the maintenance of status.

Thus the theory that knowledge of good behavior was restricted to the upper-class made a contribution to social control and was therefore of some value to society. The visible existence of a genuine lower-class (even though small) served to remind one of the necessity of leading a moral life, but the myth of a lower-class was more important than the reality. For this reason, many Coast Salish will let you understand that there are many low-class people lurking about, but you rarely find one yourself.

How could low-class groups have come into existence in Coast Salish society? At one time, most villages consisted each of a single lineage which regarded itself as descended from an ancestor left on the site by the Transformer, or dropped from the sky. Each prided itself on the antiquity and continuity of its traditional ties with its country—the village site, fishing sites, and other productive places—and hereditary rights to names and other privileges. Kinship was reckoned bilaterally but residence was patrilocal, so membership in such a lineage was usually through the male line. (With these qualifications, Boas's early use of the term "gentes" for Coast Salish villages was probably quite proper.) According to one native tradition, certain vassal villages were simply lineages whose ancestors had been assigned this status by the Transformer. According to another native explanation, the vassal villages were descendants of slaves who no longer had individual masters; and according to yet another, they were the descendants of originally high-class people who had been forced by famine to sell themselves into slavery.

I see several possible factors in the formation of lower-class groups:

1. *Private ownership of resources.* While the lineage (or village) identified itself with its country, exploitation of the most productive fishing and other sites was often in the hands of certain individuals who were able to use whatever surplus might be produced. Persons unrelated to the owners would thereby suffer some poverty. Yet some activities were unrestricted, and the development of skill—in hunting, for example—interpreted as due to the possession of spirit power might bring wealth to anyone.

2. *Primogeniture and other limitations in inheritance.* Primogeniture was often the practice and is implied by the kinship terms, which differentiate senior and junior lines of descent. Use of the term "little younger siblings" for lower-class people suggests that historically they may be the descendants of propertyless junior lines. But of course it may also be a way of extending a fictitious kinship to them when something is to be gained by doing so. However, primogeniture was not always the practice; it seems that rights such as great names often went to the child judged to be potentially the most successful. In the case of guarded knowledge such as the genealogies and family traditions contained in "advice," the child with the best memory might be the one who could later use the knowledge and assume or bestow the ancestral names. But again, a name was perhaps valued principally in relation to what was given away at the time it was assumed, so that a person with wealth might take any known ancestral name and make it great.

3. *Slavery.* Slave status was hereditary. If household slaves became too numerous they might be turned out to form a separate settlement, which might then become the nucleus of a group formed by the accretion of illegitimates, orphans, tramps, and those reduced by chance to beggary.

The taint of slave ancestry was most undesirable. A person captured and made a slave could be cleansed by a $ça^wten,$ "cleansing rite." Such ceremonies form an important class of inherited privileges. But while the paraphernalia and ritual knowledge required were restricted by primogeniture or other means to certain members of a lineage, the rite might be performed by the owner for any member of the lineage. Thus the only persons who could not be "cleansed" were those without close ties to families which had cleansing rites. Even after a cleansing rite had been performed, gossip about the taint of slavery was very important in any rivalry and made possible implicit and private rankings not usually made explicit by seating and receiving. The mere existence of a pattern of warfare and enslavement of captives led to the social evaluation of freemen.

4. *The social function of the myth of "advice."* Private property, the prevention of its dispersal through restrictions on inheritance, and the existence of slavery as a status into which freemen may fall, all these must have contributed to the differentiation of freemen into higher and lower. Still, there were mitigating factors with each. I believe that these causes are not quite sufficient to explain the existence of the strong feelings among the Coast Salish that there are (or were) high-class people and low-class people. And they are not quite sufficient to explain the particular structure that I infer for Coast Salish society—the inverted pear with the large upper-class and the small lower-class. I suggest that the additional factor needed is ideological; it is the myth that morality is the private property of the upper-class.

This myth made it necessary (or at least useful) for a lower class to exist as evidence for its truth, but the myth probably also acted as a check on the growth of the lower-class. If the lower-class grew too large, its existence would no longer be compatible with the myth; a large lower-class would be seen by the upper-class as a threat to society, and the attitude of the upper-class would become intolerable to the lower-class. The two segments of such a community could only split, or fight it out. According to traditions, both interclass fighting and the splitting of communities did occur. As to the

FIGURE 1

Stratification in a Coast Salish Community According to the Present Hypothesis

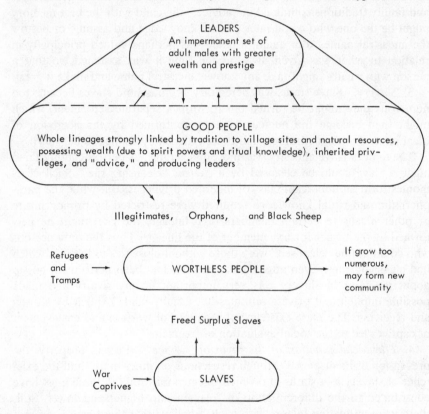

latter, Snyder (1954) has described how the rather complex tribal relations in the Lower Skagit area are the result of a process by which a community would segregate into an upper- and a lower-class and then split to form two separate communities, each of which again became stratified. Later marriages might link the more successful families of the new community with the old community. Snyder offers no explanation as to why the division was into two parts, except to suggest an underlying duality in Coast Salish culture. I believe the hypothesis presented here supports the suggestions and clarifies the process.

Let me summarize briefly. Coast Salish society consisted of three classes: a large upper-class of good people, a smaller lower-class of worthless people, and a still smaller class of slaves. Within the upper-class there were certainly differences in status, due mainly to differences in wealth. Wealth came to some persons because of their hereditary rights, to others because of spirit powers (and practical skills) acquired through their own efforts. Mobility upward within this larger class was quite possible. Moreover, there were neither clear divisions within the upper-class, nor a series of ranked individuals. There was, however, a fairly clear line dividing the upper-class from the lower-class, especially when they were spatially separated. Movement upward from the lower group was evidently much more difficult; if the group became large enough, greater separation and the formation of a new community was probably the usual way out.

I suggest, then, that when Coast Salish informants speak of social mobility and tell folktales and historic accounts of poor boys who became successful they are thinking of poor (but good) families within the upper-class, which included the bulk of the population. When they speak of "low-class people" they are thinking of the smaller worthless class. And when they hint that other families who claim high status are really low, they are thinking of possible links with the worthless people. Perhaps all families had such links, but as long as a family produced an occasional great man it was secure. At any rate, the Coast Salish myth about "advice" may have made gossip a necessity.

Kwakiutl society seems to have been organized along somewhat different lines. There is no indication that there were separate settlements of lower-class people. Within each group, many—and perhaps most—individuals held positions that were ranked in a numerical series made explicit by seating and receiving orders at potlatches. Local groups were also ranked by number in a series. This ranking had two consequences. One was that everyone stood at a different place and all differences were small; if Drucker is right (and I believe he may be right for the Kwakiutl), ranking prevented any tendency toward segregation into distinct classes. The second consequence is that ranking within a series brings into being a social unit with discernible limits, whether it is a small local group or a confederacy of tribes.

In contrast, the Coast Salish of the area that I am discussing had only a poorly-developed system of ranking in numbered series for individuals, and none for local groups. Membership in a local group was not as clear a matter as among the Kwakiutl, and there were no social units larger than the local group. Thus in one respect, Coast Salish society was more fluid than Kwakiutl society. But on the other hand, because Coast Salish society did not stress the ranking of individuals in series, it may have been easier for distinct social classes to develop.

Moreover, Kwakiutl culture does not seem to show the same emphasis on private knowledge in relation to social status as does Coast Salish culture. Among the Kwakiutl, feeling about social status seems to have been strongest at the potlatch when the relative standing of individuals was made explicit by their seating and receiving order. Among the Salish, feeling was possibly strongest when a grandparent was telling a grandchild how he should conduct himself.

I present this as one interpretation of the data at hand, in order to point out where generalizations about the Northwest Coast as a whole may be wrong. Principles of organization may be different in its different segments. We need not assume that because the Kwakiutl show the highest development of "paranoid" behavior at potlatches, they have the strongest development of social classes. I have suggested factors in Coast Salish organization which could have led to a greater development of social classes among them. I might also point to two other factors: the Coast Salish area under discussion had more varied and probably richer natural resources than did that of the Kwakiutl, and it supported a larger population (Kroeber 1939: 135); if resources and population are necessary to stratification, then the area might have supported a more stratified society.

Finally, I would urge that the relationship between the existence of a small class of worthless people and their society's ethical system, a relationship presented here more as hypothesis than as demonstrated fact, be studied in other primitive societies.

POSTSCRIPT, 1974

This paper was written in 1956. Since then I have continued to work with Coast Salish materials and I think I now see the Coast Salish more clearly than I did then, especially in the contexts of ecology and areal ethnography. (My more recent papers listed in the Bibliography are attempts at developing this understanding.) While I see no reason to change the model of social stratification presented in this paper, I would now change some of the terms I used eighteen years ago. Perhaps the term "Coast Salish" itself is misleading, since the people I was concerned with are not all of the Coast Salish but only one segment of a Coast Salish continuum that extends on to the north and to the south and southwest and exhibits cultural differences, especially between the extremes. This segment lies about at the center of the continuum and so I should have said "Central Coast Salish." The term "lineages" now seems inappropriate, since that term generally refers to the discrete descent groups found with unilineal descent, whereas the (Central) Coast Salish cognatic descent groups are non-discrete (i.e., overlapping) extended families or "stem kindreds." "Patrilocal" now seems misleading if not plain wrong, since it may imply a clearly formulated rule that a couple should live with the husband's family, whereas the (Central) Coast Salish asserted that a couple was free to live with either family. In practice perhaps two thirds (the data have not been properly pulled together) of all couples did live with the husband's family, but those who lived with the wife's family did not suffer any loss of status because of it; there was nothing like the deplorable condition of being "half-married" that was endured by Northwestern California men who lived with their wives' families. The Central Coast Salish could and did change residence according to kin and marital ties and this freedom may have been one of the ways they accommodated to local fluctuations in the abundance of resources. I would now avoid "community," since it often implies a social unit with a high degree of cohesiveness, in-group feeling, internal social control, and so forth, and the Central Coast Salish village may not have been such a unit. "Village" or simply "settlement" would be more appropriate, since these terms are more neutral in what they imply about social cohesion, and so on. I would now strike the word "primitive" from the last sentence of the paper, because of the implications of the word itself and because I should not have suggested any restriction in comparisons. In fact, my "inverted pear" image of the Central Coast Salish village could have been inspired by West's (1945) diamond-shaped representation of "Plainville, U.S.A." and/or Kroeber's (1948: 269–72) discussion of Plainville and other U.S. "communities," though I do not remember it. Finally, the term "social classes" is one I would still use, though perhaps only because I am not yet convinced that it is inappropriate. For a somewhat different view of Coast Salish social stratification see Elmendorf 1971.

Part VII

POLITICS AND CONFLICT

For decades anthropologists have classified sociocultural systems in terms of selected features. For example, people refer to "matrilineal" and "patrilineal" systems, or "agricultural" and "hunting and gathering" systems, or "monotheistic" and "polytheistic" systems. The examples could be extended almost indefinitely, but certainly one of the most common bases for such classifications has been political institutions. Anthropologists commonly speak of "bands," "tribes," "chiefdoms," "kingdoms," "states," "empires," and so forth; entire textbooks are organized around such distinctions. Usually, in such an approach, the emphasis is on describing the structure of political institutions, and the presentations are comparatively static. It has always been known, to be sure, that these were dynamic institutions, involving real people making real decisions, but this perspective was not emphasized. Recently, however, there has been a shift in interest from structure to process; or, to put it another way, the interest has shifted from describing the shape of political systems to delineating the flow of politics and conflict. Politics and conflict go hand in hand. Conflict is minimally the expression of differences of opinion as to what should be done; politics is minimally the mobilization of those factors which may be used to resolve the conflict.

This shift in interest has removed from center-stage the oft-debated questions about the universality of various political institutions (such as "law," "government," "war," and so forth). There can be no doubt that there is conflict and politics in all sociocultural systems; the question is not one of presence or absence but of form and degree. Politics and conflict can be peaceful or violent, rare or frequent, intra-familial or inter-national. Conventionally, the word "politics" has been used primarily in reference to conflict resolution at levels affecting an entire sociocultural system or some major (i.e., supra-familial) part of it; but in a very real sense, this is an arbitrary boundary. It is also generally held that the factors which are at the center of much of what is called "political" are varieties of power and coercive force. Indeed, another common definition of politics focuses on the use of force for the maintenance of order. This is, however, simply another way of saying that the flow of politics involves the mobilization of diverse resources in order to resolve conflicts of various kinds. In part, the political classification systems noted previously presume to order societies on the basis of patterned differences in the types of resources used and the kinds of conflicts resolved.

The three selections in Part VII give emphasis to political activity, although political structures are highly visible. In the first selection (Chapter 21), for example, the central theme is "only on Tuesday." As described by Roger Keesing, the Kwaio traditionally live in settlements comprised of "agnatic" (male) descent groups. Politics in these units is dominated by "big men" of the type we first encountered in Scheffler's discussion in Chapter 8. But now, at least on Tuesdays, Kwaio politics is fundamentally different. On Tuesdays, the Kwaio have chiefs.

Many factors combined to produce the change, including principally the "Pax Britannica" and World War II, with all these imply about the introduction of tax collectors, the manufacture of descent groups out of whole cloth, and the creation of cadres of officials. The most striking aspect of this process is not that it happened, for this scenario has been played out for essentially the same reasons in many places around the world. The striking fact is that the Kwaio were able to *compartmentalize* so completely what may be called their "Tuesday political culture" from their "Wednesday through Monday" culture. The effect is having one's political cake and eating it, too. And, as Keesing and others (e.g., Tessler et al. 1973) have noted, compartmentalization may represent one of the more effective ways to minimize the negative ramifications of rapid social change, especially in the areas of politics and conflict.

But perhaps one of the more basic ways to resolve conflict is to eat your adversary. Indeed, in many parts of the world, defeat is metaphorically expressed by the verb "to eat." Non-metaphorical cannibalism, however, is rare, and as Klaus-Friedrich Koch reminds us in Chapter 22, conjures images of the "mental primitiveness and diabolical inspirations of people with simple technologies." In the case of the Jale, we see people engaged in the basic acts of dispute settlement in a context where non-violent methods are weak or lacking. As a result, one violent conflict is settled by another—and so on and on. Such dispute–settling conflicts are underwritten, so to speak, by the party claiming to have been wronged, and as we have seen before, the principal leadership roles are filled by "big men" —individuals with established records in the art of leadership, including most essentially, feast-giving. The scale of the warfare is held in check by a variety of factors, not the least of which is the necessity of weeding and otherwise attending to food production requirements.

Most Jalé wars do not involve cannibalistic revenge for, as the Jalé put it, "people whose face is known must not be eaten," and many of the conflicts are in, around, and among kinsmen and neighbors whose faces are known. But, if the dispute involves groups living at a distance who are strangers, such revenge is possible—even probable. But in general, it is difficult to explain cannibalism—i.e., specify the conditions under which it is likely to occur (but see Helmuth 1973 for an extended review of this problem). In part, this is because there is rather little in the way of reliable data about such behavior, and in part, because it is seen in so many different perspectives by the participants in different societies. Views range from seeing cannibalism as a fundamental symbolic act or religious ritual to seeing it (as among the Jalé) as "mere" revenge or, even more basically, as a culinary event. Which theory you accept, at this point at least, would seem to be all a matter of taste.

Warfare and cannibalism, though dramatic and certainly not altogether rare, are by no means the most common ways for settling disputes. Arbitration, appeals to precedent, invoking sacred principles, argument, public pressure, reason—these and related practices are the dominant modes and methods for settling disputes between individuals and groups. In his article on the dispute settlement procedures among the Kpelle of Liberia (Chapter 23), James Gibbs provides several cases and their disposition in illustration of the role of the secret Kpelle Poro society. Of particular salience are the values regarding power and obedience which are inculcated into Poro society members (all men). We also see the vital role of "elders"—men in positions of power by virtue of seniority—and of chiefs. The procedures in court cases may seem abrupt, but with the intimate knowledge most people have of the matters at issue and with the strongly reinforced values of the Poro society, such adjudication procedures seem to produce decisions which, from the perspective of the Kpelle, are just and deservedly lasting.

Roger M. Keesing

21. Chiefs in a Chiefless Society: The Ideology of Modern Kwaio Politics*

The modern Kwaio pagans of Malaita, British Solomon Islands, have chiefs every Tuesday, but the rest of the week they have none. In this phenomenon I see an important clue for the behavioural scientist; and both a warning and a hope for the agent of political change.

The Kwaio form one of the last pockets of striking conservatism in the island Pacific. Some 3,000 of them still live scattered through the central mountains of the island. Despite forty years of pacification, three generations of plantation labour and use of steel tools, and long mission efforts, Kwaio retain their pagan religion in the mountainous interior, and social organization is little changed (Keesing 1965).

Fragmentation and fluidity characterize the Kwaio social order. Settlements seldom contain more than two or three households and seldom are occupied for more than four or five years. Major points of reference in this shifting scene are small territories defined in terms of focal shrines. Small descent groups, predominantly agnatic in ideology and composition but

* Reprinted with permission of author and editor from *Oceania*, vol. 38, 1968: 276–80.

A preliminary version of this paper was read at the annual meetings of the Southwestern Anthropological Association in San Francisco, March 23, 1967.

Field work on Malaita was supported by grant number 5 FI-MH 15-848 from the National Institute of Mental Health, United States Public Health Service. Helpful comments on earlier versions of the paper were received from Colin Jack-Hinton, Eugene Ogan and Richard Randolph. I am indebted to Jonathan Fifii, ethnographer and Sub-District Committee leader, for his long and remarkable collaboration.

often with a few non-agnatic affiliants, comprise ritual communities with a common primary interest in the shrine and territory. These descent groups need not be localized, and members often scatter and later nucleate again. A person can live and garden in any territory from which he has a remembered ancestor; and he maintains active ritual and kinship relations with members and ancestors of several descent groups.

A descent group frequently has a "big man" of typical Melanesian type (Sahlins 1963), though this is not a formally-labelled status. In any case, "bigness" is a matter of degree and is recognized most often in speaking of "X's section" (i.e., big man X and his descent group, perhaps augmented by a few co-resident cognates and affines). Every man is a feast-giver to some degree, and the man (if any) who is "bigger" than his fellow descent group members achieves this status by mobilizing wealth in feasts and manipulating investments and obligations. Any "political" powers he possesses derive from outstanding obligations and non-obligatory deference to him in decision-making.

However, in recent years Kwaio have organized themselves into a "Sub-District Committee" based on a radically different political ideology; and— on Tuesdays, in the meeting area—they array themselves and interact in ways that contrast strikingly with usual patterns. To comprehend this phenomenon we need some historical perspective.

Before World War II traditional patterns of social organization prevailed except for the imposition of the Pax Britannica, appointment of a Government Headman, and the collection of a small annual Head Tax. The tax-collection mechanism provides a first clue to the modern political pattern. W.R. Bell, the District Officer who introduced taxation, was familiar with north Malaita areas, especially Kwara'ae and To'abaita, where localized descent groupings were considerably larger, and fewer in number, than in Kwaio (Hogbin 1939). Apparently he sought—upon encountering several score of descent groups in Kwaio—to obtain a small list of "lines."[1] Kwaio, lacking such an ordering, apparently created one for the occasion, particularly through the efforts of village constables. These creations were based on neighbourhoods composed of descent groups linked by inter-marriage and cognatic kinship. Each was labelled with the name of an arbitrarily-chosen shrine.[2] This scheme served—and still does serve—as the basis for tax collection. Incidentally, four years later the Kwaio killed this district officer, a patrol officer, a clerk, and twelve police in one of the world's more eloquent commentaries on the introduction of taxation.

During the American occupation of Guadalcanal a movement known as

---

[1] Solomon's pidgin for "descent group", but as in New Guinea a term with a complex and unpredictable spectrum of sociological referents in various societies.

[2] A full account of this scheme, and its creation, will appear in my forthcoming monograph on Kwaio descent groups.

"Marching Rule" (properly Maasina Rule) arose among the Malaita labour force. Part of the ideology of the movement insisted that the natives should have "chiefs" to organize the people into large communal villages and represent their interests in dealing with the British government of the protectorate. For such "chiefs"—a district head chief, full chiefs, line chiefs, etc.—Kwaio adopted the term *alafa*. This is a dialectical variant of the term used for chiefs in south Malaita (Ivens 1927), and for big men in neighbouring 'Are'are. Prior to this time it seems probable that Kwaio seldom or never used this term; if they did, it designated ritual—not political—importance.

The tiny territories and small descent groups were too fragmented to serve as effective units in building communal Maasina Rule villages. So Kwaio borrowed the scheme of "tax lines" as a way of organizing these larger local groupings—though the scheme fits very poorly the facts of Kwaio social organization. Each "line" built a communal village or *buŋu 'ifi*, and was represented by its "Line Chief." These line chiefs and the full chiefs in charge of districts were mainly traditional-style big men in the realm of feasting. This form of organization prevailed from 1947 until the early 1950s.

At this point, Maasina Rule in overt form disintegrated, due in part to government pressures and increasingly millenial doctrines. In large measure this breakup was internally generated, at least in Kwaio, since the artificial scheme could not withstand fissive pressures inherent in Kwaio social organization and ecology. Kwaio life returned to the pre-war pattern.

About 1958, Maasina Rule activity in a somewhat altered form began causing a stir in neighbouring 'Are'are. This involved "Sub-District Committees" and attempts to codify and adjudicate "Custom". The movement spread to east Kwaio, and by 1962 a Sub-District Committee had been formed and genealogies were being compiled for the pagans by Christians.[3] In early 1963 a meeting house for the committee was built and several hundred pagans began to gather every Tuesday.

Since my house was adjacent to this meeting area I observed behaviour in this setting closely over a two-year period, and could compare it systematically with behaviour in "traditional" cultural settings. "Tuesday Culture" in the Sinalagu area proved to be dramatically demarcated spatially and temporally from the rest of Kwaio life.

One difference was the aggregation in a single area of several hundred persons from different descent groups and localities. In this, there was a resemblance to the gatherings at mortuary feasts or marriage feasts; and there was some transfer of principles for behaving in these traditional contexts to behaviour in this new one. But there were differences as well: a

---

[3] See Keesing 1967 for the history of relations between Christians and pagans.

feast is a time of plentiful food, where shelters, firewood, and music are provided; and there are defined appropriate activities, transactions, and emotions for the guests. A committee meeting is typically a time with little food and often poor shelter, and where diversions must be improvised. In addition, large-scale Tuesday projects using communal labour have no cultural precedent. In these respects, I presume Kwaio were reactivating patterns that had developed in the active stage of Maasina Rule.

The most striking characteristics of Tuesday Culture, however, derive from the nontraditional political ideology that brings Kwaio together in this setting. On a Tuesday, a Kwaio can tell you who his chief is (he refers to him as his *alafa* or *sifi,* the latter from Pidgin English). On Monday or Wednesday he is puzzled or offended if you ask. A whole new set of social categories is invoked, and the procedure of Sub-District Committee meetings depends on this ordering. Some phases of a meeting are restricted to chiefs. Others are open to chiefs and other men but not women and children. When women are admitted (in fact ordered) into the Committee House, they sit on the floor, not the benches. When necessary, all Kawio present can be categorized as either *sifi* or *koomani fiifulu* (English, "common people").

The committee comprises the "chief" of each line "line". In this context they have some decision-making powers binding over their "subjects". Since they are accorded the right to decide "what the custom is", their decisions are also often invoked with regard to traditional contexts. Thus, they decided at one point that a standard opening bridewealth payment of two shell valuables, comprising ten strings of discs, was mandatory—where previously the amount depended on the nature of the marriage and the outcome of haggling. This decision implied that the bride's kin could bring only ten food portions, each to be "paid for" with a sizeable amount of bridewealth by the groom's kin. In one marriage, the strong kin of a bride brought nineteen food portions instead of the specified ten. The groom's father complained to the committee, and the bride's father paid a small fine (which later had to be repaid to avoid government legal action). This fine was paid on a Tuesday in the Committee House; the demand would not have been entertained in a traditional setting. Should a leader or descent group refuse to participate in committee affairs, the committee had no formal authority or effective powers of compulsion.

The correspondence between Kwaio social organization and the pattern of "lines" and "chiefs" is far from precise. Some individuals and descent groups do not fit into this scheme at all, or are included inconsistently. Thus, it is impossible to construct an agreed list of what line each person in the area belongs to and who is the chief of each. There has been a tendency, since the earlier stages of Maasina Rule, for feast-giving "big men" to be replaced as "chiefs" by younger men more sophisticated in European ways (from plantation experiences) and more eager to divert their energies to committee projects. Still a traditional "big man" would not be excluded from the ranks of "chiefs" should he come to a meeting. Moreover, a "line" may include four or five local descent groups, and three of them may have "big men" more or less active in committee work. For such reasons, the working out of the committee ideology on the ground is far from neat.

In Kwaio culture, the roles involving secular and religious predominance in a descent group may converge in a single leader, giving him considerable authority in a wide range of settings. When such a leader also is active in committee affairs as an *alafa,* he provides a point of articulation between Tuesday Culture and behaviour in other settings. The few such leaders help give Tuesday Culture such stability and general acceptance as it has attained. Since the committee members are pagans, and many of the "chiefs" are priests, they call at times not upon an introduced ideology for their authority and powers but upon ancestral spirits for *nanamaŋaa* (Oceanic *mana*). This supernatural sanction of nontraditional activity adds a further stabilizing linkage.

Still, we may well ask whether this Tuesday Culture represents any sort of stable form. Is this only a passing phase? It is possible, of course, that Tuesday Culture could spill out across traditional life, as it did in the most active days of Maasina Rule. There has been a movement afoot for the last three years to build *buŋu 'ifi* again—not as residential units, but as meeting places. Thus Tuesday Culture is spreading to some degree into other parts of the week. What does the future hold? There seems a good chance that Tuesday Culture will dwindle in importance and gradually disappear, as the burden of one or two days diversion from regular work each week becomes oppressive, or as committee decisions are successfully flouted. However, it seems fully possible that the present pattern is stable enough to continue little changed for a decade or more, barring external interference.

Kwaio, then, are able to compartmentalize an introduced political ideology so that it operates within narrowly-defined spatial and temporal limits. Outside of these limits, the effects of the ideology are minimal and indirect. When the rules and decisions generated within this narrow context pertain to action in traditional settings, they cannot be enforced in those settings. Yet when violations take place, the authority to adjudicate or enforce is recognized again within the narrower setting; and committee rules can be violated only through abstention from Tuesday Culture.

For the behavioural scientist, this provides a neat case of contextual definition of rules for behaviour. There are roles or social identities that are occupied only in this temporal and spatial setting; and it does not trouble the actors that these roles ·and categories contrast with those of other settings. This is a striking illustration, a sort of limiting case, of the phenomenon of situational definition of social relationships. We have the conceptual equipment to handle such phenomena, but as I have asserted elsewhere, we have not paid sufficient attention to them in describing social structure (Keesing 1967).

I also read from this Kwaio case an implication for the agent or student of political change. Under favourable circumstances, far-reaching political changes may be possible precisely because of the human ability to compartmentalize, to act according to different rules in different contexts. Given a new and well-demarcated context within which an introduced ideology can operate—whether it be an election day, a legislative assembly, or a cooperative—changes may be more rapid and dramatic than most social scientists would expect. But by this very fact, changes may be less profound, and their ramifications throughout a society less pervasive, than they appear.

Klaus-Friedrich Koch

22. Cannibalistic Revenge in Jalé Warfare*

In October, 1968, two white missionaries on a long trek between two stations were killed in a remote valley in the Snow Mountains of western New Guinea, and their bodies were eaten. A few days later, warriors armed with bows and arrows gave a hostile reception to a group of armed police flown to the site by helicopter. These people, described by the newspapers as "savages living in a stone-age culture," belong to a large population of Papuans among whom I lived for nearly two years, from 1964 to 1966.

People living to the west, in the high valley of the Balim River, call them "Jalé," and this is the name that I use for them. When I read of the killing of the missionaries I was reminded of how I had first heard that the people whom I had selected for ethnographic study had anthropophagic (man-eating) predilections. After arriving at Sentani airport on the north coast, I began negotiations for transport to a mission airstrip located in the Jalémó, the country of the Jalé. "I hope the Jalé will give us permission to land," one pilot said to me. "Just a few weeks ago the airstrip was blocked because the Jalé needed the ground for a dance and a cannibalistic feast to celebrate a military victory."

Our cultural heritage predisposes many people to view the eating of human meat with extreme horror. No wonder then that the literature on the subject is permeated with grossly erroneous and prejudicial ideas about the practice. Few anthropologists have been able to study cannibalism

* Reprinted with permission from *Natural History* Magazine, February 1970. Copyright © The American Museum of Natural History 1970.

because missions and colonial governments have generally succeeded in eradicating a custom considered to epitomize, more than any other, the alleged mental primitiveness and diabolical inspiration of people with simple technologies. However, the Jalé, completely isolated from foreign influences until 1961, still practice cannibalism as an institutionalized form of revenge in warfare, which is itself an integral aspect of their life.

The Jalé live in compact villages along several valleys north and south of the Snow Mountains in east-central West New Guinea. Until the first missionaries entered the Jalémó in 1961, the Jalé were ignorant of the "outside" world. Five years later, when I left the area, many Jalé villages still had never been contacted, and culture change among the people living close to a mission station was largely limited to the acceptance of a few steel tools and to an influx of seashells imported by the foreigners.

Two weeks after I had set up camp in the village of Pasikni, a year-long truce with a neighboring village came to an end. Three days of fierce fighting ensued, during which the Pasikni warriors killed three enemies (among them a small boy), raided the defeated settlement, and drove its inhabitants into exile with friends and relatives in other villages of the region. At that time I understood little of the political realities of Jalé society, where neither formal government nor forensic institutions exist for the settlement of conflicts. Later, when I had learned their language, I began to comprehend the conditions that make military actions an inevitable consequence of the absence of an effective system of political control.

From an anthropological perspective any kind of war is generally a symptom of the absence, inadequacy, or breakdown of other procedures for resolving conflicts. This view is especially applicable to Jalé military operations, which aim neither at territorial gains and the conquest of resources nor at the suppression of one political or religious ideology and its forceful replacement by another. All armed conflicts in Jalémó occur as a result of bodily injury or killing suffered in retaliation for the infliction of a wrong. Violent redress may be exacted for adultery or theft or for a breach of obligation—usually a failure to make a compensatory payment of pigs.

Jalé warfare is structured by a complex network of kin relationships. The Jalé conceptually divide their society into two parts (moieties) whose members must marry someone from the opposite side. By a principle of patrilineal descent a person always belongs to the moiety of his father. Links between kin groups created by intervillage marriages—about half the wives in a village were born elsewhere—provide the structure of trade networks and alliance politics.

Most villages contain two or more residential compounds, or wards. One hut among the group of dwellings forming a ward is considerably bigger than all the others. This is the men's house, a special domicile for men and for boys old enough to have been initiated. Women and uninitiated boys live in the smaller huts, each of which usually houses the family of one man. The residents of a men's house constitute a unified political and ritual community, and it is this community, not the village as a whole, that is the principal war-making unit.

As in all societies, there are some individuals who have more influence over the affairs of their fellows than most. In Jalémó a man gains a position of authority (which never extends much beyond the immediate kin group) through his acquisition of an esoteric knowledge of performing rituals and through the clever management of his livestock to the benefit of his relatives, for every important event demands the exchange of pigs— to solemnify or legitimate the creation of a new status or to settle a conflict. Most disputes are over women, pigs, or gardens, and any one of them may generate enough political enmity to cause a war in which many people may lose their lives and homes.

In every Jalé war one person on either side, called the "man-at-the-root-of-the-arrow," is held responsible for the outbreak of hostilities. These people are the parties to the original dispute, which ultimately escalates into armed combat. Being a man-at-the-root-of-the-arrow carries the liability of providing compensation for all injuries and deaths suffered by supporters on the battlefield as well as by all others—including women and children—victimized in clandestine revenge raids. This liability acts as a built-in force favoring an early end of hostilities.

On rare occasions blood revenge has been prevented by delivery of wergild compensation, in the form of a pig to the kinsmen of a slain person. But only those people who, for one reason or another, cannot rally support for a revenge action and who shy away from solitary, surreptitious ambush attacks will accept such an offer if it is made at all. A negotiated peace settlement of this nature is most likely if the disputants are from the same village or if the whole settlement is at war with a common outside enemy.

When two villages are at war with each other, periods of daily combat are interrupted by short "cease-fires" during which the warriors attend to the more mundane task of garden work, but they are always prepared to counter a surprise attack launched by the enemy. After several weeks of discontinuous fighting, however, the threat of famine due to the prolonged neglect of proper cultivation induces the belligerents to maintain an informal and precarious truce. During this time small bands of kinsmen and members of the men's house of a victim whose death could not be avenged on the battlefield will venture clandestine expeditions into enemy territory, from which a successful raiding party may bring back a pig as well. It is a revenge action of this kind that often precipitates a resumption of open warfare.

Fighting on the battlefield follows a pattern of haphazardly coordinated individual engagements, which rely on the tactic of "shoot-and-run." This technique requires a warrior to advance as far as the terrain affords him cover, discharge an arrow or two, and then run back to escape from the reach of enemy shots. When one side has been forced to retreat to its village, the fighting turns into sniping from behind huts and fences. Women and children always leave the village if an invasion is imminent and take refuge with friends and relatives in other villages. As a last resort the men retreat into the men's house, which a taboo protects from being burned. When a battle reaches this stage, the victorious warriors often plunder and burn family huts. Following a catastrophe of this extent the defeated side usually elects to abandon their village, and the warfare ceases, but the hostilities linger on until a formal peace ceremony reconciles the principal parties. Arranging the ceremony, which features the ritual slaughter and consumption of a pig, may take years of informal negotiations between people who have relatives on both sides. Afterward, dances in both villages and pig exchanges on a large scale consolidate the termination of the conflict.

"People whose face is known must not be eaten," say the Jalé. Consequently, cannibalism is normally not tolerated in wars between neighboring villages, and the few incidents that did occur during the lifetime of the oldest Pasikni men are remembered as acts of tragic perversion. In wars between villages separated by a major topographic boundary such as a mountain ridge, however, cannibalistic revenge is an integral part of the conflict.

While territorially confined hostilities usually end within a few years, interregional wars may last for more than a generation. During this long period revenge parties from either side venture sporadic expeditions into hostile areas, keenly avoiding any confrontation in battle and seeking instead to surprise lone hunters or small groups of women working in distant gardens. The geography of interregional wars favors long-lasting military alliances that have a stability quite unlike the temporary and shifting allegiances that personal kin connections and trading partnerships create in local conflicts.

If an enemy is killed during a foray into hostile territory, the raiders will make every effort to bring the body home. If tactical exigencies demand that the revenge party retreat without the victim, an attempt is made to retrieve at least a limb. The avengers always present the body to an allied kin group that has lost a member in the war. In return they receive pigs and are feted at a victory dance, during which the victim's body is steam-cooked in an earth oven dug near the village. Before the butchering begins, the head is specially treated by ritual experts: eyelids and lips are clamped with the wing bones of a bat to prevent the victim's ghost from seeing through these apertures. Thus blinded, it will be unable to guide a revenge expedition against its enemies.

After the head has been severed, it is wrapped in leaves. To insure more revenge killings in the future, some men shoot reed arrows into the head while it is dragged on the ground by a piece of vine. Then the head is unwrapped and swung through the fire to burn off the hair. This is accompanied by loud incantations meant to lure the victim's kinsmen into sharing his fate.

Following this ritual overture the butchers use stone adzes and bamboo knives to cut the body apart. The fleshy portions are removed from the skull, and in an established order of step-by-step incisions, the limbs are separated from the trunk, which is split open to allow removal of the gastronomically highly prized entrails. Some small, choice cuts, especially rib sections, are roasted over the fire, but the bulk of the meat is cooked with a variety of leafy vegetables.

Before and during the operation, people who are preparing the oven, tending the fire, or just standing around appraise the victim. A healthy, muscular body is praised with ravenous exclamations, but a lesser grade body is also applauded.

When the meat is done, the pit is opened and the "owners of the body," as the Jalé call the recipients of a slain enemy, distribute much of the food among the attending relatives of the person whose death the killing has avenged. It is also distributed to the allied kin groups of a person maimed or killed in the war. Eligible people from other villages who could not participate in the celebrations are later sent pieces reserved for them. If mood so moves the Jalé, they may place some of the victim's bones in a tree near the cooking site to tell travelers of their brave deed.

In the course of the dancing and singing, a poetically gifted man may introduce a new song. If the lyrics appeal to others, it becomes a standard piece in the repertoire. The songs commemorate fortunate and tragic events from past wars, and a typical verse goes like this:

> Ngingi, your mother
> bakes only tiny potatoes for you.
> Isel, your mother too
> bakes only the ends of potatoes for you.
> We shall bake big potatoes for you
> On the day of Kingkaen's return.

Ngingi and Isel are the names of two men from a hostile village, the home of a young woman named Kingkaen who was killed in an ambush attack in September, 1964. The lines make fun of the men who, because of Kingkaen's death, have to eat poor food prepared by the inept hands of senile women.

When the festival of revenge is over, the members of the men's house group of the owners of the body arrange for the ritual removal of the victim's ghost from their village. Rhythmically voicing efficacious formulas and whistling sounds, a ceremonial procession of men carries a special arrow into the forest, as far into enemy territory as is possible without risk. A small lump of pig's fat is affixed to the arrow by an expert in esoteric lore. (Pig's fat used for ritual purposes becomes a sacred substance that is applied in many different contexts.) The arrow is finally shot toward the enemy village. This, the Jalé believe, will make the ghost stay away from their own village, but as a further precaution they block the path with branches and plants over which spells are said.

Protective rites of this kind, and the vengeance ritual described above, are the only aspects of Jalé cannibalism that may be viewed as "religious." The actual consumption of human meat and organs does not constitute an act with intrinsic "supernatural" effects. Instead, as my Jalé friends repeatedly assured me, their reason for eating an enemy's body is that man tastes as good as pork, if not better. And they added that the bad enemies in the other valley had eaten some of their people.

These descriptions of Jalé rituals and beliefs do not sufficiently explain the practice of cannibalism. To do so would necessitate the compilation of all available information about this custom from every part of the world. On the basis of these data an extensive study would have to be made of the ecological and cultural variables found to be associated with institutionalized cannibalism. Perhaps it would then be possible to recognize specific ecological and sociological features that appear to be correlated with the consumption of human meat, but the task of interpreting the custom as a sociopsychological phenomenon would still remain.

It is obvious that the enigmatic nature of cannibalism has invited many writers to speculate about its origin and its biopsychic basis. Aristotle attributed anthrophagy among tribes around the Black Sea to their feral bestiality and morbid lust. In 1688 a treatise was published in Holland entitled *De natura et moribus anthropophagorum* ("On the Nature and Customs of Anthropophagi"), and some ethnographers writing in the nineteenth century still regarded the rejection of cannibalism as the "first step into civilization." Certainly, the consumption by man of a member of his own species is as much a problem for evolutionary bioanthropology as it is for ethnology and psychology. I have made an extensive survey of the various theories proposed by earnest scholars to elucidate the phenomenon, and I have found that, at best, a few hypotheses appear plausible for the interpretation of certain aspects of some cannibalistic practices.

In Jalémó the eating of a slain enemy, in addition to its dietary value, certainly indicates a symbolic expression of spite incorporated into an act of supreme vengeance. Violent retaliation, in turn, must be seen as a consequence of certain sociopsychological conditions that determine the degree of aggressive behavior expected and tolerated in their culture. Cross-cultural studies by anthropologists have supported theories that are applicable to Jalé society. An accepted model of personality development demonstrates that societies in which boys grow up in intimate association with their mothers, who dominate a household situation in which the boy's male elders, especially their fathers, do not take part, are characterized by a high level of physical violence. Sociological models developed from large-scale comparative research predict that in societies in which small kin groups operate as relatively independent political units, warfare within the society is a common means of resolving conflict.

Both models squarely apply to Jalé society. First, young boys, separated from the community of the men's house until their initiation, are socialized in a female environment. Second, the wards of a village are not integrated by a centralized system of headmanship, and no political cooperation exists between them until they are threatened by, or faced with, actual hostility from other villages. These are the critical variables that partially determine the bellicosity and violence I have observed.

No specific hypothesis can be given to explain the cannibalism that the Jalé incorporate in their vengeance. It is certain, however, that no understanding can be achieved by applying precepts of Western thought. In a missionary's travelogue published seventy years ago, the author, speaking of an African tribe, recounted:

> Once, when told by a European that the practice of eating human flesh was a most degraded habit, the cannibal answered, "Why degraded? You people eat sheep and cows and fowls, which are all animals of a far lower order, and we eat man, who is great and above all; it is you who are degraded!"

James L. Gibbs, Jr.

23. Poro Values and Courtroom Procedures in a Kpelle Chiefdom*

Secret societies have long captured the imagination of observers of exotic cultures. This paper attempts to shed light on the subtle connection between a secret society—more properly a tribal fraternity—and legal procedures in one African culture.

Adjoining portions of Sierra Leone, Liberia and the Ivory Coast form a homogeneous culture area, long recognized as distinctive, which has recently been termed "Kru and Peripheral Mande" by Murdock (1959). One of the most significant diagnostic traits for this area, and for certain

* Reprinted with permission of author and editor from the *Southwestern Journal of Anthropology* (now: the *Journal of Anthropological Research*), vol. 18 no. 4, 1962:341–50.

The field research upon which this paper is based was carried out in Central Liberia in 1957 and 1958 and was supported by a grant from the Ford Foundation, which is, of course, not responsible for any of the views presented here. The data were analyzed while the writer was the holder of a pre-doctoral National Science Foundation Fellowship. The writer wishes to acknowledge, with gratitude, the support of both foundations. This paper was read at the Annual Meeting of the African Studies Association in New York in October, 1961.

The materials discussed here were presented initially in a dissertation directed by Philip H. Gulliver, to whom I am indebted for stimulating and provocative discussion of many of the ideas presented here. Helpful comments and suggestions have also been made by Robert T. Holt and Robert S. Merrill.

Portions of the material included were presented in a seminar on African law conducted in the Department of Anthropology at the University of Minnesota by E. Adamson Hoebel and the writer; members of the seminar were generous in their criticisms and comments.

adjoining portions of the Western Sudan, is the presence of tribal fraternities and secret societies of the Poro type which have drawn much attention because of their identification with initiation schools and exotic rites.

Analyses of the Poro and other tribal fraternities widespread in the region have demonstrated that these societies are core, integrative institutions which are inherently conservative. As d'Azevedo (1962) has indicated, one of their major functions is to preserve the status quo, even in situations of acculturation or social flux. In such situations, they attempt to maintain adherence to the traditional norms, not the competing intruding ones. This is done through the use of tribal oaths which enjoin all members of the Poro (by definition all men in the tribe) from taking certain actions; by secret trials of those who violate secret society rules, and by other social control measures (cf. Harley 1950). Such measures presuppose an unquestioning and unqualified acceptance of authority.

Authority in these cultures is exercised by elders who, in their decision making, are governed by a basic postulate which holds that power is valuable; its mere possession is its own legitimation, for it is always used for important ends, even if this is not apparent. Harley (1950), in his description of the Poro among the Mano, has shown that the graded internal structure of the society requires and reinforces submission to authority, and that this is inculcated in the initiation schools. Because officials in the Poro have ritual as well as secular duties, respect for their authority is taught in the symbolic and binding idiom of ritual, as well as through direct instruction. This makes the attitude of authoritarian submission all the more compelling.

The fusion of Poro roles with religious and political roles also results in an overlapping of Poro functions and those of other institutions. Moreover, Poro *values* with their authoritarian focus also influence the operation of other institutions. My own field research was directed toward an understanding of this latter process.

In 1957 and 1958 I carried out a field study of the legal system of the Kpelle, one of the Poro-centered cultures of West Africa. I began the study with several preliminary or sensitizing hypotheses. One of them was: that the character of the process for the formal settlement of disputes would be influenced in some manner by the presence of the Poro as a tribal fraternity. My results follow.

The Kpelle, a Mande-speaking, patrilineal group of some 175,00 rice cultivators, live in Liberia and the adjoining region of Guinea (where they are known as Guerzé). The present paper is based on field data collected among the Kpelle of Panta Chiefdom in northeastern Central Province of Liberia.

Kpelle political organization is centralized, although there is no single king or paramount chief, but a series of autonomous paramount chiefs of the same level of authority, each of whom is superordinate over district chiefs and town chiefs. Some political functions are vested in the Poro which, as indicated above, is still vigorous in the area. Thus, this form of political organization can best be termed the "polycephalous associational state."

In Liberia, the highest court of a tribal authority and the highest tribal court chartered by the Government of Liberia is that of a paramount chief. Courts of district chiefs (or "clan chiefs" as they are known in Liberia) are also chartered by the Liberian government. These are courts of original jurisdiction which also hear cases appealed from lower courts. Disputes may also be settled in non-chartered courts, those of town chiefs or ward elders. Finally, grievances are also adjusted in informal family moots, and sometimes by associational groupings such as church councils, or cooperative work groups.

The most significant of these Kpelle courts is that of a paramount chief and I undertook a study of the court of the late Chief Dolo Ken Pei, Paramount Chief of Panta Chiefdom.[1] My method was to collect case material in as complete a form as possible. Accordingly, immediately after a court session, using notes and recall, my interpreter and I would prepare verbatim transcripts of each case that we heard. These transcripts were supplemented with accounts—obtained from respondents—of past cases or cases which I did not hear litigated.

In essence, the procedures employed in a Kpelle paramount chief's court are simple. A complainant goes to the paramount chief and/or his clerk. In a casual and informal pre-trial hearing, the chief and the clerk decide whether or not the matter is justiciable. If it is, a summons is issued for the defendant. At this preliminary hearing the chief acquires his first judicial knowledge of the case, mentally sorts out the issues, and probably makes a provisional determination of how he will conduct the hearing. Normally, he hears only one party, the one who brings the complaint. In addition, he will supplement what he is told with what he may know of the case through local gossip and his knowledge of the character of the parties through personal acquaintance. His basis for deciding whether a case is justiciable, or what courtroom strategy he will follow, is necessarily somewhat limited.

The hearing itself follows four steps common to all types of Kpelle

---

[1] What follows is, then, a detailed case study of the operation of a paramount chief's court in a single chiefdom. The description and analysis are, of course, valid for that chiefdom. My visits to courts in other chiefdoms lead me to feel that, on the whole, they are valid for most of the Kpelle tribal area and particularly the Northeast, where people are traditionalists. However, the weighting of the features that characterize the courtroom hearings do vary somewhat from area to area in reflection of a chief's individuality, his judicial personality and particular relationship to his people.

Although Chief Pei is no longer living, for the sake of clearer exposition, I will present the data in the present tense.

dispute settlement. The plaintiff speaks first, making his accusation. He is then questioned by the chief and his council. Next, the defendant answers and is also questioned. Where there are witnesses, they are then called and interrogated. Finally, a decision is announced.

The transcripts of the cases heard before Dolo Ken Pei impress the Western observer as being somewhat coercive and arbitrary in tone. He will even judge (albeit informally, *in camera*) a case in which he is a party. Ground for one's intuitive feelings about the hearings in this court become apparent when the transcripts are analyzed in terms of a framework derived from both jurisprudence and ethno-law.

First, it can be noted that hearings seldom take place immediately after a breach has occurred. There is often a delay before a plaintiff can arrange to travel to the paramount chief's headquarters to institute suit. The immediacy of the hearing is important because where a hearing takes place soon after a dispute has occurred, grievance tension does not have a chance to grow and to harden to the point where it cannot be effectively dissipated (cf. Millar 1923).

Cases are heard in the paramount chief's court house, the largest building in the chiefdom, an imposing structure almost forty feet tall, although it is of wattle and daub construction.[2]

Hearings are attended by the paramount chief, sometimes one or both district chiefs, several town chiefs, and numerous spectators. A litigant thus has to air his affairs both before those who are directly involved in the case, and before a series of political notables and various "strangers." A public hearing is effective in deterring spectators from committing similar offenses, but it is also likely to inhibit litigants from fully expressing themselves (cf. Malinowski 1926 and Millar 1923:157).

Millar (1923:9) and other jurists point out that more of the pertinent points of dissension between two parties are likely to emerge when the investigatory initiative lies with the parties or their advocates, rather than with the judge. In Panta Chiefdom, the chief, as adjudicator, has investigatory initiative in his hands. The transcripts often reveal a puzzling line of questioning rooted in information which did not emerge in the courtroom testimony. Such questions are often based on community gossip or on information gained in the pre-trial hearing where only the plaintiff was present. At the same time, other points mentioned in the testimony may be ignored. Thus, in the Case of the Couple Who Used Love Charms, the wife asked for a divorce, claiming that she did not love her husband anymore. However, she did not refute his testimony that she had used love charms to cause him to love her more than his other wives and, ultimately, to drive them away. The husband, for his part, consulted a diviner, and

---

[2] Since I left the field this structure has been replaced by a building of similar size with a metal roof and cement finish.

also secured "medicine" to cause this wife to love him very much. In spite of this evident mutual concern for the marriage, the chief granted a divorce without delving into the reasons for the deterioration of the marital relationship. Since investigatory initiative lies with him, rather than with the parties, he may conduct the hearing in such a way that some grievances fail to emerge at all, while others—felt not to be pertinent—emerge, but are not ventilated.

Although Dolo Ken Pei often takes judicial notice of information which does not appear in the testimony, he usually operates with a narrow range of relevance, as noted in the reference to the Case of the Couple Who Used Love Charms. In the Case of the Wife Who Displeased the Court, another divorce case, he felt that the wife had precipitated the discord by not cohabiting with her husband and, perhaps, seeking lovers. Therefore, he ignored her denial and counter-assertion that the difficulty lay in the practice of witchcraft against her by a co-wife; witchcraft confessed by the co-wife and confirmed in court by the husband's testimony. She did not deny her husband's assertion that she stayed out late at night and had taken one lover. This, for the chief, was the crucial issue—the matter determining fault. He did not air the witchcraft matter at all. As Gluckman's (1955) Barotse study indicates, where the range of information considered pertinent is wide, the exposure of grievances is likely to be more complete. Conversely, where it is narrow, grievances are not completely aired.[3]

Dolo Ken Pei, the adjudicator, is both judge and chief, fusing judicial and political roles. He can impose a solution on the parties by backing a decision both with judicial authority and with the power underlying his political role. In the Case of the Man Who Beat His Wife, he threatened to send the defendant for his required public works duty[4] before his normal time, saying: "We always give porters to the government. If the time 'has not come for you to do porter work, you must behave yourself and not always look for trouble."

The chief presides wearing robes emblematic of his office and status and is treated with deferential etiquette. Court sessions are attended and policed by the chief's uniformed messengers known to the populace as "soldiers." These men are familiar in their roles as jailors, summoners of witnesses and persons accused of crimes such as tax delinquency. They are visible evidence of the chief's political authority, and the fact that this authority is backed by the possible application of physical force. The robes, messengers —even the courtroom itself—are all expressive symbols of his authority,

---

[3] In a Kpelle court, the range of relevance is wider than that permitted under the rules of evidence in Anglo-American common law, yet is narrower than that Gluckman describes for the Barotse courts of Northern Rhodesia (cf. Gluckman 1955).

[4] In Liberia, tribal citizens who are not permanent wage earners must work a fixed number of days on public works projects as a form of taxation (cf. Article 34 in Government of the Republic of Liberia 1949).

reminders of the ultimate judicial and political sanctions underlying the legal process. As such, they tend to inhibit litigants from a full ventilation of the issues, for their presence is mildly intimidating.

In normal circumstances in a Kpelle court, the decision must necessarily be awarded to one party. The informal reprimands and admonitions which accompany the decision are directed primarily at the losing litigant. Fining the husband as the guilty party in the Case of the Man Who Beat His Wife, the Chief said to him:

> You are behaving badly. A man lives according to his heart, and everything that a man does wrong comes from a bad heart. Therefore, you have a bad heart all the time . . . I planted greens in my own garden and my wives finished eating all of them, but I didn't say anything about it. You, little boy, what kind of wrong thing can a woman do to make you cut her?[5]

In handing down the decision on this note, the chief did not chastize the wife for her action described by the husband in an uncontested plea of self-defense, namely, that she had grabbed a stick and attempted to strike him on his penis. Dolo Ken Pei's droll reply was: "Why didn't you wait and see if she was really going to hit you?"

Such strongly unilateral ascription of blame is common in Kpelle courts, even though some fault usually lies with both parties, and it often creates resentment which raises a new reason for bad feeling between the parties. However, the decision is made less arbitrary by the lecture to the litigants. As illustrated above, it is phrased in homilies (and, often, proverbs) as a way of indicating the meaning of the decision and pointing out its roots in tradition.

Bad feeling between the parties raised by one-sided allocation of fault is often reinforced by the imposition of a harsh penalty. Such severe sanctions are more likely to be imposed by an adjudicator who holds political office and power. A most effective sanction employed by Dolo Ken Pei was to take the guilty party's fine and distribute it among the spectators in the courtroom as a windfall. Where the parties feel that the sanctions imposed as part of the settlement are unduly harsh, they will not truly concur in the solution.

The strong focus on the authority of the paramount chief in a Kpelle court is also mirrored in the fact that there is seldom a recess for deliberation between argumentation and the handing down of a decision. In fact, a decision may come very early in the proceedings, only to be finally pronounced in a formal manner at the end of a hearing. Moreover, even though a paramount chief has a "council" of lesser chiefs and elders whose

---

[5] Among the Kpelle, one's life force is felt to be located largely in the blood; therefore, a wound which breaks the skin and causes blood to flow is considered to be very serious (cf. Holas 1953:146).

formal function is to help in judicial deliberations, there is rarely a significant degree of overt consultation among them in reaching a judicial decision.

In sum, the above descriptive analysis of courtroom procedure in the Panta Chiefdom Paramount Chief's court indicates how some of the actions in the courtroom contribute to the coercive tone one notes there—and, to a certain extent, in courts in any society. Two dimensions of the dispute settlement process were studied: the completeness of the airing of grievances and the extent of party concurrence in the settlement. Each of these dimensions or rubrics presupposes several more minute attributes of a hearing which contribute to the outcome of the hearing.

It was noted that any dispute settlement is likely to be more stable when all of the grievances between the parties are completely aired. Four factors were held to contribute to this result: the immediacy of the hearing, the publicity of the hearing, the locus of investigatory initiative, and the range of relevance. Where all four of the features mark the conduct of a hearing, all of the grievances lodged between the parties are likely to be heard and adjusted.

Similarly, jurisprudence suggests that when a decision in a case is not simply imposed by the adjudicator but truly concurred in by both parties, it is more likely to be durable. We noted that the extent of party concurrence is also the result of four more detailed features of a hearing: authoritative personnel, expressive symbols of authority, unilateral ascription of blame, and sanctions of marked severity. The presence of these four features may lead to parties acquiescing in a settlement—even though it does not satisfy them. This is because the settlement is backed by authority strong enough to hand down a decision without waiting for a feeling of consensus to emerge.

Having noted the features which give hearings in this court their coercive cast, I can turn to the matter of the adequacy of the settlements reached there. Jurisprudence and ethno-law both offer guideposts by which one can measure this—albeit roughly.

Although the transcripts indicate that the hearings in the Panta Chiefdom court are arbitrary and coercive in tone, settlements effected are often satisfactory. A field period of only seventeen months does not permit meaningful conclusions as to the long term durability of settlements, but it is clear that the court is particularly effective in settling cases such as assault, theft, or possession of illegal charms. In matters like these, where the litigants are not linked in a relationship which must continue after the trial, the significant issues are isolated and the decision is announced in the form of a rule. The fact that some grievance tension remains and that the dissension sometimes spreads to other persons does not seem to undermine the decision. In short, the outcome in some types of disputes is not affected by the court's coercive tone.

However, most of the cases heard before a Kpelle paramount chief involve parties whose relationship is not transistory. They are cases of disputed rights over women. Here, the court is clearly less effective. In the majority of marital disputes brought before it, the court grants a divorce. Marital disputes seldom result in a willing reconciliation, because this requires restoration of genuine harmony between the parties. This is impossible because the coercive cast of courtroom procedures yields an incomplete airing of grievances, and faulty isolation of issues. Moreover, the coercive tone of the hearing itself *adds* to the grievance tension between the spouses and drives them farther apart. Precluded from arranging a concordant reconciliation, the court may effect an acquiescent reconciliation, perhaps by the drastic measure of threatening to jail a woman who will not return to her husband. One doubts the durability of such reconciliations.[6]

This limited role of the court in settling matrimonial cases contrasts with that of the informal moot of kinsmen which, being more conciliatory in tone, can bring about concordant reconciliations.[7]

I can now return to my initial problem and preliminary hypothesis. How does the presence of the Poro contribute to the coercive tone of the courtroom hearing in Panta Chiefdom? Some of the arbitrary nature of Kpelle court proceedings is due to the type of cases with which it has to deal. Matrimonial disputes become as cut and dried to the Kpelle judge as the Monday morning docket of drunken driving cases to an American traffic court judge. Marital disputes are handled with dispatch, which appears arbitrary, for once a judge sees that the two spouses are not reconcilable, he need not inquire further into their behavior, but proceed to arrange a divorce.

An equally significant cause of the coercive and arbitrary tone of courtroom procedure is the influence of Poro values. Respect for authority conditioned in the Poro bush leads litigants to expect a certain amount of arbitrariness in court procedures and decisions. A young man in the initiation school cannot question what he is told by the masked figures or the older men because, not having been initiated into the higher degrees, he knows little of the rationale supporting actions he is ordered to perform. He must—and does—accept on faith the notion that those who command know what is right and act with the highest moral and spiritual aims. The same attitude toward authoritarian actions is carried into the courtroom.

This is significant because it apparently limits the manner with which the court can deal with some types of disputes, especially marital disputes.

---

[6] Some of the causes and results of Kpelle marital instability are discussed in Gibbs 1960, [1962, and 1963b].

[7] Procedures in a Kpelle moot, an informal forum for dispute settlements, are described in detail and analyzed in Gibbs 1960, and [1963a]. Transcripts of the cases mentioned here and other cases as well appear in the 1960 source.

However, it also makes it possible for the court to serve as a forceful and unchallenged instrument for sanctioning deviant actions which threaten traditional values or traditional authority.

The present paper is based on the detailed and systematic analysis of a few selected cases rather than a mass of quantitative data. It uses an eclectic but organized collection of concepts to establish a relationship between one of a society's basic values, i.e., strong and unchallenged respect for authority, and the nature of that society's judicial procedures and results. An intervening variable is the presence of the Poro as a tribal fraternity which is the primary structural device through which this value is so effectively instilled and so strongly maintained.[8] The hypothesis suggested is a tentative one. Further research should involve applying the same analytical scheme to detailed case material from other Kpelle courts and courts in other Poro-centered societies and to data from societies in other world culture areas which are similarly integrated around secret societies and rituals, such as the Pueblos of the American Southwest.

---

[8] The Sande, the parallel tribal organization for women, has not been discussed here, because less is known about its operations. However, it is clear that it adheres to the same basic value, including its manifestation in feminine deference to male dominance in the courtroom and in most spheres of life.

Part VIII

RELIGION AND SYMBOLISM

In the preceding three parts of this book, we have focused on what are, by most accounts, the main organizational dimensions of human life. But by definition, all social animals—whether lions, chickens or bottle-nosed dolphins—are organized (often in ways not all that unfamiliar to us). Distinctively, however, people look for meaning in and give meaning to human life. People are also extremely creative and playful—often most intensely when undertaking this search for meaning. Thus, with the organizational dimensions as background, we turn in Parts VIII and IX to consider what are, by way of contrast, two of the most cerebral and expressive dimensions of human life—religion and symbolism, and aesthetics and recreation. Although these aspects of the human experience are themselves organized and are part of the overall pattern of social life, they also are what might be called "meta-organizational"—that is, they give organization to organization.

In the selections which follow, we will see something of the ways humans search for meaning and the ways symbols are used; we will also consider the way certain beliefs are grounded in the environment. In Part IX, we will discover that artistic, expressive efforts are "structured," and that complex messages can be—indeed, must be—sent as humans play. And in the process, these behaviors should tell us, as they tell the participants, a great deal about what is significant in a given physical and social context.

RELIGION

One of the most difficult problems in the study of religion is defining it. And yet, surprisingly, what seems to be a mandatory step may in fact be quite optional. Those who favor taking the option of not defining religion often note that definitions close off inquiry in what can only be described as unfortunate and misleading ways. Those who favor beginning with an attempt to define religion attest to the widely expressed need to start with at least a working definition of the phenomenon of interest.

Thus, although the problem is difficult and the effort can lead to unintended problems, we will follow Yinger (1957) and define religion as a "system of *beliefs* and practices by means of which a group of people struggles with [the] ultimate problems of human life" (Yinger 1957:9; italics added). The word *beliefs* is emphasized to direct attention to the way religious beliefs contrast with the more tentative ideas in non-religious systems concerned with the ultimate problems of human life (e.g., science). Beliefs, in this sense, are *presumed truths* about the nature of existence, death, and other "ultimate problems of human life." By contrast, non-religious systems operate with theories and hypotheses which by definition are continually open to refutation.

If definitions of religion pose risks, speculations about the origin of such beliefs would seem to be even more dangerous. Although serious discussions of the origin of religion have not held center stage in anthropology over the past few decades, this issue has by no means gone unconsidered (e.g., see Weston La Barre's recent major work *The Ghost Dance: The Origins of Religion*). Most thoughtful considerations of the origins of religion emphasize the well known fact that humans do not understand everything nor do they have minds which are exclusively rational. Indeed, the existence of irrationality, dreams, and other altered states of consciousness (however induced) have provided many different scholars with the groundwork for explaining the origins of religion.

The first selection in Part VIII, although not oriented specifically to the question of the origin of religion, does provide valuable insight into the role of what surely is one of the most fundamental religious figures—the *shaman*. Michael Harner, the author of the essay in Chapter 24, describes the activities and beliefs associated with the shaman in Jivaro society. With the assistance of various plant-based chemicals, a Jivaro shaman makes contact with the spirit world which, it is believed, has a vital role in the everyday affairs of people. There are many spirits in their world and, as Harner notes, there are also many shamans since a chemical assist is all that is needed to make contact with the real world of spirits. And, as Harner implies, for the Jivaro in general and the shamans in particular, it is the reality of illusions that is important, not the illusion we call reality.

From this dramatic system of belief and practice, we shift sharply in Chapter 25 to a discussion of religion in an affluent society. The analysis is presented in standard ethnographic format, complete with a description of how the field site was selected, what pseudonym was picked, and so forth. All of this is ordinary enough, of course, until we note that the field site is somewhere in the American midwest and that the ethnographer is Surajit Sinha, a citizen of India. There are, it must be admitted reluctantly, far too few non-western anthropologists and of those few, only a handful have ever given American culture an examination such as Sinha does.

In classic anthropological fashion, Sinha compares what he sees in "Mapletown" with what he knows best—the peoples and religions of India. In the course of his brief analysis, Sinha confronts several basic questions about the role of religion in any society and in highly industrialized, modern, "secular" societies in particular. As an exercise, the reader may wish to consider how the religious beliefs and behaviors Sinha observed in Mapletown over a decade ago compare with what appears to be happening in many parts of the United States today. For example, how many changes (if any) might there be in the status rankings of the various denominations? And what comparisons might Sinha make between the religious beliefs and behaviors of people in India and those of many young people today?

SYMBOLS

Symbols are an integral part of all religious systems (as well as all of the other aspects of the human experience), but analyzing them is not a task for which there is widespread agreement as to the best procedures. We will confront this problem again in Part IX, but here we will consider two facets of this topic. One approach to symbols has been provided by the great French sociologist/anthropologist Emile Durkheim. In his treatises on religion, he emphasized the role of what he called *collective representations*. These, he reasoned, were essential to the religious experience and to societies as a whole because they provided a focal point around which a society could express its sense of unity. A collective representation may be defined as a symbol or a system of symbols which expresses collective realities and which involve beliefs and rites that relate people to these symbols and to sacred beings.

In the selection by Eric Wolf (Chapter 26), we come face to face with what would seem to be one of the more significant collective representations in American life—Santa Claus. Like other such symbols, there are intriguing contradictions inherent in Santa Claus. He seems to be a sacred figure in a secular land, a mythical creature in a science oriented society, a sled-using giver of home-made toys in a jet-aged, earn-your-way, factory oriented economy. And why *do* we keep the source of our children's gifts a secret? Are we "protecting" them from the harsh reality of adult life? Are adults trying to recapture an image of youth that is no more than that —an image? And, we may ask, is Santa Claus a religious symbol? If so, what kind? If not, what kind of collective representation is he? Thoughts about these and other questions are offered by Wolf in his delightful essay.

Another approach to the analysis of symbols is offered, in Chapter 27, by Marvin Harris. We have already noted that many theories about the origin (and nature) of religion give attention to human irrationality and to the fact that much human behavior, and especially religious behavior, appears to be irrational. Although Harris discusses behavior that may seem irrational, his goal here and elsewhere is to show that what appears at first to be irrational is in fact completely rational behavior under the circumstances—primarily techno-environmental circumstances. Although he discusses many issues of this sort elsewhere (e.g., in his recent and provocative book *Cows, Pigs, Wars and Witches*), he is here concerned with the Islamic and Judaic prohibitions against eating certain animals, especially pigs. The Judaic prohibitions are found in the *Bible* in the book of Leviticus; the Islamic versions are found in the *Koran* and other sacred texts. Harris does not say so specifically, but it is apparent that his views are presented in part as a counter to the views of another anthropologist, Mary Douglas. In a paper entitled "The Abominations of Leviticus," she argues that such prohibitions

> cannot occur except in view of a systematic ordering of ideas. Hence any piecemeal interpretation of the pollution rules of another culture is bound to fail. For the only way in which pollution ideas make sense is in reference to a total structure of thought whose key-stone, boundaries, margins and internal lines are held in relation by rituals of separation" [Douglas 1970:54; original 1966].

For Harris, such total structures of thought are not only unnecessary but also wrongheaded. Instead, Harris seeks to show how such prohibitions are an outgrowth of the material conditions of the region. Thus, in Chapter 27 (which is comprised of two brief essays which appeared originally in *Natural History* magazine, the second as a retort to suggestions and comments made by those who read the first article), Harris emphasizes the reasons why pigs should not have been eaten in the Middle East at the time these prohibitions were being pronounced. But he also considers similar explanations for the other animals prohibited in Leviticus. As can be seen, his arguments make no reference to the "total structure of thought" of the religions of the region.

As with most debates of this sort, there would seem to be a viable middle position between Douglas and Harris. Surely the material conditions of the Middle East make it likely that pigs will be a prohibited animal. But it also seems just as feasible that such prohibitions may, for aesthetic, mnemonic, and "structural" reasons, be enmeshed with other ideas, including some involving environmentally uncritical prohibitions. There can be no question that humans must be alert to the contingencies of their environment if they are to survive, but in so doing, they may well respond to these limiting factors by creating symmetrical, structurally balanced conceptual systems. Indeed, given current views about the nature of the human mind, there may be no other way for humans to respond.

Michael J. Harner

24. The Sound of Rushing Water*

He had drunk, and now he softly sang. Gradually, faint lines and forms began to appear in the darkness, and the shrill music of the *tsentsak,* the spirit helpers, arose around him. The power of the drink fed them. He called, and they came. First, *pangi,* the anaconda, coiled about his head, transmuted into a crown of gold. Then *wampang,* the giant butterfly, hovered above his shoulder and sang to him with its wings. Snakes, spiders, birds, and bats danced in the air above him. On his arms appeared a thousand eyes as his demon helpers emerged to search the night for enemies.

The sound of rushing water filled his ears, and listening to its roar, he knew he possessed the power of *tsungi,* the first shaman. Now he could see. Now he could find the truth. He stared at the stomach of the sick man. Slowly, it became transparent like a shallow mountain stream, and he saw within it, coiling and uncoiling, *makanchi,* the poisonous serpent, who had been sent by the enemy shaman. The real cause of the illness had been found.

The Jívaro Indians of the Ecuadorian Amazon believe that witchcraft is the cause of the vast majority of illnesses and non-violent deaths. The normal waking life, for the Jívaro, is simply "a lie," or illusion, while the true forces that determine daily events are supernatural and can only be seen and manipulated with the aid of hallucinogenic drugs. A reality view

* Reprinted with permission from *Natural History* Magazine, June–July 1968. Copyright © The American Museum of Natural History 1968.

of this kind creates a particularly strong demand for specialists who can cross over into the supernatural world at will to deal with the forces that influence and even determine the events of the waking life.

These specialists, called "shamans" by anthropologists, are recognized by the Jívaro as being of two types: bewitching shamans or curing shamans. Both kinds take a hallucinogenic drink, whose Jívaro name is *natema,* in order to enter the supernatural world. This brew, commonly called *yagé,* or *yajé,* in Colombia, *ayahuasca* (Inca "vine of the dead") in Ecuador and Peru, and *caapi* in Brazil, is prepared from segments of a species of the vine *Banisteriopsis,* a genus belonging to the Malpighiaceae. The Jívaro boil it with the leaves of a similar vine, which probably is also a species of *Banisteriopsis,* to produce a tea that contains the powerful hallucinogenic alkaloids harmaline, harmine, d-tetrahydroharmine, and quite possibly dimethyltryptamine (DMT). These compounds have chemical structures and effects similar, but not identical, to LSD, mescaline of the peyote cactus, and psilocybin of the psychotropic Mexican mushroom.

When I first undertook research among the Jívaro in 1956–57, I did not fully appreciate the psychological impact of the *Banisteriopsis* drink upon the native view of reality, but in 1961 I had occasion to drink the hallucinogen in the course of field work with another Upper Amazon Basin tribe. For several hours after drinking the brew, I found myself, although awake, in a world literally beyond my wildest dreams. I met bird-headed people, as well as dragon-like creatures who explained that they were the true gods of this world. I enlisted the services of other spirit helpers in attempting to fly through the far reaches of the galaxy. Transported into a trance where supernatural seemed natural, I realized that anthropologists, including myself, had profoundly underestimated the importance of the drug in affecting native ideology. Therefore, in 1964 I returned to the Jívaro to give particular attention to the drug's use by the Jívaro shaman.

The use of the hallucinogenic *natema* drink among the Jívaro makes it possible for almost anyone to achieve the trance state essential for the practice of shamanism. Given the presence of the drug and the felt need to contact the "real," or supernatural, world, it is not surprising that approximately one out of every four Jívaro men is a shaman. Any adult, male or female, who desires to become such a practitioner, simply presents a gift to an already practicing shaman, who administers the *Banisteriopsis* drink and gives some of his own supernatural power—in the form of spirit helpers, or *tsentsak*—to the apprentice. These spirit helpers, or "darts," are the main supernatural forces believed to cause illness and death in daily life. To the non-shaman they are normally invisible, and even shamans can perceive them only under the influence of *natema.*

Shamans send these spirit helpers into the victims' bodies to make them ill or to kill them. At other times, they may suck spirits sent by enemy shamans from the bodies of tribesmen suffering from witchcraft-induced illness. The spirit helpers also form shields that protect their shaman masters from attacks. The following account presents the ideology of Jívaro witchcraft from the point of view of the Indians themselves.

To give the novice some *tsentsak,* the practicing shaman regurgitates what appears to be—to those who have taken *natema*—a brilliant substance in which the spirit helpers are contained. He cuts part of it off with a machete and gives it to the novice to swallow. The recipient experiences pain upon taking it into his stomach and stays on his bed for ten days, repeatedly drinking *natema.* The Jívaro believe they can keep magical darts in their stomachs indefinitely and regurgitate them at will. The shaman donating the *tsentsak* periodically blows and rubs all over the body of the novice, apparently to increase the power of the transfer.

The novice must remain inactive and not engage in sexual intercourse for at least three months. If he fails in self-discipline, as some do, he will not become a successful shaman. At the end of the first month, a *tsentsak* emerges from his mouth. With this magical dart at his disposal, the new shaman experiences a tremendous desire to bewitch. If he casts his *tsentsak* to fulfill this desire, he will become a bewitching shaman. If, on the other hand, the novice can control his impulse and reswallow this first *tsentsak,* he will become a curing shaman.

If the shaman who gave the *tsentsak* to the new man was primarily a bewitcher, rather than a curer, the novice likewise will tend to become a bewitcher. This is because a bewitcher's magical darts have such a desire to kill that their new owner will be strongly inclined to adopt their attitude. One informant said that the urge to kill felt by bewitching shamans came to them with a strength and frequency similar to that of hunger.

Only if the novice shaman is able to abstain from sexual intercourse for five months, will he have the power to kill a man (if he is a bewitcher) or cure a victim (if he is a curer). A full year's abstinence is considered necessary to become a really effective bewitcher or curer.

During the period of sexual abstinence, the new shaman collects all kinds of insects, plants, and other objects, which he now has the power to convert into *tsentsak.* Almost any object, including living insects and worms, can become a *tsentsak* if it is small enough to be swallowed by a shaman. Different types of *tsentsak* are used to cause different kinds and degrees of illness. The greater the variety of these objects that a shaman has in his body, the greater is his ability.

According to Jívaro concepts, each *tsentsak* has a natural and supernatural aspect. The magical dart's natural aspect is that of an ordinary material object as seen without drinking the drug *natema.* But the supernatural and "true" aspect of the *tsentsak* is revealed to the shaman by taking *natema.* When he does this, the magical darts appear in new forms as demons and with new names. In their supernatural aspects, the *tsentsak* are not simply objects but spirit helpers in various forms, such as giant butterflies, jaguars, or monkeys, who actively assist the shaman in his tasks.

Bewitching is carried out against a specific, known individual and thus is almost always done to neighbors or, at the most, fellow tribesmen. Normally, as is the case with intratribal assassination, bewitching is done to avenge a particular offense committed against one's family or friends. Both bewitching and individual assassination contrast with the large-scale head-hunting raids for which the Jívaro have become famous, and which were conducted against entire neighborhoods of enemy tribes.

To bewitch, the shaman takes *natema* and secretly approaches the house of his victim. Just out of sight in the forest, he drinks green tobacco juice, enabling him to regurgitate a *tsentsak,* which he throws at his victim as he comes out of his house. If the *tsentsak* is strong enough and is thrown with sufficient force, it will pass all the way through the victim's body causing death within a period of a few days to several weeks. More often, however, the magical dart simply lodges in the victim's body. If the shaman, in his hiding place, fails to see the intended victim, he may instead bewitch any member of the intended victim's family who appears, usually a wife or child. When the shaman's mission is accomplished, he returns secretly to his own home.

One of the distinguishing characteristics of the bewitching process among the Jívaro is that, as far as I could learn, the victim is given no specific indication that someone is bewitching him. The bewitcher does not want his victim to be aware that he is being supernaturally attacked, lest he take protective measures by immediately procuring the services of a curing shaman. Nonetheless, shamans and laymen alike with whom I talked noted that illness invariably follows the bewitchment, although the degree of the illness can vary considerably.

A special kind of spirit helper, called a *pasuk,* can aid the bewitching shaman by remaining near the victim in the guise of an insect or animal of the forest after the bewitcher has left. This spirit helper has his own objects to shoot into the victim should a curing shaman succeed in sucking out the *tsentsak* sent earlier by the bewitcher who is the owner of the *pasuk.*

In addition, the bewitcher can enlist the aid of a *wakani* ("soul," or "spirit") bird. Shamans have the power to call these birds and use them as spirit helpers in bewitching victims. The shaman blows on the *wakani* birds and then sends them to the house of the victim to fly around and around the man, frightening him. This is believed to cause fever and insanity, with death resulting shortly thereafter.

After he returns home from bewitching, the shaman may send a *wakani* bird to perch near the house of the victim. Then if a curing shaman sucks out the intruding object, the bewitching shaman sends the *wakani* bird more *tsentsak* to throw from its beak into the victim. By continually resupplying the *wakani* bird with new *tsentsak,* the sorcerer makes it impossible for the curer to rid his patient permanently of the magical darts.

While the *wakani* birds are supernatural servants available to anyone who wishes to use them, the *pasuk,* chief among the spirit helpers, serves only a single shaman. Likewise a shaman possesses only one *pasuk.* The *pasuk,* being specialized for the service of bewitching, has a protective shield to guard it from counterattack by the curing shaman. The curing shaman, under the influence of *natema,* sees the *pasuk* of the bewitcher in human form and size, but "covered with iron except for its eyes." The curing shaman can kill this *pasuk* only by shooting a *tsentsak* into its eyes, the sole vulnerable area in the *pasuk's* armor. To the person who has not taken the hallucinogenic drink, the *pasuk* usually appears to be simply a tarantula.

Shamans also may kill or injure a person by using magical darts, *anamuk,* to create supernatural animals that attack a victim. If a shaman has a small, pointed armadillo bone *tsentsak,* he can shoot this into a river while the victim is crossing it on a balsa raft or in a canoe. Under the water, this bone manifests itself in its supernatural aspect as an anaconda, which rises up and overturns the craft, causing the victim to drown. The shaman can similarly use a tooth from a killed snake as a *tsentsak,* creating a poisonous serpent to bite his victim. In more or less the same manner, shamans can create jaguars and pumas to kill their victims.

About five years after receiving his *tsentsak,* a bewitching shaman undergoes a test to see if he still retains enough *tsentsak* power to continue to kill successfully. This test involves bewitching a tree. The shaman, under the influence of *natema,* attempts to throw a *tsentsak* through the tree at the point where its two main branches join. If his strength and aim are adequate, the tree appears to split the moment the *tsentsak* is sent into it. The splitting, however, is invisible to an observer who is not under the influence of the hallucinogen. If the shaman fails, he knows that he is incapable of killing a human victim. This means that, as soon as possible, he must go to a strong shaman and purchase a new supply of *tsentsak.* Until he has the goods with which to pay for this new supply, he is in constant danger, in his proved weakened condition, of being seriously bewitched by other shamans. Therefore, each day, he drinks large quantities of *natema,* tobacco juice, and the extract of yet another drug, *pirípiri.* He also rests on his bed at home to conserve his strength, but tries to conceal his weakened condition from his enemies. When he purchases a new supply of *tsentsak,* he can safely cut down on his consumption of these other substances.

The degree of illness produced in a witchcraft victim is a function of both the force with which the *tsentsak* is shot into the body, and also of the character of the magical dart itself. If a *tsentsak* is shot all the way through the body of a victim, then "there is nothing for a curing shaman to suck out," and the patient dies. If the magical dart lodges within the body, however, it is theoretically possible to cure the victim by sucking. But in actual practice, the sucking is not always considered successful.

The work of the curing shaman is complementary to that of a bewitcher. When a curing shaman is called in to treat a patient, his first task is to see if the illness is due to witchcraft. The usual diagnosis and treatment begin with the curing shaman drinking *natema,* tobacco juice, and *pirípiri* in the late afternoon and early evening. These drugs permit him to see into the body of the patient as though it were glass. If the illness is due to sorcery, the curing shaman will see the intruding object within the patient's body clearly enough to determine whether or not he can cure the sickness.

A shaman sucks magical darts from a patient's body only at night, and in a dark area of the house, for it is only in the dark that he can perceive the drug-induced visions that are the supernatural reality. With the setting of the sun, he alerts his *tsentsak* by whistling the tune of the curing song; after about a quarter of an hour, he starts singing. When he is ready to suck, the shaman regurgitates two *tsentsak* into the sides of his throat and mouth. These must be identical to the one he has seen in the patient's body. He holds one of these in the front of the mouth and the other in the rear. They are expected to catch the supernatural aspect of the magical dart that the shaman sucks out of the patient's body. The *tsentsak* nearest the shaman's lips is supposed to incorporate the sucked-out *tsentsak* essence within itself. If, however, this supernatural essence should get past it, the second magical dart in the mouth blocks the throat so that the intruder cannot enter the interior of the shaman's body. If the curer's two *tsentsak* were to fail to catch the supernatural essence of the *tsentsak,* it would pass down into the shaman's stomach and kill him. Trapped thus within the mouth, this essence is shortly caught by, and incorporated into, the material substance of one of the curing shaman's *tsentsak.* He then "vomits" out this object and displays it to the patient and his family saying, "Now I have sucked it out. Here it is."

The non-shamans think that the material object itself is what has been sucked out, and the shaman does not disillusion them. At the same time, he is not lying, because he knows that the only important thing about a *tsentsak* is its supernatural aspect, or essence, which he sincerely believes he has removed from the patient's body. To explain to the layman that he already had these objects in his mouth would serve no fruitful purpose and would prevent him from displaying such an object as proof that he had effected the cure. Without incontrovertible evidence, he would not be able to convince the patient and his family that he had effected the cure and must be paid.

The ability of the shaman to suck depends largely upon the quantity and strength of his own *tsentsak,* of which he may have hundreds. His magical darts assume their supernatural aspect as spirit helpers when he is under the influence of *natema,* and he sees them as a variety of zoomorphic forms hovering over him, perching on his shoulders, and sticking out of his skin. He sees them helping to suck the patient's body. He must drink tobacco juice every few hours to "keep them fed" so that they will not leave him.

The curing shaman must also deal with any *pasuk* that may be in the patient's vicinity for the purpose of casting more darts. He drinks additional amounts of *natema* in order to see them and engages in *tsentsak* duels with them if they are present. While the *pasuk* is enclosed in iron armor, the shaman himself has his own armor composed of his many *tsentsak.* As long as he is under the influence of *natema,* these magical darts cover his body as a protective shield, and are on the lookout for any enemy *tsentsak* headed toward their master. When these *tsentsak* see such a missile coming, they immediately close up together at the point where the enemy dart is attempting to penetrate, and thereby repel it.

If the curer finds *tsentsak* entering the body of his patient after he has killed *pasuk,* he suspects the presence of a *wakani* bird. The shaman drinks *maikua* (*Datura* sp.), an hallucinogen even more powerful than *natema,* as well as tobacco juice, and silently sneaks into the forest to hunt and kill the bird with *tsentsak.* When he succeeds, the curer returns to the patient's home, blows all over the house to get rid of the "atmosphere" created by the numerous *tsentsak* sent by the bird, and completes his sucking of the patient. Even after all the *tsentsak* are extracted, the shaman may remain another night at the house to suck out any "dirtiness" (*pahuri*) still inside. In the cures which I have witnessed, this sucking is a most noisy process, accompanied by deep, but dry, vomiting.

After sucking out a *tsentsak,* the shaman puts it into a little container. He does not swallow it because it is not his own magical dart and would therefore kill him. Later, he throws the *tsentsak* into the air, and it flies back to the shaman who sent it originally into the patient. *Tsentsak* also fly back to a shaman at the death of a former apprentice who had originally received them from him. Besides receiving "old" magical darts unexpectedly in this manner, the shaman may have *tsentsak* thrown at him by a bewitcher. Accordingly, shamans constantly drink tobacco juice at all hours of the day and night. Although the tobacco juice is not truly hallucinogenic, it produces a narcotized state, which is believed necessary to keep one's *tsentsak* ready to repel any other magical darts. A shaman does not even dare go for a walk without taking along the green tobacco leaves with which he prepares the juice that keeps his spirit helpers alert. Less frequently, but regularly, he must drink *natema* for the same purpose and to keep in touch with the supernatural reality.

While curing under the influence of *natema,* the curing shaman "sees" the shaman who bewitched his patient. Generally, he can recognize the person, unless it is a shaman who lives far away or in another tribe. The patient's family knows this, and demands to be told the identity of the bewitcher, particularly if the sick person dies. At one curing session I attended, the shaman could not identify the person he had seen in his vision. The brother of the dead man then accused the shaman himself of being responsible. Under such pressure, there is a strong tendency for the curing shaman to attribute each case to a particular bewitcher.

Shamans gradually become weak and must purchase *tsentsak* again and again. Curers tend to become weak in power, especially after curing a patient bewitched by a shaman who has recently received a new supply of magical darts. Thus, the most powerful shamans are those who can repeatedly purchase new supplies of *tsentsak* from other shamans.

Shamans can take back *tsentsak* from others to whom they have previously given them. To accomplish this, the shaman drinks *natema,* and, using his *tsentsak,* creates a "bridge" in the form of a rainbow between himself and the other shaman. Then he shoots a *tsentsak* along this rainbow. This strikes the ground beside the other shaman with an explosion and flash likened to a lightning bolt. The purpose of this is to surprise the other shaman so that he temporarily forgets to maintain his guard over his magical darts, thus permitting the other shaman to suck them back along the rainbow. A shaman who has had his *tsentsak* taken away in this manner will discover that "nothing happens" when he drinks *natema.* The sudden loss of his *tsentsak* will tend to make him ill, but ordinarily the illness is not fatal unless a bewitcher shoots a magical dart into him while he is in this weakened condition. If he has not become disillusioned by his experience, he can again purchase *tsentsak* from some other shaman and resume his calling. Fortunately for anthropology some of these men have chosen to give up shamanism and therefore can be persuaded to reveal their knowledge, no longer having a vested interest in the profession. This divulgence, however, does not serve as a significant threat to practitioners, for words alone can never adequately convey the realities of shamanism. These can only be approached with the aid of *natema,* the chemical door to the invisible world of the Jívaro shaman.

Surajit Sinha

25. Religion in an Affluent Society*

This study was taken up primarily out of curiosity about a pattern of living that operates today as a powerful model for modernity and as a generator of induced change throughout the economically underdeveloped world.[1] The study deals with these problems: 1. why and how formal religion persists in the most technologically advanced country in the world, contrary to the expectations of Comte, Spencer, and Tylor; and 2. the relation between religion and secular life.

DATA COLLECTION

I sought an American village with a fairly stable core population (i.e., with a sense of local history), clear evidence of economic affluence, and a fair balance between Protestants and Roman Catholics. A population under 5,000 was desirable in order that much of the village life could be directly visible or, at least, easily approached. I found such a community, which I shall call "Mapletown," in the Midwest.

---

* Reprinted by permission of the University of Chicago Press from *Current Anthropology*, vol. 7 no. 2, 1966:189–95.

[1] There have been surprisingly few field studies of American culture by anthropologists from Afro-Asian countries. In this regard, I can think only of the publications of Francis Hsu (1953, 1961, 1963), all on the level of national character. Kluckhohn once commented: "We badly need people from India, Japan, and China to come and study our American values and *vice versa*. This is an indispensable step. We have to see a value system from this point, that point, and the other point." (Tax *et al.* 1953:340).

With my family I moved into a big modern house in the predominantly lower-middle class section. I became a member of the local chapter of the Kiwanis Club. We stayed for about 3 months—from June 5 until September 5, 1963. I revisited the village alone for about 2 weeks in May, 1964.[2]

I observed as much of the religious and related secular behavior as possible, although I collected the bulk of my data through informally guided conversation and open-ended questionnaires. Responses were often tape recorded. In framing the questionnaires, I took advantage of being a foreigner and of not knowing much about Christianity or about American society. I also did a census survey of about 10% of the families of Mapletown.

My American field experience was quite different from my earlier encounter with tribes of Central India.[3] There I studied the groups with a considerable sense of sociocultural distance, detachment, and, I must confess, condescension. In my commitment to record fully the customs of the tribe as a "natural system," I did not always pay adequate attention to the reaction of the respondents to my encroachment on the privacy of their customs and social relations. In Mapletown I was much more cautious about the sensitivities of my respondents. In tribal Central India, while I utilized the insights of exceptionally perceptive informants, the analysis of behavior was primarily done by me. In Mapletown, there were many local intellectuals who thought reflectively about the structures or processes of their community life. I could approach these specialized respondents—the priests, doctors, lawyers, educated farmers, school teachers, journalists, etc.—as fellow "intellectuals," or "learned informants." I occasionally asked selected informants for a guided tour of the village and tried to follow their mental charts of the community.

The shifting cluster of playmates around my 5½-year-old daughter often brought into relief the class structure of the community. The neighborhood children provided us with ready subjects for enquiring into the imprint of religion on 6- to 9-year-old children.

Our coming as foreigners gave us easy access to some of the marginal people who were somewhat critical of the community, such as a local newspaper reporter, the Negro leaders of the local chapter of the NAACP, and the few agnostics. In theological discussion with the local ministers, my sometimes posing contrasting alternatives from Hindu theological background stimulated discussion.

---

[2] This field study was made possible by the generous support of the Wenner-Gren Foundation for Anthropological Research and the Center for Advanced Study in the Behavioral Sciences. I am particularly grateful to Sol Tax for encouraging me in many ways to take up this study. This preliminary report will be followed by a detailed monographic account of religion in Mapletown.

[3] See my article "State Formation and Rajpur Myth in Tribal Central India" (1962).

MAPLETOWN

Mapletown became an incorporated village in 1859. The pioneering families were all Protestants from the eastern states. They worked hard, cleared large farmlands, built decent, commodious houses, and prospered.

Later immigrants to the community included members of other ethnic groups, nearly all Catholic. Of these, the Irish are no longer distinguishable from the Protestants. The other groups are: Poles, Italians, Slovaks, and Croatians. There are also 3 Jewish families, all shop-owners, and about a dozen Negro families, living mostly in the rural area.

Mapletown township today has a population of 4,939 of whom 1,967 live in rural areas and 2,972 in the village. About one-fourth of the 1,245 families in the township depends mainly or subsidiarily on farming. (Grape-growing, introduced by Southern European immigrants about 1910, is an important specialty.) The rest depend on labour, business, service, professions, and industries. Since the major industries in this township are connected with the processing of farm products, the non-farming section of the population keeps close track of what is happening to the farmers. About 100 family heads commute daily to an industrial city about 18 miles away.

To a person coming from India, Mapletown has no characteristics of a "village" other than population size. It has all the modern amenities: electricity, telephones, television, radio, supermarkets, automatic laundry, hotels, and restaurants. Within the last 30 years, the village has developed industries; it has 3 wineries, 2 juice-processing companies, 2 canning companies, 2 fish bait companies, 1 electronics factory, 1 plating company, 1 fruit-packaging company, 1 cement products company, 1 notebook and looseleaf binder company, and 1 dairy processing plant. About 1,700 people are employed by these concerns.

Two men tried to impress upon me that class structure is not very visible in the residential pattern and that there is really "no rich man towering above others in the village." Mr. D., the leading drugstore owner gave a breakdown of the class structure in terms of annual income as follows:

Level 1...Industry leaders and owners: about $100,000 or more.
Level 2...Doctors, dentists and lawyers: $15–70,000; Automobile dealers: $15–40,000; Outstanding farmers: $10–30,000.
Level 3...Salesmen, insurance agents, etc.: $10–30,000.
Level 4...Teachers: $4–10,000; medium farmers: $4–10,000.
Level 5...Skilled industrial workers: $4–8,000.
Level 6...Small farmers, unskilled industrial labourers, store clerks, retired people: $2–4,000.
Level 7...Transient laborers: $2,000.

Mr. D. estimated that about three fourths of the population of the township would belong to levels 4-6.

Nearly all the families from levels 1-5 have electricity, central heating, car, refrigerator, telephone, television, and at least 1 radio. Most of these items are also available in level 6, only a few not having a telephone. In level 7, telephones become rare and even television is missing in a number of families, and the car is usually dilapidated.

Within the upper 5 levels, variations occur in the size of the house and its lawn; lake frontage; number and quality of possessions; and ownership of special items such as record player, piano or organ, tape recorder, expensive camera, and power mower. A trip to Florida for the retired has recently become a symbol of prestige widely shared by people from levels 1-4. A pleasure trip to Europe is becoming common for the younger people from levels 1-3. A private swimming pool and horses for the children are also marks of economic distinction.

With the rising income level, increased consumption, and growth of industries, the society is aware that it is affluent, compared to its past and especially compared to other countries. However, the lower classes, from level 5 down, are aware that they are not influential in the community. They are outside the prestige churches and the prestige clubs. Although organizations like the volunteer fire department, American Legion, Masonic Lodge, and Knights of Columbus tend to blur class lines, the lower classes are involved to a lesser extent in such social activities as bridge clubs, boating, hunting, and golfing. The marginal position of these people has, of course, important bearing upon their religious behavior (Harrington 1963). They either do not go to church at all or go to the "emotional" ones that promise the coming of the Lord and the inheritance of the earth by the meek.

THE CHURCHES

Every Friday, the local newspaper publishes a Durkheimian statement: "Strong Church makes strong communities." The theme is further elaborated as follows:

> The Church is the greatest faith on earth for the building of character and good citizenship. It is a storehouse of spiritual values. Without a strong Church, neither democracy nor civilization can survive.

The full-page announcement includes church-service notices for 11 churches in the township: St. Mary's Catholic, St. Mark's Episcopal, First Presbyterian, First Methodist, Trinity Lutheran, First Baptist, Christian (Disciples of Christ), Assembly of God, Full Gospel Pentecostal, Seventh Day Adventist, and Jehovah's Witnesses.

These messages are sponsored every week by 23 industries and business establishments in Mapletown. They include a pictorial feature and a lengthy moral message obtained through a national advertising service. These announcements say much about the place of formal religion in the community: *a.* It is generally felt that church going generates the requisite individual and social ethics that support "democracy" and "civilization," which are identical; *b.* the business world is behind the church; *c.* there is considerable tolerance, on a formal level, of the various churches, denominations, and sects; and *d.* religious life in small communities is guided by a nationwide network of mass communication.

Yet the village president and the village clerk are not church members. Both of them are highly regarded by the community, not only for their official position and efficiency, but also for their general uprightness. In other words, churchgoing is not an essential indicator of normal conduct. About one fourth of the adult population of the village does not belong to any church, and another one fourth does not attend church regularly. The bulk of the unchurched comes from the low-income groups. These unchurched people, however, believe in God and want a minister to preside over their funeral ceremonies.

Six of the most important churches of Mapletown—Methodist, Presbyterian, First Baptist, Christian, Episcopal, and Catholic—were established between 1835 and 1872. The other 5 churches have been built since World War II. With 1 exception, all of these latecomers are fundamentalist churches.

The class structure of the churches is fairly explicit in broad terms, except for the Roman Catholic, which includes a wide spectrum, from industrialists to unskilled factory workers and farm laborers, but very few professionals. In terms of economic status the Protestant churches may be arranged in the following descending order: Presbyterian, Methodist, Episcopal, Christian, Lutheran, Baptist, Seventh Day Adventist, Assembly of God, and Pentecostal. The members of the first 5 churches are predominantly middle-class; while the last 4 churches (all fundamentalist) recruit members mainly from the lower classes. The Jehovah's Witnesses seem to stand apart; although predominantly of the lower-middle class, they also include stray members from the upper-middle class.

The leaders of all the above churches claim to welcome Negroes, but the latter are found only in the Baptist, Episcopal, Roman Catholic, and Jehovah's Witnesses churches.

The membership of the various churches of Mapletown is given in Table 1. St. Mary's Catholic Church is the largest single church group in the township, but the 9 Protestant churches together have more members. Among the Protestant churches, the standard churches have the bulk of the membership. (It may be mentioned here that only about 12 families of the village proper belong to the fundamentalist churches.) The unchurched include about 25% of the total number of families.

HOW THE MINISTERS VIEW THEIR CHURCHES

The ministers of the various churches in Mapletown have a number of conventional categories for describing the basic characteristics of churches:

"high" (ritualistic and formal) and "low" (informal), "conservative" (accepting literal interpretation of the Bible) and "liberal" (willing to reinterpret the letter of the scripture in terms of the spirit of modern times), "emotional" and "rational," and so on. There is also the usual distinction between the fundamentalists and the standard denominations. The fundamentalists are noted for their disregard of ritual symbolism, emotional exuberance in songs and sermons, literal interpretation of the *Bible,* belief in miraculous experiences like speaking in tongues and divine healing, strict rules of abstention, and excessive aversion to Catholicism.

By collating the views of the ministers with my observations on their religious services, the churches of Mapletown may be arranged in a variety of continua:

TABLE 1

Church Membership in Mapletown Township

Church	No. of Families	% of Total
Standard Protestant		
1. Presbyterian	160	13.0
2. Methodist	150	12.0
3. Lutheran	90	7.1
4. Episcopal	25	2.0
5. Christian	25	2.0
Total	— 450	— 36.1
Fundamentalist Protestant		
1. Baptist	15	1.2
2. Assembly of God	10	0.8
3. Seventh Day Adventist	29	2.3
4. Pentecostal	2	0.2
Total	— 56	— 4.5
Roman Catholic	400	32.1
Jehovah's Witnesses	2	0.1
Miscellaneous churches outside Mapletown	25	2.0
Jews	3	0.2
Unchurched	309	25.0
TOTAL	1,245	100.0

A. Formalistic-Informal: 1. Catholic; 2. Episcopal; 3. Lutheran; 4. Presbyterian, Methodist, and Christian; 5. Baptist; 6. Assembly of God, Seventh Day Adventist, and Pentecostal.

B. Ritualistic-Rational: 1. Catholic; 2. Episcopal; 3. Lutheran; 4. Christian; and 5. Presbyterian and Methodist. (The fundamentalist churches such as Assembly of God, Seventh Day Adventist, etc., fall outside the continuum since they are neither ritualistic nor rational.)

C. Cold-Hot: 1. Presbyterian and Methodist; 2. Christian; 3. Baptist and Lutheran; 4. Seventh Day Adventist; 5. Assembly of God; 6. Pentecostal. (The Catholic Church, although lacking the emotional exuberance of the shouting and rolling fundamentalist churches, does not share the cold intellectual persuasiveness of the rational Protestant churches.)

D. Puritanical-Permissive: 1. Assembly of God, Pentecostal, and Seventh Day Adventist; 2. Christian and Baptist; 3. Methodist; 4. Presbyterian; 5. Episcopal; and 6. Catholic. (Here "Puritanism" is judged mainly by abstention from drinking, smoking, gambling, cardplaying, etc.)

E. Authoritarian-Democratic: 1. Roman Catholic; 2. Episcopal; 3. Methodist; 4. Presbyterian and the rest. (Jehovah's Witnesses, again, do not clearly fall into any of the above continua. Like the fundamentalists, they are concerned with literal interpretation of the Bible and have "fanatical" dedication to their cause. But although their services have an informal atmosphere like that of the fundamentalist churches, there is not the same emphasis on emotional singing and shouting.)

The atmosphere of church services seemed to me distinctly non-secular in the ritualistic (i.e., Roman Catholic and Episcopalian) and in the fundamentalist churches. In the Catholic and the Episcopalian churches, the numerous esoteric symbolic elements, such as the figure of Jesus on the cross, candles, robe of the minister, and his symbolic gestures and Latin chants, create an atmosphere of sanctity quite distinct from ordinary life. The fundamentalist churches effect the separation from day-to-day life by their emotionalism: "singing of the heart," shouting of "hallelujah," and "speaking in tongues." In contrast, the "rationalist" Protestant churches give the impression of being social clubs with special emphasis on sober moralizing.

We attended a marriage ceremony in the Catholic Church and one in the Presbyterian Church. Here also the contrasts in atmosphere were quite evident—the elaborate Catholic marriage ritual ending with the couple kneeling submissively before the statue of Mary created a sacred atmosphere which was lacking in the relatively brief and contractual mode of the Presbyterian ceremony.

Below are a few statements on the position of their respective churches made by some ministers of Mapletown which will bring into relief the range of ideological positions.

The Presbyterian minister, Rev. K., whose educational background included psychology and philosophy, stated:

> Ours is very definitely a middle class church. They place heavy emphasis on education in this denomination. It is not an emotional appeal. They want a reasoned approach.

Rev. K. is proud of the fact that many of his parishioners are well-educated and that they control the power structure of the community. At the same time, he views the community as "politically and economically very conservative" and considers himself the spokesman for the young intellectuals. In his "liberal" sermons, the themes of "youth," "modernity," and "intelligence" appear repeatedly, and also an uncomfortable admission that the Christian churches tend to avoid vital issues and that "all of the good forces may be working outside the Church at the present moment." In this venture into radical ideas among an upper-middle-class congregation in a politically and socially conservative community, there is the tacit understanding between the minister and his congregation that there will be no call for action. When the previous minister of the Presbyterian church impressed upon his Board of Elders the moral necessity of letting a Negro buy a plot of land in the fashionable quarter where some of his younger influential parishioners lived, he was fired.

Brother M. of the newly established Pentecostal Church stated that the core doctrine of his church was based on the 2nd chapter of *Acts,* which prescribes communion with the Holy Ghost and speaking in tongues:

> That is the basic doctrine of our church plus holiness and righteous living. . . . our women don't put on makeup, . . . cut their hair nor adorn themselves. The Bible teaches modest dress . . . The Bible says that the Zealous of God will have to be a *peculiar* people to cut yourself [off] from the whole world. We consider ourselves as the First Church that was established in the world of God. Therefore we are not Protestants.[4] We are all labourers. The Gospel came to the Poor. And I suppose you might say we are amongst the poorest.

The Pentecostal church is also noted for its belief in ritual healing.

Father R. of St. Mary's Catholic Church stated that among the Protestant churches, he felt more at home with the standard churches than with the fundamentalists. But he complained that the former "have watered down or weakened the basic teachings":

> Historically ours is old and has "completeness" of the teachings of Christ. Their [the "liberal" Protestants'] emphasis is more on the "external," "to lead a good life," than to "a body of beliefs." . . . Whereas the Protestant churches have the idea of "serving" the people, we emphasize the idea of "receiving" the grace of God.
>
> I don't think the terms "liberal-conservative" are too applicable in describing the Catholic and the Protestant churches. Our bulk members are of lower or middle class. As lower- and middle-class people tend to vote Democratic party nationally, the majority of Roman Catholics in America are Democratic. In [Mapletown] and the surrounding areas, however, many of the Roman Catholics tend to be Republican. I don't see how a Catholic could hold to "rugged individualism" too rigorously.

The Catholic Church runs an elementary school which has about 400 students. The textbooks of this school come from the diocese. Every morn-

---

[4] Interviews with a few members of this church made it clear that the respondents felt themselves to be part of the Protestant order and were definitely against the Catholic church.

ing the students have 40 minutes of religious teaching. It appears that the Catholic school maintains stricter discipline than the local public schools. Sister D., the principal, said:

> We teach the students not to argue a point. Our children learn good discipline. You will find that our students will say 'Yes, sir,' instead of 'Yeah.'

Brother P., minister of the Jehovah's Witnesses congregation, brings out the idiosyncratic position of his church as follows:

> We are neither Protestant nor Catholic. . . . We consider ourselves as Bible students—advocates of the Truth from the Bible. The Bible puts a great emphasis on the name of God so we call him Jehovah. The cross is of pagan origin. We do not use any pagan symbol. . . . We do not salute the American flag. . . . We regard salute as an act of worship. We do not worship a flag, although we respect it. We feel that our life belongs to God who gave it to us. And for that reason we cannot give our life to any nation. So Jehovah's Witnesses refuse military service. . . . Armageddon . . . is the Great Day of Judgment of God the Almighty. Only true believers of Jehovah's Witnesses will survive the Armageddon and live happily in the new kingdom of God.

Members of all the other churches in Mapletown refer to Jehovah's Witnesses as "fanatics," "screwballs," "nuts," "pests," and so on. Only the Presbyterian minister added that the existence of such an extremist sect provided a test for religious tolerance.

Mr. B., of a neighboring village, belongs to the Spiritualist church about 50 miles away and knows 3 persons in Mapletown who occasionally attend seances and who usually attend the spiritual centers in Florida during the winter. Mr. B. explained his position as a spiritualist as follows:

> All things are controlled by one Divine Power and the object of our seances is to contact spirits who advance on different planes of life. . . . Christ was one of the greatest examples of spiritual phenomena. I have no superstition whatsoever. There are good spirits and bad spirits. I send the bad spirits back by prayer. . . . I get messages and give messages.

Mr. B. invited me to participate in a seance at his house and showed me his collection of pictures of spirits that appear before him and Mrs. B. during seances. In the state of possession, he prescribed cures for his ailing wife.

Although statistically the cult of the spiritualists does not carry any weight, its existence in a small community like Mapletown has some significance. Like the various fundamentalist groups, the spiritualists are a reminder to the rest of the community that the respectable churches have been secularized and have lost any meaningful contact with the supernatural sphere.

WHAT PEOPLE SAY THEY BELIEVE IN

Apart from interviewing 9 pastors and listening to informal conversation, I interviewed 27 adults and 5 children (ages 7 to 9) regarding their religious beliefs with the help of an open-end questionnaire. The adult respondents covered all the denominations, sects, and economic classes in the community.

Only 1 person declared himself to be an atheist. He does not believe in God, but sings in the Presbyterian choir and sends his children to Sunday School.

One person declared:

> I am not an atheist, but an agnostic. I believe there is an order behind the running of the Universe. I don't know the nature of this order. We should be concerned more with social progress than with religion.

Some who claim to be believers complain against the churches. P.L., an unchurched factory worker, said, "They look upon you in the church in a way that you don't belong there." P.M., a retired mail-carrier, raised as a German Lutheran but not now a member of any church, strongly believes in God and is now active in the American Legion and the Masonic Lodge. He stated:

> I know men, so-called pillars of the church, who are dishonest. . . . I think religion today is pretty much commercialized. I have heard ministers talk about "living like Christ." There isn't a minister in the world living like Christ.

Mrs. M., an elderly widow of Catholic descent, is bitter about the role of the churches:

> I see a lot of these people that go to church every Sunday and they are terrible people. They steal and think nothing of robbing the poor.

The theme of hypocrisy in religious behavior and divergence between what is preached and practiced is widespread in the community. The role of the aggressive village atheist, however, is dead, so that the Presbyterian minister could say: "The old struggle between science and religion is a dead issue and has been thoroughly reconciled."

In a community where there is so little overt dependence on God and where there is widespread skepticism about the depth of religious commitment, one naturally wonders how seriously the people rely on the supernatural.

From the answers of educated respondents belonging to the "liberal" Protestant churches, I got the impression that there has been a general decline of "supernaturalism,." "superstition," and "asceticism." Respondents repeatedly said: "I have no superstition." "Heaven" and "Hell" are considered states of mind rather than places. Devils and angels are ruled out as mythical and allegorical symbols. God is invisible and is an abstract ethical principle symbolizing what is best in men. Evolution is generally accepted. The *Bible* is not infallible and is not to be taken literally; the Biblical accounts are colored by the world view of the writers of those times.

The members of the Roman Catholic church in general took a less secular stand than those of the liberal Protestant churches. All Catholic respondents stated that they believed in "virgin birth," saints, and taboos on birth control and on divorce, but some of them expressed their doubts about the reality of Heaven, Hell, and the Devil and felt that at least half of the Catholic families in the town used contraceptives.

Whereas the majority of the churchgoers in the liberal churches appear as striving to preserve their belief in God along with their commitment to modernization and science, members of fundamentalist churches have a more clear commitment to God-centered beliefs. Mrs. G. of the Pentecostal church gave the following statement:

> In 1934 I believed in the Lord. It was raining hard in Missouri and the people were running away to the hills. . . . I . . . called God for help. I did not know Him but He knew me. While I was talking to the Lord, the Lord talked to my son and the storm ceased.

Such intense reliance upon the Lord is not limited to the poorly educated. B.C., who is a schoolteacher with an M.A. degree and belongs to the Church of God in a neighboring village, said:

> I believe very strongly in miracles. . . . When I was in Japan, I prayed and asked God to lead me to the right girl for my wife and He said "Don't worry about this. . . . this will be taken care of." As soon as I went home to America, I met the girl who is my present wife and I knew she was the girl right from the first time I met her.

The children I interviewed all came from Protestant families, 4 of them lower-class and 1 upper-middle-class.

The 4 children of the lower-income parents, belonging to the Baptist and Lutheran churches, conceived of God as "white-skinned, old, putting on a robe." Jesus and Mary are the father and the mother of God, and "Jesus is the best American." They vaguely believe in angels and "devils with horns." The latter sometimes "makes you shiver with cold." The sins are "to swear, drink, disobeying father and mother, and to lie." "The Sunday School teaches you to love others, to be kind and to do good to others." "Half of the world are Christians and the other half are sinners. They would go down to the Devil."

C.S. (8 years old), daughter of a lawyer who attends the Presbyterian Sunday School, strikes a more critical and rational tone. She stated:

> Nobody really knows what God looked like. Everybody says the soul goes up to the angels. Hell is not a good word to use. Some people say

there is a Devil, but I don't think so. The President and Governors are good Americans, they help to build the country, doctors also.

RELIGION AND THE SECULAR SPHERE

In a farming community with so many churches, one might expect religion to offer some support to farming activities. But the farmer, whether Roman Catholic or Protestant, does not seek divine help to solve any agricultural problems. Although in the Roman Catholic church there are formal provisions for "blessing of the grape vineyards" and for petition to God on the Rogesian days for bountiful crops, these customs have become completely obsolete in Mapletown in recent years.

According to N.H., a well-known farmer, there are still some "folk beliefs" half-heartedly adhered to by some of the old farmers in the area:

> I think there are still some people who believe that you should plant certain things in the light of the moon and others in the dark phase of the moon. My hired hand did not want to start plowing a field on Friday. It is just the fact of the old saying that if you start something on a Friday, you'll never finish.

The prevailing notions are that "God is not to be manipulated for the purpose of farming" and that "rain falls on the fields of the virtuous and the sinners alike." God is prayed to in order to build "character" with which to face one's problems. In both the Catholic school and the Protestant Sunday schools, children learn that kindliness, honesty, and obedience to parents are good and that swearing, drinking, smoking, lying, stealing, and hurting others are sins. The children begin life with a notion that God is watching their conduct. None of the churches *directly* emphasizes worldly virtues such as hard work, thrift, and cleanliness.

It is difficult to assess the role of the teaching of the churches in the maintenance of a high level of civic activity. Mapletown has had a volunteer fire department since 1868, with an excellent record of performance of which everyone is proud. The Conservation Club, whose members have built a club building and planted thousands of trees, is another example of civic cooperation. Similar effort and zeal have gone into the improvement of the local school system, the running of the village council, and the organization of the American Legion, the Farm Bureau, 4H clubs, and the Sixty Plus Club. It is customary to open these meetings by a formal prayer.

Although the Baptist minister pointed out that it is the Protestant, and not the Catholic, countries which have successfully developed industries, my respondents, whether Catholic or Protestant, did not see any direct connection between initiative in industry and Christian upbringing. A few suggested that Christian ethics provided the basis for trustworthy business transactions. People do not see their civic performance in the various voluntary associations and the level of initiative in livelihood activities as *necessarily* derived from Christian ethics. The villagers seem to imbibe their civic sense by participating in the orderly life of both secular and religious associations. Although all the churches warn against pursuit of material pleasures, it is only the fundamentalist churches that may be regarded as distinctly "otherworldly."

To a Hindu visitor, it is striking that in all the churches of Mapletown, with the exception of the Jehovah's Witnesses, the American flag is displayed as prominently as the church flag. Also, at the end of the service there is a formal prayer in which the minister invokes the blessing of God on the President and on others in power. In spite of the Protestant insistence on the separation of the church and the state, there is the underlying theme: "The church and God are the protectors of the nation." One also gains the impression that not only does the church bless the American flag, but the autonomous sacredness of the flag also lends sanctity to the church.

The ritualized repetition of the oath of allegiance to the flag in the schools, in 4H clubs, and in such voluntary associations as the Kiwanis Club, Lions Club, and American Legion is indeed impressive. A brief prize essay on "What Civil Defense means to me," written by a high school student is an example of the loyalty generated by nationalistic rituals:

> First of all . . . Civil Defense means the protecting of your country, your home and yourself from destruction by the enemy. By protecting this country you're preserving a light that is leading the free world to peace, prosperity and happiness. . . . I'm fighting for the Bill of Rights. the Constitution, the individual and the home. And all the people that make up the greatest country in the world.

Yet the leaders of the community are worried that patriotism is softening. At a Kiwanis meeting, the vice president read aloud extracts from a pamphlet, *What Happened to Patriotism,* by Max Rafferty (1963).

It appears that various nationalistic voluntary associations join forces with the churches to impress upon the people that they are indeed citizens of the most prosperous and civilized nation in the world. With prosperity, democracy, freedom, and Christian ethics, they are convinced that they have the best of everything. Protestants, Catholics, and Jews, whites and negroes, share this with equal conviction. Mapletown seems to bear out Will Herberg's observation (1960:263–4) that:

> . . . the new religiosity pervading America seems to be very largely the religious validation of the social pattern and cultural values associated with the American Way of Life.

In a recent study of the impact of religion on politics, economics, and family life in Detroit, Gerhard Lenski (1963:320–1) found a confirmation of the Weberian thesis:

White Protestants and Jews have a positive attitude toward work more often than the Negro Protestants or Catholics, especially in the upper-middle class jobs. They are likelier to believe that ability is more important than family connections; to be self-employed; to believe in intellectual autonomy and to have small families.

I did not follow up Lenski's observations by detailed study, but it is obvious that compared with the "liberal" Protestants, the Catholics are brought up in a more authoritarian elementary school system and live in more stable family units. However, an outsider is impressed with how both segments of the population are predominantly committed to rational technological orientation in agriculture and industry, in medical care, cleanliness, punctuality, and thrift.

It is true that the Catholics, most of whom are relatively recent European immigrants or their 1st-generation descendants, have not yet contributed any "professionals" to the community (with the exception of a dentist), but some of the top industrialists and businessmen belong to the Catholic church and so also do many technologically progressive farmers. Until further research is carried on, I am inclined to stick to my general impression that through their common exposure to the high school system, and to the various civic organizations, Catholics and Protestants of Mapletown share fundamentally similar secular values of economic initiative, saving, civic responsibility, and national pride. Religious upbringing does not *directly* cause any major deflection from the common American course.

CONCLUSIONS

General Impressions

This was my first field encounter with a cultural system effectively committed to technological development. The spread of economic well-being in a village like Mapletown is indeed very impressive in the contrastive perspective of an underdeveloped village in India. Also impressive is the general absence of overt violence and loud quarrels and the low level of mutual suspicion among villagers in Mapletown. The people of this village are accustomed to leave the doors of their houses unlocked even when they are away from home. The many village organizations indicate a high level of "civic culture."

Although the full roster of customs is long, one cannot escape noticing that compared to an Indian peasant community, the load of custom on the minds of the people of Mapletown is relatively light in the face of rational dedication to economic mobility. Farming is practically free of religious or esoteric customs, although some farmers still cling to the sentiment that "farming is a way of life." Many also state: "It is a matter of the almighty dollar," and "The younger generation is trying to get out of farming." The elder generation of farmers does not expect the younger generation to stay in Mapletown out of sentiment for locality and kin instead of pursuing better opportunities elsewhere.

One would expect to find the pace of life in a small community like Mapletown quite relaxed, with people meeting in many different contexts and being well acquainted. But in comparison with the Bhumij tribe of West Bengal-Bihar (India), the spontaneity of interpersonal relations in Mapletown appears considerably restrained by the discipline of a high standard of living. People are hesitant to visit one another without a formal engagement over the telephone, and everyone is aware that one should be careful not to encroach upon the time of another person. When people get together for a potluck meeting of the Sixty Plus Club or a family reunion, the affair is preceded by a planned effort and lacks the spontaneity and spirit of abandon in human interaction observed in an informal gathering of the Bhumij. One misses the spirit of *adda*[5] found in a Bengali home (even in a city like Calcutta), where people may spend hours talking on random topics without concern about the expenditure of time. It appears that a happy village like Mapletown has had to sacrifice a good portion of the "spirit of abandon" in favor of the discipline of industrialization. As a result, compared to the Indian base-line, whether tribal or peasant or urban, Mapletown gives the impression of dehydration of interpersonal sentiments.[6]

As one reads the local newspapers, attends the village council meetings, or meets people in more informal gatherings, one feels that a sense of optimism and achievement thrives in the community in spite of occasional complaints that "the younger generation is getting soft," "religion is getting hypocritical," "there is too much cut-throat competition among social climbers," and so on. The people are thoroughly convinced that they live in one of the best small communities of the best nation in the world. Good life has a vivid visual image: a clean house and a clean yard indicate that the individual has pride in himself and in his family. Although the leaders of the village continue to plan improvements in living conditions, an outsider gets the feeling that in Mapletown one has come close to the end of a fairy tale: "And they lived happily ever after."

How and Why Religion Still Holds Ground

Although I stand by my general impression that reliance on God is irreversibly on the decline, it is also true that formal religion tenaciously holds

---

[5] The Bengali word *adda* has many shades of meaning. Essentially it involves an informal get-together to spend time in leisurely and spontaneous conversation.

[6] Jules Henry (1963:25) speaks of "personality impoverishment" in contemporary America.

a residual ground. Some of the factors sustaining religion in Mapletown today are as follows:

1. Along with the numerous secular associations, the churches play an important role in the condensation of human interaction in the town and make community life vivid.

2. The churches, instead of disturbing the social structure, closely follow its contours.

3. Religion continues to provide a *certain* and coherent world view in a changing world, so that a person can conveniently think that he goes by a set of absolutes, namely, "Christian ethics."

4. Religion sanctifies the important social event of marriage and by its ritual and ideas helps people to face the crisis of death.

5. Religion is a source of aesthetic activity in the choirs and the architecture of the churches.

6. By sponsoring a series of festivals like Christmas and Easter, religion provides a vivid frame of cultural continuity between the generations.

7. Religion bolsters the common image of America as the best nation having the best ethical standards.

8. Internal competition between the various denominations and the major competition between the Roman Catholics and the Protestants maintains the vigor of social and moral commitment to the church. The Protestants cannot afford to give up while the Catholics are thriving.

Some Dysfunctional Aspects of Religion

So far I have written mainly about the extraordinarily good fit, in a value-neutral way, between religion and social structure in Mapletown. Taking a more value-laden position, one can point to some dysfunctional aspects of religion in Mapletown:

1. Although it provides the poor with the consolation of salvation and a certain emotional boost, it also pushes them to irrationality or to a symbolic acceptance of social marginality and inferiority. The upper class is perpetually charged with cynicism and hypocrisy.

2. It bolsters the national image too strongly to be desirable in the modern age.

3. By becoming too thin, it fails to provide adequate security in times of stress. The activities of the churches tend to camouflage the growing spiritual vacuum on account of lack of faith.

In facing the dilemma of how to preserve and promote secular values and yet not be spread too thinly in the spiritual realm, I feel that the Roman Catholic and the Episcopal churches have been relatively successful so far. They tend to preserve an aesthetically vivid and serene religious platform while allowing their members to imbibe the requisite secular values by directly participating in secular associations. The vows of chastity and poverty of Catholic nuns and priests help to emphasize the sacred nature of their institutions. The liberal Protestant churches, with their pride in being "rational" and "modern," are troubled with the problem of where to draw the line betwen secular idealism and belief in God.[7] Perhaps by letting secular idealism vigorously engulf almost the entire domain of the church, as is the case with Unitarianism, the liberal Protestant churches of Mapletown could find a special solution to their dilemma. But such a radical denomination is not likely to have a comfortable stay in Mapletown.

Contrasts with Hinduism

The religion of the people of Mapletown, especially of the liberal Protestant churches, contrasts with Hinduism of rural as well as urban Bengal, in the following ways:[8]

1. The role of divine intervention in natural phenomena as well as in human problems such as economics, health, and litigation is very much attenuated in Mapletown.

2. There is less of a *dependent* relation to God in the American village. Instead of praying to God to get something done, people seek divine help to build morality or character with which to face their problems.

3. The rituals in the churches of Mapletown are relatively simple.

4. Through Sunday school teachings and the general influence of the simple code of the Ten Commandments, Christian teachings tend to be more directly ethical, whereas in Hinduism the ethical elements are often immersed in pragmatic rituals.

5. Ascetic rigor and denial of "pleasures" is less emphasized in local Christianity.

6. The religious practices of the standard Christian churches, whether of the ministry or of the laity, are very close to the secular mode of life. There is little seeking of "mystical" or "transcendental" experience.

7. Religion is organized in rigid associations like the local churches,

---

[7] Here I am in agreement with the observation of the Lynds: "The Catholics, Jews, and Episcopalians, who stress ritual somewhat more and rely less upon "sermon," i.e., verbalized message, maintain a liaison between the permanent and the immediate with more dignity and less apparent sense of uneasiness than do most of the Protestant churches" (Lynd and Lynd 1937:311).

[8] These points could be considerably elaborated, but I am pointing out only the more important aspects. Needless to say, considerable simplification is involved in the process of homogenizing my complex exposure to various strata and regional versions of Bengali Hinduism. The same is true in my considering the complex range of religious behavior in Mapletown as a single entity. For a general account of peasant Hinduism see O'Malley (1935).

connected to national or international networks of organization, rather than such loose organizational units as family, temple, pilgrim centers, and so on, as in Hinduism.

8. The prescribed patterns of religious behavior of the people of Mapletown come mainly from outside, from the centers of the various church organizations, although the local pastor and the lay leaders of the congregation may give particular color to the local congregation. In the case of a Hindu village, the Great Traditions reach the small community in a much less organized way and are refracted to a much greater degree in the context of the little community, and there are also unique local cults of particular villages or of very narrow regions.[9]

9. The churches of Mapletown are strongly committed to reinforcing nationalism, in contrast to the general indifference of peasant Hinduism to nationalism.

10. There is no clear counterpart to the Hindu search for "spiritual freedom" by renunciation of worldly ties or by becoming a wandering ascetic in the distinctly more "this-worldly" religion of the Christians of Mapletown.

The Catholic Church, with its greater content of esoteric rituals, its images of Christ, and its pantheon of the saints and the Virgin Mary, comes nearer to the Hindu mode. The singers of the fundamentalist congregations remind one of the congregation of Vaishnavites singing highly emotional *Kirtana* songs, except that the contents of the latter songs, are not heavy with the concept of sin.

---

[9] McKim Marriott (1955:211) speaks about the process of "parochialization" of religious culture in Indian village communities.

Eric R. Wolf

26. Santa Claus: Notes on a Collective Representation*

Among Julian Steward's many papers is one on "The Ceremonial Buffoon of the American Indian" (1931). It bespeaks an early and abiding interest in the expression of contradictions in life and society. This paper, offered to him on the occasion of his Festschrift, deals with Santa Claus, American supernatural. What contradictions shall we find as we peer beneath Santa's superficial mask of Christmas cheer and jollity?

Who is Santa Claus? He is obviously an American, and a very noticeable American at that, and yet the investigators of American national character have hardly paid him any heed. Nor have the psychoanalysts treated him with due respect; a search of the psychoanalytic literature turned up only three references to our protagonist. Perhaps it is easier, first, to say what Santa Claus is not. Like many things American, he has European antecedents, but the process of naturalization has left few discernible European traits in his make-up. He has little in common with St. Nicholas, the fabled bishop of Myra, who initiated his career by rescuing three maidens from a fate worse than death and resuscitating three children salted away in a bathtub, to become patron saints of maidens, lovers, merchants, sailors, scholars, robbers, and children. Nor is he more than distant kin to the goodly bishop St. Nicholas who moves about among the

* Reprinted from Robert A. Manners, Editor, *Process and Pattern in Culture: Essay in Honor of Julian H. Steward* (Chicago: Aldine Publishing Company 1964); copyright © 1964 by Aldine Publishing Company. Reprinted by permission of the author and Aldine Publishing Company.

Germanic peoples and the Western Slavs on December 6th, distributing goodies to the well-behaved children and consigning the bad to his black companion, the devil. This Nicholas, for a brief period, made his home in Baltimore and among the Pennsylvania "Dutch," (Kane, 1958: 42), but did not prove viable in a country that believes in happy endings and has consigned the devil to the ashcan of history. Nor does Santa Claus have any connection with the gift-bearing Three Kings, once general all over Germany and still popular in Hispanic lands; and he would not be seen dead in the company of light-bringing and gift-bearing female spirits, such as the Swedish Santa Lucia, the Russian Babushka, or Befana, the Italian witch.

He is also a well-behaved and domesticated gentleman, compared to the sinister noise-making figure of Northern Europe who emerges from a shadowy netherworld at Christmas-time to usher in a brief reign of chaos. This figure derives in equal proportions from the Roman Saturn, in whose honor the riotous saturnalia were held at Christmas time; from the Germanic Knecht Ruprecht—the *rauhe perchta* (wild demon) who is probably none other than Woden, wild hunting master of the wild hunt; the Lord of Misrule who reigned in the villages during a brief time of license and role reversal at the end of the year; and the Boy Bishop, his ecclesiastical counterpart, who parodied and profaned the sacred functions. These were kings of a time when the rules of the normal order were turned into their opposite, and men habituated to conventional behavior donned the anonymity of masks and false noses to break through the boundaries of the conventional (Leach 1955). The Protestant revolution exorcised these demons, and domesticated these captains of riot. The Boy Bishop was forbidden in Basle in 1431, in England by Henry VIII in 1542. The town council of New Amsterdam passed a law against Christmas impersonations "to take the superstition and fables of the papacy out of the youths' heads" (Jones 1954:362). The Duke of Mecklenburg issued his edict against such mummers in 1681, to banish such features of "superstitious and ungodly popery," due *"mutatis nominibus et personis,* to darkest paganism" (quoted in Cassel 1861:226). The Elector of Prussia similarly thundered against masked impersonators of the Angel Gabriel and Knecht Rupprecht "and other similar trickery" in 1739. In medieval Christianity God and the devil, order and disorder, regularity and accident, divine spirit and gargoyle, had been in intimate communication with each other. The burgeoning Protestant world banished the disorderly, accidental and irrational in the interests of orderliness, predictability and rationality.

Santa Claus is no rebel, engaged in a "ritual of rebellion." The only noise he makes is to ring his bells and cheer on his reindeer, and his very paunch and jollity reflect his contentment with the social order. There are still faint echoes of a past cult of the dead in the celebration of Halloween, and it may even be that the presentation of gifts to children at Christmas time may have its origin in a bribe offered to incomplete souls of children to remain among the living and not to return to the spirit world (Lévi-Strauss 1952). But modern medicine has weakened the impact of child mortality, and America as a whole denies the existence of death. Santa Claus, too, is a good American, and he stands for life, for the good life, lived in the midst of abundance and plenty.

If Santa Claus is so largely an American, how was he created? Historical research has thrown increasing doubt on the popular myth that he is a creation of the Dutch settlers on New Amsterdam (Jones 1954; Emrich 1960). There is no evidence that the Santa Claus myth existed in New Amsterdam, or for a century after English occupation. To use Dr. Edgar F. Romig's phrase, "the Dutch were hagiophobic to a pre-eminent degree" (Jones 1954: 362). Moreover, the Dutch, together with other non-English settlers in New York, made up only ten percent of the New York population (Ibid.:366). There is evidence, on the other hand, that Santa is the self-conscious creation of individuals engaged in creating a new American culture. It was men like John Pintard, also responsible for making Washington's Birthday and the Fourth of July national holidays, who brought St. Nicholas to American prominence by organizing the New York Historical Society (probably 1809); Washington Irving who associated the saint with the Dutch settlers in his *Knickerbocker's History of New York* (1809) creating a mythical sentimental world of Disneyesque Dutch countryfolk and burghers; Clement Moore who wrote "Twas the Night before Christmas" in 1822, a piece of doggerel which will outlive his more notable "Observations upon Certain Passages in Mr. Jefferson's Notes on Virginia, Which Appear to Have a Tendency to Subvert Religion and Establish a False Philosophy" (Patterson 1956); and Robert W. Weir, teacher of drawing at the U.S. Military Academy at West Point, who in 1837 painted Santa Claus in the act of departing through the chimney (Vail 1951). As such, Santa seems to be a minor piece of the major effort of American myth-making that surrounded the War of Independence and its aftermath, and created the ideological charter for the newly-founded nation.

In Weir's painting, however, Santa is still a Dutchman, "a short figure without a beard, dressed in Dutch boots and stocking cap decorated with a clay pipe, traditional emblem of the saint, and wearing a red cap edged with white fur . . . a rosary and apparently also a sword for the end of the scabbard sticks out behind him. His pack contains toys for the good children along his route and switches for the bad ones, true to the Dutch tradition" (Vail 1951:340–1). "Our" Santa Claus, however, appears first in the Christmas cartoons drawn since 1863 by the famous political cartoonist Thomas Nast who created much of modern American political zoology, and who gathered the Santa drawings together in his *Christmas Drawings for the Human Race,* 1890. It was in this new stereotyped form that Santa began to appear increasingly on the Christmas cards of New York businessmen after the introduction of this new culture trait in the 1870s, from England.

An anthropologist notes a hiatus of twenty-odd years between Weir and Nast, and cannot help feeling that these years hide another, as yet missing, link in Santa's genealogy. For Nast's Santa Claus is no longer a Hollander; he is a real-life Circumpolar shaman—tailored clothing, boots, belt, beard, and all—flying through the air on a reindeer sled and entering through chimneys. He wonders whether there are not other prototypical Santa Clauses, such as the household gnomes of the Scandinavian countries—the Jultomten of Sweden and the Julnissen of Denmark and Norway. These, too, appear clad in red and wearing white beards, are associated with Christmas, punish bad conduct but are assuaged by good behavior (e.g., Spicer 1958: 30, 158, 222).

Be that as it may, each Christmas thousands of masked impersonators of this modern supernatural leave homes and barrooms to take up their appointed stations in lodges, churches, hospitals and department stores. It is the contradiction implicit in this behavior, above all, that must exercise the anthropologist, and lead him to wonder how it may be resolved. For here is a society, preeminently based on the rational exercise of science and technology, a society highly secularized in its constitution, yet paying heed each Christmas to a wholly mythical figure. A society not otherwise given to putting on masks and false noses, and yet populated at Christmas time by impersonators of an emblematic entity without rational referents. A society based on mass-production of goods, yet insisting that the toys distributed to children emanate from Santa Claus' magic workshop on the North Pole, operated on a handicraft level by non-unionized dwarfs. A society capable of distributing goods by specialized and high-powered machines, telling its children that their toys are delivered by reindeer sled and through their chimneys. A society in which goods are purchased with money and needs are prompted by massive advertising, and where children are yet told that their gifts were not bought by father or mother or Aunt Fanny, but by a mythical gentleman of extraordinary outward appearance.

The resolution of this final paradox is indeed crucial to the understanding of the myth. It has, however, gone unresolved even in the finest study of the American Santa complex to date, that by Renzo Sereno (1951). Sereno has seen clearly that it is the parents who force the children to believe in Santa Claus and that the children face the myth and ritual with discomfort, heaving a huge sigh of relief on Christmas Day when "the constant feeling of being swindled, or cheated, or lied to by parents is finally abated" (Ibid.:390). Sereno holds that "the parent needs to present the child with expensive gifts because he needs to prove to himself his own worth" (Ibid.). Why, then, the insistence that the gifts are brought by Santa, thus undoing with one hand what positive confirmation of one's self one has attempted to purchase with the other?

My first hypothesis is that the Santa Claus myth in America is part and parcel of a larger ideological complex governing the relations between adults and children. On the one hand, Americans create a special world for their children, distinct from that of adults. "The business of American parents," says Francis Hsu, "social and commercial, is their private reserve, and no trespassing by children is allowed" (1953:80). Again, "though consciously encouraging their children to grow up in some ways, American parents firmly refuse to let their youngsters enter the real world of the adults" (Ibid.). On the other hand, the world of childhood is culturally defined as a Golden Age. "It is pregenital childhood," says a French observer, "which appears most enviable in America. The adults dream of their lost childhood—the golden age which they can find only in regression" (Dolto 1954: 420).

How does this bear on the Santa myth? The adult world of America is based on the culturally induced realities of interpersonal competition in which goods and power are won by the more successful from the less successful, and in which rewards are distributed not according to wish or need but according to ability to pay. In this real world, the rich child will get an electric train, but the poor child will have to be content with a gift from the Five and Ten. Santa Claus, however, manages a magic economy in which "a letter to Santa" will produce a commensurate gift. Where the real economy operates on the principle, "from each according to his share of wealth, to each according to his ability to pay," in Santa's economy, these rules are reversed. Each recipient receives "according to his need;" scarcity has given way to true abundance, and the capitalist realities are confronted with a utopian dream. Santa thus exemplifies Hsu's dictum that "in summary, American parents face a world of reality while their children live in the near ideal realm of the fairy tales where the rules of the parental world do not apply, are watered down, or are even reversed" (Ibid.:82).

To discover that there is no Santa Claus therefore has deeper meaning. It is the American equivalent of the fall from grace that befell Adam when he ate the apple from the tree of knowledge. For to know that Santa Claus is a fraud, is to know that childhood and the magical economy of childhood are dreams and that the true reality is that of the world of adults in which men are pitted against each other in endless competition. Here, too, is one of the reasons why adults insist that children believe in Santa Claus. For as long as they maintain this belief they can be socially defined as "happy," just as adults can convince themselves that they, too, were once "happy." Insisting that innocence is possible, they can loose themselves for a fleeting moment in the creation of a myth of innocence, longing for an infantile world that never was. "Yes, Virginia, there is a

Santa Claus," wrote Francis P. Church in his editorial in the *New York Sun*. To believe otherwise, would be to extinguish "the eternal light with which childhood fills the world."

But if Santa Claus manages the magical economy of childhood and distributes its products to his eager customers—in apparent autonomy of the competitive world of adults—why is he himself an adult, and not a gigantic super-child? He is, in fact, a special kind of adult, an old man; and this fact, too, requires a functional explanation. He is not a father, that much is clear; indeed, father must don the guise of Santa Claus should he wish to play the mythical role, and turn himself into a not-father. Is Santa Claus, then, a grandfather? The relation between grandfather and grandchild is certainly more Santa Claus-like than the relation between father and child. In cultures like ours, where grandparents are deprived of authority, the relation between them is indulgent and free-flowing, the relation between father and child is charged with the ambivalence of discipline (Apple 1956). Moreover, grandfather and grandchild are linked by a common dysphoria in dealing with the intermediate generation.

Yet Santa Claus is certainly not somebody's grandfather *in partitcular;* he stands outside the kin network altogether. Is he then like other old men depicted in popular mythology, like the kindly old men played by Edmund Gwenn in the movies who—in their role as social bystanders—lend their aid in making things come out for the protagonists (as, indeed, in *The Miracle of 34th Street* by Valentin Davies)? These old men, too, are mythical, in that their story-book role contrasts sharply with the uncertain real role of the aged in America. Like the other aged, they are no longer involved in competition and in the struggle for status; like them, too, they have neither families nor much involvement with kin. Yet they glow with contentment and satisfaction, and get their pleasure from a pixyish beneficial intervention in the lives of others. Santa Claus has something in common with these jolly post-mature men also. Like them he is kindly, and in him, also, the lean frame that bespeaks the competitive man of action and his aggressive masculinity has become overlaid by fat and transmuted into the jollity of a substantial paunch.

Yet Santa Claus is neither jolly old bystander, nor kindly grandfather, nor manager of a golden world of childhood alone. Santa Claus also has another side. He is a guardian and promoter of morality. For he exacts from the recipients of his gifts what each can give "according to his ability," the promise to be good. Only then will he be given "according to his need," only then find fulfillment of his wishes. The children trade moral behavior for goods; and it is Santa Claus who guides the input and out of this economy.

Perhaps he is old, in part, because as a guardian of morality he is an after-image of God the Father, the greater arbiter of morality, whom the industrial and commercial revolutions of our times have relegated to the role of an otiose deity. Like God the Father, Santa Claus is male, old, bearded—and Caucasian (there is no Negro Santa Claus!). But, unlike God, Santa Claus is a secular saint, and hence acceptable to a society that must perpetuate a morality without God. The departure of God has left an ideological vacuum which, as Tillich has put it,

> is occupied by the humanistic idea, *the emotional motive of which is the appeal to obedience and law, and the actual character of which is 'conformity to bourgeois conventions.'* (Tillich 956:202; my italics).

Santa Claus is not God; in Nietzsche's words, "God is dead." But as God has been replaced by society, so the word of God has been replaced by the morality of the market place that governs the production and distribution of goods. Of this morality Santa Claus is both emblem and agent. No wonder then that the Catholic clergy of Dijon, France, should—in 1951—have organized an auto-da-fé in front of the cathedral and burned Santa in effigy (Lévi-Strauss 1952:1572), nor that the clerical weekly *l'Osservatore della Domenica* should thunder against Santa as "a monstrous substitute that offends the faith and reason" (*New York Times*, Dec. 17, 1961: 29).

Where previously we saw Santa Claus as steward of a mythical world of happy children, we have now unmasked him as a protagonist of the world of adults. Yet the contradiction is only apparent: for childhood may be a golden age in which the realities of the adult world are not yet perceived; but it is also the age in which behavior proper to the adult world is learned, and in which the appropriate motivations are inculcated. Under the aegis of Santa Claus, the proposition "if you make a wish, you will receive goods" is linked to another stating that "if you are good, your wish will be fulfilled," to form the paradigm "if you are good," i.e., if you conform to the prevailing canons of morality, "you will receive goods."

This paradigm, too, however, enshrines a myth. According to this formulation, the child is pictured as a participant in the market, prepared to offer good behavior, the way other participants offer shoes or cloth or labor power. This is the market of capitalist society, as seen through the eyes of Adam Smith, rather than through those of Karl Marx or Lord Keynes, and based on views of economy and society harkening back to the early days of capitalism, only poorly applicable to its present functioning. A long time ago Marx criticized the "commodity fetishism" of Smith and his followers, their tendency to conceptualize the dance of commodities as a reality independent of the social relations that make up the market. In Santa Claus, this commodity fetishism has found an appropriate collective representation. But we may doubt whether Adam Smith and Horatio Alger are fit guides to an uncertain future, and this doubt, too, must reflect on the mythical figure under discussion. For we have seen that the outward mask of jollity hides a veritable prophet of regression to an individual childhood that never was, to a collective infancy that offers no guidance to the realities of tomorrow. We need not scorn the humble Arunta; for the jolly figure whose throne is raised up each Christmas in the department store around the corner dispenses annually our own dream of the mythical *alchera* times.

Marvin Harris

27. The Riddle of the Pig*

I

When the God of the ancient Hebrews told them not to eat pork, He must have realized that generations of scholars were going to try to figure out why. From my ecological perspective, I would like to offer an explanation that relates Jewish and Muslim attitudes toward the pig to the cultural and natural ecosystems of the Middle East.

Naturalistic explanations for the taboo on pork go back to Maimonides, who lived in the twelfth century. Maimonides said that God had intended the ban on pork as a public health measure since swine's flesh "had a bad and damaging effect upon the body." This explanation gained favor in the mid-nineteenth century when it was discovered that there was a parasite present in undercooked pork that caused trichinosis.

Impressed by this rational answer to the ancient riddle, American Jews who belonged to the reformed congregations proceeded forthwith to revoke the scriptural taboo on the grounds that if properly cooked, pork no longer menaced the community's health. But Maimonides's explanation has a big hole in it: the flesh of all undercooked domestic animals can serve as a vector for human diseases. Cattle, sheep, and goats, for example, transmit brucellosis and anthrax, both of which have fatality rates as high as that of trichinosis.

* Adapted with permission of author and publisher from "The Riddle of the Pig," *Natural History* Magazine, October 1972, and from "Riddle of the Pig, II," *Natural History* Magazine, February 1973. Copyright © The American Museum of Natural History 1972 and 1973.

Although Maimonides's explanation must be rejected, I think he was closer to the truth than modern anthropologists, including Sir James Frazer, renowned author of *The Golden Bough*. Frazer declared that pigs, like "all so-called unclean animals were originally sacred; the reason for not eating them was that many were originally divine." This doesn't help us very much since the sheep, goat, and cow were also once worshipped in the Middle East, and yet their meat is much enjoyed by all ethnic and religious groups in the area.

Other scholars have suggested that pigs, along with the rest of the foods prohibited in the *Bible*, were the original totem animals of the Hebrew clans. But why interdict the consumption of a valuable food resource? After all, eagles, ravens, spiders and other animals that are of only limited significance as a source of human food are also used as clan totems.

Maimonides at least tried to place the taboo in a natural context in which definite, intelligible forces were at work. His mistake was that he conceived of public health much too narrowly. What he lacked was an understanding of the threat that the pig posed to the integrity of the broad cultural and natural ecosystem of the ancient Hebrew habitat.

I think we have to take into account that the protohistoric Hebrews—the children of Abraham—were adapted to life in the rugged, sparsely inhabited arid lands between Mesopotamia and Egypt. Until their conquest of the Jordan Valley in Palestine, which began in the thirteenth century B.C., they were primarily nomadic pastoralists, living almost entirely on their sheep, goats, and cattle. But like all pastoral peoples they maintained close relationships with sedentary agriculturalists who held the oasis and fertile river valley.

From time to time certain Hebrew lineages adopted a more sedentary, agriculturally oriented mode of existence, as appears to have been the case with the Abrahamites in Mesopotamia, the Josephites in Egypt, and the Isaacites in the western Negev. But even during the climax of urban and village life under David and Solomon, the herding of sheep, goats, and cattle continued to play a vital, if not predominant, economic role everywhere except in the irrigated portions of the Jordan Valley.

Within the overall pattern of this mixed farming and pastoral complex, the divine prohibition against pork constituted a sound ecological strategy. During periods of maximum nomadism, it was impossible for the Israelites to raise pigs, while during the semi-sedentary and even fully village farming phrases, pigs were more of a threat than an asset. The basic reason for this is that the world zones of pastoral nomadism correspond to unforested plains and hills that are too arid for rainfall agriculture and that cannot easily be irrigated. The domestic animals best adapted to these zones are the ruminants—cattle, sheep, and goats. Because ruminants have sacks anterior to their stomachs, they are able to digest grass, leaves, and other foods consisting mainly of cellulose more efficiently than any other mammals.

The pig, however, is primarily a creature of forests and shaded river banks. Although it is omnivorous, its best weight gain is from food low in cellulose—nuts, fruits, tubers, and especially grains, making it a direct competitor of man. It cannot subsist on grass alone and nowhere in the world do fully nomadic pastoralists raise significant numbers of pigs. The pig has the further disadvantage of not being a practical source of milk and of being difficult to herd over long distances.

Above all, the pig is ill-adapted to the heat of the Negev, the Jordan Valley, and the other biblical lands. Compared to cattle, goats, and sheep, the pig is markedly incapable of maintaining a constant body temperature when the temperature rises.

In spite of the expression "to sweat like a pig," it has now become clear that pigs can't sweat through their relatively hairless skins. Human beings, the sweatiest of all mammals, cool themselves by evaporating as much as three ounces of body liquid per hour from each square foot of body surface. The best a pig can manage is one-tenth ounce per square foot, and none of this is sweat. Even sheep evaporate twice as much body liquid through their skins as pigs. And sheep have the advantage of thick white wool, which both reflects the sun's rays and provides insulation when the ambient temperature rises above body temperature. According to L. E. Mount of the Argicultural Research Council Institute of Animal Physiology in Cambridge, England, adult pigs will die if exposed to direct sunlight and air temperatures over 97 degrees F. In the Jordan Valley, air temperatures of 110 degrees occur almost every summer and there is intense sunshine throughtout the year.

To compensate for its lack of protective hair and its inability to sweat, the pig must dampen its skin with external moisture. It usually does this by wallowing in fresh, clean mud, but if nothing else is available, it will cover its skin with its own urine and feces. Mount reports that below 84 degrees F. pigs kept in pens deposit their excreta away from their sleeping and feeding areas, while above 84 degrees they excrete throughout the pen.

Sheep and goats were the first animals to be domesticated in the Middle East, possibly as early as 9000 B.C. Pigs were domesticated in the same general region about 2,000 years later. Bone counts conducted by archeologists at early prehistoric village farming sites show that sheep and goats were in the majority while the domesticated pig was almost always a relatively minor part—about 5 percent—of the village fauna. This is what one would expect of a creature that ate the same food as man, couldn't be milked, and had to be provided with shade and mudholes. Domesticated pigs were from the beginning an economical and ecological luxury, especially since goats, sheep, and cattle provided milk, cheese, meat, hides, dung, fiber, and traction for plowing. But the pig, with its rich, fatty meat, was a delectable temptation—the kind, like incest and adultery, that mankind finds difficult to resist. And so God was heard to say that swine were unclean, not only as food, but to the touch as well. This message was repeated by Mohammed for the same reason: it was ecologically more adaptive for the people of the Middle East to cater to their goats, sheep, and cattle. Pigs tasted good but they ate you out of house and home and, if you gave them a chance, used up your water as well. Well, that's my answer to the riddle of why God told the Jews and the Muslims not to eat pork. Anyone have a better idea?

II

A number of readers were critical of my essay "Riddle of the Pig" ("Hogwash," wrote one wag). I hope that the following discussion will clarify the issues and meet some of the objections that have been raised. . . .

Several readers insisted that the reason for the taboo was simply that the pig is, in fact, a dirty and disgusting animal. Pierre Gringoire, for example, reminded me of "the pig's habit of eating with great relish and many delighted grunts human excrement." Another correspondent, even more graphically inclined, told of once being surrounded by pigs before he could leap back over the stone wall behind which he had chosen to squat. Other commentators pointed out that pigs will even eat carrion, "which obviously seems unclean," as Dorothy Muegel put it. Reader Paul Squibb neatly summed up these sentiments with the observation that "the Mosaic injunction was something like: 'You mustn't eat any part of your sewer system.' "

The reason I didn't mention this aspect of "piggishness" is that, among domestic animals, it is scarcely peculiar to the pig. In South American Indian groups, for example, the role of fecal and carrion scavenger was monopolized by the dog. Friends who have studied among the Eskimo tell of Rabelaisian encounters between themselves and their host's huskies whenever they had to step outside the igloo during the winter night. Dogs, of course, are eaten in many societies throughout the world. So the consumption of carrion or human feces by a domestic animal is not by itself sufficient reason for placing a ban on the consumption of its flesh.

Nothing in nature "obviously seems unclean," least of all the pig. Millions of people in Latin America, Asia, and Oceania enjoy eating pigs, even though they know the animals have consumed substantial amounts of carrion and human feces. In New Guinea and Melanesia, the pig, far from being regarded as loathsome, is thought to be the most sacred and beautiful of all nature's creations. Incidentally, the conditions for raising pigs in such places—heavy rainfall and lots of trees—are the direct opposite of those in the Middle East.

The assumption made by several readers that pigs in the Middle East were loathsome because they were primarily fecal scavengers leads back to the ecological factors stressed in my theory. Restriction of pigs to rations consisting primarily of human excrement obviously imposes drastic limits on the size of the pig population relative to the human population. We would need, therefore, to explain why the pig was raised in this manner, rather than by extensive swineherding or by an intensive grain supplement. In other words, we would have to explain why the pig ate more sewage in the Middle East than elsewhere. The explanation is the same as the one I gave for why the pig in the Middle East had to cool itself by wallowing in its own excreta rather than in fresh water: the pig is an ecological anomaly in the hot and arid Middle Eastern heartlands.

Another group of correspondents dismissed my ecological solution to the riddle of the pig because it failed to explain all the other food taboos mentioned in the Bible. William Alkus accused me of perpetuating the common error "that the forbidden food or those things unkosher are primarily the pig." I concede that I should have taken more care to explain why I was emphasizing the pig. I was not unaware that many other animals are banned in Leviticus and Deuteronomy. But the ban on pork has always seemed the most difficult to understand in rational and ecosystem terms. Of all the animals whose flesh is forbidden in the Five Books of Moses, the pig is the only one that is a domesticated animal bred primarily for the value of its meat. Therefore, the taboo on pork initially seems utterly baffling and entirely a result of scientifically unknowable causes.

I fail to see why I should be expected to explain all the other food taboos in the Bible as a reward for having offered a plausible solution to the riddle of the pig. Some years ago I offered an ecological explanation, which has since been largely confirmed, of the Hindu taboo on the consumption of beef (*see* "The Myth of the Sacred Cow," *Natural History,* March 1967). "Ah!" said the skeptics. "But what about the Chinese aversion to milk?" And when I showed how that, too, could be given an ecological explanation, I was told, "Oh, yes. But what about the Hebrew and Moslem taboo against pork?" Unfortunately, I just don't seem able to resist these challenges, so here comes an ecological explanation for the entire set of creatures whose flesh is forbidden in the Mosaic code.

Cultural ecological theory predicts that religiously supported food taboos seldom, if ever, decrease total energetic and nutritional efficiency; actually, such taboos often constitute ideological barriers against food practices that might tend to degrade specific ecosystems or impair their bioenergetic productivity. I maintain, in conformity with this principle, that the great majority of forbidden flesh in Leviticus and Deuteronomy belongs to feral mammals, birds, reptiles, fish, and insects whose retention in the ancient Hebrew diet would not have significantly raised, and could easily have lowered, the capability of the seminomadic pastoral and farming complex to support human life.

Let us start with the interdiction against eating beasts that have "paws." The animals most likely to have been included in this ban consisted of predators, such as weasels (specifically mentioned), wildcats, foxes, and wolves, plus domestic cats and dogs. It seems unlikely that a people who raised large numbers of sheep, goats, and cattle would often want to be in a position to dine on carnivorous predators. The whole object of pastoral management is to exterminate predators or at least to keep them far away from one's herds and flocks. Dogs in such ecosystems are used primarily to herd and hunt; for meat production, anything fed to a dog would be better put into the mouth of a goat. As for cats, which were primarily house pets, they are a sorry source of protein under the best of circumstances.

Among animals specifically mentioned in Leviticus 11 we find the chameleon, lizard, and mole, and, by implication, the snake. Avoidance of such difficult to catch and/or calorically insignificant tidbits cannot conceivably constitute a nutritional loss for people who keep meat- and milk-producing ruminants—although such animals might very well constitute a net caloric loss if they were the object of serious culinary attention.

Another large category of forbidden creature, which is not designated by species, consists of water dwellers without fins or scales. By implication, the interdicted species are usually understood to include eels, shellfish, whales, porpoises, and several "scaleless" fish, perhaps including sturgeons, lumpsuckers, lampreys, hagfish, and catfish. It seems to me that pastoralists were well advised to forget about hunting for whales or sturgeon or collecting clams or devoting much effort to difficult to catch, difficult to eat, or relatively rare fish. Similar observations apply, I believe, to the tortoise and snail, which are mentioned specifically.

I come now to birds, the largest group of specifically identified forbidden creatures. The list is dominated by such unlikely sources of human food energy as eagles, ospreys, vultures, ravens, hawks, swans, storks, herons, and lapwings. Bats are included among the birds and exemplify the same principle of nutritional triviality.

Turning to the category "insects," we find a surprising exception to the general taboo. Four kinds of locusts are specifically recommended as good to eat. Is it an accident that locusts also happen to be nutritionally significant in the biblical heartlands? I think not. Locusts were not only abundant but they also tended to become available under circumstances that recommended they be consumed without ado; namely, when swarms had stripped the fields and locusts were the only thing left to eat.

The remaining category consists of the animals that "part not the hoof," or "chew not the cud." Although not mentioned specifically, the domesticated horse and donkey are usually thought to have been among the species implicated by that formula. I find little to ponder in the case of the horse. This animal was bred for aristocratic and military purposes. It was a great luxury, even for the royalty of Egypt and Babylonia, and could never have provided meat for more than a tiny fraction of the ancient Hebrew population. I am less confident of the status of donkeys; still, these animals were bred for portage, not for food, and I am unaware of any culture in which donkey meat is regularly on the menu.

That leaves, among domesticated species, the camel, whose flesh the Bible specifically prohibits. Several correspondents were particularly concerned about what the taboo on camel flesh did to my ecological explanation. ("Can Professor Harris dare say the camel is not adapted to the Middle East?")

Although some of the ancient Hebrews kept flocks of camels, these animals are pre-eminently creatures of the deep desert. They are associated with a fully migratory Bedouin life-style, not with the semisedentary adaptation of the ancient Hebrews. Throughout most of the Mosaic period, camel flesh was probably no more abundant than horse flesh. But the camel is an extremely important test of the ecological approach in another sense. Mohammed specifically reaffirmed the Mosaic taboo against only one animal, the pig. And he specifically rescinded the Mosaic taboo against only one animal, the camel.

This was no mere whim. Indeed, it is difficult to imagine how the subsequent history of the world could have been quite the same had Islam maintained the ban on camel flesh. The Arabian tribesmen who were Mohammed's earliest supporters were camel nomads. They depended upon the camel for their entire livelihood; camel flesh was for them an emergency ration without which they could never have ventured forth on their spectacular journeys across the desert.

I have not quite exhausted all the animals that were specifically interdicted in the Mosaic code (the taxonomic identity of several species remains unresolved). But in any case, I do not intend the preceding analysis to be anything other than a series of hypotheses that merit consideration before one finally concludes, along with several of my correspondents, that "no logical explanation of food taboos is possible." It has been my lifelong experience with pronouncements about the inexplicability of human events that such pronouncements are themselves often the chief obstacle to the advance of anthropological knowledge.

Part IX

AESTHETICS AND RECREATION

There are artists in all societies. Their efforts not only provide us with pleasurable moments but also give us valuable insights about many aspects of particular times and places. Fundamentally, an artist (even when expressing deep personal concerns) must communicate with others by using special symbols in a very subtle language. Our effort to understand aesthetics does have much in common with our previous effort to understand language, but artistic styles are even more difficult to grasp than linguistic grammars. As Bohannan puts it (1963:47), ". . . there would seem to be more 'parts of painting' than there are parts of speech."

The anthropological study of human aesthetic efforts has come into its own once again after a period of relative quiesence. Some efforts have involved the use of form and style as part of a general index of cultural complexity and historical continuity (e.g., see the summary of the massive "cantometrics" project as presented in *Folk Song Style and Culture* by Alan Lomax 1968). Others have turned to music and other art forms as a means of exploring human nature, and especially the structure of the human mind as it may be inferred from the way humans express themselves (e.g. see *How Musical Is Man?* by John Blacking, 1973).

Undoubtedly, however, one of the oldest and still most active areas of interest within the anthropology of aesthetics is the study of folklore (and related forms of "oral literature" such as poetry, riddles, myths, proverbs, and so on). Within this field, few have had the breadth of vision or the impact of the French anthropologist Claude Lévi-Strauss. It is virtually impossible to exaggerate his popularity. He is a national hero of France; composers have written choral pieces using passages from his books; scholars have favorably compared him to Darwin, Freud and Marx. At the same time, and in some ways as further proof of his position of eminence in the discipline, there are many who completely discount what he says, and there are even more who have serious reservations about his theories and his handling of the data he marshals in support of these. Edmund Leach, who must be judged as one of the more informed admirers of Lévi-Strauss' work has suggested (1970:53) that "Lévi-Strauss on myths has much the same fascination as Freud on the interpretation of dreams, and the same kind of weaknesses, too."

Some of the reasons for the fascinataion with Lévi-Strauss can be seen in Chapter 28 in his analysis of four Winnebago myths. This essay follows a pattern that is basic to most of his attempts to understand myths and folktales. He uses the essential elements from a diverse array of folktales to identify fundamental "oppositions." In the case of the four Winnebago myths analyzed here, there are several closely related oppositions involving either the contrast between an ordinary life and an extraordinary one (and particularly the heroic life), or the contrast between final death and undulations between life and death. For his devoted followers, the magic of his analysis is revealed in his ability to incorporate the distinctive fourth myth into the pattern established in the first three. For his "devoted detractors," it is precisely at such points that he seems to be playing mere tricks on us by saying, in essence, 'if it doesn't work one way, turn it upside down or inside out and then it will probably fit.' In many cases, his critics come very close to spoiling Lévi-Strauss' performance but often they are insufficiently sensitive to the level of his analyses for, as in this essay, he reminds us only in passing that "the kind of analysis I intend to offer is no alternative to Radin's own analysis. It lies on a different level, logical rather than historical. . . ." Lévi-Strauss is attempting to find the unconscious meanings in myths (the problems they try to resolve). Sometimes, so it is claimed, these meanings may be transformations of the conscious content of a given myth. And, of course, it is here that we come back to the suggestion made by Leach—the trouble with Lévi-Strauss, as with Freud, is that very often one wonders whether it is ever possible to prove him wrong.

In some ways, it is more difficult to define "play" than it is to define religion. Some very insightful observations about play have been made, however, by the anthropologists Gregory Bateson (1970) and Clifford Geertz (1973). After observing some monkeys playfully nipping at each other, Bateson suggested that the behavior could not have occurred the way it did unless the monkeys had been able to exchange signals carrying the message "this is play." Such a simple sounding message is actually rather complex. Taking the example of the monkeys Bateson observed, the "this is play" message says, in effect, "the . . . nip denotes the bite, but it does not denote what would be denoted by the bite" (Bateson 1970:180). This expanded rendering of the message "this is play," if stated in very general terms, gives us a useful working definition of play itself. Thus, play is an activity for which the following message-statement is valid: " 'These actions, in which we now engage, do not denote what would be denoted by those actions which these actions denote' " (Bateson 1970: ibid).

Superficially, this expanded definition may seem to say, only, that play is an activity which is not serious. But in fact it says a great deal more than this. When play is defined in this way we can work through the apparent paradox posed by the well known phenomenon of play that seems to be (or even is) serious.

One of the most enthralling illustrations of serious play is the extended analysis by Clifford Geertz of the Balinese cockfight (Geertz 1973:412–53). Geertz effectively argues that cockfighting, which he calls a form of "deep" play,

> is like playing with fire only not getting burned. You activate village and kingroup rivalries and hostilities, but in "play" form, coming dangerously and entrancingly close to the expression of open and direct interpersonal and intergroup aggression (something which . . . almost never happens in the normal course of ordinary life), but not quite, because, after all, it is "only a cockfight" [1973:440].

To put it in Bateson's terms, the cockfight denotes the "bite" of status rivalries and kingroup hostilities, but it does not denote what would be denoted by actual status rivalries and kingroup hostilities. The excitement of the cockfighting drama lies in the fact that in well-arranged matches, the "this is play" message is extremely subtle (indeed, only the experienced *aficionados* may really get it) and yet it is absolutely essential if the play is not to degenerate into something else. In the case of Balinese cockfighting, as Geertz stresses repeatedly, the message always gets through. Bateson describes something very similar to this when he discusses the "more complex form of play" in which the game "is constructed not upon the premise 'This is play' but rather around the question 'Is this play?' " (Bateson 1970:182). Such play activities, because they are more complex and subtle in this communicational sense, are almost always more exciting.

It is just such exciting, complex, deep play that is described so interestingly by Robin Fox in his essay (Chapter 29) on Pueblo baseball. For most participating Americans, baseball may seem to be "pure fun [play]" but only a few minutes at a Little League game is needed to put this notion to rest. The same may be said for baseball as played by the peaceful, cooperative Pueblos. At issue is not whether the Braves and Redskins are playing but *what* they are playing. What does the play denote? Or, to put it more completely, what do the games described by Fox *not* denote which would be denoted by those actions which the games *do* denote?

Claude Lévi-Strauss

28. Four Winnebago Myths: A Structural Sketch*

Among the many talents which make him one of the great anthropologists of our time, Paul Radin has one which gives a singular flavor to his work. He has the authentic esthetic touch, rather uncommon in our profession. This is what we call in French *flair:* the gift of singling out those facts, observations, and documents which possess an especially rich meaning, sometimes undisclosed at first, but likely to become evident as one ponders the implications woven into the material. A crop harvested by Paul Radin, even if he does not choose to mill it himself, is always capable of providing lasting nourishment for many generations of students.

This is the reason why I intend to pay my tribute to the work of Paul Radin by giving some thought to four myths which he has published under the title *The Culture of the Winnebago: As Described by Themselves* (Radin 1949). Although Radin himself pointed out in the Preface: "In publishing these texts I have only one object in view, to put at the disposal of students, authentic material for the study of Winnebago culture," and although the four myths were each obtained from different informants, it seems that, on a structural level, there was good reason for making them the subject of a single publication. A deep unity underlies all four, notwithstanding the fact that one myth, as Radin has shown in his introduction and notes, appears to differ widely in content, style, and structure

* Reprinted with the author's permission from *Culture in History: Essays in Honor of Paul Radin,* Stanley Diamond, ed., Columbia University Press, 1960:351–62.

"Four Winnebago Myths," from *Structural Anthropology,* Volume II, by Claude Lévi-Strauss, to be published in 1975 by Basic Books, Inc., Publishers, New York.

from the other three. My purpose will be to analyze the structural relationships between the four myths and to suggest that they can be grouped
together not only because they are part of a collection of ethnographic
and linguistic data referring to one tribe, which Radin too modestly claimed
as his sole purpose, but because they are of the same genre, i.e., their
meanings logically complement each other.

The title of the first myth is "The Two Friends Who Became Reincarnated: The Origin of the Four Nights' Wake." This is the story of two
friends, one of them a chief's son, who decide to sacrifice their lives for
the welfare of the community. After undergoing a series of ordeals in the
underworld, they reach the lodge of Earthmaker, who permits them to
become reincarnated and to resume their previous lives among their relatives and friends.

As explained by Radin in his commentary (Ibid:41, para 32), there is
a native theory underlying the myth: every individual is entitled to a specific quota of years of life and experience. If a person dies before his time,
his relatives can ask the spirits to distribute among them what he has
failed to utilize. But there is more in this theory than meets the eye. The
unspent life-span given up by the hero, when he lets himself be killed by
the enemies, will be added to the capital of life, set up in trust for the
group. Neverthless, his act of dedication is not entirely without personal
profit: by becoming a hero an individual makes a choice, he exchanges
a full life-span for a shortened one, but while the full life-span is unique,
granted once and for all, the shortened one appears as a kind of lease
taken on eternity. That is, by giving up one full life, an indefinite succession of half-lives is gained. But since all the unlived halves will increase
the life expectancy of the ordinary people, everybody gains in the process:
the ordinary people whose average life expectancy will slowly but substantially increase generation after generation, and the warriors with shortened but indefinitely renewable lives, provided their minds remain set on
self-dedication.

It is not clear, however, that Radin pays full justice to the narrator
when he treats as a "secondary interpretation" the fact that the expedition
is undertaken by the heroes to show their appreciation of the favors of
their fellow villagers (Ibid:37, para. 2). My contention is that this motive
of the heroes deserves primary emphasis, and it is supported by the fact
that there are two war parties. The first one is undertaken by the warriors
while the heroes are still in their adolescent years, so they are neither
included in, nor even informed of it; they hear about the party only as a
rumor (Ibid.:37, paras. 11-14), and they decide to join it uninvited. We
must conclude then that the heroes have no responsibility for the very
venture wherein they distinguish themselves, since it has been instigated
and led by others. Moreover, they are not responsible for the second war

party, during which they are killed, since this latter foray has been initiated by the enemy in revenge for the first.

The basic idea is clear: the two friends have developed into successful social beings (Ibid.:37, paras. 66–70), accordingly, they feel obliged to repay their fellow tribesmen who have treated them so well (Ibid.: para. 72). As the story goes, they set out to expose themselves in the wilderness; later they die in an ambush prepared by the enemy in revenge for the former defeat. The obvious conclusion is that the heroes have willingly died for the sake of their people. And because they died without responsibility of their own, but instead that of others, those will inherit the unspent parts of their lives, while the heroes themselves will be permitted to return to earth and the same process will be repeated all over again. This interpretation is in agreement with information given elsewhere by Radin: i.e., in order to pass the test of the Old Woman who rids the soul of all the recollections belonging to its earthly life, each soul must be solicitous not of its own welfare but of the welfare of the living members of the group.

Now at the root of this myth we find—as the phonologist would say —a double opposition. First there is the opposition between *ordinary life* and *heroic life,* the former realizing a full life-span, not renewable, the latter gambling with life for the benefit of the group. The second opposition is between two kinds of death, one "straight" and final, although it provides a type of unearthly immortality in the villages of the dead; the other "undulating," and swinging between life and death. Indeed one is tempted to see the reflection of this double fate in the Winnebago symbol of the ladder of the afterworld as it appears in the Medicine Rite. One side is "like a frog's leg, twisted and dappled with light-and-life. The other [is] like a red cedar, blackened from frequent usage and very smooth and shiny" (Ibid.:71, paras. 91–93; see also Radin 1945, especially the author's illuminating comments on pp. 63–65).

To sum up the meaning of the myth so far: if one wants a full life one gets a full death; if one renounces life and seeks death, then one increases the full life of his fellow-tribesmen, and, moreover, secures for oneself a state composed of an indefinite series of half-lives and half-deaths. Thus we have a triangular system:

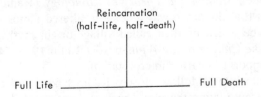

The second myth, entitled "The Man Who Brought His Wife Back from Spiritland," is a variation on the same theme, although there is a significant difference involved. Here too, we find a hero—the husband—ready to sacrifice his unspent life-span; not, as in the first myth, for the benefit of the group, but rather for the benefit of only one individual, his beloved wife. Indeed, the hero is not aware at first that by seeking death he will secure a new lease on life for both his dead wife and himself. Had he been so aware, and this holds equally for the protagonists in the first myth, the essential element of sacrifice would have been missing. In both cases the result is similar: an altruistic loss of life means life regained, not only for the self-appointed victim, but also for the one or more persons to whom the sacrifice was consecrated.

The third myth, "The Journey of the Ghost to Spiritland, as Told in the Medicine Rite," belongs, as the title suggests, to a religious society. It explains how the members of the Medicine Rite, after death, undergo (as do the protagonists of the other myths) several tests in Spiritland, which they overcome, thus gaining the right to become reincarnated.

At first sight this situation seems to differ from the others, since nobody sacrificed his life. However, the members of the Medicine Rite actually spend their lives in symbolic sacrifice. As Radin has shown, in *The Road of Life and Death* and elsewhere, the Medicine Rite follows the familiar pattern of letting oneself be "killed" and then "revived." Thus the only departure consists in the fact that whereas in the first and second myths the heroes are willing to die once and, so they anticipate, permanently, the heroes of the third myth (the members of the Rite) repeatedly, though symbolically, have trained themselves to self-sacrifice. They have, so to speak, mithridatized themselves against a full death by renouncing a full ordinary life which is replaced, in ritual practice, by a lifelong succession of half-lives and half-deaths. Therefore we are entitled to assume that, in this case too, the myth is made up of the same elements, although Ego— and not another person, nor the group as a whole—is conceived as the primary beneficiary.

Let us now consider the fourth myth, "How an Orphan Restored the Chief's Daughter to Life," a tale which has given Radin some concern. This myth, he says, is not only different from the other three, its plot appears unusual relative to the rest of Winnebago mythology. After recalling that in his book *Method and Theory of Ethnology* (Radin 1933:238–45), he suggested that this myth was a version, altered almost beyond recognition, of a type which he then called village-origin myths, he proceeds to explain in *The Culture of the Winnebago* (Radin 1949:74 ff) why he can no longer support this earlier interpretation.

It is worthwhile to follow closely Radin's new line of reasoning. He begins by recapitulating the plot—such a simple plot, he says, that there is practically no need for doing so: "The daughter of a tribal chief falls in love with an orphan, dies of a broken heart and is then restored to life by the orphan who must submit to and overcome certain tests, not in spiritland but here, on earth, in the very lodge in which the young woman died" (Ibid.:74).

If this plot is "simplicity itself," where do the moot points lie? Radin lists three which he says every modern Winnebago would question: 1. the plot seems to refer to a highly stratified society; 2. in order to understand the plot one should assume that in that society women occupied a high position and that, possibly, descent was reckoned in the matrilineal line; 3. the tests which in Winnebago mythology take place, as a rule, in the land of ghosts occur, in this instance, on earth.

After dismissing two possible explanations—that we are dealing here with a borrowed European tale or that the myth was invented by some Winnebago radical—Radin concludes that the myth must belong to "a very old stratum of Winnebago history." He also suggests that two distinct types of literary tradition, divine tales on the one hand and human tales on the other, have merged while certain primitive elements have been reinterpreted to make them fit togethter (Ibid.:74–77).

I am certainly not going to challenge this very elegant reconstruction backed by an incomparable knowledge of Winnebago culture, language, and history. The kind of analysis I intend to offer is no alternative to Radin's own analysis. It lies on a different level, logical rather than historical. It takes as its context the three myths already discussed, not Winnebago culture, old or recent. My purpose is to explicate the structural relationship—if any—which prevails between this myth and the other three.

First, there is a theoretical problem which should be noted briefly. Since the publication of Boas's *Tsimshian Mythology,* anthropologists have often simply assumed that a full correlation exists between the myths of a given society and its culture. This, I feel, is going further than Boas intended. In the work just referred to, he did not suppose that myths automatically reflect the culture, as some of his followers seem always to anticipate. Rather, he tried to find out how much of the culture actually did pass into the myths, if any, and he convincingly showed that *some* of it does. It does not follow that whenever a social pattern is alluded to in a myth this pattern must correspond to something real which should be attributed to the past if, under direct scrutiny, the present fails to offer an equivalent.

There must be, and there is, a correspondence between the unconscious meaning of a myth—the problem it tries to solve—and the conscious content it makes use of to reach that end, i.e., the plot. However, this correspondence should not always be conceived as a kind of mirror-image, it can also appear as a *transformation.* If the problem is presented in "straight" terms, that is, in the way the social life of the group expresses and tries to solve it, the overt content of the myth, the plot, can borrow its elements from social life itself. But should the problem be formulated, and its solution sought for, "upside down," that is *ab absurdo,* then the overt content will become modified accordingly to form an inverted image of the social pattern actually present to the consciousness of the natives.

If this hypothesis is true, it follows that Radin's assumption that the pattern of social life referred to in the fourth myth must belong to a past stage of Winnebago history, is not inescapable.

We may be confronted with the pattern of a nonexistent society, contrary to the Winnebago traditional pattern, only because the structure of that particular myth is itself inverted, in relation to those myths which use as overt content the traditional pattern. To put it simply, if a certain correspondence is assumed between A and B, then if A is replaced by $-A$, B must be replaced by $-B$, without implying that, since B corresponds to an external object, there should exist another external object $-B$, which must exist somewhere: either in another society (borrowed element) or in a past stage of the same society (survival).

Obviously, the problem remains: why do we have three myths of the A type and one of the $-A$ type? This could be the case because $-A$ is older than A, but it can also be because $-A$ is one of the transformations of A which is already known to us under three different guises: $A_1, A_2, A_3,$ since we have seen that the three myths of the assumed A type are not identical.

We have already established that the group of myths under consideration is based upon a fundamental opposition: on the one hand, the lives of ordinary people unfolding towards a natural death, followed by immortality in one of the spirit villages; and, on the other hand, heroic life, self-abridged, the gain being a supplementary life quota for the others as well as for oneself. The former alternative is not envisaged in this group of myths which, as we have seen, is mostly concerned with the latter. There is, however, a secondary difference which permits us to classify the first three myths according to the particular end assigned to the self-sacrifice in each. In the first myth the group is intended to be the immediate beneficiary, in the second it is another individual (the wife), and in the third it is oneself.

When we turn to the fourth myth, we may agree with Radin that it exhibits "unusual" features in relation to the other three. However, the difference seems to be of a logical more than of a sociological or historical nature. It consists in a new opposition introduced within the first pair of opposites (between "ordinary" life and "extraordinary" life). Now there are two ways in which an "extraordinary" phenomenon may be construed as such; it may consist either in a *surplus* or in a *lack*. While the heroes of the first three myths are all overgifted, through social success, emotions or wisdom, the heroes of the fourth myth are, if one may say so, "below standard," at least in one respect.

The chief's daughter occupies a high social position; so high, in fact, that she is cut off from the rest of the group and is therefore paralyzed when it comes to expressing her feelings. Her exalted position makes her a defective human being, lacking an essential attribute of life. The boy is also defective, but socially, that is, he is an orphan and very poor. May we say, then, that the myth reflects a stratified society? This would compel us to overlook the remarkable symmetry which prevails between our two heroes, for it would be wrong to say simply that one is high and the other low: as a matter of fact, each of them is high in one respect and low in the other, and this pair of symmetrical structures, wherein the two terms are inverted relative to each other, belongs to the realm of ideological constructs rather than of sociological systems. We have just seen that the girl is "socially" above and "naturally" below. The boy is undoubtedly very low in the social scale; however, he is a miraculous hunter, i.e., he entertains privileged relations with the natural world, the world of animals. This is emphasized over and over again in the myth (see paras. 10–14, 17–18, 59–60, 77–90).

Therefore may we not claim that the myth actually confronts us with a polar system consisting in two individuals, one male, the other female, and both exceptional insofar as each of them is overgifted in one way $(+)$ and undergifted in the other $(-)$.

	Nature	Culture
Boy	+	−
Girl	−	+

The plot consists in carrying this disequilibrium to its logical extreme; the girl dies a *natural* death, the boy stays alone, i.e., he also dies, but in a *social* way. Whereas during their ordinary lives the girl was overtly above, the boy overtly below, now that they have become segregated (either from the living or from society) their positions are inverted: the girl is below (in her grave), the boy above (in his lodge). This, I think, is clearly implied in a detail stated by the narrator which seems to have puzzled Radin: "On top of the grave they then piled loose dirt, placing everything in such a way that nothing could seep through." (Ibid.:87, para. 52). Radin comments: "I do not understand why piling the dirt loosely would prevent seepage. There must be something else involved that has not been mentioned" (Ibid.:100, n. 40). May I suggest that this detail be correlated with a similar detail about the building of the young man's lodge: ". . . the bottom was piled high with dirt so that, in this fashion, they could keep the lodge warm." (Ibid.:87, para. 74). There is implied here, I think, not a reference to recent or past custom but rather a clumsy attempt to emphasize that, relative to the earth's surface, i.e., dirt, the boy is now above and the girl below.

This new equilibrium, however, will be no more lasting than the first. *She who was unable to live cannot die;* her ghost lingers "on earth." Finally she induces the young man to fight the ghosts and take her back among the living. With a wonderful symmetry, the boy will meet, a few years later, with a similar, although inverted, fate; "Although I am not yet old, he says to the girl (now his wife,) I have been here (lasted) on earth as long as I can. . . ." (Ibid.:94, para. 341). *He who overcame death, proves unable to live.* This recurring antithesis could develop indefinitely, and such a possibility is noted in the text, (with an only son surviving his father, he too an orphan, he too a sharpshooter) but a different solution is finally reached. The heroes, equally unable to die or to live, will assume an intermediate identity, that of twilight creatures living under the earth but also able to come up on it; they will be neither men nor gods, but wolves, that is, ambivalent spirits combining good and evil features. So ends the myth.

If the above analysis is correct, two consequences follow: first, our myth makes up a consistent whole wherein the details balance and fit each other nicely; secondly, the three problems raised by Radin can be analyzed in terms of the myth itself; and no hypothetical past stage of Winnebago society need be invoked.

Let us, then, try to solve these problems, following the pattern of our analysis.

1. The society of the myth appears stratified, only because the two heroes are conceived as a pair of opposites, but they are such both from the point of view of nature *and* of culture. Thus, the so-called stratified society should be interpreted not as a sociological vestige but as a projection of a logical structure wherein everything is given both in opposition and correlation.

2. The same answer can be given to the question of the assumed exalted position of the women. If I am right, our myths state three propositions, the first by implication, the second expressly stated in myths 1, 2 and 3, the third expressly stated in myth 4.

These propositions are as follow:

a. Ordinary people live (their full lives) and die (their full deaths).
b. Positive extraordinary people die (earlier) and live (more).
c. Negative extraordinary people are able neither to live nor to die.

Obviously proposition c offers an inverted demonstration of the truth of a and b. Hence, it must use a plot starting with protagonists (here, man and woman) in inverted positions. This leads us to state that a plot and its component parts should neither be interpreted by themselves nor relative to something outside the realm of the myth proper, but as *substitutions* given in, and understandable only with reference to *the group made up of all the myths of the same series.*

3. We may now revert to the third problem raised by Radin about myth 4, that is, the contest with the ghosts takes place on earth instead of, as was usually the case, in spiritland. To this query I shall suggest an answer along the same lines as the others.

It is precisely because our two heroes suffer from a state of *underlife* (in respect either to culture or nature) that, in the narrative, the ghosts become a kind of *super-dead*. It will be recalled that the whole myth develops and is resolved on an intermediary level, where humans become underground animals and ghosts linger on earth. It tells about people who are, from the start, half-alive and half-dead while, in the preceding myths, the opposition between life and death is strongly emphasized at the beginning, and overcome only at the end. Thus, the integral meaning of the four myths is that, in order to be overcome the opposition between life and death should be first acknowledged, or else the ambiguous state will persist indefinitely.

I hope to have shown that the four myths under consideration all belong to the same *group* (understood as in *group theory*) and that Radin was even more right than he supposed in publishing them together. In the first place, the four myths deal with extraordinary, in opposition to ordinary, fate. The fact that ordinary fate is not illustrated here and thus is reckoned as an "empty" category, does not imply, of course, that it is not illustrated elsewhere. In the second place, we find an opposition between two types of extraordinary fate, positive and negative. This new dichotomy which permits us to segregate myth 4 from myths 1, 2 and 3 corresponds, on a logical level, to the discrimination that Radin makes on psychological, sociological, and historical grounds. Finally, myths 1, 2 and 3 have been classified according to the purpose of the sacrifice which is the theme of each.

Thus the four myths can be organized in a dichotomous structure of correlations and oppositions. But we can go even further and try to order them on a common scale. This is suggested by the curious variations which can be observed in each myth with respect to the kind of test the hero is put to by the ghosts.

In myth 3 there is no test at all, so far as the ghosts are concerned. The tests consist in overcoming material obstacles while the ghosts themselves figure as indifferent fellow travelers. In myth 1 they cease to be indifferent without yet becoming hostile. On the contrary, the tests result from their overfriendliness, as inviting women and infectious merry-makers. Thus, from *companions* in myth 3 they change to *seducers* in myth 1. In myth 2 they still behave as human beings, but they now act as *aggressors,* and permit themselves all kinds of rough play. This is even more evident in myth 4, but here the human element vanishes; it is only at the end that we know that ghosts, not crawling insects, are responsible for the trials of the hero. We have thus a twofold progression, from a *peaceful* attitude to an *aggressive* one, and from *human* to *nonhuman* behavior.

This progression can be correlated with the kind of relationship which the hero (or heroes) of each myth entertain with the social group. The hero of myth 3 belongs to a ritual brotherhood: he definitely assumes his (privileged) fate as member of a group, he acts with and in his group.

The two heroes of myth 1 have resolved to part from the group, but the text states repeatedly that this is in order to find an opportunity to achieve

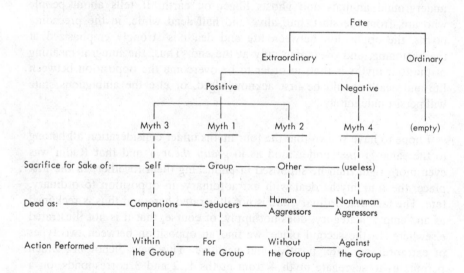

something beneficial for their fellow tribesmen. They act, therefore, for the group. But in myth 2 the hero is only inspired by his love for his wife. There is no reference to the group. The action is undertaken independently for the sake of another individual.

Finally, in myth 4, the negative attitude toward the group is clearly revealed; the girl dies of her "uncommunicativeness," if one may say so. Indeed she prefers to die rather than speak; death is her "final" exile. As for the boy, he refuses to follow the villagers when they decide to move away and abandon the grave. The segregation is thus willfully sought on all sides; the action unrolls against the group.

The accompanying chart summarizes our discussion. I am quite aware that, in order to be fully convincing, the argument should not be limited to the four myths considered here, but include more of the invaluable Winnebago mythology which Radin has given us. But I hope that by integrating more material the basic structure outlined has become richer and more complex, without being impaired. By singling out one book which its author would perhaps consider a minor contribution, I have intended to emphasize, in an indirect way, the fecundity of the method followed by Radin, and the lasting value of the problems he poses for the anthropologist.

Robin Fox

29. Pueblo Baseball: A New Use for Old Witchcraft*

The ideals of harmony and cooperation and the outlawing of competition among the Pueblo Indians have become an anthropological commonplace during the past few decades. Ruth Benedict's confusion of institutions with personality traits, which led her to believe that the Pueblos were "harmonious" people, has since been cleared up. Such books as *Sun Chief: The Autobiography of a Hopi Indian* vividly show the amount of hate, aggression, and suspicion that lies behind the conscious harmony of Pueblo social life. If interpersonal relations in the Pueblos could be summed up in one word, "cautious" would be it. The power of public opinion, of "what people will say," in these crowded little communities is the strongest force for social conformity, and manifests itself in an extreme fear of witchcraft accusations. Indeed, the fear of being accused is greater than the fear of actual witchcraft. Informants are vague about the powers and practices of witches and often complain that they have forgotten what witches are supposed to do—"only the old people remember what the *kanatya* do." But everyone agrees that the most terrible thing that can be said of one is that "everyone knows he [or she] is a witch." Thus, while the cultural trappings and elaborations surrounding witch behavior have largely been forgotten, the motivational basis for this projective system remains strong. It exists, as it were, in the raw.

---

* Reprinted from *Encounter with Anthropology* by Robin Fox (Harcourt Brace Jovanovich, Inc. 1973) with permission of Robin Fox and The American Folklore Society. Originally published in the *American Journal of Folklore* 1961, 74:9–16.

Everyone is suspect. The Sun Chief of Oraibi suspected his own mother on her deathbed of being a "two-heart" (witch). All interpersonal relations are fraught with danger, and there are few people who can be wholly trusted. Women in particular do not trust one another. With the Don Juanism of the males and the relative promiscuity of the women, no woman can be sure that any other woman is not her husband's lover, or has not been at one time. A woman can trust her sisters, more or less, and of course her mother, primarily because it would be difficult for members of the same household group to carry on affairs. Affines are much mistrusted, often with good reason.

What is involved is not so much sexual jealousy as, again, the fear of "talk." This is not just fear of gossip. Words have power and are not to be used lightly. Bad thoughts are believed to have tremendous repercussions in the real world. Bad words, as the manifestations of bad thoughts, "poison the air of the pueblo." There are real repercussions to accusation and insults and they do disturb pueblo peace. In societies based on extended kin groupings it is impossible to insult only one person. Any accusation may lead to a widespread split-up of the village, and this fear of internal dissension is a strong motive for not making open accusations, or at least for toning them down. In the case of a philandering husband caught *flagrante delicto,* relatives on both sides will try to patch the matter up or persuade the pair to part quietly. In the old days a woman could be rid of her husband fairly easily by ordering him out of her house. This is becoming impossible today because men are now more likely than women to be the house owners. The Catholic Church complicates matters for the Rio Grande Pueblos by forbidding divorce and remarriage. A wronged woman, taking her children, will often go to live with her sister or mother, but life is hard because she cannot remarry and she risks priestly censure if she takes another mate.

These limitations to direct action cause much frustration and bitterness among the women, so that witchcraft accusations are more likely to involve women than men. In the past, the war captains, ceremonial police of the Pueblos, would usually deal with the witches, once they had gathered sufficient proof of their activities. Death or exile would have been the punishment. Today, however, nothing would be done. One Indian said, "People just get mad and don't speak to each other, or they leave the village." Today, too, the relatively sophisticated Cochiti Indians realize that white people think these beliefs silly, and they tend to shrug them off or deny them. Some members of the ultra-Catholic progressive faction share the white man's contempt for these beliefs. But beneath the careless disbelief and outright denial lies the unchanged motivational and social basis for interpersonal fear.

Formal Pueblo institutions are a counter to, rather than an acting out of, the personality forces. People must dance together, work together, play together. They are enjoined to think good, harmonious thoughts so as not to spoil the air of the pueblo; bad thoughts are as dangerous as bad deeds. Drunkenness is feared for the aggressive impulses it lets loose. All forms of overt hostility are taboo.

In Cochiti, the intricate crisscrossing of clans, societies, the two kivas, extended families, church, and other groups helps to ensure that no permanent oppositions and cleavages can occur to channel hostilities into armed camps. The factional split between conservatives and progressives early in this century came nearest to open war, but the crosscutting of these divisions by others (particularly extended families) saved the village from complete disintegration. As long as any two groups continue to exchange women in Cochiti, it is difficult for them to remain in hostile opposition. All formal divisions within the village are divisions of labor, not of enmity. As the co-operation between the kivas is essential to the proper performance of public ceremonies, they in no way compete with each other. All medicine societies complement each other's work—there are never two societies for one cure. A careful political balance is struck so that every group is evenly represented on the council. The village is small and roles overlap, so that, despite continually recurring conflicts, there is no permanent discord.

Following this principle, the old competitive games of the pueblo were never played between any two formal groups. For races and shinny games, teams consisted of married versus unmarried, or of young men picked according to a count-out method. The social groupings were never competitively aligned and teams were not permanent. Since the advent of baseball in Cochiti, however, a new situation has arisen. The pueblo now has two baseball teams playing in the same league (Inter-Pueblo Baseball League) and in open competition with each other. The original team, now called the "Redskins," was formed many years ago; old photographs testify to the Pueblos' long-standing interest in baseball. Most men now playing grew up in a society that was already enthusiastic about the sport. Support comes from all sections of the population, including old medicine men and the ceremonial heads of the kivas. The current cacique, the religious leader of the tribe, was for a long time a pitcher for the second team. When he assumed office, the medicine men forbade him to continue playing ball because they did not think this consonant with the dignity of his office—but he is the only exception. The Redskins, first known as the "Eagles," were the focus of interest for many years; but with the return of servicemen to Cochiti after World War II, a second team, called the "Silversmiths," was formed. This team, now the Braves, claimed independent status, built its own ball park and entered the league in competition with the Redskins. The Silversmiths were immediately successful and won the championship three years in succession. Thus a new and potentially dangerous situation occurred—the two teams had to meet each other in the village and fight it out twice a year. This was wildly at variance with the whole Pueblo ethos.

During the first game, all went reasonably well on the field, but there were fights on the sidelines—between the mothers of the players. As the momentum of the game increased, these women began to abuse one another, to brawl, and finally to do open battle. The horrified Pueblo council immediately banned all future games between the teams in the pueblo.

An examination of the original membership of the two teams shows that, because of the voluntary nature of the recruitment, the teams were a perfect breeding ground for factions. One was not constrained to join either team by kinship ties, initiation, or any other automatic factor. The Braves, when they broke away from the Redskins, broke away by family groups; that is, several families of players left the one and formed the other. Thus the choice was made not by individuals, but by families. Within living memory, there had always been two ill-defined groups of extended families that formed opposing blocks on the basis of quarrels now forgotten. Previously, these two blocks had never had occasion or excuse to come out in opposition to each other, since there had been no basis for such an oppositional grouping, and the two groups even cut across the conservative-progressive factional boundaries—but in the baseball split there was a unique opportunity for the old latent hostilities to erupt. Allegiance to the team is predominantly patrilineal, as it is in the kivas, but the two teams are by no means coterminous with the kivas. They represent a dual alignment of families for purely competitive purposes. Families that mistrusted or disliked each other would readily line up on opposite sides. And the infection spread even to families not committed to either side. The crosscutting tendency in Pueblo institutions mitigates this, as it did with the factions, but the essential factor of the exchange of women has not had time to work itself out. What is more, the away games of the teams have increased the chances of young men to meet girls from outside the village and hence have increased the number of outmarriages. The wives of these marriages, having no female relatives in Cochiti, tend to become assimilated into the husband's mother's extended family and this widens the gap between the two teams. One year, out of eight marriages, three were to girls from San Juan Pueblo—results of the popular away game. It is not the young wives, however, but the older women who are the troublemakers. These women would formerly have had little chance to attack other women they disliked without invoking the frightening subject of witchcraft. Now they had an excuse and an opportunity to do battle royal over their sons and grandsons. The epithet "cheater" quickly became a virtual synonym for witch.

The council ban against baseball was effective in preventing open war in the village for a time, but it served only to drive the feelings underground. By 1959 antagonism had spread to the players. That year the

Braves indulged in a series of rule-breaking episodes that flared into open quarrels. These were accentuated by the fact that after a trial game the year before, which rumbled but went off without incident, the council had reluctantly decided that the annual games could continue to be played. Significantly, the games were scheduled for the beginning of the week of the annual Corn Dance, on the feast day of the village saint, Bonaventure. Thus they came at a time when "all hearts are in harmony," when everyone was bending his efforts toward the success of the great communal dance for rain, good harvest, and long life.

The Braves, according to their opponents, had not behaved properly. A Redskin commented, "Rules don't mean nothing to them; they don't care." It seems that the Braves had gone to town with the rule book. They had: 1. used people in the finals who had not played five consecutive games; 2. failed to turn up for games but refused to forfeit the points for not doing so; 3. used men who had previously played for other sides and refused to relinquish them even after threats of suspension; 4. cheated in the games; 5. threatened umpires (unspecified); 6. attempted to maim opponents. The rule that the Braves and their female supporters are said to have broken most often was not in the official book: influencing the course of the game by occult means—witchcraft. Particularly, it seems, they attempted to cause "accidents," to make the ball hit a runner, et cetera. When I asked why they hadn't been suspended or denied the replays, I was told, "They get their own way because the other teams are scared of them." San Juan had a good claim to two forfeited games but gave in because "they were scared." The manager of the Braves is feared as the Kwirena *nawa,* head of the powerful Kwirena, one of the "managing" societies in Pueblo ceremonials. He is also head of the Pumpkin Kiva. Some of the Redskins spoke out against the Braves' conduct at meetings of the league, and in a confused bit of political maneuvering the Braves were suspended, reinstated, quit the league, then rejoined it. By the time of the Cochiti games they were in again but had to forfeit points for two games.

The 1959 Cochiti games, set on Sunday, were to have been a doubleheader—the first game in the morning after Mass, the second in the afternoon before the kiva practice for the Corn Dance. Mysteriously, the Braves did not show up for the morning game. In an attempt to be friendly and accommodating, the Redskins agreed to play the game on the following Saturday. Several of their female relatives muttered that the game should have been claimed ("The men are too soft"). But the men were making a conscious, if nervous, effort to keep things going smoothly. Several said they would not watch the game: "They'll only fight, those ladies; they'll just yell and shout and upset everybody; people don't forget easily. They don't care about the game; they just want to fight and upset other people." Some predicted that "they won't speak to each other for a year or more," others that "they are just mad in the season, they forget it in the winter."

The Redskins' supporters could name only one Braves family that was consistently friendly with any Redskin family. Asked why this antagonism didn't exist between kivas, they said, "Why should it? They don't have nothing to fight about." But no one could explain why the antagonism was there in the first place—or no one was willing to risk the analysis for fear of reaching conclusions too unpleasant to bear about his beloved village. All the men agreed that it was the fault of "them old ladies. I guess they just like fighting."

The afternoon game was played in a fit of nerves. To lend weight to the authority of the council, both the governor and the lieutenant governor sat together, and the war captain and his assistant placed themselves strategically between the supporters of the two sides. The men of the village deliberately chose a neutral spot behind the wire and huddled there, while the women of the teams stood around their respective dugouts.

The game progressed in a lively fashion, the women gathering force as it went on. Their comments, at first mild—"Get him glasses, he can't see"; "He can't hit what he can't see; he's blind"—became bitter, personal, and finally obscene. The men, meanwhile, made polite comments and factual observations. At one point the women became so noisy that the Redskins' manager, at his team's request, had to hurry over to quiet them. This had no noticeable effect. However, the game passed without any unruly incident, although the players were so nervous they made a phenomenal number of errors. There was some relaxation of tension because there was a neutral umpire and because the game was never in doubt. The Redskins went into an early lead and won, 18 to 8. Everyone left the ball ground quickly. Irate old ladies were hustled away by sons and grandsons.

All the following week tension mounted toward the second game. Many declared they would stay away; others were just as sure they wouldn't miss it for anything. The latter were usually women. "There's going to be a lot of accidents," a Redskin mother said, " 'cause them Braves is sure mad they lost last Sunday." In the Corn Dance of midweek, opposing families had to dance together in the communal prayer for harmony and happiness. But Saturday morning the tension was high again. Many actually did stay away. Those that came watched mostly from inside their pickups and cars. Some Redskins had just returned from drinking in the local Spanish-American town of Peña Blanca. The lieutenant governor, not a regular fan, sat between the two blocks of women and invited me to join him.

I did not have long to wait. After the game had been tied up at 1 to 1 for four innings, the skies suddenly darkened, lightning flashed and thunder rolled, but no rain fell. A huge wind swept across the valley, lifting clouds of sand so that the whole field was obliterated. Players crouched down to avoid being binded by the stinging grains. I took refuge in a Redskin car, where it was quickly pointed out to me that if the other ground had been used (the Redskins') this would not have happened, because there was less loose soil there. But the Braves had insisted on using their own inferior ground, "so that they could work more of their magic." (Twice in the previous week I had been cautioned to watch out for their, the Braves', "magic.") I failed to see how this complete halt was to the Braves' advantage.

The game should have been stopped until the sand cleared, but the Braves insisted on continuing to play. They played between sharp bursts of wind, swirling sandstorms, and the crashing of thunder. And still no rain fell. Sun Chief says that if, instead of rain at the end of a *katsina* dance, only a strong wind blows, spreading sand, this shows that those who sent for the *katsinas* had done evil. This was the feeling at the Cochiti game, amid the storm clouds and dead dust and absence of rain. One Redskin going out to bat fell on his knees, crossed himself, and muttered a prayer.

There was a nonneutral umpire of the Redskin faction, but he was courting the daughter of a prominent Braves family. The only reason he was made umpire was that he was on leave from the Navy and so would be taking any bad feelings away with him when he left. He gave a faulty-seeming decision that cost the Redskins a base. Immediately the Redskin women called out to him: "Some of her dirt has rubbed off on you! She's got you under her skin, that girl." Among themselves they used epithets other than "girl," and muttered about "influences." But it stopped there; the umpire was the son of the lieutenant governor, whom no one wished to offend.

In between sandstorms the game continued; the score leveled to 2 to 2 at the bottom of the eighth inning. In the final innings the Redskins seemed to go to pieces as the sand lashed their faces, while the Braves hit two runs to win the game, 4 to 2. The players ran to shake hands, although some refused—an unheard-of thing in previous games. The male participants tried to keep things calm. The Braves women were screaming with delight at the victory of their side. The Redskin women went away tight-lipped and furious, convinced that dirty work had been done. The storm, the "influenced" umpire, the unaccountable reversal of the Redskins (an admittedly superior team under normal conditions), all added up to—witchcraft.

In the weeks following the games, rival families went about not speaking. About three weeks later, an incident occurred that reactivated the whole business. The Redskins had just lost a game and were returning home disconsolate when a Braves mother accosted one of them entering his house. The burden of her remarks seemed to be that he had lost the game because his love life was sapping his strength. All this was said in the presence of the Redskin's wife, who was furious but remained mute. The Redskin spat out a few replies and went indoors. The Braves mother had not finished, however; she stood on her own rooftop and hurled insults across at the neighbor. The Redskin took his whole family to the governor's house and asked for the council's protection against these onslaughts. That evening a council meeting was called, and, in typical Pueblo fashion, the combatants were told to shake hands and apologize to each other. An announcement was made to the pueblo to the effect that this antagonism over baseball would have to cease or the sport would be discontinued. This was a desparate measure and a test of the council's authority. The young people were not at all likely to give up baseball, whatever the council said. However, as harvest and winter approached and the baseball season drew to a close, hard feelings began to soften. There would be time during the winter to forget the summer's quarrels.

Competitive Western games that have been introduced into primitive societies have usually taken the place of more violent forms of competition. For example, football in New Guinea replaced intervillage spear-fighting. But baseball in the pueblos was a competitive intrusion into an essentially noncompetitive socal system. As long as competition remains between villages, no untoward events occur, as this is in line with tradition, but competition within villages is potentially destructive. Pueblo institutions are constructed to eliminate and nullify aggressive conflict by placing individuals in automatically determined, overlapping-role situations. The baseball teams, based on voluntary recruitment and stressing competition, allow the acting out of competitive and aggressive tendencies. The Pueblos have taken various steps to neutralize this effect but the participants seem just as bewildered by these steps as by the turn of events that necessitates them. Resort to naked authority in the settlement of interfamilial disputes is a new thing to Cochiti and, in a way, a confession of weakness in the social system, previously so ingeniously adequate to deal with conflict. It looks as if the male forces of authority and order may be able to keep the peace. But the women have married the old witch fears to the new sport and thus directed a whole body of deep-rooted motivations into new channels. When the tension is high, the old cry of "Witch!" flies from the women and long-suppressed rages are given full vent. Of course, it may prove therapeutic.

Part X

CONTINUITY AND CHANGE

In previous chapters we have considered some of the main methodological and conceptual elements of anthropology, discussed the principle human adaptive processes, examined the organizational patterns of human societies, and explored some of the ways humans strive to find meaning in life. We turn now (or, in a sense, return full circle) to themes touched upon briefly and in passing in other sections of the book but which are so important that they require separate treatment. These are the themes of continuity and change.

For many, the words "continuity" and "change" may seem to be antonyms. They seem to be two sides of a coin; as one goes up the other goes down. What could be more clear-cut in this era of rapid social change? Isn't it obvious that the more change there is, the less continuity there can be? Would it not, therefore, have been more appropriate to call Part X "Continuity *or* Change" rather than "Continuity *and* Change"? Although evidence could be marshaled in support of a positive answer, I think the better answer is "no." This view rests on several assumptions. In the first place, change is not a new phenomenon; it is now and always has been a fact of human social life. Second, although the rate of change is accelerating, continuity does not rise or fall simply as a function of rate of change. But most importantly, this view emphasizes the contrast between "authentic change"—that is, change which builds on the past—and change which is alien and unauthentic. In a very real sense, continuity itself is a type of change. It is change that builds on the past—not the general past that underlies change in any evolving system, but the specific remembered past that is so relevant to any group of people. The urgent problem today, therefore, is not "simply" one of understanding and controlling change (although this should be done), but of maximizing continuity—authentic change. In part, then, the five cases which follow illustrate the extent to which changes faced by people in most societies are "authentic." As will be seen, continuity—i.e., authentic change—is a comparatively rare phenomenon.

371

MONEY

In 1944, the economist Karl Polanyi wrote a very significant book called *The Great Transformation*. Although it continues to be controversial, one of the central theses in it is very relevant to the first case of social change to be considered—Paul Bohannan's description of the impact of money on an African subsistence economy (Chapter 30). This particular thesis suggests that at a certain point, namely when market principles of exchange become firmly established in a society, there is a transformation in the nature of social life which is not simply a matter of degree but of a fundamental kind. The change is so sweeping and fundamental that the very fabric of social life is forever changed. Re-stated in terms of authenticity, we may say that even though such a transformation may seem to be based on a specific local context, it is so radical that whatever authenticity it may have pales beside its scope and impact.

One major element of any full-scale market economy is "money." As Bohannan reminds us at the beginning of his essay, money has several purposes, although not all known forms of money serve all these purposes. Those that do are termed "general purpose" monies; those that do not are termed "special purpose" monies. Perhaps the most important function of money is to serve as a "medium" of exchange. To serve this purpose, all parties to the exchange must agree that the item being exchanged for money can be priced in terms of it. The range of things which can be priced in terms of a particular form of money varies greatly from society to society. In the case of the Tiv, as described by Bohannan, the various forms of money were limited in the range of things they could price. Indeed, the limits were so great it could be said the Tiv had a "multi-centric" economy, with each sphere being essentially separate from the other and each involving different pricing traditions.

Of particular importance in this system was the exchange of items in the highest ranking sphere, the "item" being women. Women were exchanged for marriage purposes and if it could be said they were "priced" at all, it was in terms of other women. But with the introduction of western, general purpose money, and a general increase in trade, the separate spheres were merged into one since all the items in all the spheres were priced in terms of the same money. As a result, it became possible (indeed, it was impossible to do otherwise) to price women in the same terms that one priced red peppers. The distortions this change introduced into Tiv social life in general were enormous. Truly, as Bohannan notes, "Money is one of the shatteringly simplifying ideas of all time." And, it would seem, for most people money is not primarily simplifying; it is "simply" shattering.

CARGO

An old science fiction film depicts what happens "When Worlds Collide." In a sense, Peter Worsley's essay in Chapter 31 is about an equally dramatic collision, only this time it is two cultures worlds apart. In New Guinea, and elsewhere, many people respond to rapid, sweeping, and, in a very real sense, unauthentic change, by developing complex millenial religious and political organizations of the type described by Worsley. The behavior of the members of these movements seems, at first glance, to be completely irrational. At best the men in the "control tower" would seem to be stone-age victims of "future shock." And for many, their behavior only confirms deeply held suspicions that "primitive" people really are incapable of understanding how the "civilized" world produces all that "cargo." But is this really the central implication of their behavior? Might it not be that the whole exploitative situation they are faced with is perfectly clear to them and, since they are powerless to do anything about it, they struggle in the best way they know how to make sense out of nonsense?

STEEL

The experience of the Mohawk, as described by Morris Freilich in Chapter 32, offers a striking contrast to the experiences of the Tiv and of the people of New Guinea described by Worsley. Why? Why should the Mohawk shift from hunting and warfare to climbing on high structural steel? What greater shift is there than hunters becoming steel workers? If worlds have ever collided, the world of the Mohawk hunters and bridge-building hardhats would seem to be it. The solution to this seeming paradox is that the demands on men working in high structural steel are not so very different from the demands of traditional Mohawk life. The change was rapid and great but it was also authentic. As Freilich puts it, "participation in the structural steel industry enabled the Mohawks to closely duplicate their pre-reservation period social structure." In a word, the values necessary for a successful life making steel bridges and buildings were nearly the same as those necessary for a successful life making war and hunting—at least the way the Mohawks did these things. The result is successful, rapid, sweeping authentic change.

SISAL

Often, many areas of the rapidly changing world seem to be faced with only two choices, one of them bad and the other worse (and neither of them very authentic). The discussion of the "great" sisal project in Brazil by Daniel Gross in Chapter 33 illustrates this all too well. For the people of the *sertão,* the semi-arid region in northeast Brazil, the choice seemed to be between sticking with traditional subsistence agriculture and face periodic famines or grow a cash crop and face continual fluctuations in world prices and malnutrition.

Traditionally, the cowboys of the *sertão* could put together a life—a civilization of leather, as Gross calls it—in this remote and difficult part of Brazil by hard work and a willingness to adjust to shifts in climatic conditions. But the advantages of this lifestyle were too meager to argue against accepting a new life in search of Brazil's green gold—sisal. But as with so many other development projects, the full picture was only dimly perceived, if at all. The work was dangerous, the market conditions were highly variable, the crop made turning back to subsistence farming almost physically impossible, and the production process, in order to be competitive, was almost inherently exploitative. As a result what started as a boon soon became a bust. Standards of living did not rise; indeed, standards of eating and health fell. Was this an "authentic" change? What could have been done to make it so, if anything?

WRETCHED

The last essay in Part X—which is the concluding chapter in Frantz Fanon's masterpiece, *The Wretched of the Earth*—is a complex of emotions and ideas which in many ways summarize the mix of negative frustration and positive assertion that is so predominant in much of the Third World. We have said that change is ever-present. But only recently has the pressure to change come from a single source as powerful as the industrial west. Fanon speaks for millions when he asserts that there are better things to do than follow the pathway blazed by the west. Can the people of the Third World accept themselves, he asks, if all they do with the opportunities and challenges before them is create yet a third Europe (America being the second)? And, he is quick to remind us, if there is to be a new direction, if the stasis of the west is to be left behind, it will not be achieved by returning to "Nature." Rather, and more concretely, it is a matter of "not dragging men toward mutilation, of not imposing upon the brain rhythms which very quickly obliterate it and wreck it." It is, in our terms, a search for a fundamentally new but still authentic direction. The goal is to go forward, not from the foundations laid by the west, but from those nurtured in other parts of the world. Whether or not this can be done remains to be seen, but it may well be that if they do not succeed, we all, together, will fail altogether.

AMERICA

Before turning to the essays in Part X, we must consider some very pernicious themes which are explicit in some and implicit in most discussions of sociocultural change. These themes have their roots, apparently, in many facets of the American ethos, especially as it pertains to our notions of "progress" in general and economic development in particular. To begin to see what these themes are and to appreciate how they can influence our reactions to the case material presented here (and elsewhere), we may recall how these themes were expressed in the social sciences in the 1960s.

In the 1960s, social scientists by the hundreds (including me) went to all parts of the world to find out how the less developed societies were "modernizing." Then, as now, the word "modern" had several meanings, but in most renderings, it was suggested that modern societies were populated by people who desired rapid and continual change, who readily accepted change, and who even felt a kind of urgency regarding the importance of change. It was assumed (and still is for all anyone can tell) that the Third World was not modern but that America was. As a corollary, it was suggested that the values, attitudes and beliefs of people in the Third World led to their non-modern behavior and that if these beliefs were to change they would become more receptive to change (i.e., more modern). In this, too, America was the implicit (if not explicit) model.

But is it correct to say that the people of the Third World find themselves in the position they do because of the attitudes and beliefs they hold? Is it correct, even, to say that they have resisted change, or that they tend to resist change more than is typical of "modern" Americans? And more fundamentally, do Americans exhibit any greater willingness to accept change when those changes are comparable to those being brought *to* the Third World? And how do Americans accept change that is brought *to* them? These are questions which are difficult to answer with precision and to the satisfaction of all, but consider the following observations when working to reach your own conclusions.

In the cases presented in Part X and in other parts of this book (as well as in whole libraries of anthropological case material), one can see examples of very fundamental changes of all kinds being accepted by peoples throughout the Third World. These changes, which seem to come in clusters rather than singly, are accepted only with difficulty in many cases. But change can be very difficult (perhaps it is generally); are we to equate difficulty with resistance? To answer this, we must consider the kinds of changes we are talking about. In recent years in the Third World, these have involved changes in such things as language, government, monetary systems, land-owning policies, marital practices, dispute settlement procedures, law, educational practices, kinship rules, interpersonal relationship norms, subsistence activities, counting systems, weights and measures, time reckoning standards, and religion—to name but the most prominent. Should people faced with such changes even be judged as to whether they are "resistant"? And if they accept these changes, as millions of people have, can they possibly be called resistant?

When, in the last century or so, have Americans faced comparable changes? How do Americans react, for example, to suggestions about changing to the metric system for weights and measures? How do Americans react when it is suggested that we change our mode of transportation to and from work? How do Americans react when they are urged to reduce energy consumption or children production? How do Americans react when courts order changes in the schools children should attend? And how would Americans react if they were made to feel, as so many millions of people have felt as a result of European and American behavior abroad, that their language, political system, marital practices, laws, money system, religions, and so on were inferior and should be replaced by other institutions? How are American men reacting to the shift in power between the sexes? Are there really that many differences between the newly "liberated men" in the cities of Africa and their counterparts in the bedroom suburbs of America?

And finally and perhaps most tellingly, how are Americans reacting to the "infusion" (as we call it nowadays) of Third World capital into American business and industry? How do the captains of industry and molders of opinion in the media suggest we should respond to this sudden inflow of capital? With open arms? Receptively? The sad fact appears to be that the Americans who are most committed to the notion that the people of the Third World are resistant to change, backward, inhospitable, suspicious and uninterested in development are the very same Americans who are themselves resistant to internal change, and are inhospitable to and suspicious of foreign investors. Who, in the final analysis, is receptive to change and who is not?

Paul Bohannan

30. The Impact of Money on an African Subsistence Economy*

It has often been claimed that money was to be found in much of the African continent before the impact of the European world and the extension of trade made coinage general. When we examine these claims, however, they tend to evaporate or to emerge as tricks of definition. It is an astounding fact that economists have, for decades, been assigning three or four qualities to money when they discuss it with reference to our own society or to those of the medieval and modern world, yet the moment they have gone to ancient history or to the societies and economies studied by anthropologists they have sought the "real" nature of money by allowing only one of these defining characteristics to dominate their definitions.

All economists learned as students that money serves at least three purposes. It is a means of exchange, it is a mode of payment, it is a standard of value. Depending on the vintage and persuasion of the author of the book one consults, one may find another money use—storage of wealth. In newer books, money is defined as merely the means of unitizing the purchasing power, yet behind that definition still lie the standard, the payment, and the exchange uses of money.

It is interesting that on the fairly rare occasions that economists discuss primitive money at all—or at least when they discuss it with any empirical referent—they have discarded one or more of the money uses in framing

* Reprinted with permission of the author and the Economic History Association from *The Journal of Economic History*, vol. 19, 1959:491–503.

their definitions. Paul Einzing (1949:319–26), to take one example for many, first makes a plea for "elastic definitions," and goes on to point out that different economists have utilized different criteria in their definitions; he then falls into the trap he has been exposing: he excoriates Menger for utilizing only the "medium of exchange" criterion and then himselfs omits it, utilizing only the standard and payment criteria, thus taking sides in an argument in which there was no real issue.

The answer to these difficulties should be apparent. If we take no more than the three major money uses—payment, standard and means of exchange—we will find that in many primitive societies as well as in some of the ancient empires, one object may serve one money use while quite another object serves another money use. In order to deal with this situation, and to avoid the trap of choosing one of these uses to define "real" money, Karl Polanyi (1957:264–66) and his associates have labeled as "general purpose money" any item which serves all three of these primary money uses, while an item which serves only one or two is "special purpose money." With this distinction in mind, we can see that special-purpose money was very common in pre-contact Africa, but that general purpose money was rare.

This paper is a brief analysis of the impact of general purpose money and increase in trade in an African economy which had known only local trade and had used only special purpose money.

The Tiv are a people, still largely pagan, who live in the Benue Valley in central Nigeria, among whom I had the good fortune to live and work for well over two years. They are prosperous subsistence farmers and have a highly developed indigenous market in which they exchanged their produce and handicrafts, and through which they carried on local trade. The most distinctive feature about the economy of the Tiv—and it is a feature they share with many, perhaps most, of the pre-monetary peoples—is what can be called a multi-centric economy. Briefly, a multi-centric economy is an economy in which a society's exchangeable goods fall into two or more mutually exclusive spheres, each marked by different institutionalization and different moral values. In some multi-centric economies these spheres remain distinct, though in most there are more or less institutionalized means of converting wealth from one into wealth in another.

Indigenously there were three spheres in the multi-centric economy of the Tiv. The first of these spheres is that associated with subsistence, which the Tiv call *yiagh*. The commodities in it include all locally produced foodstuffs: the staple yams and cereals, plus all the condiments, vegetable side-dishes and seasonings, as well as small livestock—chickens, goats and sheep. It also includes household utensils (mortars, grindstones, calabashes, baskets and pots), some tools (particularly those used in agriculture), and raw materials for producing any items in the category.

Within this sphere, goods are distributed either by gift giving or through marketing. Traditionally, there was no money of any sort in this sphere—all goods changed hands by barter. There was a highly developed market organization at which people exchanged their produce for their requirements, and in which today traders buy produce in cheap markets and transport it to sell in dearer markets. The morality of this sphere of the economy is the morality of the free and uncontrolled market.

The second sphere of the Tiv economy is one which is in no way associated with markets. The category of goods within this sphere is slaves, cattle, ritual "offices" purchased from the Jukun, that type of large white cloth known as *tugudu,* medicines and magic, and metal rods. One is still entitled to use the present tense in this case, for ideally the category still exists in spite of the fact that metal rods are today very rare, that slavery has been abolished, that European "offices" have replaced Jukun offices and cannot be bought, and that much European medicine has been accepted. Tiv still quote prices of slaves in cows and brass rods, and of cattle in brass rods and *tugudu* cloth. The price of magical rites, as it has been described in the literature, was in terms of *tugudu* cloth or brass rods (though payment might be made in other items); payment for Jukun titles was in cows and slaves, *tugudu* cloths and metal rods (B. Akiga Sai 1939: 382 and passim).

None of these goods ever entered the market as it was institutionalized in Tivland, even though it might be possible for an economist to find the principle of supply and demand at work in the exchanges which characterized it. The actual shifts of goods took place at ceremonies, at more or less ritualized wealth displays, and on occasions when "doctors" performed rites and prescribed medicines. Tiv refer to the items and the activities within this sphere by the word *shagba,* which can be roughly translated as prestige.

Within the prestige sphere there was one item which took on all of the money uses and hence can be called a general-purpose currency, though it must be remembered that it was of only a *very limited range.* Brass rods were used as means of exchange *within the sphere;* they also served as a standard of value within it (though not the only one), and as a means of payment. However, this sphere of the economy was tightly sealed off from the subsistence goods and its market. After European contact, brass rods occasionally entered the market, but they did so only as means of payment, not as medium of exchange or as standard of valuation. Because of the complex institutionalization and morality, no one ever sold a slave for food; no one, save in the depths of extremity, ever paid brass rods for domestic goods.

The supreme and unique sphere of exchangeable values for the Tiv contains a single item: rights in human beings other than slaves, particularly rights in women. Even twenty-five years after official abolition of exchange marriage, it is the category of exchange in which Tiv are emotionally most entangled. All exchanges within this category are exchanges of rights in human beings, usually dependent women and children. Its values are expressed in terms of kinship and marriage.

Tiv marriage is an extremely complex subject (see Akiga 1939:120–27; Laura and Paul Bohannan 1953:69–78 and 1958:384–444). Again, economists might find supply and demand principles at work, but Tiv adamantly separate marriage and market. Before the coming of the Europeans all "real" marriages were exchange marriages. In its simplest form, an exchange marriage involves two men exchanging sisters. Actually, this simple form seldom or never occurred. In order for every man to have a ward (*ingol*) to exchange for a wife, small localized agnatic lineages formed ward-sharing groups ("those who eat one Ingol"—*mbaye ingol i mom*). There was an initial "exchange"—or at least, distribution—of wards among the men of this group, so that each man became the guardian (*tien*) of one or more wards. The guardian, then, saw to the marriage of his ward, exchanging her with outsiders for another woman (her "partner" or *ikyar*) who becomes the bride of the guardian or one of his close agnatic kinsmen, or—in some situations—becomes a ward in the ward-sharing group and is exchanged for yet another woman who becomes a wife.

Tiv are, however, extremely practical and sensible people, and they know that successful marriages cannot be made if women are not consulted and if they are not happy. Elopements occurred, and sometimes a woman in exchange was not forthcoming. Therefore, a debt existed from the ward-sharing group of the husband to that of the guardian.

These debts sometimes lagged two or even three generations behind actual exchanges. The simplest way of paying them off was for the oldest daughter of the marriage to return to the ward-sharing group of her mother, as ward, thus cancelling the debt.

Because of its many impracticalities, the system had to be buttressed in several ways in order to work: one way was a provision for "earnest" during the time of the lag, another was to recognize other types of marriage as binding to limited extents. These two elements are somewhat confused with one another, because of the fact that right up until the abolition of exchange marriage in 1927, the inclination was always to treat all nonexchange marriages as if they were "lags" in the completion of exchange marriages.

When lags in exchange occurred, they were usually filled with "earnests" of brass rods or, occasionally, it would seem, of cattle. The brass rods or cattle in such situations were *never* exchange equivalents (*ishe*) for the woman. The only "price" of one woman is another woman.

Although Tiv decline to grant it antiquity, another type of marriage occurred at the time Europeans first met them—it was called "accumulating a woman/wife" (*kem kwase*). It is difficult to tell today just exactly what it consisted in, because the terminology of this union has been adapted to describe the bridewealth marriage that was declared by an administrative fiat of 1927 to be the only legal form.

Kem marriage consisted in acquisition of sexual, domestic and economic rights in a woman—but not the rights to filiate her children to the social group of the husband. Put in another way, in exchange marriage, both rights *in genetricem* (rights to filiate a woman's children) and rights *in uxorem* (sexual, domestic and economic rights in a woman) automatically were acquired by husbands and their lineages (Laura Bohannan 1949:273–87). In *kem* marriage, only rights *in uxorem* were acquired. In order to affiliate the *kem* wife's children, additional payments had to be made to the woman's guardians. These payments were for the children, not for the rights *in genetricem* in their mother, which could be acquired only by exchange of equivalent rights in another woman. *Kem* payments were paid in brass rods. However, rights in women had no equivalent or "price" in brass rods or in any other item—save, of course, identical rights in another woman. *Kem* marriage was similar to but showed important differences from bridewealth marriage as it is known in South and East Africa. There rights in women and rights in cattle form a single economic sphere, and could be exchanged directly for one another. Among Tiv, however, conveyance of rights in women necessarily involved direct exchange of another woman. The Tiv custom that approached bridewealth was not an exchange of equivalents, but payment in a medium that was specifically not equivalent.

Thus, within the sphere of exchange marriage there was no item that fulfilled any of the uses of money; when second-best types of marriage were made, payment was in an item which was specifically not used as a standard of value.

That Tiv do conceptualize exchange articles as belonging to different categories, and that they rank the categories on a moral basis, and that most but not all exchanges are limited to one sphere, gives rise to the fact that two different kinds of exchanges may be recognized: exchange of items contained within a single category, and exchanges of items belonging to different categories. For Tiv, these two different types of exchange are marked by separate and distinct moral attitudes.

To maintain this distinction between the two types of exchanges which Tiv mark by different behavior and different values, I shall use separate words. I shall call those exchanges of items within a single category "conveyances" and those exchanges of items from one category to another "conversions" (Steiner 1954:118–29). Roughly, conveyances are morally neutral; conversions have a strong moral quality in their rationalization.

Exchanges within a category—particularly that of subsistence, the only one intact today—excite no moral judgments. Exchanges between categories, however, do excite a moral reaction: the man who exchanges lower category goods for higher category goods does not brag about his market luck but about his "strong heart" and his success in life. The man who exchanges high category goods for lower rationalizes his action in terms of high-valued motivation (most often the needs of his kinsmen).

The two institutions most intimately connected with conveyance are markets and marriage. Conveyance in the prestige sphere seems (to the latter-day investigator, at least) to have been less highly institutionalized. It centered on slave dealing, on curing and on the acquisition of status.

Conversion is a much more complex matter. Conversion depends on the fact that some items of every sphere could, on certain occasions, be used in exchanges in which the return was *not* considered equivalent (*ishe*). Obviously, given the moral ranking of the spheres, such a situation leaves one party to the exchange in a good position, and the other in bad one. Tiv say that it is "good" to trade food for brass rods, but that it is "bad" to trade brass rods for food, that it is good to trade your cows or brass rods for a wife, but very bad to trade your marriage ward for cows or brass rods.

Seen from the individual's point of view, it is profitable and possible to invest one's wealth if one converts it into a morally superior category: to convert subsistence wealth into prestige wealth and both into women is the aim of the economic endeavor or individual Tiv. To put it into economists' terms: conversion is the ultimate type of maximization.

We have already examined the marriage system by which a man could convert his brass rods to a wife: he could get a *kem* wife and *kem* her children as they were born. Her daughters, then, could be used as wards in his exchange marriages. It is the desire of every Tiv to "acquire a woman" (*ngoho kwase*) either as wife or ward in some way other than sharing in the ward-sharing group. A wife whom one acquires in any other way is not the concern of one's marriage-ward sharing group because the woman or other property exchanged for her did not belong to the marriage-ward group. The daughters of such a wife are not divided among the members of a man's marriage-ward group, but only among his sons. Such a wife is not only indicative of a man's ability and success financially and personally, but rights in her are the only form of property which is not ethically subject to the demands of his kinsmen.

Conversion from the prestige sphere to the kinship sphere was, thus, fairly common; it consisted in all the forms of marriage save exchange marriage, usually in terms of brass rods.

Conversion from the subsistence sphere to the prestige sphere was also usually in terms of metal rods. They, on occasion, entered the market place as payment. If the owner of the brass rods required an unusually large amount of staples to give a feast, making too heavy a drain on his wives' food supplies, he might buy it with brass rods.

However, brass rods could not possibly have been a general currency.

They were not divisible. One could not receive "change" from a brass rod. Moreover, a single rod was worth much more than the usual market purchases for any given day of most Tiv subsistence traders. Although it might be possible to buy chickens with brass rods, one would have to have bought a very large quantity of yams to equal one rod, and to buy an item like pepper with rods would be laughable.

Brass rods, thus, overlapped from the prestige to the subsistence sphere on some occasions, but only on special occasions and for large purchases.

Not only is conversion possible, but it is encouraged—it is, in fact, the behavior which proves a man's worth. Tiv are scornful of a man who is merely rich in subsistence goods (or, today, in money). If, having adequate subsistence, he does not seek prestige in accordance with the old counters, or if he does not strive for more wives, and hence more children, the fault must be personal inadequacy. They also note that they all try to keep a man from making conversions; jealous kinsmen of a rich man will bewitch him and his people by fetishes, in order to make him expend his wealth on sacrifices to repair the fetishes, thus maintaining economic equality. However, once a conversion has been made, demands of kinsmen are not effective—at least, they take a new form.

Therefore, the man who successfully converts his wealth into higher categories is successful—he has a "strong heart." He is both feared and respected.

In this entire process, metal rods hold a pivotal position, and it is not surprising that early administrators considered them money. Originally imported from Europe, they were used as "currency" in some part of southern Nigeria in the slave trade. They are dowels about a quarter of an inch in diameter and some three feet long; they can be made into jewelry, and were used as a source of metal for castings.

Whatever their use elsewhere, brass rods in Tivland had some but not all of the attributes of money. Within the prestige sphere, they were used as a standard of equivalence, and they were a medium of exchange; they were also a mode for storage of wealth, and were used as payment. In short, brass rods were a general purpose currency *within the prestige sphere*. However, outside of the prestige sphere—markets and marriage were the most active institutions of exchange outside it—brass rods fulfilled only one of these functions of money: payment. We have examined in detail the reasons why equivalency could not exist between brass rods and rights in women, between brass rods and food.

We have, thus, in Tivland, a multi-centric economy of three spheres, and we have a sort of money which was a general purpose money within the limited range of the prestige sphere, and a special purpose money in the special transactions in which the other spheres overlapped it.

The next question is: what happened to this multi-centric economy and to the morality accompanying it when it felt the impact of the expanding European economy in the 19th and early 20th centuries, and when an all-purpose money of very much greater range was introduced?

The Western impact is not, of course, limited to economic institutions. Administrative organizations, missions and others have been as effective instruments of change as any other.

One of the most startling innovations of the British administration was a general peace. Before the arrival of the British, one did not venture far beyond the area of one's kinsmen or special friends. To do so was to court death or enslavement.

With government police systems and safety, road building was also begun. Moving about the country has been made both safe and comparatively easy. Peace and the new road network led to both increased trade and a greater number of markets.

Not only has the internal marketing system been perturbed by the introduction of alien institutions, but the economic institutions of the Tiv have in fact been put into touch with world economy. Northern Nigeria, like much of the rest of the colonial world, was originally taken over by trading companies with governing powers. The close linkage of government and trade was evident when taxation was introduced into Tivland. Tax was originally paid in produce, which was transported and sold through Hausa traders, who were government contractors. A few years later, coinage was introduced; taxes were demanded in that medium. It became necessary for Tiv to go into trade or to make their own contract with foreign traders in order to get cash. The trading companies, which had had "canteens" on the Benue for some decades, were quick to cooperate with the government in introducing a "cash crop" which could be bought by the traders in return for cash to pay taxes, and incidentally to buy imported goods. The crop which proved best adapted for this purpose in Tivland was beniseed (*sesamum indicum*), a crop Tiv already grew in small quanities. Acreage need only be increased and facilities for sale established.

There is still another way in which Tiv economy is linked, through the trading companies, to the economy of the outside world. Not only do the companies buy their cash crops, they also "stake" African traders with imported goods. There is, on the part both of the companies and the government, a desire to build up "native entrepreneurial classes." Imported cloth, enamelware and ironmongery are generally sold through a network of dependent African traders. Thus, African traders are linked to the companies, and hence into international trade.

Probably no single factor has been so important, however, as the introduction of all-purpose money. Neither introduction of cash crops and taxes nor extended trading has affected the basic congruence between Tiv ideas and their institutionalization to the same extent as has money. With the introduction of money the indigenous ideas of maximization—that is, conversion of all forms of wealth into women and children—no longer leads to the result it once did.

General purpose money provides a common denominator among all the spheres, thus making the commodities within each expressible in terms of a single standard and hence immediately exchangeable. This new money is misunderstood by Tiv. They use it as a standard of value in the subsistence category, even when—as is often the case—the exchange is direct barter. They use it as a means of payment of bridewealth under the new system, but still refuse to admit that a woman has a "price" or can be valued in the same terms as food. At the same time, it has become something formerly lacking in all save the prestige sphere of Tiv economy—a means of exchange. Tiv have tried to categorize money with the other new imported goods and place them all in a fourth economic sphere, to be ranked morally below subsistence. They have, of course, not been successful in so doing.

What in fact happened was that general purpose money was introduced to Tivland, where formerly only special purpose money had been known.

It is in the nature of a general purpose money that it standardizes the exchangeability value of every item to a common scale. It is precisely this function which brass rods, a "limited-purpose money" in the old system, did not perform. As we have seen, brass rods were used as a standard in some situations of conveyance in the intermediate or "prestige" category. They were also used as a means of payment (but specifically not as a standard) in some instances of conversion.

In this situation, the early Administrative officers interpreted brass rods as "money," by which they mean a general-purpose money. It became a fairly easy process, in their view, to establish by fiat an exchange rate between brass rods and a new coinage, "withdraw" the rods, and hence "replace" one currency with another. The actual effect, as we have seen, was to introduce a general purpose currency in place of a limited purpose money. Today all conversions and most conveyances are made in terms of coinage. Yet Tiv constantly express their distrust of money. This fact, and another—that a single means of exchange has entered all the economic spheres—has broken down the major distinctions among the spheres. Money has created in Tivland a unicentric economy. Not only is the money a general-purpose money, but it applies to the full range of exchangeable goods.

Thus, when semi-professional traders, using money, began trading in the foodstuffs marketed by women and formerly solely the province of women, the range of the market was very greatly increased and hence the price in Tiv markets is determined by supply and demand far distant from the local producer and consumer. Tiv react to this situation by saying that foreign traders "spoil" their markets. The overlap of marketing and men's long-distance trade in staples also results in truckload after truckload of

foodstuffs exported from major Tiv markets every day they meet. Tiv say
that food is less plentiful today than it was in the past, though more land
is being farmed. Tiv elders deplore this situation and know what is happening, but they do not know just where to fix the blame. In attempts to do
something about it, they sometimes announce that no women are to sell
any food at all. But when their wives disobey them, men do not really feel
that they were wrong to have done so. Tiv sometimes discriminate against
non-Tiv traders in attempts to stop export of food. In their condemnation
of the situation which is depriving them of their food faster than they are
able to increase production, Tiv elders always curse money itself. It is
money which, as the instrument for selling one's life subsistence, is responsible for the worsened situation—money and the Europeans who brought it.

Of even greater concern to Tiv is the influence money has had on marriage institutions. Today every woman's guardian, in accepting money as
bridewealth, feels that he is converting down. Although attempts are made
to spend money which is received in bridewealth to acquire brides for one's
self and one's sons, it is in the nature of money, Tiv insist, that it is most
difficult to accomplish. The good man still spends his bridewealth receipts
for brides—but good men are not so numerous as would be desirable. Tiv
deplore the fact that they are required to "sell" (*te*) their daughters and
"buy" (*yam*) wives. There is no dignity in it since the possibility of making
a bridewealth marriage into an exchange marriage has been removed.

With money, thus, the institutionalization of Tiv economy has become
unicentric, even though Tiv still see it with multicentric values. The single
sphere takes many of its characteristics from the market, so that the new
situation can be considered a spread of the market. But throughout these
changes in institutionalization, the basic Tiv value of maximization—converting one's wealth into the highest category, women and children—has
remained. And in this discrepancy between values and institutions, Tiv
have come upon what is to them a paradox, for all that Westerners understand it and are familiar with it. Today it is easy to sell subsistence goods
for money to buy prestige articles and women, thereby aggrandizing oneself
at a rapid rate. The food so sold is exported, decreasing the amount of subsistence goods available for consumption. On the other hand, the number
of women is limited. The result is that bridewealth gets higher: rights in
women have entered the market, and since the supply is fixed, the price of
women has become inflated.

The frame of reference given me by the organizer of this symposium
asked for comments on the effects of increased monetization on trade, on
the distribution of wealth and indebtedness. To sum up the situation in
these terms, trade has vastly increased with the introduction of general
purpose money but also with the other factors brought by a colonial form
of government. At the same time, the market has expanded its range of
applicability in the society. The Tiv are, indigenously, a people who valued

egalitarian distribution of wealth to the extent that they believed they bewitched one another to whittle down the wealth of one man to the size of that of another. With money, the degree and extent of differentiation by wealth has greatly increased and will probably continue to increase. Finally, money has brought a new form of indebtedness—one which we know, only too well. In the indigenous system, debt took either the form of owing marriage wards and was hence congruent with the kinship system, or else took the form of decreased prestige. There was no debt in the sphere of subsistence because there was no credit there save among kinsmen and neighbors whose activities were aspects of family status, not acts of moneylenders. The introduction of general purpose money and the concomitant spread of the market has divorced debt from kinship and status and has created the notion of debt in the subsistence sphere divorced from the activities of kinsmen and neighbors.

In short, because of the spread of the market and the introduction of general-purpose money, Tiv economy has become a part of the world economy. It has brought about profound changes in the institutionalization of Tiv society. Money is one of the shatteringly simplifying ideas of all time, and like any other new and compelling idea, it creates its own revolution. The monetary revolution, at least in this part of Africa, is the turn away from the multicentric economy. Its course may be painful, but there is very little doubt about its outcome.

Peter M. Worsley

31. Cargo Cults*

Patrols of the Australian Government venturing into the "uncontrolled" central highlands of New Guinea in 1946 found the primitive people there swept up in a wave of religious excitement. Prophecy was being fulfilled: The arrival of the Whites was the sign that the end of the world was at hand. The natives proceeded to butcher all of their pigs—animals that were not only a principal source of subsistence but also symbols of social status and ritual preeminence in their culture. They killed these valued animals in expression of the belief that after three days of darkness "Great Pigs" would appear from the sky. Food, firewood and other necessities had to be stock-piled to see the people through to the arrival of the Great Pigs. Mock wireless antennae of bamboo and rope had been erected to receive in advance the news of the millennium. Many believed that with the great event they would exchange their black skins for white ones.

This bizarre episode is by no means the single event of its kind in the murky history of the collision of European civilization with the indigenous cultures of the southwest Pacific. For more than 100 years traders and missionaries have been reporting similar disturbances among the people of Melanesia, the group of Negro-inhabited islands (including New Guinea, Fiji, the Solomons and the New Hebrides) lying between Australia and the open Pacific Ocean. Though their technologies were based largely upon bone and wood, these peoples had highly developed cultures, as measured by the standards of maritime and agricultural ingenuity, the complexity of their varied social organizations and the elaboration of religious belief and ritual. They were nonetheless ill prepared for the shock of the encounter with the Whites, a people so radically different from themselves and so infinitely more powerful. The sudden transition from the society of the ceremonial stone ax to the society of sailing ships and now of airplanes has not been easy to make.

After four centuries of Western expansion, the densely populated central highlands of New Guinea remain one of the few regions where the people still carry on their primitive existence in complete independence of the world outside. Yet as the agents of the Australian Government penetrate into ever more remote mountain valleys, they find these backwaters of antiquity already deeply disturbed by contact with the ideas and artifacts of European civilization. For "cargo"—Pidgin English for trade goods— has long flowed along the indigenous channels of communication from the seacoast into the wilderness. With it has traveled the frightening knowledge of the white man's magical power. No small element in the white man's magic is the hopeful message sent abroad by his missionaries: the news that a Messiah will come and that the present order of Creation will end.

The people of the central highlands of New Guinea are only the latest to be gripped in the recurrent religious frenzy of the "cargo cults." However variously embellished with details from native myth and Christian belief, these cults all advance the same central theme: the world is about to end in a terrible cataclysm. Thereafter God, the ancestors or some local culture hero will appear and inaugurate a blissful paradise on earth. Death, old age, illness and evil will be unknown. The riches of the white man will accrue to the Melanesians.

Although the news of such a movement in one area has doubtless often inspired similar movements in other areas, the evidence indicates that these cults have arisen independently in many places as parallel responses to the same enormous social stress and strain. Among the movements best known to students of Melanesia are the "Taro Cult" of New Guinea, the "Vailala Madness" of Papua, the "Naked Cult" of Espiritu Santo, the "John Frum Movement" of the New Hebrides and the "Tuka Cult" of the Fiji Islands.

At times the cults have been so well organized and fanatically persistent that they have brought the work of government to a standstill. The outbreaks have often taken the authorities completely by surprise and have confronted them with mass opposition of an alarming kind. In the 1930s, for example, villagers in the vicinity of Wewak, New Guinea, were stirred by a succession of "Black King" movements. The prophets announced that the Europeans would soon leave the island, abandoning their property to the natives, and urged their followers to cease paying taxes, since the government station was about to disappear into the sea in a great earthquake. To the tiny community of Whites in charge of the region, such talk was dangerous. The authorities jailed four of the prophets and exiled three others. In yet another movement, that sprang up in declared opposition to the local Christian mission, the cult leader took Satan as his god.

Troops on both sides in World War II found their arrival in Melanesia heralded as a sign of the Apocalypse. The G.I.'s who landed in the New Hebrides, moving up for the bloody fighting on Guadalcanal, found the natives furiously at work preparing airfields, roads and docks for the magic ships and planes that they believed were coming from "Rusefel" (Roosevelt), the friendly king of America.

The Japanese also encountered millenarian visionaries during their southward march to Guadalcanal. Indeed, one of the strangest minor military actions of World War II occurred in Dutch New Guinea, when Japanese forces had to be turned against the local Papuan inhabitants of the Geelvink Bay region. The Japanese had at first been received with great joy, not because their "Greater East Asia Co-Prosperity Sphere" propaganda had made any great impact upon the Papuans, but because the natives regarded them as harbingers of the new world that was dawning, the flight of the Dutch having already given the first sign. Mansren, creator of the islands and their peoples, would now return, bringing with him the ancestral dead. All this had been known, the cult leaders declared, to the crafty Dutch, who had torn out the first page of the Bible where these truths were inscribed. When Mansren returned, the existing world order would be entirely overturned. White men would turn black like Papuans. Papuans would become Whites; root crops would grow in trees, and coconuts and fruits would grow like tubers. Some of the islanders now began to draw together into large "towns"; others took Biblical names such as "Jericho" and "Galilee" for their villages. Soon they adopted military uniforms and began drilling. The Japanese, by now highly unpopular, tried to disarm and disperse the Papuans; resistance inevitably developed. The climax of this tragedy came when several canoe-loads of fanatics sailed out to attack Japanese warships, believing themselves to be invulnerable by virtue of the holy water with which they had sprinkled themselves. But the bullets of the Japanese did not turn to water, and the attackers were mowed down by machine-gun fire.

Behind this incident lay a long history. As long ago as 1857 missionaries in the Geelvink Bay region had made note of the story of Mansren. It is typical of many Melanesian myths that became confounded with Christian doctrine to form the ideological basis of the movements. The legend tells how long ago there lived an old man named Manamakeri ("he who itches"), whose body was covered with sores. Manamakeri was extremely fond of palm wine, and used to climb a huge tree every day to tap the liquid from the flowers. He soon found that someone was getting there before him and removing the liquid. Eventually he trapped the thief, who turned out to be none other than the Morning Star. In return for his freedom, the Star gave the old man a wand that would produce as much fish as he liked, a magic tree and a magic staff. If he drew in the sand and stamped his foot, the drawing would become real. Manamakeri, aged as he was, now magically impregnated a young maiden; the child of this union was a miracle-child who spoke as soon as he was born. But the maiden's parents were horrified, and banished her, the child and the old man. The trio sailed off in a canoe created by Mansren ("The Lord"), as the old man now became known. On this journey Mansren rejuvenated himself by stepping into a fire and flaking off his scaly skin, which changed into valuables. He then sailed around Geelvink Bay, creating islands where he stopped, and peopling them with the ancestors of the present-day Papuans.

The Mansren myth is plainly a creation myth full of symbolic ideas relating to fertility and rebirth. Comparative evidence—especially the shredding of his scaly skin—confirms the suspicion that the old man is, in fact, the Snake in another guise. Psychoanalytic writers argue that the snake occupies such a prominent part in mythology the world over because it stands for the penis, another fertility symbol. This may be so, but its symbolic significance is surely more complex than this. It is the "rebirth" of the hero, whether Mansren or the Snake, that exercises such universal fascination over men's minds.

The 19th-century missionaries thought that the Mansren story would make the introduction of Christianity easier, since the concept of "resurrection," not to mention that of the "virgin birth" and the "second coming," was already there. By 1867, however, the first cult organized around the Mansren legend was reported.

Though such myths were widespread in Melanesia, and may have sparked occasional movements even in the pre-White era, they took on a new significance in the late 19th century, once the European powers had finished parceling out the Melanesian region among themselves. In many coastal areas the long history of "blackbirding"—the seizure of islanders for work on the plantations of Australia and Fiji—had built up a reservoir of hostility to Europeans. In other areas, however, the arrival of the Whites was accepted, even welcomed, for it meant access to bully beef and cigarettes, shirts and paraffin lamps, whisky and bicycles. It also meant access to the knowledge behind these material goods, for the Europeans brought missions and schools as well as cargo.

Practically the only teaching the natives received about European life came from the missions, which emphasized the central significance of religion in European society. The Melanesians already believed that man's activities—whether gardening, sailing canoes or bearing children—needed magical assistance. Ritual without human effort was not enough. But neither was human effort on its own. This outlook was reinforced by mission teaching.

The initial enthusiasm for European rule, however, was speedily dispelled. The rapid growth of the plantation economy removed the bulk of the able-bodied men from the villages, leaving women, children and old men to carry on as best they could. The splendid vision of the equality of all Christians began to seem a pious deception in face of the realities of the color bar, the multiplicity of rival Christian missions and the open irreligion of many Whites.

For a long time the natives accepted the European mission as the means by which the "cargo" would eventually be made available to them. But they found that acceptance of Christianity did not bring the cargo any nearer. They grew disillusioned. The story now began to be put about that it was not the Whites who made the cargo, but the dead ancestors. To people completely ignorant of factory production, this made good sense. White men did not work; they merely wrote secret signs on scraps of paper, for which they were given shiploads of goods. On the other hand, the Melanesians labored week after week for pitiful wages. Plainly the goods must be made for Melanesians somewhere, perhaps in the Land of the Dead. The Whites, who possessed the secret of the cargo, were intercepting it and keeping it from the hands of the islanders, to whom it was really consigned. In the Madang district of New Guinea, after some 40 years' experience of the missions, the natives went in a body one day with a petition demanding that the cargo secret should now be revealed to them, for they had been very patient.

So strong is this belief in the existence of a "secret" that the cargo cults generally contain some ritual in imitation of the mysterious European customs which are held to be the clue to the white man's extraordinary power over goods and men. The believers sit around tables with bottles of flowers in front of them, dressed in European clothes, waiting for the cargo ship or airplane to materialize; other cultists feature magic pieces of paper and cabalistic writing. Many of them deliberately turn their backs on the past by destroying secret ritual objects, or exposing them to the gaze of uninitiated youths and women, for whom formerly even a glimpse of the sacred objects would have meant the severest penalties, even death. The belief that they were the chosen people is further reinforced by their reading of the Bible, for the lives and customs of the people in the Old Testament resemble their own lives rather than those of the Europeans. In the New Testament they find the Apocalypse, with its prophecies of destruction and resurrection, particularly attractive.

Missions that stress the imminence of the Second Coming, like those of the Seventh Day Adventists, are often accused of stimulating millenarian cults among the islanders. In reality, however, the Melanesians themselves rework the doctrines the missionaries teach them, selecting from the Bible what they themselves find particularly congenial in it. Such movements have occurred in areas where missions of quite different types have been dominant, from Roman Catholic to Seventh Day Adventist. The reasons for the emergence of these cults, of course, lie far deeper in the life-experience of the people.

The economy of most of the islands is very backward. Native agriculture produces little for the world market, and even the European plantations and mines export only a few primary products and raw materials: copra, rubber, gold. Melanesians are quite unable to understand why copra, for example, fetches 30 pounds sterling per ton one month and but 5 pounds a few months later. With no notion of the workings of world-commodity markets, the natives see only the sudden closing of plantations, reduced wages and unemployment, and are inclined to attribute their insecurity to the whim or evil in the nature of individual planters.

Such shocks have not been confined to the economic order. Governments, too, have come and gone, especially during the two world wars: German, Dutch, British and French administration melted overnight. Then came the Japanese, only to be ousted in turn largely by the previously unknown Americans. And among these Americans the Melanesians saw Negroes like themselves, living lives of luxury on equal terms with white G.I.'s. The sight of these Negroes seemed like a fulfillment of the old prophecies to many cargo cult leaders. Nor must we forget the sheer scale of this invasion. Around a million U. S. troops passed through the Admiralty Islands, completely swamping the inhabitants. It was a world of meaningless and chaotic changes, in which anything was possible. New ideas were imported and given local twists. Thus in the Loyalty Islands people expected the French Communist Party to bring the millennium. There is no real evidence, however, of any Communist influence in these movements, despite the rather hysterical belief among Solomon Island planters that the name of the local "Masinga Rule" movement was derived from the word "Marxian"! In reality the name comes from a Solomon Island tongue, and means "brotherhood."

Europeans who have witnessed outbreaks inspired by the cargo cults are usually at a loss to understand what they behold. The islanders throw away their money, break their most sacred taboos, abandon their gardens and destroy their precious livestock; they indulge in sexual license or, alternatively, rigidly separate men from women in huge communal establishments. Sometimes they spend days sitting gazing at the horizon for a glimpse of the long-awaited ship or airplane; sometimes they dance, pray and sing in mass congregations, becoming possessed and "speaking with tongues."

Observers have not hesitated to use such words as "madness," "mania," and "irrationality" to characterize the cults. But the cults reflect quite logical and rational attempts to make sense out of a social order that appears senseless and chaotic. Given the ignorance of the Melanesians about the wider European society, its economic organization and its highly developed technology, their reactions form a consistent and understandable pattern. They wrap up all their yearning and hope in an amalgam that combines the best counsel they can find in Christianity and their native belief. If the world is soon to end, gardening or fishing is unnecessary; everything will be provided. If the Melanesians are to be part of a much wider order, the taboos that prescribe their social conduct must now be lifted or broken in a newly prescribed way.

Of course the cargo never comes. The cults nonetheless live on. If the millennium does not arrive on schedule, then perhaps there is some failure in the magic, some error in the ritual. New breakaway groups organize around "purer" faith and ritual. The cult rarely disappears, so long as the social situation which brings it into being persists.

At this point it should be observed that cults of this general kind are not peculiar to Melanesia. Men who feel themselves oppressed and deceived have always been ready to pour their hopes and fears, their aspirations and frustrations, into dreams of a millennium to come or of a golden age to return. All parts of the world have had their counterparts of the cargo cults, from the American Indian ghost dance to the communist-millenarist "reign of the saints" in Münster during the Reformation, from medieval European apocalyptic cults to African "witch-finding" movements and Chinese Buddhist heresies. In some situations men have been content to wait and pray; in others they have sought to hasten the day by using their strong right arms to do the Lord's work. And always the cults serve to bring together scattered groups, notably the peasants and urban plebeians of agrarian societies and the peoples of "stateless" societies where the cult unites separate (and often hostile) villages, clans and tribes into a wider religio-political unity.

Once the people begin to develop secular political organizations, however, the sects tend to lose their importance as vehicles of protest. They begin to relegate the Second Coming to the distant future or to the next world. In Melanesia ordinary political bodies, trade unions and native councils are becoming the normal media through which the islanders express their aspirations. In recent years continued economic prosperity and political stability have taken some of the edge off their despair. It now seems unlikely that any major movement along cargo-cult lines will recur in areas where the transition to secular politics has been made, even if the insecurity of prewar times returned. I would predict that the embryonic nationalism represented by cargo cults is likely in future to take forms familiar in the history of other countries that have moved from subsistence agriculture to participation in the world economy.

Morris Freilich

32. Cultural Persistence among the Modern Iroquois*

INTRODUCTION

In 1886 the Dominion Bridge Company hired some Mohawks to work as unskilled laborers on the Victoria Tubelar Bridge. The bridge which abutted on reservation land brought about the first contact Mohawks had with the structural steel industry. As of today, the great majority of Mohawk males between the ages of 18 and 60 are skilled structural steel workers. These facts suggest the following problems: firstly, why did the Mohawks as a tribe take up steel work? Secondly, why have they remained in this occupation for seventy years? I will attempt to show, and substantiate with field work information, that given certain historical accidents, specific cultural factors made it, as it were, necessary for the Mohawks to go into structural steel. Further, that once in structural steel, specific cultural factors kept them there.

Analytically, we have to deal with two major variables: culture and environment. We hypothesize a connection between general environmental change and cultural change. The exact nature of such a connection we hope to discover after an analysis of the following:

* Reprinted with permission of author and editor from *Anthropos*, vol. 53, 1958: 473–83.

Before 1721, the term Iroquois is used to refer to the Five Nations: Mohawk, Oneida, Onandaga, Cayuga and Seneca. After 1721 the Tuscarora became a member of the League of the Iroquois and the confederacy was often referred to as the Six Nations.

1. Mohawk males prior to their "continuous first hand contact" with the white man.
2. The changes in their environment during the intermittent period.
3. The way of life of Mohawk males today.

HISTORICAL MOHAWK

From sources which deal with the Mohawks historically (Morgan, Colden, Fenton, Jenness), we get the following information:

Mohawks, aboriginally, lived in palisaded villages. Each village contained several Long Houses. Within the Long House lived several matrilocally extended families and "the longhouse took the name and insignia of the clan of its dominant family." (Quain 1937:256, quoting Fenton). The society was matrilineal, and women were mainly responsible for subsistence activities.

The men hunted to provide the extra delicacies of meat and fish, but they were mainly concerned with politics and war. They lived in a world of men, where prestige was obtained by the great warrior, and where women were considered inferior. As Morgan (1901:320) tells us: "The warrior despised the toil of husbandry and held all labor beneath him."

Warfare most frequently took place on a small group level. A renowned warrior would suggest a particular enterprise and then try to interest others in it. At this time a war dance was held and past exploits were recounted to arouse the interest of the males. Colden (1904-I:xxii-xxiii) describes war party formation as follows:

> When any of the young men of these Nations have a mind to . . . gain a reputation among their countrymen, by some notable enterprise against their enemy, they first communicate their design to two or three of their most intimate friends; and if they come into it an invitation is made in their names to all the young men in the castle. . . , the promoters of the enterprise set forth the undertaking in the best colours they can; they boast of what they intend to do and incite others to join from the glory there is to be obtained.

No one had the authority to order another to go on the warpath. Authority was not of the lineal type, as in the European tradition, but rather similar to the pattern among the Fox Indians (see Miller 1955), where acceptance of directives by executants in collective action, was considered a matter of choice. Colden (1904-I:xxviii) states "The Five Nations have such absolute notions of Liberty that they allow no kind of superiority of one over another."

When the warriors returned from the warpath, they received definite social applause.

They had the opportunity to recite deeds of valor publicly at the victory dance . . . , each [war leader] had a war post on which he made pictographs to commemorate his deeds . . . , and success . . . is said to have influenced the possibilities of winning a beautiful wife [Quain 1937: 268–69].

From around 1640 to the end of the eighteenth century, the men spent increasingly more time at warfare and less in subsistence activities. Fenton (1940:159–251) divided this part of Iroquois history into two warring periods:

1. The period of Iroquoian wars for the fur trade;
2. The period of colonial wars.

The fact that the women took care both of subsistence activities and the home made it possible for the men to keep going off to war. It was the women who stored the grain, so that when a man returned from war there was always food to eat, be it in his wife's house or his mother's.[1] Should the men drift into any Iroquois village, the principle of hospitality required that they be fed. Fenton (in Quain 1937:254, n.2) suggests that "hospitality may have helped solve the problems of a military economy."

If we examine Mohawk society, a model can be constructed which has the following characteristics:

A matrilineal society composed of matrilocally extended families with women supplying the community with essential foods, having fixed residence, and taking care of home and family. Their relationships with each other are relatively constant for long periods of time.

The men lived in a world of men where [non-matron] women were useful appendages who looked after the mundane parts of life, provided food and shelter, cared for the children and were available for men's sexual pleasures. Men had brittle, intermittent relationships with each other. These were formed around different warrior chiefs and created strong bonds only for the duration of a particular war party. Here in the world of men, one could fight, boast, talk men's talk and be a warrior. To a great extent men were their own masters; no one could order them to do anything (except in retribution for criminal offenses). The men chose whether they would join a war party, and could leave it any time they so desired, suffering only the loss of public esteem. The great prestige of the warrior status made for frequent war parties. Colloquially speaking the warrior returned to the tune of "Home the Conquering Hero Comes," and to hear it again and again, he necessarily had to keep leaving for war.

---

[1] Snyderman tells us that women were frequently instrumental in starting war parties. He states "there were many instances where the matron solicited, cajoled, bullied or paid with wampum, individual warriors to take to the war path in order that prisoners be brought back for adoption" (1948, p. 19). We would differentiate the matrons (clan mothers) from non-matron women. The former had considerable status in the tribe; they elected and disposed of *sachems* (civil chiefs); initiated some war parties and disposed of prisoners.

ENVIRONMENTAL CHANGES

The environment (the total milieu) had been slowly changing ever since contact with the white men, but the drastic changes took but a comparatively short time.

> At the time of the French defeat at Quebec . . . the basic configurations of Six Nation society were still maintained . . . ; before the end of the eighteenth century, the Nations of the Confederacy were already located on reservations [Noon 1949:16].

The Iroquois' alliance with the British, and Washington's decision to lay waste to the Indians' fields and lands were important factors which led to the rapid changes.

The problem for the Mohawk male was simply one of adjustment to a reservation situation. The hunter now had little opportunity to hunt, the warrior was forbidden the warpath.

> Let us examine what the Mohawks actually did. They "became voyageurs for the fur companies. Their expeditions took them in quest of furs to the country beyond Red River, and soon after 1798, a Mohawk party had skirmished with the Blackfoot . . . Meanwhile on the St. Lawrence . . . [others] furnished raftsmen and lumberjacks to the timber industry" [Fenton 1940:212].

As canoe men, guides and carriers, they accompanied Franklin and Richardson to the Polar Seas. That the male still yearned for the role of warrior can be deduced from the following:

> On September 23, 1812, Granger, [the Indian agent at Buffalo Creek] reported that the young men of the Nation [the Iroquois] could not be restrained from fighting—that if the United States declined their services they would fight under the British Flag [Babcock 1927:27].

It is important to note that it is not loyalty to a cause, which led the Iroquois into battle, but rather *the desire to fight*. And fight they did at every opportunity.

> Along with the Canadians they defeated the American Invaders at the Battle of Chateaugay in 1813, and in 1838 they defeated Nelson's partisans who were marching on Montreal [Cory 1955:61].

In the last half of the nineteenth century, the Mohawks were engaged in timber rafting, river boating, dock work and circus work. In 1886, they took to structural steel work and soon this became the occupation *par excellence* for Mohawk males.

How is it, we ask, that the great majority of Mohawk men found their niche in structural steel? Our answer is simply that participation in the structural steel industry enabled the Mohawks to closely duplicate their pre-reservation period social structure. Let us then examine the way of life of modern Mohawks to demonstrate the similarities with the past.

MODERN MOHAWK

The Caughnawaga Mohawks live in several small communities in Eastern Canada and the United States. The Caughnawaga reservation is about 10 miles south of Montreal and is considered by one and all as home. For seventy years now, the men have been leaving Caughnawaga to do structural steel work in Canada, Alaska and the United States. Until recently women remained on the reservation taking care of home and children and awaiting the return of their menfolk.

Two decades ago (1938 in Brooklyn) small Mohawk communities were formed in a few American cities, New York (Brooklyn), Detroit, and Buffalo.

On the reservation mothers and their married daughters tend to live near each other, frequently owning adjacent houses. In Brooklyn, the matrilaterally extended family is often found either in the same apartment house or in adjacent apartment houses. Practically all the Mohawks in Brooklyn live within short walking distance of each other.

The Mohawk male remains in school just long enough to fulfill minimum requirements. He is usually intelligent and shows leadership abilities in sports. He can rarely be interested in continuing his schooling; he wishes to become a steel worker.[2]

Structural steel work requires little formal training. A boy reaching the age of 17 or so is brought into a gang by his father, uncle, cousin or brother who happens to be the foreman or a close relative or friend of the latter. The initiate is "broken in" or "shown the ropes." For a short time he earns apprentice wages; however, as soon as he can do a full man's job, he demands and gets full pay ($150.00 per week). Construction work entails remaining at a job in a given area for a relatively short time. When the job is finished, another is found somewhere else. Not to be frequently out of work necessitates keeping in close touch with the rest of the Mohawk steel workers any one of whom may learn of a job.

In the early days of steel, this meant that the reservation at Caughnawaga was the central information center. After the completion of one or more jobs, the men would go home, see their families and get together with the boys to swap stories of narrow escapes off the "ledges," of the women they "had" in different towns, and to find out about future work opportunities. Usually "pushers" (foremen) would have jobs lined up and be looking for gangs. Soon it would be time for the men who fearlessly worked up high to leave for another job so that they could later return victorious.

They left with their gang, consisting of age mates, and a "pusher," an older, more experienced steel worker. As in the case of the warriors, there was the chance that some of them would not return alive, for this was

---

[2] This information was received from teachers of the schools that Mohawk children attended in Brooklyn, New York. It was confirmed by informal interviews of many Mohawk boys between the ages of 8 and 16.

dangerous men's work. Men worked, played, lived and died with men. The women tried (and still try) to get as much of the money the men brought home as possible. They still keep up the home and take care of the children. In essence they still "store the grain." The men, left alone, would drink away their earnings.

Comparing the models of Mohawk society, past and present, we find the following characteristics common to both:

A. Women: 1. Maintaining a fixed residence.
2. Looking after the home and children.
3. Storing the "grain" (be it maize or money).
4. Living in close contact with the matrilineal family.
5. Having constant relationships with other Mohawk women.
6. Providing hospitality for their males and gang.

B. Men: 1. Leaving a home base to be able to return as conquering heroes.
2. Bringing of booty home as a sign of a successful expedition (slaves or goods by the warrior; a new car or a large "wad" of money by the steel worker).
3. Achieving certain observable accomplishments, which can be spoken of at length and greatly exaggerated ("We laid low the Erie lands" or "We built the Empire State Building").
4. Working in an all-male group under the leadership of a more experienced tribesman.
5. Being subject to the minimum of lineal authority, under a leader that one picked; for short periods of time (length of the war party or job assignment—in both cases the Mohawk leaves any time he wants to).
6. Becoming a full member of the group without having to undergo a long, formal learning period.
7. Having chances to display daring and courage and thereby gain personal prestige both from the whole community and from the group one fought or worked with.
8. Having excitement as an ever present ingredient.
9. Leaving the maintenance of home and family to the women.
10. Forming short and brittle bonds around a leader (war chief or "pusher").

It is of interest to note that all the occupations the Mohawk took up prior to steel work, to wit, river navigation, lumberjacking, railroading, dock-working, and circus work, necessitated leaving home for lengthy periods of time. Further, that there was in each case little or no directive authority. The Mohawk of today, like his forebears, does not like being told what to do. If the "pusher" gives too many orders, the Mohawk leaves the gang.

I have explained above why the Mohawk stayed in steel by showing a continuity in Mohawk social structure from aboriginal times until today.

The question remains how did the Mohawk get into steel? In part, at least, this requires a historical explanation.

In 1886, an accident (from the point of view of the Mohawk), the building of the Victoria Tubelar Bridge brought the Mohawk and structural steel together. Then, as now (with the St. Lawrence Seaway), local labor was needed to supplement the imported labor force, and Mohawks went to work as unskilled laborers. The bravado and excitement-seeking aspects of the warrior role led Mohawks to climb girders even when they did not have to. This is the kind of daredevil activity in which Mohawk males still participate. Some examples from my field work including driving 90 miles per hour on a winding road at night in the mountains of New York State in an old car while inebriated; accepting a dare to go faster than the speedometer could register and two men having sexual intercourse with a girl while her fiancé was asleep beside her.

But, back to the past. Seeing the Mohawks' *apparent* lack of fear of heights, some of the foremen on the job decided to teach a few of them riveting, firing, welding, etc. As soon as a few Mohawks were proficient structural steel workers, they taught their sons, brothers, cousins and friends construction work. Here was a means by which the status of warrior and most of the complex attached to it could be well duplicated, in the absence of warfare.

The Mohawk steel worker had no difficulty getting his tribe into steel. For to be a man—if you could not be a warrior, steel work was a close second best. To get someone into steel was similar to getting him into his first war party. Frequently, Mohawks have boasted to me: "I got Angus his first job," or "Didn't I break in Bob," or "I taught Joe steel work," etc. As more and more males got into steel, it was progressively easier to get other Indians in. The "In group" was the steel workers. This, just as being a warrior, was a way of life; it meant living in a male world. That the formula *"to be a man = to be a warrior"* changed in a relatively short time period to *"to be a man = to be a steel worker"* was due to the similarities in the essence of the two ways of life.

MOHAWK "WARRIORS" TODAY

Before giving a short account of what the Indians themselves think of steel, let me present the environment in which my fieldwork was done.

A large percentage of my time was spent in the Longhouse[3] bar in

---

[3] The names used are fictitious but refer to actual places and people.

Brooklyn, New York. This is a club room, recreation hall, central information center and home to the Indian steel workers and their friends. Periodically, the Indians tear the place apart; they feel it their right, since it is their home. If outsiders give any sign of attempting to make it their clubroom, too, blood flows fast and furious.

The Longhouse is perhaps the Brooklyn symbol of the fusion of warrior and steelworker. As one enters, "Custer's Last Stand" is prominently displayed, and around the room drawings of Iroquois warriors are intermingled with helmets of structural steel workers. It is at the Longhouse, too, that the Indians meet every Friday night during the summer to leave for the reservation. Why they spend 25 hours in a car (round trip to Caughnawaga) nearly every week, to be on the reservation for a day was something that puzzled me greatly. The answer came in the theme of "home the conquering hero."

My position in the Longhouse came to be that of a guy who liked to drink and hang around with the Indians and who spent week-ends with them on the reservation. Several other non-Indians have similar status around the bar, so once I got to know a few Mohawks, there was a place for me in Longhouse society.

As to the Mohawks' feeling about steel work, one Indian (Joe Smith) told me: "For steel you need guts—you gotta be strong—you have to have it here" (pointing to his brain). He went on: "I'm a big chief, you know. I have an Oldsmobile, money in the bank, two homes, a yacht (not true), and a farm (not true). I'm a real red Indian. Feel my face—I don't have to shave. I have red skin but I'm a foreman."

Foreman or "pusher" is equated with big chief by Joe Smith and many other middle-aged Indian pushers. The equation *"foreman = big chief"* is derived from the fact that both lead a party of young Indians to an assignment where booty and prestige are to be acquired.

Another Indian, Sam Johnson said with pride: "Caughnawaga Indians are the best steel workers in the world. It's in their blood." The statement, "Steel is in our blood," is perhaps the closest the Indians come to understanding the role continuity in steel, of the strong, daring, home-leaving warrior. The statement is frequently made and always with tones of pride and superiority over other peoples.

Joe Redson speaking to John Bull about steel work, said, for example: "It's in your blood, ain't it? You want your freedom, outside in the fresh air, don't you?" That freedom, meaning lack of the lineal authority which directs, is here important and not fresh air, can be deduced from the fact that the Indians never appear to be bothered by the scarcity of fresh air in the Longhouse bar, where they often sit for hours on end.

John Bull spoke of the little money Indians had in the bank because of "bumming around and drinking"; and how he had often considered getting another job where he would make less but live on a budget and save money. Joe Redson replied, "No, you'll stay in steel. No one tells you to, but you do . . . I did not tell my son to go into construction work, but that's what he is doing."

As to the men not in steel work, direct questions about them lead to answers such as: "That's their business," or "They like something else." But indirect questioning led to comments such as "Jack was no good, he was scared to be on the bars," or quoting Mrs. Peters, "Some Indians are not in steel work—*they couldn't make it.*"

Their definition of a real man is in terms of the warrior transplanted into the steel situation. "Now Bob," said Russel, "was a real man. He was a pusher and did not call up and say, 'Do so-and-so'—he came up and showed you. He would often swing around just hanging by his feet and when he pushed a pin in, it went. He could push them in with his bare hands."

Like most fearless, daredevil warriors, "pusher" Bob died with his boots on, and his glory is still frequently recounted. He fell off a girder.

As to whether the Mohawks lack a fear of heights (a belief held by many people both anthropologists and laymen), I was fortunate enough to be around when a few Indians in the Longhouse were discussing this very subject. Russel said, "I pray every morning that I'll come back alive." The others agreed that when you are up there on the outside of a building, you are afraid. Joe Ringer said, "I've yet to meet the man who's not afraid up there . . . if you were not afraid, you would not be a good steel worker as you would not be careful." The group were fairly inebriated during this discussion. Usually, it is impossible to get them to admit fear of heights for two reasons. Firstly, the Indian has completely accepted the white man's stereotype of him as "the surefooted Indian." Secondly, *a warrior is not afraid.* A frequent statement of the Mohawks is, "Indians are afraid of nothing." Their fear of heights is the normal one of men who know that work on the girders is dangerous; however, just as the possibility of death did not deter the warrior from the warpath, it does not deter his descendant from structural steel work. In both cases, participating in dangerous activities is the sign of being a man.

If the role of warrior persisted (though modified), we would expect it to show up at other times as well as at work. This expectation is justified, as the following examples will show.

The preferred service for the Mohawks was the United States Marines. A number volunteered, not only for this "toughest of outfits," but also for direct assignment for overseas combat duty.

Over and over again, I have been told by the Mohawks, "An Indian never backs away in a fight," or while discussing cowardly actions, "You'd never see an Indian do that."

Jack (an informant) proudly related to my wife and me how he and his friend had "beaten up a couple of guys" in Canada. He was completely unconcerned that one of the fellows that he stabbed was in the hospital on the critical list. He expressed his real concern as follows: "I can't go back to Canada as the cops are looking for me." In reply to my question as to why he got involved in such a mess, he replied, "I like to fight . . . that's how I have fun." Jack is not unique; most of the younger men like to fight, and they relate with great pride how they got rid of many Puerto Ricans and Negroes who started to frequent their bar. On a number of occasions, Mohawks have attempted to pick a fight with me, and only a great deal of pride-swallowing prevented me from being beaten up. The evidence which could be multiplied, shows at every turn the structural continuity between the way of life of the warrior and that of the Mohawk steel worker.

SUMMARY AND CONCLUSIONS

I have attempted to show why the Mohawks went into and stayed in structural steel work. That a bridge was built which partly rested on reservation land was a historical accident; however, for the Mohawks to show off their fearlessness by running around on rafters was not an accident. This was a new variation of a culturally accepted manner of achieving prestige, to wit, through acts of daring. Because of this behavior, a few Mohawks were taught construction work, which, being group or gang work, allowed the trained Mohawks to form gangs of their own. The ability to form gangs, to work well together on a group assignment, to learn the work in a gang situation, all came from the already culturally patterned behavior of the warriors going off together on the warpath. Thus it was that the Mohawks got into steel and once in, the similarity of roles, authority patterns, etc., in short, the ability to maintain a similar way of life to that of the warrior, has kept the Mohawk in steel.

Daniel R. Gross

33. The Great Sisal Scheme*

In northeastern Brazil, the lush green coastal vegetation almost hides the endemic human misery of the region. Unless you look closely, the busy streets of Salvador and Recife and the waving palm trees mask the desperation of city slums, the poverty of plantation workers. When you leave the well-traveled coastal highways and go—usually on a dusty, rutted road—toward the interior, the signs of suffering become more and more apparent.

The transition is quick and brutal. Within 50 miles the vegetation changes from palm, tropical fruit, and dark-green broad-leafed trees to scrawny brush only slightly greener than the dusty earth. Nearly every plant is armed with spines or thorns. The hills are jagged, with hard faces of rock exposed. This is the *sertão,* the interior of northeastern Brazil.

If the *sertão* were honest desert, it would probably contain only a few inhabitants and a fair share of human misery. But the *sertão* is deceitful and fickle. It will smile for several years in a row, with sufficient rains arriving for the growing seasons. Gardens and crops will flourish. Cattle fatten. Then, without warning, another growing season comes, but the rains don't. The drought may go on, year after dusty year. Crops fail. Cattle grow thin and die. Humans begin to do the same. In bad droughts, the people of the *sertão* migrate to other regions by the thousands.

---

* Reprinted with permission from *Natural History* Magazine, March 1971. Copyright © The American Museum of Natural History 1971.

The bandits, the mystics, the droughts and migrants, the dreams and schemes of the *sertão* hold a special place in Brazilian folklore, literature, and song. Even at its worst, the *sertão* has been a fertile ground for the human imagination.

For two years, I studied the impact of sisal crops—a recent dream and scheme—on the people of the *sertão*. Taking an ecological approach, I found that sisal, which some poetic dreamers call "green gold," has greatly changed northeastern Brazil. But the changes have not been what the economic planners anticipated. And misery has not left the *sertão*.

I lived in Vila Nova, a small village with a population of less than 500 about an hour's drive from the town of Victoria in Bahia State. Vila Nova is striking only for its drabness. Weeds grow in the middle of unpaved streets. Facing the plaza is an incomplete series of nondescript row houses. Some have faded pastel façades, others are mud brown because their owners never managed to plaster over the rough adobe walls. The village looks decadent, yet the oldest building is less than 20 years old and most were built after 1963.

Cattle raisers settled the *sertão* 400 years ago when the expanding sugar plantations of the coast demanded large supplies of beef and traction animals. A "civilization of leather" developed, with generations of colorful and intrepid cowboys (*vaqueiros*) clad entirely in rawhide to protect themselves against the thorny scrub vegetation. As the population of the *sertão* grew, many *sertanejos* settled down to subsistence farming. Gradually the entire region became a cul-de-sac, with many small and medium-sized estates occupied by descendants of the *vaqueiros* and others who had drifted into the region.

Life was never easy in this thorny land, for the work was hard and the environment cruel. Yet cooperation and mutual assistance provided assurance of survival even to the poorest. The chief crops were manioc, beans, and corn, and most of what was grown was consumed by the cultivator's family. Most families received some share of meat and milk, and consumed highly nutritious foods like beans and squash, in addition to starchy foods like manioc flour.

When droughts menaced the region all but the wealthiest ranchers migrated temporarily to the coast to work on the sugar plantations. When the rains came again to the *sertão,* they nearly always returned, for the work in the cane fields was brutal and labor relations had not changed greatly from the time when slaves worked the plantations.

Originally from Mexico, sisal was introduced to Brazil early in this century and reached the *sertão* in the 1930's. Farmers found sisal useful for hedgerows because its tough, pointed leaves effectively kept out cattle. The cellulose core of the long sisal leaf contains hard fibers, which can be twisted together into twine and rope. When World War II cut off the supply of Manila hemp to the United States, buyers turned to Brazil for fiber. At first only hedgerow sisal was exploited, but the state of Bahia offered incentives for planting sisal as a cash crop. Since sisal plants require about four years to mature, Brazil did not begin to export the fiber in significant quantities until 1945. The demand persisted, and by 1951, Brazil was selling actively in the world market as prices rose.

In Vila Nova, a young entrepreneur who owned a mule team, David Castro, heard about the prices being paid for sisal fiber and planted the first acres of sisal in 1951. By 1968, in the county of Victoria, where Vila Nova is located, so many people had caught "sisal fever" that half of the total land area was planted in the crop. Sisal is easily transplanted and cultivated, requires little care, and is highly resistant to drought. It has some drawbacks as a cultivated plant, however. At least one annual weeding is necessary or else the field may become choked with thorn bushes, weeds, and suckers (unwanted small sisal plants growing from the base of parent plants). A field abandoned for two years becomes unusable, practically unreclaimable. Despite these difficulties, many landowners planted sisal, especially in 1951 and 1962, years of high prices on the world market.

From the outset, sisal produced differential rewards for those who planted it. Owners of small plots (ten acres or less) planted proportionately more of their land in sisal than did large landowners. Many who owned just a few acres simply planted all their land in sisal in expectation of large profits. This deprived them of whatever subsistence they had managed to scratch out of the ground in the past. But work was easy to find because the need for labor in the sisal fields grew rapidly. When, after four years, the crops were ready to harvest, many small landholders discovered to their dismay that prices had dropped sharply, and that harvest teams did not want to work small crops. They had planted sisal with dreams of new clothes, new homes, even motor vehicles purchased with sisal profits, but found their fields choked with unusable sisal and became permanent field laborers harvesting sisal on large landholdings. In this way, sisal created its own labor force.

The separation of sisal fiber from the leaf is known as decortication. In Brazil, this process requires enormous amounts of manual labor. The decorticating machine is basically a spinning rasp powered by a gasoline or diesel motor. Sisal leaves are fed into it by hand, and the spinning rasp beats out the pulp or residue leaving only the fibers, which the worker pulls out of the whirling blades. Mounted on a trailer, the machine is well adapted to the scattered small-scale plantations of northeastern Brazil.

The decortication process requires constant labor for harvesting the year round. Sisal leaves, once cut, must be defibered quickly before the hot sun renders them useless. Each decorticating machine requires a crew of about seven working in close coordination. The first step is harvesting. Two cutters move from plant to plant, first lopping off the needle-sharp thorns from the leaves, then stooping to sever each leaf at the base. A transporter, working with each cutter, gathers the leaves and loads them on a burro. The leaves are taken to the machine and placed on a low stage for the defiberer to strip, one by one. A residue man removes the pulpy mass stripped from the leaves from under the motor, supplies the defiberer with leaves, and bundles and ties the freshly stripped fiber. Each bundle is weighed and counted in the day's production. Finally, the dryer spreads the wet, greenish fiber in the sun, where it dries and acquires its characteristic blond color.

For the planters and sisal buyers, this method of decortication operates profitably, but for the workers it exacts a terrible cost. The decorticating machine requires a man to stand in front of the whirling rasp for four or five hours at a shift, introducing first the foot and then the point of each leaf. The worker pulls against the powerful motor, which draws the leaf into the mouth of the machine. After half of each leaf is defibered, the defiberer grasps the raw fiber to insert the remaining half of the leaf. There is a constant danger that the fiber will entangle his hand and pull it into the machine. Several defiberers have lost arms this way. The strain and danger would seem to encourage slow and deliberate work; but in fact, defiberers decorticate about 25 leaves per minute. This is because the crew is paid according to the day's production of fiber. Although the defiberer is the highest-paid crew member, many of them must work both morning and afternoon shifts to make ends meet.

A residue man's work is also strenuous. According to measurements I made, this job requires that a man lift and carry about 2,700 pounds of material per hour. The residue man, moreover, does not work in shifts. He works as long as the machinery is running. The remaining jobs on the crew are less demanding and may be held by women or adolescents, but even these jobs are hard, requiring frequent lifting and stooping in the broiling semidesert sun.

With their own fields in sisal, to earn money the villagers had to work at harvesting sisal for large landowners. And because wages were low, more and more people had to work for families to survive. In 1968 two-thirds of all men and women employed in Vila Nova worked full time in the sisal decorticating process. Many of these were youths. Of 33 village boys between the ages of 10 and 14, 24 worked on sisal crews. Most people had completely abandoned subsistence agriculture.

Sisal brought other significant changes in the life of Vila Nova. Because most villagers no longer grew their food, it now had to be imported. Numerous shops, stocking beans, salt pork, and manioc flour, grew up in the village. A few villagers with capital or good contacts among wholesalers in the town of Victoria built small businesses based on this need. Other villagers secured credit from sisal buyers in Victoria to purchase sisal decorticating machinery.

The shopkeepers and sisal machine owners in the village formed a new economic class on whom the other villagers were economically dependent. The wealthier group enjoyed many advantages. Rather than going to work on the sisal machines, most of the children of these entrepreneurs went to school. All of the upper group married in a socially prescribed way: usually a church wedding with civil ceremonies as well. But among the workers, common-law marriages were frequent, reflecting their lack of resources for celebrating this important event.

The only villagers who became truly affluent were David Castro and his cousin. These men each owned extensive sisal plantations and several decorticating units. Most importantly, each became middlemen, collecting sisal in warehouses in the village and trucking the fiber into Victoria. David, moreover, owned the largest store in the village. Since the village was located on David's land, he sold house plots along the streets. He also acted as the representative of the dominant political party in Victoria, serving as a ward boss during elections and as an unofficial but effective police power. There was a difference between David and the large ranch owners of the past. While wealthy men were formerly on close terms with their dependents, helping them out during tough times, David's relations with the villagers were cold, business-like, and exploitative. Most of the villagers disliked him, both for his alleged stinginess and because he never had time to talk to anyone.

During my stay in Vila Nova I gradually became aware of these changes in the social and economic structure. But I hoped to establish that the introduction of sisal had also resulted in a quantitative, ecological change in the village. At the suggestion of Dr. Barbara A. Underwood of the Institute of Human Nutrition at Columbia University, I undertook an intensive study to determine what influence sisal had on diet and other factors of a few representative households. When I looked at household budgets, I quickly discovered that those households that depended entirely on wages from sisal work spent nearly all their money on food. Families with few or no children or with several able-bodied workers seemed to be holding their own. But families with few workers or several dependents were less fortunate. To understand the condition of these families, I collected information not only on cash budgets but also on household *energy budgets*. Each household expends not only money, but also energy in the form of calories in performing work. "Income" in the latter case is the caloric value of the foods consumed by these households. By carefully measuring the amount and kind of food consumed, I was able to determine the total inflow and outflow of energy in individual households.

For example, Miguel Costa is a residue man who works steadily on a sisal unit belonging to a nearby planter. He lives in Vila Nova in a two-room adobe hut with his wife and four small children, ranging in age from three to eight. During the seven-day test period, Miguel worked at the sisal motor four and a half days, while his wife stayed home with the children. I was able to estimate Miguel's caloric expenditures during the test period. During the same period, I visited his home after every meal where his wife graciously permitted me to weigh the family's meager food supplies to determine food consumption. Each day the supply of beans diminished by less than one-half pound and the weight of the coarse manioc flour eaten with beans dropped by two or three pounds. Manioc flour is almost pure starch, high in calories but low in essential nutrients. At the beginning of the week about half a pound of fatty beef and pork were consumed each day, but this was exhausted by midweek. The remainder of the family's calories were consumed in the form of sugar, bread, and boiled sweet manioc, all high in calories but low in other nutrients.

Calorie Budget of a Sisal Worker's Household

	Average daily caloric intake	Minimum daily caloric requirements	Percent of need met	Percent of standard weight of children
Household	9,392	12,592	75	
Worker	3,642	3,642	100	
Wife	2,150	2,150	100	
Son (age 8)	1,112	2,100	53	62
Daughter (6)	900	1,700	53	70
Son (5)	900	1,700	53	85
Son (3)	688	1,300	53	90

Estimating the caloric requirements of the two adults from their activities and the children's by Food and Agriculture Organization minimum requirements, the household had a minimum need of 88,142 calories for the week. The household received only 65,744 calories, or 75 percent of need. Since the two adults did not lose weight while maintaining their regular levels of activity, they were apparently meeting their total calorie requirements. Miguel, for example, had been working steadily at his job for weeks before the test and continued to do so for weeks afterward. Had he not been maintaining himself calorically, he could not have sustained his performance at his demanding job. Despite his small stature (5 feet, 4 inches) Miguel required some 3,642 calories per day to keep going at the job. And Miguel's wife evidently also maintained herself calorically—pregnant at the time of my visit, she later gave birth to a normal child.

The caloric deficit in Miguel's household, then, was almost certainly being made up by systematically depriving the dependent children of sufficient calories. This was not intentional, nor were the parents aware of it. Nor could Miguel have done anything about it even if he had understood this process. If he were to work harder for longer to earn more money, he would incur greater caloric costs and would have to consume more. If he were to reduce his food intake to leave more food for his children, he would be obliged by his own physiology to work less, thereby earning less. If he were to provide his household with foods higher in caloric content (for example, more manioc), he would almost certainly push his children over the brink into a severe nutritional crisis that they might not survive for lack of protein and essential vitamins. Thus, Miguel, a victim of ecological circumstances, is maintaining his family against terrible odds.

Miguel's children respond to this deprivation in a predictable manner. Nature has provided a mechanism to compensate for caloric deficiencies during critical growth periods: the rate of growth simply slows down. As a result, Miguel's children, and many other children of sisal workers, are much smaller than properly nourished children of the same age. The longer the deprivation goes on the more pronounced the tendency: thus Miguel's youngest boy, who is three, is 90 percent of standard weight for his age. The five-year-old boy is 85 percent; the six-year-old girl, 70 percent; and the oldest boy, at eight, is only 62 percent of standard weight. Caloric deprivation takes its toll in other ways than stunting. Caloric and other nutritional deficiencies are prime causes of such problems as reduced mental capacity and lower resistance to infection. In Vila Nova one-third of all children die by the age of 10.

When I surveyed the nutritional status of the people of Vila Nova, I found a distinct difference between the average body weights of the two economic groups formed since the introduction of sisal (shopkeepers and motor-owners on the one hand, and workers on the other). Since the introduction of sisal the upper economic group exhibited a marked improvement in nutritional status (as measured by body weight) while the lower group showed a decline in nutritional status. The statistics showed that while one group was better off than before, a majority of the population was actually worse off nutritionally.

This conclusion was unexpected in view of the widespread claim that sisal had brought lasting benefits to the people of the *sertão,* that sisal had narrowed the gap between the rich and the poor. Clearly, changes had come about. Towns like Victoria had grown far beyond their presisal size.

But outside the towns, in the villages and rural farmsteads, the picture is different. Having abandoned subsistence agriculture, many workers moved to villages to find work on sisal units. In settlements such as Vila Nova wages and profits depend on the world price for sisal. When I arrived in 1967, the price was at the bottom of a trough that had paralyzed all growth and construction. Wages were so low that outmigration was showing signs of resuming as in the drought years. In spite of local symbols of wealth and "development," my observations revealed a continuation of endemic poverty throughout most of the countryside and even an intensification of the social and economic divisions that have always characterized the *sertão.*

Sisal is not the only example of an economic change that has brought unforeseen, deleterious consequences. The underdeveloped world is replete with examples of development schemes that brought progress only to a privileged few. The example of sisal in northeastern Brazil shows that an ecological approach is needed in all economic planning. Even more important, we must recognize that not all economic growth brings social and economic development in its true sense. As the sisal example shows, a system may be formed (often as part of a worldwide system) that only increases the store of human misery.

Frantz Fanon

34. The Wretched of the Earth: Conclusion*

Come, then, comrades; it would be as well to decide at once to change our ways. We must shake off the heavy darkness in which we were plunged, and leave it behind. The new day which is already at hand must find us firm, prudent, and resolute.

We must leave our dreams and abandon our old beliefs and friendships from the time before life began. Let us waste no time in sterile litanies and nauseating mimicry. Leave this Europe where they are never done talking of Man, yet murder men everywhere they find them, at the corner of every one of their own streets, in all the corners of the globe. For centuries they have stifled almost the whole of humanity in the name of a so-called spiritual experience. Look at them today swaying between atomic and spiritual disintegration.

And yet it may be said that Europe has been successful in as much as everything that she has attempted has succeeded.

Europe undertook the leadership of the world with ardor, cynicism, and violence. Look at how the shadow of her palaces stretches out ever further! Every one of her movements has burst the bounds of space and thought. Europe has declined all humility and all modesty; but she has also set her face against all solicitude and all tenderness.

---

* Reprinted by permission of Grove Press and MacGibbon and Kee, Ltd. from *The Wretched of the Earth* ("Conclusion," pages 311–16, Black Cat Edition). Copyright © 1963 by *Présence Africaine*. This chapter is taken from Frantz Fanon's *The Damned* (translated by Constance Farrington), published by *Présence Africaine*, Paris, 1963 (and subsequently as *The Wretched of the Earth* by other houses).

She has only shown herself parsimonious and niggardly where men are concerned; it is only men that she has killed and devoured.

So, my brothers, how is it that we do not understand that we have better things to do than to follow that same Europe?

That same Europe where they were never done talking of Man, and where they never stopped proclaiming that they were only anxious for the welfare of Man: today we know with what sufferings humanity has paid for every one of their triumphs of the mind.

Come, then, comrades, the European game has finally ended; we must find something different. We today can do everything, so long as we do not imitate Europe, so long as we are not obsessed by the desire to catch up with Europe.

Europe now lives at such a mad, reckless pace that she has shaken off all guidance and all reason, and she is running headlong into the abyss; we would do well to avoid it with all possible speed.

Yet it is very true that we need a model, and that we want blueprints and examples. For many among us the European model is the most inspiring. We have therefore seen in the preceding pages to what mortifying setbacks such an imitation has led us. European achievements, European techniques, and the European style ought no longer to tempt us and to throw us off our balance.

When I search for Man in the technique and the style of Europe, I see only a succession of negations of man, and an avalanche of murders.

The human condition, plans for mankind, and collaboration between men in those tasks which increase the sum total of humanity are new problems, which demand true inventions.

Let us decide not to imitate Europe; let us combine our muscles and our brains in a new direction. Let us try to create the whole man, whom Europe has been incapable of bringing to triumphant birth.

Two centuries ago, a former European colony decided to catch up with Europe. It succeeded so well that the United States of America became a monster, in which the taints, the sickness, and the inhumanity of Europe have grown to appalling dimensions.

Comrades, have we not other work to do than to create a third Europe? The West saw itself as a spiritual adventure. It is in the name of the spirit, in the name of the spirit of Europe, that Europe has made her encroachments, that she has justified her crimes and legitimized the slavery in which she holds the four-fifths of humanity.

Yes, the European spirit has strange roots. All European thought has unfolded in places which were increasingly more deserted and more encircled by precipices; and thus it was that the custom grew up in those places of very seldom meeting man.

A permanent dialogue with oneself and an increasingly obscene narcissism never ceased to prepare the way for a half delirious state, where intellectual work became suffering and the reality was not at all that of a living man, working and creating himself, but rather words, different combinations of words, and the tensions springing from the meanings contained in words. Yet some Europeans were found to urge the European workers to shatter this narcissism and to break with this unreality.

But in general, the workers of Europe have not replied to these calls; for the workers believe, too, that they are part of the prodigious adventure of the European spirit.

All the elements of a solution to the great problems of humanity have, at different times, existed in European thought. But the action of European men has not carried out the mission which fell to them, and which consisted of bringing their whole weight violently to bear upon these elements, of modifying their arrangement and their nature, of changing them and finally of bringing the problem of mankind to an infinitely higher plane.

Today we are present at the stasis of Europe. Comrades, let us flee from this motionless movement where gradually dialectic is changing into the logic of equilibrium. Let us reconsider the question of mankind. Let us reconsider the question of cerebral reality and of the cerebral mass of all humanity, whose connections must be increased, whose channels must be diversified and whose meassages must be re-humanized.

Come, brothers, we have far too much work to do for us to play the game of rearguard. Europe has done what she set out to do and on the whole she has done it well; let us stop blaming her, but let us say to her firmly that she should not make such a song and dance about it. We have no more to fear; so let us stop envying her.

The Third World today faces Europe like a colossal mass whose aim should be to try to resolve the problems to which Europe has not been able to find the answers.

But let us be clear: what matters is to stop talking about output, and intensification, and the rhythm of work.

No, there is no question of a return to Nature. It is simply a very concrete question of not dragging men toward mutilation, of not imposing upon the brain rhythms which very quickly obliterate it and wreck it. The pretext of catching up must not be used to push man around, to tear him away from himself or from his privacy, to break and kill him.

No, we do not want to catch up with anyone. What we want to do is to go forward all the time, night and day, in the company of Man, in the company of all men. The caravan should not be stretched out, for in that case each line will hardly see those who precede it; and men who no longer recognize each other meet less and less together, and talk to each other less and less.

It is a question of the Third World starting a new history of Man, a history which will have regard to the sometimes prodigious theses which

Europe has put forward, but which will also not forget Europe's crimes, of which the most horrible was committed in the heart of man, and consisted of the pathological tearing apart of his functions and the crumbling away of his unity. And in the framework of the collectivity there were the differentiations, the stratification, and the bloodthirsty tensions fed by classes; and finally, on the immense scale of humanity, there were racial hatreds, slavery, exploitation, and above all the bloodless genocide which consisted in the setting aside of fifteen thousand millions of men.

So, comrades, let us not pay tribute to Europe by creating states, institutions, and societies which draw their inspiration from her.

Humanity is waiting for something from us other than such an imitation, which would be almost an obscene caricature.

If we want to turn Africa into a new Europe, and America into a new Europe, then let us leave the destiny of our countries to Europeans. They will know how to do it better than the most gifted among us.

But if we want humanity to advance a step further, if we want to bring it up to a different level than that which Europe has shown it, then we must invent and we must make discoveries.

If we wish to live up to our peoples' expectations, we must seek the response elsewhere than in Europe.

Moreover, if we wish to reply to the expectations of the people of Europe, it is no good sending them back a reflection, even an ideal reflection, of their society and their thought with which from time to time they feel immeasurably sickened.

For Europe, for ourselves, and for humanity, comrades, we must turn over a new leaf, we must work out new concepts, and try to set afoot a new man.

CONCLUSION

Understanding Variety:
Conclusions about
Anthropology and the
Human Experience

Increasingly, I find, people want to know *in general* what anthropologists think the nature of the human experience is. Readers are usually fascinated by ethnographic facts and descriptions, but they also very much want an overview of anthropology as it is disciplined and human life as it is experienced. They want to know what assumptions, conclusions and general interests currently animate anthropolgy. And, more importantly, they want to know where we are uncertain and where we disagree in our efforts to understand variety in the human experience.

But are there any general lessons and agreements at all? Some may argue that there are none or, failing this, that our assumptions are obvious, our agreements trivial, our arguments banal, and our conclusions foregone. I think, however, that the accumulated record of anthropological research, of which there is a small but reasonably representative sample in this book, leads to numerous valuable insights about the human experience. It is neither necessary nor possible to review all of them here. I am convinced there is value, none the less, in making an effort to summarize what I believe are the major assumptions, conclusions, and areas of agreement and disagreement within anthropology today. If nothing else, these statements will serve as points for discussion and debate, in classrooms and elsewhere. Recalling the introduction to this book, the following overview will be structured in terms of the three basic questions anthropologists ask about human behavioral variety.

WHY IS THERE VARIETY IN HUMAN SOCIETIES?

As noted in the introduction, the question which asks why there is variety in human societies was given its most fundamental answer by John Locke in the eighteenth century. To summarize briefly, he said that people behave differently not because they have different "natures" or different innate ideas but because they have had different *experiences*. But in order to see the full implications of Locke's revolutionary argument, it will be helpful to consider why organisms in general vary so much in their behavior.

In order to behave, organisms utilize "information" (to use a purposefully general term). But what is this information? Where is it located? From where does it come? As is well known now, much of an organism's information is stored ("encoded") in its genes. The concrete physical reality of an organism (the phenotype) is an expression of the organism's genetically encoded information (its gentoype). An organism *inherits* this information in an event that happens only once—at the very outset of the organism's life. With rare exceptions, this information does not change for the remainder of that life.

But organisms also acquire information of a different type through another general process; this process is called *learning*. Information which is acquired through learning is encoded in the neural structures of the organism. Learned information is acquired throughout the lifetime of the organism, and it may vary significantly in content over this span. Although there are similarities, genetically encoded information is very different from non-genetically encoded information. Some of these differences will be spelled out later.

The ratio of genetic to non-genetic information varies from one type of organism to the next. In general, the greater the portion of information which is non-genetic, the more "advanced" and less specialized the organism may be said to be. This is because the organism's behavioral range is usually far more variable and flexible when it is able to acquire and utilize large amounts of non-genetic information. Experience is one of the key events in learning (i.e., the acquisition of non-genetic information) and now, obviously, we are back again to Locke.

Learning processes are complex and are not yet fully understood. For our purposes, however, it will be helpful to describe three broad and rather different kinds of learning processes. These are: "situational," "social," and "symbolic" learning (these terms are taken from Fried's very useful discussion; Fried 1967:5–6). As Fried suggests, situational learning is a very common and elementary way for an organism to acquire information. It is characterzed by a direct physical encounter between an organism and an environmental stimulus. Information acquired by an organism that can only learn situationally cannot be passed on to other organisms. At the death of the organism, the information is destroyed.

"Social learning" is also very common. Unlike situational learning, an organism capable of social learning may acquire information without having direct physical encounters with an environmental stimulus. Rather, it is able to perceive the encounters of other organisms and can learn (i.e., encode information) from their experiences. In this way, it is possible for an organism to acquire a great deal of information (far more than is typical under ordinary circumstances with only situational learning). It is even possible, in effect, for such an organism to "pass on" information to its offspring. As a consequence, as Fried puts it (1967:6), an organism or a group of such organisms can "stockpile" responses for situations not yet encountered directly.

"Symbolic" learning is the least common variety. As Fried states (1967:6), "the crux of symbolic learning is the omission of the original situation." In symbolic learning, the organism does not encounter a physical stimulus directly (this is situational learning) nor does it directly perceive another organism encountering such a stimulus (that is social learning). Rather, "the stimulus situation is not present but is *represented* by something else—by a *symbol*" (Fried 1967:6; italics added). And, it is vital to note, the symbol is itself a form of encoded information. Thus, organisms which learn symbolically encode this information in their neural structures but it is also encoded in the symbol. As Bohannan puts it (1973), this is *doubly encoded* information. Organisms that can learn symbolically have many advantages, the principal ones being that they can accumulate very large amounts of information in a lifetime, they can store it neurally and symbolically (i.e., extra-somatically), and they can pass it on directly to other organisms.

There are those who would assert that only humans are capable of symbolic learning. This is both a risky and an unnecessary assertion. There is increasing evidence that chimpanzees and other animals may be able to learn symbolically, but what is most important is not the exclusive possession of such a capacity but the extent of it. Humans appear to have more extensive capabilities for symbolic learning than any other organism. Thus, along with Fried, Bohannan and many other anthropologists, the word "culture" (and its derivations) might most usefully be limited to symbolic information, including both its neural and extra-somatically encoded (stored) forms. Since the word culture still carries so many meanings, it will not often be used in this discussion; this is done to facilitate communication.

Thus organisms, including humans, behave the way they do and as differently as they do because of the diversity of the information they have —whether it is in their genes, in their neural structures, or in extra-somatic symbols. It has been noted, however, that human societies (to return to the main focus of attention) may be assumed to have essentially similar sets of genetically encoded information. Therefore, a *partial* explanation of group or societal differences in behavior is that there are differences in the non-genetic, primarily symbolically learned information encoded, ultimately, in the neural structures of the humans in the societies being compared.

This is only a *partial* answer to our original question because no sooner is it given than another equally critical question emerges—namely, why are there the particular differences we find? After all, in his charge to those who would seek a "universal history" (a charge since adopted by many anthropologists), Turgot urged the identification of "the detailed causes" which have shaped the human experience.

In discussing what some of these specific causes may be, we must begin by noting that in general, the diversification of the behavior of human societies appears to be a type of evolutionary process. And, by implication, the non-genetic, primarily symbolically learned information encoded in symbols and in the neural structures of the people in those societies (i.e., "culture" in one of the senses of that term) also diversifies this way. The mechanism of this process is a form of natural selection. In particular, basic features of an environment, including temperature, rainfall, terrain, raw materials, population density, natural and human competitors, etc., present situations (experiences) which exert pressures on societies (or, more precisely, on the people who comprise a society). These pressures tend, in the long run, to select for or preserve that information which leads to behavior that contributes to the survival of the group. Similarly, information tends not to be preserved if it does not contribute to survival (or, more forcefully, if it contributes to the destruction of the group). These selection pressures are similar to but *not* the same as natural selection in the biological world. The principal differences may be summarized by recalling that genetic and non-genetic information, though similar, are not the same. When genetic information does not provide an adequate basis for survival, the organisms generally die (or their reproductive rate suffers), but when non-genetic information proves inadequate, the organisms that have it may well not die (and their reproductive rate may just as easily go up as down). One significant consequence of this is that selection pressures produce change in genetic information slowly over great spans of time and at the cost, often, of countless dead organisms; change in non-genetic information (especially that acquired through symbolic learning) is comparatively rapid and is achieved at the more modest cost of countless dead ideas (not dead people).

The question which asks why there is variety in human populations has always been a double edged issue, although one side—the one which has just been discussed—has been emphasized. It needs to be recalled, however, that natural selection is not all there is to an evolutionary system. There are limits to what can happen to items (e.g., genes) in the face of selection pressure if they are unchanging. There must also be a mechanism for generating variety within the materials being selected for or against by the pressures of selection (natural or otherwise). There are, in a word, different species because there are mechanisms for producing different organisms which can be selected for and against over long periods of time. Similarly, there are populations of humans that exhibit different behaviors because there are mechanisms for producing different behaviors which can be selected for or against over time. Obviously, the major source of such variation is the creative human mind. Other factors, such as the chance spread of ideas from neighboring groups, are also important. The mix of these factors and their relevant importance vis-à-vis selection pressures are not matters about which there is uniform opinion within anthropology as yet.

WHAT ORDER CAN BE DISCOVERED IN AND/OR GIVEN TO THIS VARIETY?

Anthropologists have gone about the truly monumental task of ordering our knowledge about the variety of human societies (and of the behavior of the people that make them up) in almost as many ways as there are societies. Beyond any doubt, this has been the most active, productive and stimulating area of anthropology, especially in the last forty years or so. Three broad types of ordering activities will be discussed here. Each of these has several sub-varieties which in their own right are major fields of inquiry. Most of these sub-varieties will also be discussed. For lack of better terms, the three main types may be termed "taxonomic," "systemic," and "formal."

TAXONOMIC

An early and basic ordering activity engaged in by anthropologists has been the effort to classify human societies taxonomically. This classification process is roughly analogous to the process which produced the so-called Linnaen taxonomic system in biology. In both, the goal is to examine the variety of societies (or living things, in the case of biology) and order them in a way which utilizes selected and presumably distinctive features (see Sokal 1974 for an informative discussion of this).

There are several reasons for this interest in such an ordering framework. In the first place, and this is perhaps the most basic reason for any kind of ordering activity, these systems make it easier to deal with the sheer volume of available data. Second, the taxonomic schemes of Linnaeus and his successors played a key role in the development of the theory of biological evolution by natural selection. Linnaeus, of course, did not explicitly use such a theory when creating his taxonomy, but the arrangement did facilitate a more organized assault on the question of why there were so many different things (species). Third, societies of behaving humans and the non-genetic, primarily symbolic information implied therein, may, according to some, be organizable only in terms of some sort of evolutionary-taxonomic system.

These taxonomic schemes generally reflect a continuous change in some of the more critical features; this change has the appearance of being directional. In biological taxonomies, for example, the order is reflective of increasing complexity, especially in the neural structures of the organisms. Similarly, the taxonomies of societies are often thought to reflect a general trend toward increasing complexity, as measured, for example, by the diversity of roles or size of population. Others have suggested that taxonomic orderings of societies reflect increasing energy production and utilization (e.g., Leslie White's famous energy "laws"). In all of these observations, it is dangerously easy to assume that these trends point to some sort of "end" or "goal" and that there is, in the common-sense meaning of the word, a "purpose" in the evolution of sociocultural systems. This is most emphatically not the case at all—*if* the system is truly evolutionary. Views to the contrary rest on an inadequate understanding of the open-ended nature of evolutionary systems. Evolutionary systems are "blind." They are "planless plans." This is a crucial issue for those who would understand the nature of the human experience. Many seek trends in our past in the hope that the future can be predicted. A complete reading of our evolutionary future, however, is not possible. We can get clues from the past, but that is about all.

At this point, it will be useful to consider other limitations in the effort to develop taxonomies of societies and their associated cultures. For example, the significance of the difference between organizing societies according to some taxonomic-evolutionary conceptual scheme and trying to identify the specific mechanisms of that evolutionary process should be emphasized. Although it oversimplifies the contrast a bit, it is analogous to the difference between Linnaeus and Darwin. The former gave sensible order to the variety while the latter provided a reasonable hypothesis about the mechanisms that produced this variety. Both contributions, it should also be emphasized, have proven to be very valuable to science and to humanity, but they are by no means the same.

The goal of taxonomic ordering in anthropology can be misunderstood and misused in other ways. These problems are generally an outgrowth of the tendency, especially among non-anthropologists, to overlook the ways in which the phenomena being ordered by anthropologists differ from that being ordered by biologists.

Ostensibly, taxonomic systems in biology order the variety of living organisms (in the past and present), but in fact they order the diverse genetic information implicit in this phenotypic variety. In anthropology, taxonomic systems ostensibly order behaviorally distinct societies, but in fact they order the diverse non-genetic, primarily symbolically learned information implicit in this variety. Because of the nature of genetic information, we find that biological taxonomies reflect historical connection (in part because gene flow only occurs across generation lines). But since non-genetic information acquired through symbolic learning flows in all directions, anthropological taxonomies cannot be assumed to reflect historical connections (although from time to time such connections may well be shown by one or another of these taxonomies). Moreover, the biological taxonomies give order to phenomena which have (or can and do have) very definite boundaries. At the species level and above, no genetic material can viably be exchanged. Humans are most certainly a single species in a genetic sense but it is less often realized that they are, in an analogous way, a single species in the non-genetic sense. There are no truly complete barriers to the transfer of non-genetic, symbolic information among humans (indeed, much of the symbolic information humans have is, for all intents and purposes, timeless!).

Consequently, taxonomies of societies cannot help but be very different than those constructed by biologists. Ordering systems widely in use in anthropology—for example, those which distinguish such societies as "bands," "tribes," "chiefdoms," "states" and the like—appear far more precise and neat than they really are. Generally, those who propose such conceptual frameworks are fully aware of this, but not always; similarly with those who read about such ordering frameworks.

Finally, this observation about the difference between biological and anthropological taxonomic systems provides a context for offering an even more general comment about the tendencies toward misue of the analogy in question. For almost a century, anthropologists have been attempting to establish parallels between biological and cultural evolution. In this effort, however, we have made the strategic error of trying to gain insights from the wrong portion of the analogy. Biological evolution has not only produced many species but, by implication, many living forms whose differences are far greater than species-level differences. By comparison, the diversity of symbolic non-genetic information, while great, has not reached (nor, probably, can it ever reach) even the species level of difference. If anything, then, the effort to gain insight from the analogy between biological and cultural systems should be focused on the nature of change and variety formation at the sub-species level in the biological world. This, it may be noted, is indeed where much of the interest lies in contemporary anthropology in the effort to explain why there is variety; the concern is with localized adaptive processes.

SYSTEMIC

The first general type of ordering activity, as we have just seen, is directed to discovering ways of arranging societies taxonomically. By contrast, the second kind of ordering activity (which I have chosen to call "systemic") seeks ways of ordering the behavior of people *within* a society. In some cases, however, these efforts also contribute rather directly to the search for ways to order groups taxonomically. This is because taxonomic classification systems, as we have said, utilize data about certain features of the things to be classified. Linnaeus and his successors could do what they did because of the availability of extensive morphological and physiological data about the living things of the world. Distinctive features of morphology and physiology were used in creating the biological taxonomies.

In part because such data are needed for anthropological comparisons and taxonomic orderings, anthropologists have worked to provide detailed information about the distinctive features of particular societies. One of the most common of such efforts, in fact, utilizes a biological analogy involving morphology and physiology. This approach suggests there is an analogy between the vital parts and processes of a living organism and the behavior (especially "institutions") found in societies. This analogy may well have almost as many weaknesses as it does strengths (some have argued that it has no strengths at all). For example (and perhaps most significantly), if a vital organ fails, the organism is usually doomed to die. But if an analogously vital institution of a society "fails," it seldom happens that the people and the society fail (die) with it. Using this analogy for our own purposes for a minute, we may say that societies not only can tolerate a great range of "organ transplants," but entirely different (rather than the same but new or repaired) "organs" can be put in the place of the ones that fail. Those who find the analogy useful have noted that such "radical transplants" (something like giving gills to a dog) seem to force radical adjustments in the nature and relationships of other "organs" in the society. These supporters of the analogy may also note that, in a sense, the failure of an "organ" really does destroy a society because the radically new "organ" effectively creates a new type of society (this would be something like turning a puppy into a guppy).

This analogy was developed early in the history of thought about the human experience. The anthropological versions of it received their greatest early elaboration by Herbert Spencer (in the late nineteenth century). By the mid-twentieth century, those using this analogy (often more implicitly than explicitly) were (and still are) known as "functionalists." The label gives empasis to the tendency of proponents of this analogy to suggest that human social systems had internal order which corresponded to the internal order of living organisms. Often these views led to suggestions that such vital "organs" as the family, law, marriage, etc., were necessary for the survival of a society. These statements then led some people to suggest that changing such vital organs was bad (or impossible). Such views posed obvious problems in a world characterized, as it has been especially since World War II, by extensive, rapid and broad changes in the behavior of people in societies. These arguments also constituted a major form of anthropological "explanation" (but not, generally, for explaining variety, which was the concern in the previous section). Unfortunately, however, many of these explanatory statements were sloppy and not true to the analogy upon which they were ostensibly based (for example, anthropologists sometimes made statements which are analogous to "explaining" the existence of "lungs" by saying animals need them in order to breathe). All in all, these "functionalist" efforts provided more in the way of excellent records about the behavior of people in societies than they did in the way of explanations of that behavior.

Another widespread and closely related way of giving order to the variety of behavior found in societies is to postulate (on a number of bases) "human universals." Many of these approaches have been based on an old and fundamental part of the discipline of anthropology—the study of humans as a type of animal (the major anthropological sub-field known as "physical anthropology" and including the relatively new, stimulating, and publicly popular field of "ethology"). In such contexts, efforts are made to link behavioral tendencies among humans to distinctive human biophysical characteristics (e.g., upright posture, binocular vision, opposable thumb, continuous sexuality, pronounced sexual dimorphism, prolonged infancy-immaturity, and so forth). And, of course, it is clear that we are animals (although some people still hold that humans are "special creations") and that we must, *therefore,* satisfy certain basic animal needs (for food, sex, nurture, etc.). Such links are clearly real (for example, why else, ultimately, do people eat?), but these arguments have weaknesses which too often are minimized.

In the first place, the effort inevitably requires continual definitional updating so that the "universals" will still be "universal" (that is, until the next "exception" come along). The effort to continually redefine "marriage" or "law" (for example) in such a way so as to make it possible to claim that all known human societies have these institutions is analogous (roughly) to continually redefining what lungs are so that it can be claimed that all living things have them. We will have to live with the fact that not all human societies have had or will have all of the major and admittedly widespread institutionalized human behaviors. To assume that they do or should or will is to fly in the face of the nature of the reality which is being examined. There are, as we have just noted, institutions in societies which are very common and it is true that by altering our definitions we have seen commonalities that were previously missed. But if carried to extremes, the process tends to produce what are really "empty universals." If anything, it is preferable to ask, "given this or that definition of 'law' or 'marriage,' tell me how many of the known, organized populations of humans have 'law' and 'marriage'." For in so doing, we can avoid the morass of proclaiming uniformity and get on with the more informative and exciting business of explaining and ordering the variety.

In the second place, such an enterprise gives insufficient emphasis to the nature and role of symbolically learned non-genetic information and to the statistical nature of the principal unit of investigation—a society.

The role of such information, as Geertz emphasizes, is *to complete* the process of humanizing humans. Because of the nature of the information and the diversity of environments, this process *of necessity* leads to fundamental variety and diversity in human societies. Talking about universals may help give order to our inquiry (even the topical labels for the parts in this book are in some cases "universals"), but it can be carried to extremes that mislead us into thinking we know what all human societies *must* be and this, I contend, is something we do not know.

Perhaps the most general and inclusive statements of an order-seeking sort made about single or small numbers of societies are those which have been made by anthropologists known, generally, as "configurationists." Undoubtedly, the most widely known of such anthropologists is Ruth Benedict whose book, *Patterns of Culture,* has probably been read by more people than any other book by an anthropologist. She and many others since have attempted to do systematically what people throughout history have done on a more casual basis—characterize societies on the basis of a few general principles or themes. The resulting descriptions were called "configurations" (hence the name for these anthropologists) or "patterns" or "national character." (Today, similar interests are sometimes given expression by studies of ethnic "identity.") Many of these efforts to characterize a society or sometimes even a whole region or continent in terms of a few principles have come under heavy criticism from inside and outside anthropology. However, and in spite of the weaknesses these studies at times have, anthropologists still assume that the lifeways of people in a society are, to a significant degree, integrated (even if by mutual hostilities), patterned, wholes, and that themes expressed in one institutionalized set of behaviors can also be discovered in many of the other behaviors occurring in the society.

Another common anthropological approach to ordering data about behavior within a society is to seek statistical patterns and trends in these behaviors. This important activity is widely utilized in anthropology and is illustrated in several of the articles in this volume. Although this ordering activity is complex, difficult, and often becomes an end in itself, I think most anthropologists engaged in it see these patterns and statistics as contributing, ultimately, to other kinds of ordering activities at the more general level of comparing and classifying (whether taxonomic, configurational or otherwise) the variety of societies found in the world, now and in the past.

FORMAL

One of the newer approaches to finding order in the variety comes from insights gained through the study of human speech. The arguments about these insights are fierce and the points of view are complex (in this volume, the articles by Lévi-Strauss, Burling, and Farb presented some of these views). Many of the arguments against the approach are similar to those used against anthropologists who in the past used the organismic analogy; in short, it is argued that the analogy between how people are able to speak and how they are able to behave is simply more confusing than enlightening. It remains to be seen whether this criticism will be sustained.

It is neither feasible nor necessary to review the entire analogy. Perhaps the most vital part of it involves Noam Chomsky's observation that it is difficult to account for the ability of children to learn to speak since they grow up hearing only a rather unrepresentative (and often ungrammatical) sample of the language they eventually do learn to speak. It is difficult, that is, unless it is *postulated* that the human mind has certain *innate* structures which together provide the child with the *capacity* for learning to speak meaningfully. Importantly, when this is said (and supported with impressive data and argument), it also follows that all of the many mutually unintelligible speech communities (languages) of the world are, in certain ways, fundamentally alike (since the human mind is everywhere the same).

Although the step is a giant one, anthropologists have taken off from this point and suggested that humans exhibit in their non-speech as well as speech behavior, certain fundamental universal patterns which are a reflection of the nature of the human mind. Finding these universals is not an easy process, either in linguistics or anthropology (indeed, it may be easier in the latter than in the former). The effort has produced great controversy but also high expectation. The most notable efforts to date are those of the French anthropologist Claude Lévi-Strauss. He and other "like-minded" structuralists have emphasized the search for fundamental structures in such diverse aspects of life in human societies as the way humans organize themselves and the way they organize themes in their myths (indeed, the term "organize" may be too strong since behavior which emerges from innate mental structures would seem to be "expressed" rather than organized in the usual sense of that term). The areas of agreement are small at this early stage of the inquiry, but much attention and interest continues to be given to the search for binary oppositions (fundamentally, a division of things into + and − in the same way that the binary counting system involves only two digits—0 and 1). Example seem to have been found everywhere, from the relationships of totem animals, to the colors of traffic "stop-and-go" signals. Although such examples seem to reflect the binary character of the human brain, the potential of alternative views of brain function (e.g., the exciting analog model proposed by Powers 1973) are just beginning to be assessed.

Another type of "formal" inquiry based on the analogy between speech and other human behavior is illustrated above in the article by Burling

(Chapter 5). Suffice it to note here that proponents of this view argue that other forms of human behavior besides speech may be "grammatical." It has long been suggested, in anthropology, that institutionalized behavior in human societies (especially "rituals") are themselves a kind of "message." If they aren't done correctly, the "message" is at least garbled; in extreme cases, the wrong meaning altogether will be communicated. Some anthropologists, taking off from this point, have sought to find the "messages" hidden in all behavior. Others have sought to account for behavior in terms of the rules which "generate" it (in much the same way that the grammatical rules of a language are thought to "generate" meaningful sentences). Others have sought to discover the various ways ritualized behavior can be carried out and still be meaningful (something like trying to see how many different ways one can express the same thought in a particular language). All of these efforts have their problematic aspects, but they all appear to hold out great promise for a new understanding of the patterns, order, and meaning in the behavior of humans in societies.

Still another linguistically stimulated inquiry which seeks to order the behavior of humans is designed, essentially, to record the ways other people have developed for classifying and ordering reality (including human behavior). In short, one type of ordering activity engaged in by anthropologists is describing the types of ordering activities engaged in by other people (who usually are not anthropologists). Here, too, the search has just begun, complete with acrimonious debate and controversy. Some have argued that these efforts have been trivial (the most often cited example probably being the description of how people in a particular society classify or give order to firewood). But others note that the description of "folk classification systems" has produced more impressive results. For example, Berlin and Kay (1969) have evidence which suggests that the number of basic color terms seems to increase with changes in the overall complexity of a sociocultural system.

In all of these efforts to order the variety of societies and the behavior of the people in them, with all of the problems and pitfalls, the general finding is overwhelming—the human experience is ordered, patterned, and meaningful. The outlines are only dimly in view and many seemingly fruitful leads and strategies have not lived up to expectations, but the general order is yielding to anthropological scrutiny.

HOW MUCH VARIETY IS THERE?

Anthropologists have long considered it important to try and answer the question which asks how much variety there is in the behavior exhibited by humans in societies (and, by implication, in culture in the sense of non-genetic, primarily symbolically learned information stored extrasomatically and in the neural structures of the people in those societies).

For a long time, it was assumed, if not in word then certainly in deed, that the recording of behavior from all parts of the world was an end in itself. Although this has produced data of value, it is more common for such unguided efforts to produce data of little value. Often, the bits and pieces compare poorly with the things "pot-hunters" and "grave-robbers" bring to archaeological museums. At best some of these data can be considered a sort of low-grade ore which can be turned to when all else fails (or when the need for particular bits of data is so pressing that it will be considered worthwhile to sift through tons of "slag" to get the gems we hope are there).

Anthropologists have been known for their apparent "love" of the exotic, unusual, atypical, surprising elements in human life. There is a certain ill-defined and, for many, an ill-received tradition within the discipline which leads people to work to find exotic behavior, and then to talk about it and listen to it being described with a studied solemnity and detachment that I find almost as bizarre as the exotica attributed to other people. There are many good reasons for this stance (e.g., as a counter to the all too common tendency to inject morals into the inquiry in ways that prevent understanding), but one particular reason for this interest in the exotic should be mentioned in this context. Anthropologists want to get some idea of the limits (thus far) of human behavior. Just how far can these beings be stretched and still be human? All the data which appear to come from around the edge of the range are of great interest for this reason; they give us clues about human limits and human "nature." There can never really be a final answer to this. This is not to say there are not limits, but only that within those limits set by our biology and our environment, there are few if any limitations on the variety. All limits are hypothetical in an ongoing system.

One other traditionally cited reason for recording the full variety of human societies deserves evaluation. Small-scaled societies have been compared to "endangered species" and, to be sure, it is sadly true that they are endangered. But anthropology is not, as some have erroneously concluded, endangered as a result. It is essential that anthropology have a representative record of the range of human societies if it is to comment and generalize about all of humanity, but given the nature of the causes of this variety and of the thing which varies, we may safely assume that so long as there is humanity there will be variety and, I suppose, anthropologists to study it.

In all of this, we are presented repeatedly with three paradoxes which for centuries have plagued and entranced those who have reflected upon the nature of the human experience. First, by nature, both humans in general and scientists in particular seek the unique and then classify it away. Second, while there are limits to what humans can be and must do, human behavior within those limits is, for all practical purposes, limitless.

And third, anthropology, as a science, cannot explain the unique; but its subjects are beings who, as Geertz has reminded us, must be unique if they are to be human at all!

A SUMMING UP

Anthropology, then, is not simply the science of humanity. It is, distinctively, the science oriented to answering at a pan-human level, three very general questions about *human behavioral variety*. These questions ask *why* there is variety in societies, *what order* there is in this variety, and *how much* variety there is. These questions have been asked for centuries to be sure, but more intensely and on a more inclusive scale by anthropologists than by any other group of scholars.

The decades since World War II have been, in anthropology, an incredibly intense and complex period. Each of the three basic questions has had periods of dominance, with perhaps most of the spotlight belonging to those asking derivations of the first question. This can be seen especially during the 1950s and 1960s when most of the world was in the throes of anti-colonial nationalism. There will be argument, of course, but I think the spotlight now belongs to those searching out answers to derivations of the second question—especially "structuralist" derivations. But the great lesson of the past few decades is that each of these questions is essential and contributes to our knowledge of the human experience. Some anthropologists appear to be asserting that the first question noted above, because of its historic priority, should continue to have priority today. Regardless of the validity of the historical claim, there are surely other, better reasons for asking a question about the human experience than because our intellectual forebears began by asking it. Anthropology has never been as single-minded as is sometimes believed. An anthropological consideration of the human experience, I think, requires a full exploration of all three of these basic questions. If any question is to be dominant or, more appropriately in my view, if any set of questions is to be dominant, then it should be the one whose answers can reasonably be expected to lead to a general improvement in the quality of the human experience or, even more basically but pessimistically, to contribute to its preservation at all.

Finally, it may be noted that most of the general assumptions, conclusions and disputes summarized here are deceptively simple. For many, this review may be more of a bore than a challenge or a platform. To this, however, I can only respond with a challenge of my own. If these assumptions and conclusions seem simple or obvious, please reread and rethink them now and again—not immediately, necessarily, but perhaps after an interval of some length. For as Geertz notes at the outset of his essay in Chapter 1, explanation in anthropology often consists of "substituting complex pictures for simple ones while striving somehow to retain the persuasive clarity that went with the simple ones." But more than this, and again citing Geertz (who, in this instance, draws upon the philosopher, Whitehead), the maxim for the natural sciences may well be "seek simplicity and distrust it," while for the social sciences, it probably should be "seek complexity and order it." In writing this essay as well as in deciding what to include as selections for this book, I have tried to face and to help the reader face the complexity of both anthropology and the human experience. If, by the time you have finished this book, you think my view of either seems simple, then distrust it; if both seem complex but ordered, then we are on the way to comprehending them.

References Cited

Abegglen, J.C.
  1958   *The Japanese Factory*. Glencoe, Ill. Free Press.
Adams, W.Y.
  1963   *Shonto: A Study of the Role of the Trader in a Modern Navaho Community*. Washington, D.C.: Smithsonian Institution, Bureau of American Ethnology, Bulletin 188.
Akiga, B. Sai (B. Akiga Sai)
  1939   *Akiga's Story*. Translated by Rupert East. London: Oxford University Press for the International African Institute.
Akinola, R.N.
  1964   "The industrial structure of Ibadan." *The Nigerian Geographical Journal* 7:115–30.
Apple, Dorrian
  1956   "The social structure of grandparenthood." *American Anthropologist* 58:656–63.
Arensberg, Conrad M.
  1955   "American communities." *American Anthropologist* 57:1143–62.
Armstrong, W.R. and T.G. McGee.
  1968   "Revolutionary change and the Third World city: A theory of urban involution." *Civilisations* 28:353–78.
d'Azevedo, Warren L.
  1962   "Common principles of variant kinship structures among the Gola." *American Anthropologist* 64:504–20.
Babcock, Louis L.
  1927   *The War of 1812 on the Niagara Frontier*. Buffalo, N.Y.: The Buffalo Historical Society.

Bakan, David
    1968   *On Method: Toward a Reconstruction of Psychological Theory.* San Francisco: Jossey-Bass.

Barnett, H.G.
    1955   *The Coast Salish of British Columbia.* University of Oregon.

Barth, Fredrik
    1960   "The land use pattern of migratory tribes of South-Persia," in *Norsk Geografisk Tidsskrift,* v.17.
    1961   *Nomads of South-Persia.* Oslo University Press; New York: Humanities Press.

Bateson, Gregory
    1970   *Steps to an Ecology of Mind.* New York: Ballantine Books.

Beattie, J.
    1960   *Bunyoro: An African Kingdom.* New York: Holt, Rinehart & Winston.
    1964   *Other Cultures: Aims, Methods, and Achievements in Social Anthropology.* New York: Free Press of Glencoe.
    1965   *Understanding an African Kingdom: Bunyoro.* New York: Holt, Rinehart & Winston.

Beidelman, Thomas O.
    1963   "Witchcraft in Ukaguru." In *Witchcraft and Sorcery in East Africa,* John Middleton and E.H. Winter, eds., New York: Praeger (pp. 57–98).

Belshaw, C.W.
    1965   *Traditional Exchange and Modern Markets.* Englewood Cliffs, New Jersey: Prentice-Hall.

Benedict, Ruth
    1934   *Patterns of Culture.* Boston: Houghton Mifflin.
    1938   "Continuities and discontinuities in cultural conditioning." *Psychiatry* 1:161–67.

Benet, F.
    1963   "Sociology uncertain: The ideology of the rural-urban continuum." *Comparative Studies in Society and History* 6:1–23.

Berlin, B. and P. Kay
    1969   *Basic Color Terms: Their Universality and Evolution.* Berkeley: University of California Press.

Blacking, John
    1973   *How Musical is Man?* Seattle: University of Washington Press.

Boas, Franz
    1894   "Indian tribes of the Lower Fraser River." *British Association for the Advancement of Science* 64:456–63.

Bode, Carl
    1958   *The Anatomy of American Popular Culture 1840–1861.* Berkeley: University of California Press.

Boeke, J.H.
    1953   *Economics and Economic Policy of Dual Societies as Exemplified by Indonesia.* New York: Institute of Pacific Relations.

Bohannan, Laura
    1949   "Dahomean marriage: A revaluation." *Africa XIX:273–87.*

Bohannan, Laura and Paul Bohannan
  1953   *The Tiv of Central Nigeria.* London: International African Institute.
Bohannan, Paul J.
  1955   "Some principles of exchange and investment among the Tiv." *American Anthropologist* 57:60–70.
  1963   *Social Anthropology.* New York: Holt, Rinehart & Winston.
  1973   "Rethinking culture: A project for current anthropologists." *Current Anthropology* 14(4):357–65; 371–72.
Bohannan, Paul and Laura Bohannan
  1958   "Three Source Notebooks in Tiv Ethnography." New Haven: Human Relations Area Files.
Brooks, Van Wyck
  1944   *The World of Washington Irving.* New York: Dutton.
Brownell, Charles De Wolfe
  1853   *The Indian Races of North and South America.* Chicago: American Publishing Co.
Bruner, Edward M.
  1956   "Cultural transmission and culture change." *Southwestern Journal of Anthropology* 12:191–99.
Burling, Robbins
  1963   *Rengsanggri: Family and Kinship in a Garo Village.* Philadelphia: University of Pennsylvania Press.
Busia, K.A.
  1950   *Report on a Social Survey of Sekondi-Takoradi.* London: Crown Agents.
Cassel, Paulus
  1861   *Weinachten: Ursprung, Bräuche und Aberglauben.* Berlin: Ludwig Rauh.
Chayanov, A.V.
  1966   *The Theory of Peasant Economy.* Daniel Thorner, R.E.F. Smith, and B. Kerblay, eds., Homewood, Illinois: Irwin.
Chomsky, Noam
  1957   *Syntactic Structures.* The Hague: Mouton.
  1972   *Language and Mind.* New York: Harcourt Brace Jovanovich.
Codere, Helen
  1957   "Kwakiutl society: Rank without class." *American Anthropologist* 59:473–86.
Colden, Cadwallander
  1904   *The History of the Five Indian Nations of Canada* (2 vols.). New York: New Amsterdam Book Co.
Cory, David M.
  1955   *Within Two Worlds.* New York: Friendship Press.
Dalton, George
  1972   "Peasantries in anthropology and history." *Current Anthropology* 13:385–415.
Davies, Valentin
  1947   *Miracle on 34th Street.* (Screenplay by George Seaton, 20th Century Fox.) New York: Harcourt Brace.

Devereux, George
1967 *From Anxiety to Method in the Behavioral Sciences.* The Hague: Mouton.

Dewey, A.G.
1962 *Peasant Marketing in Java.* Glencoe, Illinois: Free Press.

Dolto, Francoise
1955 "French and American children as seen by a French child analyst." In *Childhood in Contemporary Cultures,* Margaret Mead and Martha Wolfenstein, eds., Chicago: University of Chicago Press (pp. 408–23).

Douglas, Mary
1966 *Purity and Danger: An Analysis of Concepts of Pollution and Taboo.* London: Kegan Paul. Baltimore, Md.: Pelcan Books, 1970.

Edgerton, Robert B.
1971 *The Individual in Cultural Adaptation.* Berkeley and Los Angeles: University of California Press.

Einzig, Paul
1949 *Primitive Money in its Ethnological, Historical, and Economic Aspects.* London: Eyre and Spottisworde.

Elmendorf, William W.
1971 "Coast Salish status ranking and intergroup ties." *Southwestern Journal of Anthropology* 27:353–80.

Emrich, Duncan
1960 *A Certain Nicholas of Patara.* American Heritage 12:22–27.

Fenton, William N.
1940 *Problems Arising from the Historic Northeatsern Position of the Iroquois.* Washington, D.C., Smithsonian Misc. Collection 100, pp. 159–251.
1951 *Symposium on local diversity in Iroquois culture.* Washington, D.C.: Bureau of American Ethnology, no. 149.

Firth, R.
1946 *Malay Fishermen: Their Peasant Economy.* London: Routledge and Kegan Paul.
1951 *Elements of Social Organization.* London: Watts.

Firth, R. and B.S. Yamey, eds.
1964 *Capital, Savings and Credit in Peasant Societies.* London: Allen and Unwin.

Franciscan Fathers, The
1910 *An Ethnologic Dictionary of the Navaho Language.* Arizona, St. Michaels.

Franklin, S.H.
1962 "Reflections on the peasantry." *Pacific Viewpoint* 3:1–26.
1965 "Systems of production, systems of appropraition." *Pacific Viewpoint* 6:145–66.
1969 *The European Peasantry, The Final Phase.* London: Methuen.

Frazer, Sir James
1910 *Totemism and Exogamy.* 4 vols. London: Macmillan and Co.

Fried, Morton
1967 *The Evolution of Political Society.* New York: Random House.

Friedl, Ernestine
   1956   "Persistence in Chippewa culture and personality." *American Anthropologist* 58:814–25.
Geertz, Clifford
   1963   *Peddlers and Princes: Social Change and Economic Modernization in Two Indonesian Towns.* Chicago: The University of Chicago Press.
   1973   *The Interpretation of Cultures.* New York: Basic Books.
Gibbs, James L., Jr.
   1960   "Some judicial implications of marital instability among the Kpelle." Unpublished Ph.D. dissertation, Harvard University.
   1962   "Some judicial implications of Kpelle marital instability." Paper read at the annual meeting of the African Studies Association, November.
   1963a "The Kpelle moot: A therapeutic model for the informal settlement disputes." *Africa* XXXIII:1–11.
   1963b "Marital instability among the Kpelle: Towards a theory of epainogamy." *American Anthropologist* 65:552–73.
Gluckman, Max
   1955   *The Judicial Process among the Barotse of Northern Rhodesia.* Manchester: Manchester University Press.
Goldenweiser, Alexander A.
   1922   *Early Civilization.* New York: A.A. Knopf.
Goldschmidt, Walter
   1950   "Social class in America—a critical review." *American Anthropologist* 52:483–98.
Goodenough, Ward
   1963   *Cooperation in Change.* New York: Russell Sage Foundation.
Goody, J.
   1957   "Anomie in Ashanti?" *Africa* XXVII:356–63.
Gould, H.
   1970   "Some preliminary observations concerning the anthropology of industrialization." In *Peasants in Cities: Readings in the Anthropology of Urbanization.* W. Mangin, ed., Boston: Houghton Mifflin.
Government of the Republic of Liberia
   1949   "Revised laws and administrative regulations for governing the hinterland." Mimeographed edition of "The revised interior administrative regulations passed by Legislative Enactment and approved December 22, 1949" issued in 1952 by the Department of the Interior, Monrovia.
Greenland, C.
   1957   "A study of the correspondence addressed to an" 'Advice Column' in 1953. *Case Conference* III:255–62.
Gulliver, Philip
   1966   *The Family Herds.* London: Routledge and Kegan Paul (2nd edition).
Gunther, Erna
   1927   "Klallam Ethnography." University of Washington Publications in *Anthropology* 1(5):171–314.
Haeberlin, H. and E. Gunther
   1930   "The Indians of Puget Sound." University of Washington Publications in *Anthropology* 4(1):1–84.

Hallowell, A.I.
1955 *Culture and Experience.* Philadelphia: University of Pennsylvania Press.

Harley, George W.
1950 "Masks as agents of control in Northeast Liberia." Cambridge: Peabody Museum Papers, vol. 22, no. 2.

Harrington, M. Eleanor
1921 "Captain John Deserontyou and the Mohawk Settlement at Deseronto." Ontario, Canada: Bulletin of the Department of History and Political and Economic Science, Queens University.

Harrington, Michael
1963 *The Other America.* Baltimore: Penguin Books.

Harris, Marvin
1964 *The Nature of Cultural Things.* New York: Random House.
1968 *The Rise of Anthropological Theory: A History of Theories of Culture.* New York: Thomas Y. Crowell Company.
1974 *Cows, Pigs, Wars, and Witches: The Riddles of Culture.* New York: Random House.

Hebb, D.O. and W.R. Thompson
1968 "The social significance of animal studies." In *The Handbook of Social Psychology.* 5 vols. G. Lindzey and E. Aronson, eds., Reading, Mass.: Addison-Wesley.

Helmuth, Hermann
1973 "Cannibalism in paleoanthropology and ethnology." In *Man and Aggression,* Ashley Montagu, ed., London: Oxford University Press (pp. 101–19).

Henry, Jules
1963 *Culture Against Man.* New York: Random House.

Herberg, Will
1960 *Protestant, Catholic, Jew.* New York: Doubleday Anchor Books.

Herskovits, Melville J.
1955 *Cultural Anthropology.* New York: Alfred A. Knopf, Inc.

Higgins, B.
1956 "The dualistic theory of underdeveloped areas." *Economic Development and Cultural Change* 4:99–115.

Hill-Tout, Charles
1902 "Ethnological studies of the Mainland Halkomelem, a division of the Salish of British Columbia." British Association for the Advancement of Science 72:355–449.

Hodge, Fred Webb, ed.
1913 *Handbook of American Indians North of Mexico.* Washington, D.C.: Smithsonian Institution Bureau of American Ethnology, no. 30.

Hogbin, H.I.
1939 *Experiments in Civilization: The Effects of European Culture on a Native Community of the Solomon Islands.* London: G. Routledge and Sons, Ltd.

Holas, B.
1953 "Décès d'une femme Guerzé." *Africa* XXIII:145–55.

Homans, George C. and David H. Schneider
  1955   *Marriage, Authority and Final Causes.* Glencoe, Illinois: The Free Press.
Hopkins, K., ed.
  1971   *Hong Kong: The Industrial Colony, A Political, Social and Economic Survey.* Hong Kong: Oxford University Press.
Hsu, Francis L.K.
  1953   *Americans and Chinese: Two Ways of Life.* New York: Abelard-Schuman.
  1961   "American core values and national character." In *Psychological Anthropology: Aspects of Culture and Personality,* F.L.K. Hsu, ed., Homewood, Ill.: Dorsey Press.
  1963   *Clan, Caste and Club.* Princeton: Van Nostrand.
Hunt, George T.
  1940   *The Wars of the Iroquois.* Madison: University of Wisconsin Press.
Huxley, Julian
  1955   "Evolution, cultural and biological." In *Current Anthropology: A Supplement to Anthropology Today.* William L. Thomas, Jr. Chicago: University of Chicago Press.
Imanishi, K.
  1961   "The origin of the human family—A primatological approach." *Japanese Journal of Ethnology* 25:119–30.
Ivens, W.
  1927   *Melanesians of the South-east Solomon Islands.* London: K. Paul, Trench, Trubner & Co., Ltd.
Jahoda, G.
  1958   "Boys' images of marriage partners and girls' self-images in Ghana." *Sociologus* VIII:155–69.
Jenkinds, Charles Rivington
  1949   "Caughnawaga Mohawk." Unpublished M.A. thesis, Columbia University.
Jenness, Diamond
  1932   *Indians of Canada.* Bulletin 65, National Museum of Canada, Anthropology Series 15.
  1955   "The faith of a Coast Salish Indian." *Anthropology in British Columbia,* Memoir 3.
Jeromin, U.
  1966   *Die Uberseechinesen, Ihre Bedeutung für die wirschaftliche Entwicklung Südostasiens.* Stuttgart: Gustav Fischer Verlag.
Johnson, Samual
  1931   *Johnson on Shakespeare.* London: Oxford University Press.
Jones, Charles W.
  1954   "Knickerbocker Santa Claus." *New York Historical Society Quarterly* 38:357–83.
Kane, Harnett F.
  1958   *The Southern Christmas Book.* New York: David McKay Co.
Kaplan, D.
  1965   "The Mexican marketplace then and now." In *Essays in Economic Anthropology Dedicated to the Memory of Karl Polanyi.* June Helm,

ed., Seattle: Proceedings of the Annual meeting of the American Ethnological Society.

Kaufman, J.H.
1965 "A three-year study of mating behavior in a free-ranging band of rhesus monkeys." *Ecology* 46:500–12.

Keesing, R.M.
1965 "Kwaio marriage and society." Unpublished Ph.D. dissertation, Harvard University.
1966 "Ambilineal descent and contextual definition of status: The Kwaio Case." Paper read at the American Anthropological Association Annual meetings, November.
1967 "Christians and pagans in Kwaio, Malaita." *Journal of the Polynesian Society* 76:82–100.

Kimble, H.
1956 "A reading survey in Accra." *Universitas* II:77–81.

Kluckhohn, Clyde
1944 *Navaho Witchcraft*. Boston: Beacon Press.
1945 *The Personal Document in Anthropological Science*. New York: Social Science Research Council, Bulletin no. 53.
1953 "Universal categories of culture." In *Anthropology Today*, A.L. Kroeber, ed., Chicago: University of Chicago Press (pp. 507–23).
1962 *Culture and Behavior*. New York: Free Press of Glencoe.

Kroeber, A.L.
1939 *Cultural and Natural Areas of Native North America*. University of California Publications in American Archaeology and Ethnology 38.
1948 *Anthropology*. New York: Harcourt Brace and Company.

Kroeber, A.L. and Clyde Kluckhohn
1952 *Culture: A Critical Review of Concepts and Definitions*. New York: Random House.

La Barre, Weston
1970 *The Ghost Dance: The Origins of Religion*. New York: Doubleday & Company.

Ladd, J.
1957 *The Structure of a Moral Code*. Cambridge: Harvard University Press.

Lambton, A.K.S.
1953 *Landlord and Peasant in Persia*. London: Oxford University Press.

Leach, E.R.
1951 "The structural implications of matrilateral cross cousin marriage." *Journal of the Royal Anthropological Institution* 81:23–55.
1955a *Political Systems of Highland Burma*. Cambridge: Harvard University Press.
1955b "Time and false noses." *Explorations* 5:30–35.
1970 *Claude Lévi-Strauss*. New York: The Viking Press.

Lenski, Gerhard
1963 *The Religious Factors: A Sociological Enquiry*. New York: Doubleday Anchor Books.

Lévi-Strauss, Claude
1952 "Le Père Noël Supplicié." *Les Temps Modernes*, year 7, no. 77: 1572–90.

1953   "Social structure." In *Anthropology Today*. Alfred L. Kroeber, ed. Chicago: University of Chicago Press.

1960   "The family." In *Man, Culture and Society*. L. Shapiro, ed., New York: Oxford University Press.

1961   *The New York Times*, Dec. 17.

Lewis, I.M.

1961   *A Pastoral Democracy*. London: Oxford University Press.

Linton, Ralph, ed.

1940   *Acculturation in Seven American Indian Tribes*. New York: Appleton-Century.

Lomax, Alan

1968   *Folk Song and Style in Culture*. Washington, D.C.: American Association for the Advancement of Science, publication no. 88.

Lovejoy, Arthur O.

1960   *Essays in the History of Ideas*. New York: G.P. Putnam's Sons, Capricorn books (orig. 1948).

Lowie, Robert H.

1956   "Boas once more." *American Anthropologist* 58:159–64.

Lupri, E.

1967   "The rural-urban variable reconsidered: The cross-cultural perspective." *Sociological Ruralis* 7:1–20.

Lydekker, John W.

1938   *The Faithful Mohawk*. New York: I.J. Friedman.

Lynd, Robert S. and Helen M. Lynd

1937   *Middletown in Transition: A Study in Cultural Conflicts*. New York: Harcourt, Brace.

Malinowski, B.

1961   *Argonauts of the Western Pacific*. New York: Dutton. (orig. 1922).

1926   *Crime and Custom in Savage Society*. New York: Harcourt Brace.

Mangin, W., ed.

1970   *Peasants in Cities: Readings in the Anthropology of Urbanization*. Boston: Houghton Mifflin.

Marriott, McKim

1955   "Little communities in an indigenous civilization." In *Village India*, McKim Marriott, ed., American Anthropological Association Memoir 83:171–222.

Maugham, W. Somerset

1934   "The book bag." In *East and West: The Collected Short Stories of W. Somerset Maugham*. Garden City: Garden City Publishing Company.

Mayer, P.

1962   *Tribesmen or Townsmen—Conservatism and the Process of Urbanization in a South African City, Cape Town*. London: Oxford University Press.

McGee, T.G.

1964   "The rural-urban continuum debate: The preindustrial city and rural-urban migration." *Pacific Viewpoint* 5:159–81.

1970a   *Hawkers in Hong Kong: Preliminary Tables*. Hong Kong: Center of Asian Studies, University of Hong Kong.

1970b *Hawkers in Selected Asian Cities.* Hong Kong: Center of Asian Studies, University of Hong Kong.

1971a "Catalysts or cancers? The role of cities in Asian society." In *Urbanization and National Development.* L. Jakobsen and V. Prakash, eds., South and Southeast Asia Urban Affairs Annual, I. Beverly Hills: Sage Publications.

1971b *The Urbanization Process in the Third World: Explorations in Search of a Theory.* London: G. Bell and Sons.

1973 *Hawkers in Hong Kong: A Preliminary Study of Policy and Planning in a Third World City.* Forthcoming. Hong Kong: Center of Asian Studies, University of Hong Kong.

Mead, Margaret
1949 *Male and Female.* New York: Morrow.

Millar, Robert
1923 "The formative principles of civil procedure." *The Illinois Law Review* 18:1–36; 94–117; 150–68.

Miller, Walter W.
1955 "Two concepts of authority." *American Anthropologist* 57:271–89.

Mintz, S.W.
1971 "Men, women, and trade." *Comparative Studies in Society and History* 13:247–69.

Mitchell, Joseph
1949 Mohawks in high steel. *New Yorker,* vol. 25, no. 30.

Monboddo, St. G.
1744 *Of the Origin and Progress of Language, vol. 1.* Edinburgh: J. Balfour and T. Cadell.

Morgan, Lewis H.
1877 *Ancient Society.* New York: World Publishing.

1901 *League of the Ho-De-No-Sau-Nee, or Iroquois.* New Haven, Conn.: Human Relations Area Files, 1954.

Murdock, George P.
1937 "Comparative data on the division of labor by sex." *Social Forces* 15:551–53.

1949 *Social Structure.* New York: Macmillan.

1959 *Africa: Its People and their Culture History.* New York: McGraw-Hill.

Murdock, George P. and J.W.M. Whiting
1951 "Cultural determination of parental attitudes: The relationship between the social structure, particularly family structure and parental behavior." In *Problems of Infancy and Childhood: Transactions of the Fourth Conference,* March 6–7, 1950, M.J.E. Senn, ed., New York: Josiah Macy, Jr. Foundation.

Nash, M.
1966 *Primitive and Peasant Economic Systems.* San Francisco: Chandler Publishing Co.

Noon, John A.
1949 "Law and Government of the Grand River Iroquois." New York: Viking Fund Publications in *Anthropology,* no. 12.

Noyes, Robert W. and Eleanor M. Chapnick
  1964   "Literature on psychology and infertility: A critical analysis." *Fertility and Sterility* 15:543–56.
O'Malley, L.S.S.
  1935   *Popular Hinduism.* Cambridge: Cambridge University Press.
Pahl, R.E.
  1966   "The rural-urban continuum." *Sociological Ruralis* 6:299–327.
  1967   "The rural-urban continuum: A reply to Eugeun Lupri." *Sociological Ruralis* 7:20–28.
Parsons, T., R.F. Bales, et al.
  1955   *Family, Socialization and Interaction Process.* Glencoe, Ill.: Free Press.
Patterson, Samuel W.
  1956   *The Poet of Christmas Eve: A Life of Clement Clarke Moore, 1779–1863.* New York: Morehouse-Gorham Co.
Polanyi, Karl
  1944   *The Great Transformation: The Political and Economic Origins of Our Time.* New York: Rinehart and Winston. Boston: Beacon Press, 1957.
  1957   "The economy as instituted process." In *Trade and Market in the Early Empires,* Conrad M. Arensberg and Harry W. Pearson, eds., Glencoe, Ill.: The Free Press and The Falcon's Wing Press.
Porter, Peter A.
  1896   *A Brief History of Old Fort Niagara.* Buffalo, New York.
Potter, J.M., M.N. Dias, and G.M. Foster, eds.
  1967   *Peasant Society: A Reader.* Boston: Little Brown.
Powers, William
  1973   *Behavior: The Control of Perception.* Chicago: Aldine.
Purcell, V.
  1965   *The Chinese in Southeast Asia.* London: Oxford University Press.
Quain, B.H.
  1937   "The Iroquois." In *Cooperation and Competition among Primitive Peoples.* Margaret Mead, ed., New York: McGraw-Hill.
Radcliffe-Brown, A.R.
  1952   *Structure and Function in Primitive Society.* Glencoe, Ill.: The Free Press.
Radin, Paul
  1933   *Method and Theory of Ethnology: An Essay in Criticism.* New York: Basic Books (1966).
  1945   *The Road of Life and Death: A Ritual Drama of North American Indians.* New York: Bollingen Series, vol. V, Pantheon Books.
  1949   "The culture of the Winnebago: As described by themselves." *Memoir 2* of the *International Journal of American Linguistics,* pp. iv, 1–119. (Also published as a Special Publication of the Bollingen Foundation, vol. I, and Baltimore: Waverly Press.
Rafferty, Max
  1953   *What Happened to Patriotism?* West Orange, New Jersey: Economic Press.

Ray, Verne F.
1955   "Review of *Franz Boas: The Science of Man in the Making.*" *American Anthropologist* 57:138–40.
1956   "Rejoinder." *American Anthropologist* 58:164–70.

Redfield, R.
1953   *The Primitive World and Its Transformations.* Ithaca: Cornell University Press.
1956   *Peasant Society and Culture.* Chicago: University of Chicago Press.

Reichard, G.A.
1963   *Navaho Religion: A Study of Symbolism.* New York: Pantheon Books, Bollingen Series XVIII.

Ruyle, Eugene E.
1973   "Slavery, surplus, and stratification on the Northwest Coast: The ethnoenergetics of an incipient stratification system." *Current Anthropology* 14:603–17; 624–31.

Sade, Donald Stone
1968   "Inhibition of son-mother mating among free-ranging rhesus monkeys." *Science and Psychoanalysis* 12:18–38.

Sahlins, Marshall
1960   "The origin of society." *Scientific American* 48:76–89.
1963   "Poor man, rich man, big-man, chief: Political types in Melanesia and Polynesia." *Comparative Studies in Society and History* 5:285–303.

Santos, M.
1971   *Les Villes du Tiers Monde.* Paris: Editions M., Th. Genin.
1972   "Economic development and urbanization in underdeveloped countries: The two flow systems of the urban economy and their spatial implications." Unpublished manuscript.

Scheinfeld, A.
1944   *Women and Men.* New York: Harcourt, Brace.

Sereno, Renzo
1951   "Some observations on the Santa Claus Custom." *Psychiatry* 14:387–96.

Sinha, Surajit
1962   "State formation and Rajput myth in tribal central India." *Man in India* 42(1):35–80.

Skinner, G.W.
1957   *Chinese Society in Thailand: An Analytical History.* Ithaca: Cornell University Press.

Snyder, Sally
1954   "Class growth and distinctions and their relation to tribal shifts in Northern Puget Sound." Paper read at the Northwest Anthropological Conference, Vancouver.

Snyderman, George S.
1948   "Behind the Tree of Peace." *Bulletin* of the Society for Pennsylvania Archaeology.

Sokal, Robert R.
1974   "Classification: Purposes, principles, progress, prospects." *Science* 185:1115–23 (September).

Spencer, Paul
    1965   *The Samburu: A Study of Gerontocracy in a Nomadic Tribe.* Berkeley
            and Los Angeles: University of California Press.
Spiro, M.E.
    1956   *Kibbutz: Venture in Utopia.* Cambridge: Harvard University Press.
    1961   "An overview and a suggested reorientation." In *Psychological
            Anthropology,* F.L.K. Hsu, ed., Homewood, Ill.: The Dorsey Press.
Steele, J.
    1963   *A preliminary analysis of the Burmese Rorschachs.* Unpublished ms.
Steiner, Franz
    1954   "Notes on comparative economics." *British Journal of Sociology*
            5:118–29.
Steward, Julian
    1931   "The ceremonial buffoon of the American Indian." Papers of the
            Michigan Academy of Science, Arts and Letters 14:187–207.
Suttles, Wayne
    1960   "Affinal ties, subsistence, and prestige among the Coast Salish." *American Anthropologist* 62:296–305.
    1962   "Variation in habitat and culture on the Northwest Coast." *Akten des
            34.* internationalen Amerikanistenkongrasses, Wien, 1960. Vienna:
            F. Berger. Reprinted in *Man in Adaptation: The Cultural Present,*
            Yehudi A. Cohen, ed., Chicago: Aldine (pp. 93–106; 1968).
    1963   "The persistence of intervillage ties among the Coast Salish." *Ethnology* 2:512–25.
    1968   "Coping with abundance: Subsistence on the Northwest Coast." In
            Man the Hunter. Richard B. Lee and Irven DeVore, eds., Chicago:
            Aldine (pp. 55–68).
Tax, Sol, Loren C. Eisley, Irving Rouse and C.F. Voegelin
    1953   *An Appraisal of Anthropolgy Today.* Chicago: University of Chicago
            Press.
Terman, L.M. and Catherine C. Miles
    1936   *Sex and Personality.* New York: McGraw-Hill.
Tessler, Mark A., William M. O'Barr and David H. Spain
    1973   *Tradition and Identity in Changing Africa.* New York: Harper & Row.
T'ien, J-K.
    1953   "The Chinese of Sarawak: A Study of Social Structure." Monograph
            13. London: University of London, Department of Anthropology.
Tillich, Paul
    1956   *The Religious Situation.* New York: Meridian Books.
Tokuda, K.
    1961-62 "A study on the sexual behavior in the Japanese monkey troop."
            Primates 3:1–40.
Turgot, A.R.J.
    1844   *Plan de Deux Discours sur l'Histoire Universelle Oruvres de Turgot.*
            Paris: Guillaumin (original 1750).
Uchendu, V.C.
    1965   *The Igbo of Southeast Nigeria.* New York: Holt, Rinehart and Winston.

Vail, R.W.G.
1951 "Santa Claus visits the Hudson." *New York Historical Society Quarterly* 35:337–43.

Voget, P.
1951 "Acculturation at Caughnawaga." *American Anthropologist* 53:220–31.
1953 "Kinship changes at Caughnawaga." *American Anthropologist* 55:385–94.

Wagley, Charles
1951 "Cultural Influences on Population: A Comparison of Two Tupí Tribes." *Revista do Museu Paulista, N.S.,* vol. 5.

Ward, B.E.
1956 "Some observations on religious cults in Ashanti." *Africa* XXVI:47–60.

West, James
1945 *Plainville, U.S.A.* New York: Columbia University Press.

Westermarck, Edward
1922 *The History of Human Marriage.* 3 vols. London: Macmillan and Company.

White, Leslie A.
1948 "The definition and prohibition of incest." *American Anthropologist* 50:416–35.

Whyte, W.F.
1964 *Street Corner Society.* Chicago: University of Chicago Press.

Wolf, Arthur P.
1966 "Childhood association, sexual attraction, and the incest taboo: A Chinese case." *American Anthropologist* 68:883–98.
1968 "Adopt a daughter-in-law, marry a sister: A Chinese solution to the problem of the incest taboo." *American Anthropologist* 70:864–74.

Wolf, E.R.
1966 *Peasants.* Englewood Cliffs, New Jersey: Prentice-Hall.

Yinger, J. Milton
1957 *Religion, Society, and the Individual: An Introduction to the Sociology of Religion.* New York: Macmillan.

INDEX

Index